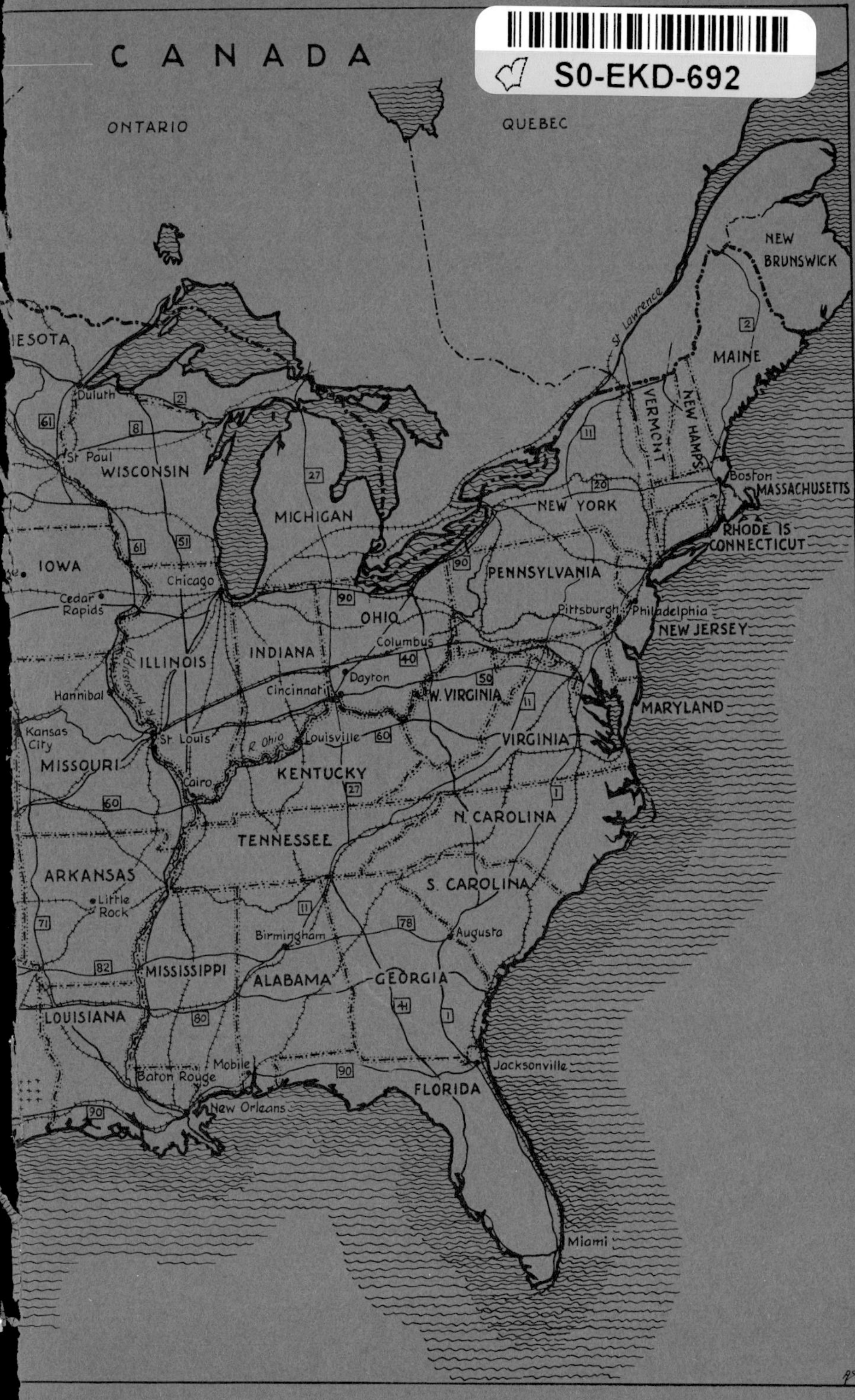
CANADA
ONTARIO
QUEBEC
NEW BRUNSWICK
MAINE
VERMONT
NEW HAMPS
St Lawrence
Boston
MASSACHUSETTS
RHODE IS
CONNECTICUT
NEW YORK
PENNSYLVANIA
Pittsburgh
Philadelphia
NEW JERSEY
MARYLAND
W. VIRGINIA
VIRGINIA
N. CAROLINA
S. CAROLINA
Augusta
GEORGIA
FLORIDA
Jacksonville
Miami
ALABAMA
Birmingham
Mobile
MISSISSIPPI
LOUISIANA
Baton Rouge
New Orleans
ARKANSAS
Little Rock
TENNESSEE
KENTUCKY
Louisville
R. Ohio
OHIO
Columbus
Dayton
Cincinnati
INDIANA
ILLINOIS
Chicago
Cairo
St. Louis
R. Mississippi
MISSOURI
Kansas City
Hannibal
IOWA
Cedar Rapids
WISCONSIN
St Paul
Duluth
MICHIGAN
NESOTA
2
8
61
27
51
90
40
50
11
60
1
20
78
71
82
80
41

HARD TRAVELLIN'

WANTED!

3,000 LABORERS

On the 12th Division of the

ILLINOIS CENTRAL RAILROAD

Wages, $1.25 per Day.

Fare, from New-York, only - - $4.75

By Railroad and Steamboat, to the work in the
State of Illinois.

Constant employment for two years or more
given. Good board can be obtained at two
dollars per week.

This is a rare chance for persons to go
West, being sure of permanent employment
in a healthy climate, where land can be
bought cheap, and for fertility is not surpassed
in any part of the Union.

Men with families preferred.

For further information in regard to it, call
at the Central Railroad Office,

173 BROADWAY,

CORNER OF COURTLANDT ST.

NEW-YORK.

R. B. MASON, Chief Engineer.

H. PHELPS, Agent,

July, 1853.

The lure West: how the labourers were drawn into motion. Railroad
poster, 1853.

HARD TRAVELLIN'

The hobo and his history by

Kenneth Allsop

The New American Library

BY THE SAME AUTHOR

Adventure Lit Their Star
The Angry Decade
Rare Bird
The Bootleggers
Scan

Copyright © 1967 by Kenneth Allsop
All rights reserved

First Printing

Published by The New American Library
1301 Avenue of the Americas, New York, N. Y. 10019

Originally published in Great Britain
by Hodder and Stoughton Limited

Library of Congress Catalog Card Number: 68-15278
Printed in the United States of America

For

MIREK VITALI

I been hittin' some hard travellin', I thought you knowed.
I been hittin' some hard travellin', way down the road.
I been hittin' some hard travellin', hard ramblin', hard gamblin'.
I been hittin' some hard travellin', Lord.

I been ridin' them fast rattlers, I thought you knowed.
I been ridin' them flat wheelers, way down the road.
I been ridin' those dead enders, blind passengers, kickin' up
$\qquad\qquad\qquad\qquad\qquad\qquad\qquad$ *cinders.*
I been hittin' some hard travellin', Lord.

Well, I been hittin' some hard-rock minin', I thought you
$\qquad\qquad\qquad\qquad\qquad\qquad\qquad$ *knowed.*
I been leanin' on a pressure drill, way down the road.
Hammer flyin', airhose suckin',
An' six feet of mud an' I sure been a-muckin',
I been hittin' some hard travellin', Lord.

I been workin' at Pittsburgh Steel, I thought you knowed.
I been dumpin' red-hot slag, way down the road.
I been blastin', I been firin',
I been pourin' that red-hot iron,
An' I been hittin' some hard travellin', Lord.

I been layin' in a hard-rock jail, I thought you knowed.
I been layin' out ninety days, way down the road.
Mean old judge, he says to me,
"It's ninety days for vagrancy."
An' I been hittin' some hard travellin', Lord.

Well, I been hittin' some hard harvestin', I thought you knowed.
North Dakota to Kansas City, way down the road.
Cuttin' that wheat and a-stackin' that hay,
Tryin' to make about a dollar a day.
I been hittin' some hard travellin', Lord.

I been walkin' that Lincoln Highway, I thought you knowed.
I been hittin' that Sixty-six, way down the road
Heavy load and a worried mind,
Lookin' for a woman that's hard to find,
An' I been hittin' some hard travellin', Lord.

$\qquad\qquad\qquad\qquad\qquad\qquad\qquad\qquad$ Woody Guthrie

Englishman to American on trans-Atlantic liner: *"Who was it who discovered America?"*
American: *"Christopher Columbus."*
Englishman (later, after three days on train): *"Who was it, old boy, who discovered America?"*
American: *"Christopher Columbus."*
Englishman: *"He could hardly miss the bloody place, could he?"*

Joke on Station WWNC, Nashville

Hobo, hobo, where did you come from?

American children's chant

PREFATORY NOTE

The shock-trooper of the American expansion, the man with bed-roll on back who free-lanced beyond the community redoubts, building the canals and roads and rights-of-way, spiking rails, felling timber, drilling oil, digging mines, fencing prairie, harvesting wheat, was the hobo.

He was homeless and unmarried. He freeloaded on the freight trains whose tracks he laid and whose tunnels he blasted. He lived in bunk houses or tents or jungle camps or city flophouses. He was a marginal, alienated man, capriciously used and discarded by a callous but dynamic system, yet he was proud of the mode he devised out of an imperative mobility. He was a unique and indigenous American product.

He formed the moving labor corps which followed the advancing line across the continent, and he answered the market demand for manpower where none existed in the new, rough country. He staked down with his hammer the provisional frontier.

In one of his aspects he was the Ancient Mariner of this oceanic land, the albatross of failure hung about his neck. In his militant political role, as a Wobbly, a red card carrier of the Industrial Workers of the World, he was "half industrial slave, half vagabond adventurer ... the *francs tireurs* of the class struggle."

He often got drunk and squandered the money he had sweated for. He was a wild and recalcitrant wayfarer, bothersome to the settled citizen who disapproved of him and perhaps secretly envied him. Out there in the offing he developed his own distinct life and philosophy: tough, reckless, radical, sardonic. A romantic essence of the hobo's style has impregnated American song, literature and outlook.

Considering the degree to which it has, he has been surprisingly neglected as a subject of study. Information about him is scattered, piecemeal, throughout seventy years of autobiography, fiction, poetry, folk song, sociology and economic surveys, yet his genesis was really much earlier, and few attempts have been made, and none in recent years, to examine his origins, the type and the influence of the wandering worker in America.

His habitat has changed but his habits have not, not all that much. For he is still there, a sundry part of the tidal restlessness of American life; and the hobo idea, or impulse, is even more widely present, the eagerly seized inheritance of the young of an urbanized society in which the hobo is theoretically obsolete.

There are no agreed forms or consistency for the plural and abbreviation of hobo. When the words occur within quotation marks I have kept to the originals, so that such variations as hobos and hoboes, bos and boes, 'bo and bo occur in the text. Similarly: boxcar, box-car and box car. Pedantically, Skid Road is the correct early vernacular, but the corruption skid row is now normal, and this I have used. Okies – the Dust Bowl refugees from Oklahoma – is not infrequently misspelt as Oakies; when it occurs thus in quotation I have again kept to the original.

K.A.

ACKNOWLEDGEMENTS

The information of greatest value to me in preparing this book came from passing strangers scattered about the continent of the United States, men who unlike me – a temporary transient – were permanently on the road: hobos, loggers, iron workers, oilmen, cowhands, fruit pickers and unemployed drifters, Americans on the move encountered hitching on the highways, dropping off freight trains, anaesthetizing themselves in wine bars, laboring on construction sites, cutting softwoods on peaks, harvesting vegetables, and doing nothing in city skid rows and mission hostels.

However, many official bodies and individuals generously gave me access to their own specialist records and knowledge, and those to whom I am indebted include the U.S. Department of State, and Angeline M. Pascuzzi of the Bureau of Educational and Cultural Affairs; Sophia Cooper and Glenn Halm of the U.S. Department of Labor; Charles M. Clendenen of the U.S. Department of Agriculture; the Library of Congress, Washington; Louise Heinze of the Tamiment Library, New York University Libraries; the library staff of the Labadie Collection, University of Michigan, Ann Arbor; Mrs. Clifford R. Miller of the International Center, University of Michigan; Herbert Gutman of the State University of New York; Bertram Gottlieb and Marvin Friedman of the American Federation of Labor; Archie Green and Barbara D. Dennis of the Institute of Labor and Industrial Relations, University of Illinois; John Hope Franklin of the University of Chicago; Paul S. Taylor, William H. Metzler and Melville Dalton of the University of California; Joseph G. Rayback of the University of Alberta; the State of California Department of Industrial Relations; Sam J. Allen of the National Council of Churches; the Association of American Railroads; Colonel George W. Svodoba and Lt. Joe Nocerino of the U.S. Corps of Engineers, Magdalen G. H. Flexner, Maggie Haferd and Edward J. McHale of the American Embassy, London; Nancy Phillips and the staff of the U.S. Information Service Library, London; George Evans of the Hertfordshire County Library and R. G. Murray of the Cambridgeshire College of Arts.

I am also grateful for the personal hospitality and help in New York to Michael and Stephanie Harrington, Tim Seldes, Mr. and Mrs. Benjamin B. Ferencz, Francis Brown of the New York *Times* and Shirley Lentz of CBS; in Chicago to Nelson Algren and Carl Keller; in Little Rock to Jack and Ellen Smith; in Los Angeles to John and Margery Edwards; in Nashville to Bill Churchill and John Seigenthaler; in Custer, South Dakota, to Ken Adkins; in Klamath Falls, Oregon, to Jack Wolff and Al Carlson; in Walla Walla, Washington, to Larry Brown. Also I am especially grateful to the Ford Motor Company who so kindly furnished the Galaxie which kept me mobile over 9,000 miles of turnpike and Main Street, mountain pass and desert road, and never blew a gasket.

I would like to thank the following authors and publishers for permission to quote from their books: Cassell and Company Ltd. for permission to quote from *Been Here and Gone* by Frederic Ramsey Jr.; Harold Ober Associates Inc. for permission to quote from the poem *Florida Road Workers* by Langston Hughes, copyrighted 1927 by Alfred A. Knopf, renewed 1955 by Langston Hughes; Alan Lomax for permission to quote from *Folk Songs of North America*; Essex Music Limited for permission to quote *Hard Travellin'* by Woody Guthrie, copyrighted 1957 by Ludlow Music Inc., New York; Harmony Music Limited and Tom Paxton for permission to quote from *My Ramblin' Boy*, copyrighted 1963 by Cherry Lane Music Inc., *I'm Bound for the Mountains and the Sea*, copyrighted 1962 by Cherry Lane Music Inc., and *I Can't Help but Wonder*, copyrighted 1963 by Cherry Lane Music Inc., all written by Tom Paxton; Harcourt, Brace and World, Inc. for permission to quote from *Land of the Free* by Archibald MacLeish, copyrighted 1938, 1966; Mrs. E. L. Masters for permission to quote from the poem *Abel Melveny* in *Spoon*

River Anthology by Edgar Lee Masters, published by Macmillan Company 1914, 1942; Houghton Mifflin Company for permission to quote from *Songs of the Outland : Ballads of the Hoboes and Other Verse* by Herbert Knibbs; The University of Chicago Press for permission to quote from *The Hobo and Men on the Move* by Nels Anderson, and from *Wobbly* by Ralph Chaplin; André Deutsch for permission to quote from *The Gravel Ponds* by Peter Levi; E. P. Dutton and Co., Inc. for permission to quote from *Bound for Glory* by Woody Guthrie, copyrighted 1943; Irving Shepard for permission to quote from *The Road* by Jack London; Liveright Publishing Corporation for permission to quote from *The River* by Hart Crane; and Paul S. Taylor for permission to quote from *An American Exodus*.

Most of all, my thanks to my wife for her tireless navigation, both on the road and through the research.

K.A.

CONTENTS

ILLUSTRATIONS

following page 224

"Hard travellin' "[7]
American rolling stone[12]
Leaving town[7]
Stoop Labour[8]
Child labour[2]

Key to acknowledgements
[1] Illinois Central Railroad Public Relations
[2] George Eastman House Collection
[3] Culver Pictures, Inc.
[4] Chicago, Burlington and Quincy Railroad Company Public Relations
[5] Brown Brothers
[6] Sante Fe Railway Photo
[7] Library of Congress Collection
[8] United Press International Photo
[9] From *Industrial Worker*, April 23, 1910
[10] From *The Man Who Never Died*
[11] J. H. Ward, Lamar, Colorado
[12] E. O. Hoppé

PART ONE

STRANGERS AND SOJOURNERS

*The land is mine; for ye are
strangers and sojourners with me.*

God to Moses : Leviticus, 25 : 23

I : SOME PEOPLE JUST GOT THAT ROAMIN' BLOOD IN THEM

At worst, one is in motion; and at best,
Reaching no absolute, in which to rest,
One is always nearer by not keeping still.

Thom Gunn : *On the Move*

TWELVE miles from a crossroads store and gas station, given on the map the unwarranted importance of being named Spotted Horse, and fifty miles more from the nearest small town, a dilapidated 1950 Plymouth is juddering along the switchbacks of Highway 14 between the lean, rocky hills of Wyoming. The Plymouth's fender and chrome radiator grill hang and shake like a broken jaw, and across the flaking *eau-de-Nil* paintwork on the doors, boot and bonnet is stencilled in black capitals, six times over

WORK
WANTED
ANYTHING

The car's driver has a two-day stubble and a sweat-blackened straw stetson is crushed down on his eyebrows. His name is Harold Myers. He is thirty-three. All his upper front teeth are missing (not because of decay, is the impression, but because of a collision some time or other with a hard object, perhaps a fist). He is wearing, as well as the stetson, a dirty gray work shirt, threadbare Levis secured by a wide leather belt with a swaggery silver buckle, and high tooled cowhand boots.

"They call people like me rubber tire tramps," Harold Myers says when he has drawn into the wayside. He tears off the zip opener from one of the Budweiser beer cans lined up along the back seat, and takes a long swig. "I bought this heap three months ago in Milwaukee, thirty-five dollars. I paint this sign on whatever auto I have when I take to the road. Every spring I

21

get this fever. Can't sit no more. I have to get on the road again, and see people, hit new experiences. That sign's my promoter. When the car breaks down I just leave it where it is and travel on the thumb.

"I've got another sign in my suitcase: RIDE WANTED PLEASE. I hang out my shingle at the roadside. That shows courtesy and motorists respond.

"Right now I been herding cattle, breaking horses, plowing land, all that, here in Wyoming, and before that I was doing ranch work up at Kelispell, Montana, and now I got the urge again. Figured I'd go down to Florida, taking charter boats out with deep-sea fishermen for Captain White, down in Miami. I worked for him back in 1961.

"I was born in Michigan but I been what you might call driftwood, just jetsam, since me and my wife split up in 1956, working through the fruit belt in California, through the wheat belt in Kansas, farmhand in Virginia and Georgia, going out on the shrimp boats up the whole Eastern seaboard.

"I don't carry much, just a razor and a change of pants and shirt, and I have a picture of my wife and kids, and a little twenty-four hour prayer book which was my wife's, it's got twenty-four hour thoughts, prayers and meditations. Okay, I'm a hobo. A ramblin' man ain't too welcome in towns – not unless you got fifty bucks to spend, then you're welcome, then you're a goddam good boy and they don't give a shit if you're wanted for murder. But if you're broke, if you don't have that almighty dollar, the towns are cruel places.

"That don't worry me too much. You know what I think of the Good Life? It stinks, boy. I don't want any part of this organized deal. Let me tell you, rubber tire tramps like me are basically honest. If we see shit we don't take it. We're not running from fear. We're running from the corrupt rotten standards this country has built up.

"Automation is pushing a lot of good men outside society. This is modern America, not the supermarkets and Chambers of Commerce. Ranch hands like me just live like vagabonds. We live well if we've got the money. If we haven't, well, there's always another valley over the hill.

"I get a lot of happiness out of this life, more satisfaction than

22

the guys who've got this pisspoor deal of trying to squeeze along providing the milk and the corn, all the middlemen getting their rake-offs and cuts. I may be an outcast but I've cast myself out. I figure it'll take me three weeks to get to Florida; but if it's three months, I can spare the time."

———————

FRESNO COUNTY, California, is the world's most bountiful agricultural dominion: 6,000 square miles tightly patterned into 8,340 farms; 221 commercial crops with a turnover of one million dollars a day. There are many millionaires in the top echelon of Fresno agribusiness, the term used here to distinguish this scale of operation from old-fashioned farming.

In this transitional prelude to total mechanization agribusiness still needs human hands. In the peak three weeks of the year, the September grape crop, there is work for 50,000 seasonal immigrants. It is a hit-and-miss system. Now with the grape harvest yet to start there are 500 men around the town, without jobs or shelter.

One who has found both after a fashion is across in the derelicts' quarter where the freeway overpass strides across on concrete stilts. On the Mission chapel wall, beneath a huge blurry mural of an open Bible, Edward Wayne Mollett is painstakingly painting in the words from the 107th Psalm: "They wandered in the wilderness in a solitary way; they found no city to dwell in."

He is a big sprawling man with cropped pepper-and-salt hair and a ravaged nice face. "I'm fifty-four," he says, "and I was doing swell until the war. I started out as a Western Union messenger. I went into the grocery business and rose from clerk to be manager of San Francisco's first drive-in Safeway supermarket in 1937.

"I went to night-school and qualified as a welder and earned some big money in the shipyards. I bought a 65,000 dollar apartment house and eight sets of flats. I was happily married for thirteen years. Then my wife and small son were killed in an automobile accident.

"Through remorse and the tragedy I began drinking and for fifteen years I was on the wine. I went round the world twice on ships and sailed on a lumber schooner and oil tankers and I mooched around every state in the union on freight trains.

"Part of the year I'd follow the vegetable harvests on the trains, to wherever I could drive a tractor or cut and bale hay. A crowd of us would go up to Chicago and get shipped 500 miles up into Michigan, living in a caboose doing pick and shovel labor on renewing track for a dollar-fifty a day. But you can't do that kind of work if you drink. Your nerves are too shaky.

"Down in Sacramento I cut up old autos with a torch and in summer I'd take off to pick apricots and cherries, then up picking apples in Washington. I'd get back into town with 500 dollars and just soak it up for a couple of months. Then I'd hit the trains again and probably get thrown in the hoosegow by the detectives, the rest of the time living in cardboard box jungles down by the riverside.

"When you've got a gallon of wine you feel happy for a few hours, but it's a sewer; it's a dirty pointless life. You have no friends, only drinking acquaintances who, same as you, are frightened, discouraged men. You're in a rut, stuck in the mud.

"You say 'Let's go to Tucson, Arizona, let's go to New York to look at the World Fair, let's go up to Seattle' – but you take your troubles with you from state to state. It's a life of a thousand jails and a thousand flophouses. All the time, wherever you go, you got your own skid row right there inside your head."

2 : KING OF THE ROAD

*Oh, highway ... you express me
better than I can express myself!*

Walt Whitman

A FEW years ago I was in Florida with ten days spare before
my next appointment in Los Angeles. I had been to the
United States previously, to New York, to Chicago, to Los Angeles, to San Francisco, to Dallas, to New Orleans – but always
these visits had been for specific, usually journalistic, reasons.
There had never been free time for sloping off into impromptu
exploration. I had been slotted into a jet at one metropolitan
airport and shot back the same way. The immense hinterland of
America remained utterly unknown to me, concealed and in-
communicado under that cloud haze. It seemed to me a mystery,
a secret continent which tantalized my imagination.

On that spring morning of 1962 I boarded a Greyhound bus
which would take me from Fort Lauderdale across the Deep
South, around the rim of the Gulf of Mexico and along the Mexican border, then tacking up across the West to California
through ground floor America, bus station America. The great
metal capsule pounded, day and night, between pine scrub and
orange groves, cotton and rice fields where egrets fed, and endlessly through the billboards, sub-division housing, trailer parks,
pennant-frilled gas stations, scrapped car heaps, and the motel,
snack bar and supermarket signscape at the approach to every
town – "like badger holes, ringed with trash," is John Steinbeck's phrase. Wherever we halted for refueling and a meal
break, whether an oil city with refinery tanks and pipe com-
plexes, shimmering white satin in the sun, or a few streets of
shabby grayish clapboard houses washed with mimosa, in each
Greyhound Post House all around me was the swill and flux of
this strange American life.

There in the concrete bazaar were always the banks of lockers,
the news-stand racks displaying *True Romances*, *Sad Sack*,
Stumbo the Giant and *The Adventures of Jerry Lewis*, luggage

stickers and Confederate flag postcards. There was the lunch-counter offering cheeseburgers, hot roast beef sandwiches and DuB-L-Burgers. Around the ticket office and the big central precinct with its rows of benches was the tide of passengers, constantly replenished as it was drained off by the next connecting bus: mothers with babies, fathers with families, single girls and solo men, parties in seersuckers with smart matching fiberglass baggage sets and men in striped mechanics' hats with haversacks of tools, soldiers with duffle bags and farm hands in straw slouch hats or carrying plaid mackinaws for the Northern woods. On the benches some were curled up asleep or slumped in a half-dozing daze, sitting it out for a dawn schedule; others weaved and strolled around the crowded, butt-smudged floor, swigging Cokes or chewing hot-dogs. Under the raw strip lights there was always the frowsty, stained look of an over-used transient place, the temporary shelter of travellers with fifty miles to go, or 3,000.

In the wash room at Mobile, after an all-night run, there were two men freshening up. One was sluicing cold water into his carroty hair, which he then combed and kneaded into Byzantine helixes. He was asking the other, in a white T-shirt emblazoned with racing cars and a DAYTONA BEACH crest, who was shaving with a plastic pocket kit open on the basin, if Route 80 would take him straight through to the West Coast, or would he have to go into New Orleans? "Figured I'd see if there's any pruning up there," he said.

The other gave him expert directions: "Baby, I been out to the Coast a hunnerd times. Why spend your dough on a bus? You could thumb your way right through. You'd make it in less than a week."

This was America, the federal entity, the United States, but they talked of those sumless spaces fanning out North and West like two prospectors colliding in unconstituted territory.

Later I rode for a day through Texas with a boy who joined the bus at Baton Rouge and who was also bound for the Golden State. He wore a peaked cap and a shiny black mock-leather windcheater decorated with pretty flowers of verdigrised tin studs, and on the rack overhead he had a bed-roll tucked in at each end and tied with sash cord. He chain smoked king-size menthol cigarettes, a routine interrupted only when he scooped a harmonica from the zip breast pocket and sucked and blew some desolate hillbilly music. He was seventeen and, he said, had decided to split out of Louisiana. "My daddy used to ride the freight trains when he was a kid," he told me, "and he got around this country plenty. Felt I'd like to try it myself. I had enough money to buy a ticket as far as San Diego and after that I'll do just what comes nat'rly. Man, I can't wait to get to ole California. That's where the gold is, everybody knows." He played a tune which he announced as *Teardrops On Your Letter*, learned from a very big record of 1959 by Hank Ballard and The Midnighters.

These brushes, the glimpses of an unbeholden truancy along just one strand of roadway, really began this book by momentarily bringing to life an essence of American life which had always fascinated me from a distance: the fluctuating ground swells Westward as the frontier was thrust back; the transcontinental zig-zagging by nomadic laboring men at the height of the hobo epoch when they rode the boxcars in hundreds of thousands; the *Grapes of Wrath* period when a million rural refugees, dispossessed by dust storms and slump, were on the road; the symbolism of the train, both as the way out to the possibility of better things and as the poignant reminder of a distant home, as in Thomas Wolfe's

> *The rails go westward in the dark.*
> *Brother, have you seen the starlight on the rails?*
> *Have you heard the thunder of the fast express?*

And in the Negro blues:

> *I'm just from the country, never been in your town before,*
> *Lord, I'm broke and hungry, ain't got no place to go.*
> *I was raised in the country, I been there all my life,*
> *Lord, I had to run off and leave my children and wife.*

But how true was any of this still? How representative were these Greyhound riders? Then there were about four million unemployed (that summer it fell a fraction) and it was estimated, with less statistical certainty, that there were thirty-five million people living below poverty line. On the other hand there were seventy-five million in the total work force and that thirty-five million had to be viewed in relation to a population of 198 million enjoying, overall, a state of prosperity and ease hitherto unknown to mankind. Had the American economy stabilized, the old sliding about calmed, the melting pot simmered down? Economists have defined four post-war "spending tiers," the fourth and present being "the life-enriching stratum." America urbanized, standardized, a consumers' cornucopia garlanded with telephone wire and television beam, was hardly the picture of a hobo jungle. Was it that the vigor and impatience, the bustle and striking out, as well as the directionless scrambling for a position on that fourth stratum, all the dynamic of the American dream, had – as has been said – clotted into the American trance?

I was unsure what I would find although it seemed likely that it would not be the hobo, neither the old freight train rider, banking on luck and muscle to get through the most arduous circumstances, nor even many of the Greyhound transients I had briefly encountered. All the official agencies assured me that this phase of American life was over and done with. The endlessly helpful Washington departments which guided me to big construction projects and on to the seasonal routes of the semi-organized armies of harvest migrants explained that, while mobility was a vital nerve in the nation's functioning, it no longer took the old vagabond form: the hobo was extinct, the Java Man of industrial history.

That I retained some scepticism about those statements was due, flimsily enough, to a record which popped into the hit parade as I was making plans for my trip. My hunch was that despite the improbable gaiety of Roger Miller's *King of the Road*, it must have some significance to the average American if it had been elected a best-seller. It began, with a lazy lilt:

> *Trailers for sale or rent,*
> *Rooms to let, fifty cents,*
> *No 'phone, no pool, no pets,*
> *Ain't got no cigarettes.*

28

It continued to explain with sunny resignation that two hours of "pushin' broom" brought in enough to take a four-bit room and, the inference was, an enviable contentment known only to the happy-go-lucky bum. If it had struck the chord it had in fourth-stratum America it seemed to me that it might have more relevance than mere romantic nostalgia for the idea of a departed wayfaring freedom. Perhaps I might find that there were still many, from choice or necessity, itinerant under the floorboards of the Great Society.

In fact, I did not have to search far, only in the right places, and usually just a few blocks away from any town's Department of Labor and Department of Agriculture buildings — beside the railroad tracks where the freight trains delivered their human cargo to the skid row district of bars, rooming houses and missions, the makeshift palaces of the real kings of the road.

My starting point was not the belief that mobility is unique to America, only that America has a unique kind of mobility. I need not have moved out of my own patch of England to find a fluid hotchpotch of race. The tuft of chimneys I can see as I write, across the county border in Bedfordshire, is a brickfield staffed mostly by young immigrant Italians. Farming nearby is a Pole who stayed on after flying with Bomber Command. Several streets in the small market town three miles away have been colonized by West Indians and Pakistanis. The motorway extension just beyond is being built by Irish construction gangs. A Scottish boy in the village recently married a Spanish girl from the Canaries, and the shop is run by a Yorkshire couple.

Man has ever, and everywhere, been on the move. The ticker-tape of the human race's occupation of our planet is an endless message of invasion and retreat, ebb and flow, flux and reflux. Always concomitant within the nature of man has been on the one hand the need to push down roots and to have the security of a center, a homestead, and on the other the restless chafing against these very ties. The warring of these two compulsions had produced the fluctuations of migration, settlement, secondary surge.

There are medical terms designed to cover wanderlust in its pathological forms. Dromomania is the desire to travel pushed to

29

the point of abnormality, an obsession for roaming, and drapeto-mania is an insane or uncontrollable impulse to wander away from home. But although these conditions may disguise themselves under good reasons, my impression is that they are rare beside the causes for most men being on the road. Behind each drive and drift there has usually been the primary need for food. Violent climatic changes, such as the opening of a glacial period and the southerly curve of rain belts dispersed game and crops, so man adjusted – with the flexibility that has made him a successful survivor – and followed. Races and tribes were nudged out by an advancing ice-cap or roasted out of drying deserts by cycles of fiercer heat. Other more sophisticated or emotional reasons have propelled populations into new ground: greed for plunder and the greener fields of others, the stubborn adherence to outlawed religious or totemic principles, revolt against political oppression, the draw of adventure and action: all have inextricably mingled.

Distance lengthened between image and reality, between experience and desire. It was amid the smoke and degradation of nineteenth-century factory enslavement that the poignancy of the lost labor, of the *idea* of a natural life in the glades and the wheatfields – for the reinlessness of the happy rover, the tramp, the road mender, the shepherd, the gipsy – became most confused and most acute.

Both the ideal and the actuality of mobility, of free-ranging in unfenced countryside and across distances of pulse-quickening scale, have survived in America long beyond the time when they had become a literary convention, a cliché of the imagination, in Europe. Perhaps the nearest similarity to the American pattern was the briefer, and pedestrian or horse-borne, span of the Australian sundowner, who humped his bluey in the outback and like the American hobo glorified himself in song and legend: the "jolly swagman," the squatter and free selector, the gold digger and the shearer and the other itinerant bush-workers, as in *The Ramble-eer* of the 1890s.

> For I am a ramble-eer, a rollicking ramble-eer
> I'm a roving rake of poverty, and son-of-a-gun for beer.

30

(One of the earliest American hobo songs was *The Son of a Gambolier* which began:

*I'm a rambling rake of poverty
From Tippery Town I came.*)

Tremendous though the upheavals and shifts of people in Europe during and after the war were, they were an aberration. Despite the heterogeneity in my own ordinary country area there is a family in the village which has been here since the thirteenth century (when the records start, so it may well be even longer), and to look down the parish registers is to see, from the seventeenth century onward, familiar name after familiar name, whose descendants are present neighbors. In America it is the exception to talk to a person who was born in the place where you meet him. Furthermore it is statistically likely that he will have flitted off if you call in at that town a few years later.

To risk a large generalization, which I shall be attempting to justify, no matter how he may rhapsodize about the rover and picture himself within the golden pastoral mode – or its rolled-gold substitute – to the European entrenchment is good. To the European impermanence and change are bad, restlessness reveals the flaw of instability; whereas to an American restlessness is pandemic; entrenchment means fossilization, a poor spirit. Of course both outlooks are held there, as historical parallels in the edificial scheme of the traditional regionalists of the Old South, and in the chafing and fidgetiness of those who thrust deeper into inner America; both are mixed unsettlingly in the individual. Lerner makes the point that to understand America these are the two elements – "double beat of migration and the sense of place" – which must be seen as facets of each other. "In a big country you run the risk of feeling lost, of being anonymous, and a sense of place is a way of riveting yourself down." But the lostness and the longing for trustworthy attachments – Thomas Wolfe's "a stone, a leaf, an unfound door" – has usually in America succumbed to the greater fear of being caught.

So the search is continued, the Faustian spirit of the endless

31

quest, the temptation to top the next hill, which became the tropistic quality of the American migrations – indeed, of American institutions themselves, whose very nature has evolved in terms of flexibility and acceptance of the new to the point of dread of anything – car, building or mind – that is not of the latest styling.

The present Europeans are those who stayed, who were, whichever way it may be seen, content or steady or faint-hearted. The present Americans are the Europeans, or their descendants, who got out, the mavericks and the refractory and the bold (or the duds and fugitives: again, however it may be seen). They keep that bloody-mindedness green and they preserve within their adopted borders the right to move on to new ground if the old is intolerable, infertile, or just too stalely familiar.

Fluidity in America is prized and praised, both kinds of fluidity: that which is physical and horizontal about the land, and the other which is vertically social, up, and down, the economic grease-pole. They cannot be discussed unrelatedly because each is implicit in the metabolism of the other.

The highly-paid white-collar executive who moves from a ranch-style house in St. Paul, Minnesota, will, with luck, be moving to a bigger ranch-style house in Westchester County. So, although he is a dot on the geographical mobility chart, he is simultaneously acting out the social mobility myth and proving it true in his case. The "gipsy" truck driver who pulls on hire one of those monster aluminium cargo vans 3,000 miles across country, howling down the highways with twin exhausts jutting like snorkels above the cabin, hopes soon to be sitting in an office sending out others on the long hauls.

There are seventy-five million motor vehicles in America, sixty-eight million of those being private cars, and there are more than ninety million licensed drivers. Every year 400 billion miles of motor traveling is done on American roads.

The Americans also take to the road with trailers and caravans swaying behind. There are 350,000 now on wheels, as distinct from those positioned like semi-permanent bungalows. More and more Americans go off in camping vans and in metal housing units mounted on three-quarter-ton trucks, bedrooms projecting like nose gun-turrets over the driving compartment.

In Colorado I saw one family camper-truck, placarded across the radiator THE NOMADS, towing a Volkswagen – the dinghy for use when anchored in the programed forest bower. Overnight campers in the national parks and forests have risen from fifteen million in 1960 to twenty-three million a year. Additionally, the inter-city buses now match the railroads in total passenger miles. The Greyhound Scenicruisers and the Continental Trailways Silver Eagles, the two biggest lines, together log eleven billion miles a year. Nearly as much mileage again is mopped up by the shorter-hop bus services.

The drive-in banks, the supermarket plazas, the open-air restaurant stalls where your order, dictated over a window-side telephone or microphone, is brought by a waitress to the car door (an odd sensation of having public breakfast in bed), the throw-in machines which catch your coins in a metal wicket-keeper's mitts at the toll road gateway – all these are the superficial but intelligent adjustments to a social order built, like an auto's bodyshell itself, around the internal combustion engine, accessories which have evolved out of a mobile behavior and which in turn aid and extend that mobile behavior.

Much of this ferment in America is frivolous and frothy ("freedom plus groceries"), a splurging away of gasoline and tire rubber at a rate that never fails to make a frugal European's heart quail. At base, though, there is the condition which the American accepted when he rejected Europe and came to the new shore, indeed the very condition that drew him there: space and its kinetic scope.

Forty million Americans, almost a fifth of the population, change places of residence every year. A move may mean just across town (if those status ascent cogs are engaging as they should) but it is likelier to be farther, even across the continent. The average American family moves house every five years, eighteen in every thousand long-distance. (The Nashville *Tennessean* – a local daily newspaper – publishes a New Neighbors list. On the day I glanced down it among the thirty-six families who had moved into town the previous day, eleven were from other, different states.) The trend for twenty-five years has been sharply away from the country. In 1940 farm population was nearly one-quarter of the total; today it is less than one-eighth.

Thirty-five years ago one farm worker produced food for ten people; today he produces enough for twenty-three. The cities have not absorbed this surplus as an additional work force: this is the social drop-out factor. These are the men shoved over to and beyond the perimeter, the drifters without gyroscopes.

Yet by and large Americans continue to value mobility as a high performance fifth gear over most standard economies' four-speed boxes. In the Chicago Employment Office last year, Rodger Wilson explained to me that because "ever-increasing complexity of economic living hampers the movement of un-employed workers," his department was beginning a Congress-authorized experimental project "to increase mobility." *Increase* it. The British attitude, reflected in Margot Jeffery's 1954 survey, is perhaps predictably more conservative. "It is impossible to regard the willingness of the labor force to make changes as an unmixed asset; since such willingness may reflect not merely a satisfactory measure of personal adaptability to changing cir-cumstances, but the restlessness which comes from a failure to find satisfying work."

Actually there are American economists and sociologists who concur. As long ago as 1938 Anderson wrote: "The casual-labor market is an economic luxury because of the trial-and-error principle upon which it operates. Workers go here and there in a chance search for jobs. Such a hit-and-miss search occupies the attention of many more workers than are needed. Many are busy in the search, but few are busy at work."

It had by then become clear to all who would look it in the eye – and ignoring the wanderlust that may incubate it and the romance that is its by-product – that migrant casual labor is horribly wasteful of human energy and resources. The general turmoil of the past is known about: indeed, the dust has still not settled. The question here is not only "Is it necessary?" but "Is it good?" When the frontier closed, the West strung itself with barbed wire and the railroads from East to West embraced – goodbye adventure! But in the nineteenth century came the call for a style of movement different to that of the frontier scout and the inaugural plowman. What was now needed was an industrial labor force without impediment, to be transferred and distributed like troops on a fluid battleground. So the busi-

34

ness world created "an ideology of stir and movement, jostling the pick-up-and-sadly-go spirit of the immigrant, using whatever allies it could find in the ever-upward doctrine of religion, science and progress, linking democracy to them and to unending change."

Yet there is nothing in the American Republic as a political institution to say that change in itself is good. The Founders permitted change but made it pretty hard to accomplish. Existing religions have rarely looked kindly on unsettledness: it is the typical terrain of messiahs. "Thus government, science, and religion are not by themselves supporters of the doctrine of mobility and change," writes de Grazia. "Like the Indian following the buffalo, the American follows his job."

The Indians and the buffaloes are tamed and penned; the American is not yet, entirely.

PART TWO

STONES IN MY PASSWAY

I got stones in my passway, and my
  road is dark at night . . .

I got to keep moving, blues falling down like hail
Can't keep no money, hellbound on my trail.

From two blues recorded by Robert
Johnson in 1936, the year before he
was murdered.

3: EXTINCT (OFFICIAL)

Now alien, I move forlorn, an uprooted tree.
And at dawn, irresolutely,
into the void ...

From *Worker Uprooted* by Joseph Kalar,
a lumbermill poet of the Thirties.

"UNCLE" Purl Stockton spent forty-five years singing the gospel around the United States, praising the Almighty in blazing baritone in hundreds of revivalist tents and store-front churches. When in 1958 he was asked if he would start a rescue mission for derelicts, drifters, lolligaggers, alki stiffs, scrubs and winos in Little Rock, he replied that any man who hadn't more sense than to get drunk should look after himself.

"The Lord changed my mind right quick."

He has been running the Union Rescue Mission at Little Rock since then. He is now seventy-seven, a massive, powerful, unstoppable redeemer with flossy white hair and chromium-rimmed spectacles. He is crouched restlessly at the desk under a framed SERVICE TO MANKIND AWARD in his office beside the Rock Island tracks. He houses nearly 200 homeless men at a time. He gets income by putting those unable to find jobs around town (yard work, picking cucumbers, loading sugar trucks, chopping cotton) on to cutting up newspapers which sell for wrapping at a dollar a hundred sheets. He has an ex-bootlegger just out of the penitentiary running an electrical shop where broken television sets, radios and refrigerators, donated to the mission, are doctored up and resold.

"This isn't a hobo jungle or a drunks' paradise or a loafers' retreat," Uncle Purl lets it be known in his melodious bellow. "This is a rescue mission. I tell any man who comes in here 'We're trying to keep you from going to hell. HELL! You can stay here as long as you want to if you're trying to find yourself and find Christ and find a job.

" 'If you aren't interested you're nothing but a bum, and I'm not going to take money from God's people to feed a bum, so git! If you get drunk that's *your* business but if you come here drunk that's *my* business. We've sent a thousand men to jail for getting drunk. You can feed here and rest here and you come to church every day. I'm not trying to jam religion down your throat because if I did that you'd puke it up – but, brother, *you come to church.*' That's what I tell them.

"We call them travelers. We don't use the word hobo – unless I get mad at them. Why do they come here? Because of broken homes, because they've lost their jobs, because their firm moved someplace else, because they're old.

"Some are running from the law, some are running from themselves. Seventy per cent are drunks. The word goes round in the boxcars about our Mission. Only the other day, I was told, three men were eating some breakfast in Cheyenne, Wyoming, and one said he was heading South for winter, and another said 'Be sure you hit Little Rock, Arkansas. The old man there'll treat you right if you treat him right, and if you don't he'll beat the hell out of you.'"

Uncle Purl chuckles. "The police don't bother them. They work with me. They know these men won't wander around the town panhandling and bumming money. We make sure they behave themselves while they're here, then they move on. They ramble around. They got ants in their pants. Just ramble around. The freight trains bring them in and the freight trains take them out."

The previous night seven new travelers had checked in at the Little Rock Rescue Mission from five different states, two from Tennessee, two from Texas, and from Kentucky, Indiana and Oklahoma; the day before, ten men from seven different states; the day before that, eight from seven different states, the day before that, six from six different states, the day before that, seven from six different states, the day before that, fourteen from four different states, the day before that, eleven from seven different states. Among them were laborers, truck drivers, roofers, carpenters, sailors – whatever they chose to call themselves. As their "home" they gave, for the register, the state where perhaps they had been born and may have seen since only when traversing it on a link freight or a redball passenger but not inside "on the cushions."

In Tulsa at a rail crossing a man in check cotton shirt and denims, and with a newspaper parcel under his arm, eyes the New Jersey license plate on my car and strolls over, rolling a cigarette from a handful of dog ends.

"Any work up there in New Jersey? Well, I just wondered. I'd try anywhere. I been on the road three years now. Maybe I just wanted to see what else there was. I'm a planer and floor polisher, just got in from California.

"There were fifteen of us riding in that boxcar, and maybe another thirty on that train. I figure there're more men on the road now than there ever was. I don't know where I'll head next. A lot of employers think you're a loafer and it's hard to convince them that you won't quit after a coupla days. Anyway they give what jobs there are to local men, guess that's understandable.

"I hear there are jobs up in Chicago and New York but what happens if you arrive without a cent? You can't walk through from one end of a city to another without a cent for car fare."

———————

OFFICIALLY that man does not exist, not, at least, as a permanent transient. Men may move from one place to another, changing jobs, but they don't hobo now. Not officially. The railroads have erased the hobo as a problem.

The Association of American Railroads describes the present situation in this way: "In the days of steam locomotive operation the railroads were used rather extensively by hobos but the coming of diesel locomotive power and the newer types of cars, coupled with high speed train operations, have contributed greatly to a considerable curtailment of hobo traffic by rail."

Some scattered enquiries confirm that this official picture is general. From Mobile, Alabama, the Gulf, Mobile and Ohio Railroad Company reports: "This situation has changed materially in the past twenty years in that comparatively few hobos ride trains in this modern day. This is a rather minor duty of the Special Agents Department. The present type of person riding trains or loitering in out-of-the-way places around a railroad today could be classified as migrant labor although most of these are derelicts, alcoholics, and a very low class of the human race. Modern railroading in the United States does not lend itself the benefit of the old time transient who used to ride from one town to another or follow the harvest each year. This is a thing of the past."

J. L. Hastings, manager of the Atchison, Topeka and Santa Fe Railway System in Chicago, recalls: "I started with the Santa Fe in 1937 as a Special Officer at Needles, California, a freight and passenger division point. We used to handle between 600 and 1,000 transients riding our trains every month.

"Our policy was to endeavor to sell them tickets on our passenger trains to discourage their riding. We would have had the jails full if we had arrested all of them. Some were arrested. This was a small town, and the railroad police department had keys to the city jail. We could lock up our own prisoners.

"Our reasons for trying to discourage these people from riding was because some used to break into boxcars, and principally because of the possibility of their receiving personal injuries – some of which would turn out to be fatalities. We always endeavored to take them off the trains and get them back on the highway rather than back on a freight train.

"The economy of our country being as it is people are able to make some sort of living – but this was difficult during the depression years. Today at that same station I doubt that three active men would find more than fifty transients in any one month."

That might seem to be that. Furthermore as recently as 1966 Lou Menk, president of the Chicago, Burlington and Quincy Railroad, ordered the line's police force to "forget about chasing hobos, concentrate instead on reducing freight damage." Unarguably the streamlining of rolling stock has thinned out the freight train riders. The new locomotives – the diesel-electric, the gas-turbine which develops up to 8,500 horse power, the ignitron

42

rectifier electric, the silicon rectifier electric and the diesel-hydraulic – are all hotshots, or fast runners. They stop infrequently for water or fuel; they pass at speeds defeating the most practised jumper. Also, America's railroads are being trimmed and rationalized.

Perhaps the solstice of the railroad age, and therefore also of the hobo, was December 2, 1927, when a million sightseers stormed a certain building in Detroit, when mounted police fought off crowds in Cleveland and a mob rushed the city hall in Kansas City.

They were all there to worship the new tutelary god, the car, personified by the unveiled Ford Model "A." In 1919 there had been six million cars in the United States; ten years later there were twenty-three million. In that decade the face of America was re-cast.

In 1923 the investigators of "Middletown," the sociologists' quintessential American community – it was Muncie, Indiana – found that already about half the working class residents had cars, although many had no bath. This was not a luxury: it was the blessed new means of access to jobs and free-ranging animation for a mercurial people.

The steam age gave way to the gasoline age. Instead of riding Pullman you rode Marmon or Pierce-Arrow, and the third-class passengers went by Model "A."

But the rods underneath the trains were still packed because the broad ramification of the railroads remained: the hobo could still span North, East, South and West in his customary scot-free style. But less and less could he exercise nuances of choice from a weft of local spurs and branchlets and from a skein of trunk lines of competing systems. His wings, if not quite clipped, were cramped, for unless he took to hitch-hiking, which few establishment sticklers were prepared to do, areas of the country fell out of reach ,and he was increasingly canalized onto the remaining main lines.

The slimming continues. Since 1959 the Interstate Commerce Commission has authorized eighteen railroad mergers involving thirty-four lines, and is investigating another nine requests for marriage, including the consolidation of the Pennsylvania Railroad, the nation's biggest, and the New York Central, its third biggest.

The Chesapeake and Ohio has integrated with the Baltimore and Ohio, the Norfolk and Western with the Wabash and Nickel Plate. Throughout the nation since the 1916 peak of 254,000 miles the railroads have been shedding their fat, 40,000 miles lopped off in the past fifty years.

In 1911 there were 1,312 separate, privately owned railroads in America. Today there are fewer than a hundred. Once there were just two types of wooden freight car, flat and box, both mostly open and accessible. The modern freight car, forty feet long and capable of loads up to 300 tons, is built of steel or aluminium. There are tank cars, automatically regulated refrigerator cars, gondolas, open and closed-top hopper cars, well cars, container cars, poultry cars, furniture cars, ore cars, milk cars, pulpwood cars, cattle cars, cars made to carry highway trailers piggyback, bi-level passenger cars and tri-level flat cars stacked with tiers of new automobiles and trucks – almost all locked, proofed and insulated.

The marshaling grounds today are centralized, supervised by closed circuit television and IBM 360 computers, sorted by the yardmaster in his watchtower by remote-control switches, and linked with the yards of other cities by private microwave to dovetail and speed freight movements.

Clearly the railroad hobo is being outsmarted by technology.

All the same every day in the year there are about 15,000 freight trains wiggling about. On the 214,000 miles of track every one of the nearly two million serviceable freight cars averages more than 16,000 miles a year; there are about 50,000 freight terminals in moderate to hectic use; and, despite all the sleek manifest whizzers, you don't have to cast your eye far down any line to see strings of the old hospitable side-door wooden boxcars rocking at a comfortable jog along a branch line or through a siding.

The hobo still has the means of staying alive and moving. He is not utterly out of business yet. Persistently he has been declared to be.

In the November 1922 issue of *Hobo News* was reprinted a

"capitalist press idea of a bum," an article from an unspecified capitalist newspaper in which an Arthur S. Hadaway completed his survey of hoboing: "With the disappearance of the American frontier, the hoped-for eradication of looseness and negligence in the operation of most of our railroads, and a tightening of the purse strings of the gullible and overcredulous honest worker ... the bum may soon go the way of the stage driver and the Mississippi Pilot."

Milburn declares with melancholy certainty: "Both tramps and hoboes are anachronisms bound for extinction. It does not take a particularly astute observer to see the imminent doom of the hoboes, the migratory workers ... for two years now, like the buffalo herds before them, the hoboes have failed to come through. No especial determination or fortitude is required to qualify as a tramp nowadays, and presently the tramping fraternity, with all its lore, must break up."

In fact at the very time – 1929 – that Milburn was grieving at the dwindling away of his troubadors and for the wilting of "hobo poesy," another great hobo resurgence, the waves of workless splattered in every direction from the Wall Street crash, was just about beginning.

In 1938 Anderson reproved one Jeff Davis, who was running the International Itinerant Migratory Workers' Union in Cincinnati, for "romanticizing the hobo" (although he conceded that this was not "without a basis in reality, and his poetic interest in the species arose from experience") for, like it or not, the hobo's day was over. Davis, he complained, had "placed on a pedestal a man who belongs to the past."

Then in the 1961 reissue of his original study Anderson said that this "in-between worker" – the man who completed the actual engineering of the territory overrun by 1890 – was already disappearing when his book appeared in 1923: when the automobile came in, he went out.

In the 1940s Ben Benson, on the road since 1898, was writing: "If this was the beginning of the century I was talking to you boys: I would advise you all to 'hit the road'. For many men and boys who had the right stuff – sometimes called the American Rugged Individualism – made good. But, I regret to say, 'them days are gone forever!'"

Twenty years later De Grazia was saying, with a tinge of regret: "There used to be a kind of person in America who openly proclaimed his aversion to work. The type, though not already gone from sight, seems to be going fast. He is or was called the hobo."

Almost from his embryo stage the hobo has regularly and finally been bade farewell. His numbers and habits have varied but he has created regular renewals of surprise as, like a social coelacanth, once again he swims into sight from the deeps of the past, an immanent creature.

4 : LEATHERSTOCKING OF THE FREIGHT CARS

It is a sacrament to walk the streets as an American citizen. Being an American is a sacred mission.

From a Presbyterian circular of the 1900s.

AT Delano on Route 99, which slots a cement backbone up the middle of California, a man is standing beside a battered blue valise in the ferocious afternoon sun. At each approaching car he languidly flags a briefcase labeled SACRAMENTO, which is about 400 miles distant. Snappy blonde moustache shaved down to a shrimp's whisker, broad-brimmed straw sombrero, white windcheater and pistol tietack in black silk cravat, all combined with a round-shouldered spindliness and wavering blue eyes, give a curious indecisive air that is both dashing and disconsolate.

Yet Thomas Carlson talks with confidence enough – with a stagey pokerfaced bitterness. "You could say I'm an artist on wings," he says. "I goof off all the time but I keep up my art work."

Riding along he unclips his briefcase and displays his art work, done around the skid row taverns and burlesques of Houston, Texas, his last port of call. They are vapid drawings of alcoholics, hobos, prostitutes and stockmen; he also has a separate sheaf of "pin-ups," mildly erotic but inaccurate nudes.

He is, he says, twenty-six, the son of an entomologist at the University of California. "I was born in Washington state and brought up at Woodland, beyond San Francisco. I've worked at a few things, I ran an art gallery and I was employed by a television station, but we were on strike most of the time. Mostly I do laboring, any odd jobs along the road, and selling my art work. I charge seventy dollars for a drawing. That's my price. I won't take any less.

"I like to move, I like to have wings. I'm a gambler at heart.

47

I take chances. I get bored staying in one place. For instance one night in Los Angeles I said to two guys I'd met 'Man, I'd like to make a trip', so we did right then. We goofed off up to Canada and Alaska, and did some traveling on dog-sled, then turned around right through Nevada and Texas and down to Mexico City. I went back to Mexico a year later, went round the peninsula in a ship and we brought back a load of contraband stuff.

"A lot of guys on the move are just bums, lush-heads. They drift from town to town, hiding from sight in the shadows, afraid of life, trying to hide themselves in a bottle. They bum, steal, kill, do anything. They're *crazy*. That's why I don't ride the freights. I did when I was seventeen and got into a fight with a queer alcoholic in the same boxcar. I just dropped him over my shoulder out through the door. I never did know what happened to him. I'd never again go on a train, not without a gun.

"I hitch-hike all the time but hiking days are about through in America. Motorists are afraid to pick you up because of crime. It's a pisspoor attitude – they think anyone who hasn't got a car is a bum. On this trip one night I sat beside the highway all night without getting a ride. Right now the last meal I had was a can of beans twenty-four hours ago.

"You wanna know the reason people move around so much in this country? I'll tell you. Because they're restless, because they've done everything worth doing in the average squaresville. It's the ones who stay put who become the bastards of the world, who give you the cold-shoulder deal.

"I've always been looking for something – yeah, that dream world we hear so much about – but I prefer to go it alone. You know how the timber wolf lives alone and just comes down out of the woods for food or a mate? That's like me. But one of these days I'm gonna do it in style."

At Fresno he humps his cases across the verge to the freeway and the North-bound traffic, calling over his shoulder: "Take it easy and make like a timber wolf."

THE hobo matrix was as indivisibly a part of nineteenth-century American capitalism as John D. Rockefeller. The hobo was the unemployed spoil cast aside by a bold and ruthless *laissez faire* system. In 1879 Henry George wrote: "The 'tramp' comes with the locomotive, and almshouses and prisons are as surely the marks of 'material progress' as are costly dwellings, rich warehouses, and magnificent churches."

It was the size of the continent and its distant limbo of lumber camps and wheat prairies that allowed room for the hobo to spin off into a remote anonymity. It was the railroads which gave him his identity and style of life in a distinctive clan of homeless floating laborers. Yet the hobo became more than that. He became a tribal totem – and, what is most astonishing, remains so.

It was the respectable citizen's muddle of guilt and envy that elevated the hobo to both a folk and a culture hero. He saw the hobo as a betrayer of the open economy. There it was extending Horatio Alger's "ladder to the stars" for all with the diligence to climb it, and some pig-headedly stayed below rung one, poor and hungry, their only benefit being to substantiate social Darwinism's postulate of hardy individualism and the survival of the fittest.

At the same time, perhaps in his secret doubts the true-blue citizen saw the hobo as a reproach to the economy. Additionally he suspected, with covetous resentment, that the hobo had by unfair thaumaturgical means retained an independence which had somehow drained out of his own successful career. So in his more sentimental moods he indulged himself with wistful yearning for the vagabond contentment he erratically invested in the hobo.

It was in the floodtime of immigration – migrations from the Old World, migrations from farm to town – that created the volatile society which, in Thernstrom's words, "made a hero of the man on the road, heading for the Great West or the Great City." Increasingly at the center of the folklore current was the equation of movement with clicking big. "The hero was on the make as well as on the move."

America could not have been made without these squads

ready to sign up for shipping out to any quarter. The hobo may have been the "rather pathetic figure ... wracked by strange diseases and tortured by unrealized dreams that haunt his soul" (one retrospective view) but he had as well as the muscle a certain spirit crucial to those preparatory stages of capitalism through the Middle West to the Pacific Coast.

In a society so censorious of failure, which in editorial, on political platform and from pulpit nagged pitilessly – and defensively – about the shiftless who squandered their opportunities, the failure had to hold on to a remnant of self-esteem. Accordingly he conjured for himself a substitute role. This was partially an acceptance of the merry wayfarer image imposed upon him, derived from imported literary ideas about the greenwood and the *Nut Brown Maid*, and naturalized in Walt Whitman's *Song of the Open Road*. This was not entirely untrue. At a stiff price the hobo was, as the industrial revolution roared forward, prolonging the frontier dynamic. As the actual frontiers closed and the fences went up, on the narrow steel trail of the railroad the hobo was Fenimore Cooper's Natty Bumppo with a second lease of life, the Leatherstocking of the freight cars, beholden to no one.

The other element in the synthesis of the hobo was his pride and self-respect as a worker. He may have been stripped of environment, of an outlet for his limited skills, but he doggedly clung to his membership of "the productive classes." The hobo might not seem, when begging at a back door or dozing on a sunny ditch bank, to qualify; nor could status in the jungle shanties over the tracks and outside the community structure appear, from above, anything but a fairly chimerical conceit; but the hobo always insisted on the distinction. Among many who, out of despair or drink, had sunk too low to fret, the hobo tenaciously regarded himself as a working joe temporarily out of a job and out of luck. Also, he could often argue his case in political and philosophical terms – in broad, slapdash outlines, at any rate – and did. Whether he was later a Wobbly – a member of the Industrial Workers of the World or not – hoboism was his union; he wore the badge with a swagger.

There began with the American roving worker what Pittard, in his study of gipsies, has called "ceremonial nomadization."

This class consciousness, or "underclass" consciousness, developed in the United States one of the few instances of political solidarity as well as a sense of social entity, and produced such movements as the Hobo Colleges and the songs and doggerel of alienation which inevitably call to mind the *Corporations de Gueuserie* of medieval Europe, the beggars' guilds which adopted their own cant lingo, jurisprudence, territorial rights and – as the hobo Wobblies of the IWW centred themselves upon Chicago and Seattle and Spokane – set up their "States General," or legislative bodies, in La Vendée and Languedoc.

Although it was the railroad system which, by uniquely providing a rootless working stiff with 254,000 miles of ready-made promenade, gave the hobo his particular flavor and a structure to his "ceremonial nomadization," the raw material from which he was fashioned had been there for a long time. The raw and hasty makeshift conditions which were his blueprint have changed, or anyway modified, yet the hobo's perpetuation is the natural outcome of a hyperglandular belief, still intrinsic to the American writ, that the race must be to the swiftest – never summarized more pungently than by the public war whoop of one nineteenth-century industrial concern: "Let buffalo gore buffalo and the pasture go to the strongest," whereupon the company was, with consummate aptness, gored into the dust by its competitors.

America was the "open door" to forty millions from 1800 to 1950, eighty-five per cent of them from Europe. From the earliest beginnings the chancers from Europe were not only shut inside habit and kinship but confronted by formidable physical confines, the walls of forest and mountain and wilderness. They had to hack their way into the heartland, probing and clearing every mile of the immeasurable adventure. A mist then hid the New World. America was the last territory to which European settlers went in droves before the geographers and surveyors.

The transfer of populations began in the seventeenth century; it was far into the nineteenth before the mist was dispersed from the continent, and it loitered in pockets for longer. There was little scope for the drifting scrimshanker in the early colonial days. Every muscle had to function.

The modern tramp who has either opted out from choice, or fallen out because of lack of grip, still needs the infrastructure of society. His crumbs must fall from somewhere. The men who pushed inland from the thin rind of settlement on the Atlantic seaboard were on their own. They had to grapple their way forward with axe and hoe and gun.

It was a working passage all the way, for the first trails were stitched together by fur traders and hunters and scouts, and the smudges in the dust were beaten broader by the creaking carts of homesteaders, the prospectors and missionaries and woodsmen and tyro ranchers, and whole communities which were mobile, pausing for rest and replenishment, then, like a circus, folding and moving on.

This was a total break with the pattern of nomadic people in the Old World, whose journeyings were scratchings across starved soil, never more than a few steps ahead of depletion. Here, the mist was rolled back upon tumultuous wealth. The decision to be taken was what and where to seize. In the mind of every man who struck out into "the golden America" was a certainty of sovereignty. They were working princes, their accession was merely temporarily held in escrow.

Concurrently within the established townships of Massachusetts and Virginia and Pennsylvania and Maryland, a different kind of movement was interweaving, limited in diagram and purpose. The first colonists were Englishmen, prosperous bourgeois merchants and aristocrats. Their instinct was to reproduce on this empty page the formal typography of the feudal class gradations at home. Not many of them stayed personally in the God-forsaken treasure chest. Nor, incidentally, did many of their retainers and free immigrants.

The heavy backlash migration, the two-way traffic, mounted. Huge numbers of European poor – probably one in three – stayed in the New World just long enough, much as Italians go to Germany and Britain now, to accumulate enough capital to buy a farm or cut a dash back in the old country.

Most of these later immigrants who were deliberately flooded into the steel labor market as scabs were single men, willing to work for nine dollars weekly, pig it in communal boarding houses, then return permanently to their homelands with a few hundred dollars saved.

These nineteenth-century short-term lodgers in America were a crucial factor in crippling young unionism and protracting the working man's insecurity for they were eagerly recruited as strike breakers.

Not all went back; many stayed and learned the bleak truth about being a new American and remained alienated men – "alienated from the culture they had left and from the one that had not yet wholly welcomed them and that they did not understand, and alienated finally from themselves," says Lerner. Despite the excitement and ferment, "the immigrant experience was thus somber and tragic."

None the less the intaglio introduced by the early return trippers marked their successors and their indentured servants borne over in cattle boat consignments. Fifty per cent of the white population came to the colonies as wageless servants – but usually voluntarily, the progenitors of the present seemly white slave traffic in upper-class English girls who flock to Manhattan as secretaries or smart home helps.

Of the thirty-five million people who shifted from Europe to America between 1800 and 1914 only five million were English, but the mold of their influence lasted like a fossilized footprint. The old life persisted despite the aspirations of most who had crossed the ocean to slip the collar of restrictions. Even by 1728 the back country "had already developed the free and easy ways of the squatter world, shiftless, lubberly, independent, but animated by hostility towards the aristocratic Old Dominion."

There was a lively scurry of men on the move – but on circuit, separate from the outward bound who were beginning to penetrate the frontier curtain of the Appalachians, to bore into the Kentucky forests, and slog on pack-horses and Conestoga wagons through the Cumberland Gap and across the Pennsylvania peaks.

On the Atlantic coastal plain the servants freed from indenture left to grab parcels of land where they could set themselves up as yeoman farmers in the Connecticut River valley and in the hills of New Hampshire and Vermont. In the German settlements along the Delaware and Schuylkill rivers, the Quaker colonies in South-East Philadelphia, the Scotch-Irish caravans halted in Central Pennsylvania, and the trial plantations in the back country of Georgia and the Carolinas, there was an increasing urgent call for skills and goods.

Specialization changed to jack-of-all-trades ingenuity. The carpenter mended shoes and cut wheels. The printer wrote as well as set up type, sold books and ink, made paper. The doctor and the lawyer went in the saddle to find customers. Such itinerant preachers as the Wesley brothers, the Quaker Thomas Chalkley and the Anglican Charles Woodmason, set the prescription fulfilled still by the migrant ministry infiltrating the migrant fruit pickers' camps, by the hell-busting revivalists whose marquees and scary promises of damnation can be seen erected on spare lots beside the motels and lunch counters in the Bible Belt. The first Swedes toured the fringe hamlets building houses from squared-off timbers, which became the hallmark of the American frontierscape, and of modern mountain resort motels and pancake drive-ins: the log cabin.

In these conditions of scattered centers of an agrarian economy the floating laborer was born. He was then the wandering "mechanick." He arrived at a farmstead with his kit of tools, was furnished with board and wages, built the lean-to or bedsteads, repaired a wagon or plow, cured hides and made dresses, all with materials supplied by the farmer, then strode on when the job was done.

There was a wide open barter area for the handyman with skills to hawk. The floating laborer was for a long time in relatively piping times. Wage rates were high for the "beste sorte of laborers," thirty to one hundred per cent above the British workers'.

There was an acute shortage of artisans, bespoke and nomadic. If disagreement or boredom entered, not far down the turnpike another job awaited. The relationship between hirer and hired was, until the eighteenth century, harmonious. They worked on intimate terms, temporarily under the same roof.

It was a free life that the craftsman lived, unhampered by union protocol or unemployment, and work proceeded at a leisurely pace and in attractive variety.

To meet the shortage of labor the colonies ignored the embargo clamped by the British government on the emigration of skilled artisans and imported boatloads. They also imported glass-workers from France and Italy, flax workers from the North of Ireland, miners, masons and carpenters from Germany, potters brick makers, tanners and lime burners from Sweden, cowmen from Poland, silk workers from Italy, sawyers from Holland, and also peasant biceps from all of Europe for the strong-arm toil done in the South by African slaves.

Although the British apprenticeship system had been borrowed, this did not feed through enough trained labor, even combined with that lured from Europe. Consequently there was rapacious hijacking between the colonies. Advertisements jostled in the news sheets. Agents offered such fringe benefits as a no-tax honeymoon period, exemption from militia service and immunity from compulsory labor service on public roads and building projects.

Unionism began piecemeal, hugger-mugger, usually as extemporaneous alliances to tackle a local wrangle or organize a turn-out, and which dissolved when a particular matter was disposed of.

Although the shoemakers of Philadelphia and the New York printers made groping attempts to form permanent "associations" in the 1790s, it was not until the second decade of the nineteenth century that there was a serious attempt to organize a drive, met head-on by employers' resistance to wage demands and by prosecutions under an old English common law against "conspiracies in restraining of trade."

The craft guild, the one combination legal in Britain, never took hold – and this was as much due to employee as to employer. In 1648 Massachusetts chartered a shoemakers' guild and a coopers' guild, but neither charter was renewed after the three-year term, largely because of the clamor from rural artisans at this move to "hinder a free trade." A weavers' guild in New York, and chartered cordwainers' and tailors' guilds in Philadelphia were similarly strangled in infancy.

Elsewhere there were efforts to enforce guild regulations, such as the leather industry's rule that butchers, tanners, shoemakers and carriers should not trespass on allied crafts. Boston prohibited the opening of a workshop by a non-qualified journeyman. And many cities tried to limit tradesmen to one craft and to prevent farmers poaching on other trades in slack seasons.

Thus from the start of the American experiment the proto-type of the free laborer, the casual all-rounder, was embodied in the economic blueprint – and endorsed by the man himself.

The important difference between the American craftsman and his nearest counterpart in Britain was that the American had no union life-line to guide him in his ventures. In Britain the tramping system lasted for two hundred years, becoming the way of life of many unions.

It existed in Germany and France too but there the *Wander-pflcht* and the *tour de France* of the *compagnons* were deve-loped to burnish a craftsman's education with ecumenical ex-perience.

In Britain by the mid-Victorian period there were networks of "stations" – houses of call still marked in familiar pub signs, the Bricklayers' Arms, the Masons' Arms, and so on, where the lodges were set up. Walking was the approved "provident" means of circulation, and it was a single man's business.

Calico printers report trips of 1,400 miles; the compositors' itinerary covered 2,800 miles in the 1850s, and there is one case of a compositor who left London in March 1848 and returned a year later having tramped to Brighton, round the South coast to Bristol, up to Birmingham, Liverpool and Carlisle, into Scot-land, across to Belfast, Dublin and nineteen Irish towns, and back to London via Liverpool, Yorkshire and Cambridge, having received relief in seventy towns and worked in three. All this by foot: no rods for them to ride.

An original purpose was to slacken off the screws in zones and times of unemployment and to lighten the load on strike funds, so strengthening the union's endurance and bargaining power. But the crucial point here is that the "sacrificed" man (the printer's phrase) was not a castaway.

The emblem of the ironfounders depicted a tramping molder, pack on back and ash staff in hand, saying "Brother craft, can you give me a job?" and receiving the answer: "If we cannot, we will assist you." He carried with him a card of identity, his credential and introduction, and a book of relief checks cashable at each branch. Monthly circulars listing men on the road paved his way, so that a niche could be held ready or advice given on prospects ahead. If there was no job, he could depend upon lodging, food and probably beer.

The navvies – the millions of heavy laborers from Lincolnshire and Yorkshire, Scotland and Ireland, who in the eighty years from 1822 onward built 20,000 miles of railways in Britain – were a distinct tribe, an "anarchic élite of laborers" who moved from cantonment to cantonment along the new embankments, who dressed in moleskin trousers, velveteen square-tailed coats and gaudy neckerchiefs, and who drank and fought ferociously.

There is an 1855 sketch showing a navvy on the tramp, his shoulders loaded not only with personal kit but also with wheelbarrow, pick and shovel, lamp, ale-flask and sword. Coleman writes: "This was the age of lives spent in factories and sweat shops, but the navvy, with all his hardships, worked mostly in the open and between contracts he was on the tramp. His life was a strange one, isolated and free ... They were nomads. At one time there were 200,000 thousand of them, yet to ordinary people they were practically unknown, and this increased the fear and the legend."

That is a strikingly similar social situation to that which was happening to the navvy's counterpart across the Atlantic, where the hobo ganger was both romanticized and outlawed. On the other hand the British navvy seems never to have freeloaded on the trains he made way for, as did his American opposite number. Instead of riding the rods or snagging a boxcar he either walked it or bought a third-class ticket "because they loved to see what they called the course of the country" – an American migrant worker would never, on principle, have parted with money to the railroad companies.

British craftsmen of all kinds were constantly semi-nomadic, often spending a lifetime pack-on-back. But the system, with its traces of medieval wayfaring, eventually crumpled under the massive stresses of modern capitalism. Indeed unions grew steadily less keen on subsidizing those whom they came to view as their giddy fly-by-night membership. There was also a profound change of mind toward crisis and slump, as it was slowly borne upon them that these were no longer parochial eddies which could be walked out of, but national and even wider.

Further, as Hobsbawn puts it, "the tram replaced the tramp" – from the 1880s urban transport made it possible for a worker to renounce long-range wandering, for, without changing residence or lodgings, he had within reach a larger labor market to explore.

Even so the tramping artisan did benefit from the security that the system contained, as well as contribute to it. The British migrant spread trade unionism, not only by disseminating news of wages and conditions elsewhere but by stirring colleagues to found branches and by leaving conversions in his wake. The brotherhood sustained him and he nurtured the brotherhood, with a staunchness that was to become a class solidarity, absent from the American experience.

The immigrants who had continued to leave the British Isles on the North Atlantic trade route were largely those who had not qualified by aptitude or opportunity for this bottom dog élite, and they took with them little knowledge of or loyalty toward the traditions of journeyman unionism. This continued up to the very end of the great migrational waves. Of the million immigrants who arrived in 1910, four out of five had earned their living in their homeland as laborers. They had much to gain. Shortage of labor kept wages high, and the early Eastern industrialists tried to stem the flow West. But as the reinforcements from Europe surged in, increasingly the new merchant capitalists of America found this an aid to pegging costs by recruiting the untrained peasants, and the women and children.

A free-for-all economic scramble was the prevailing and accepted state, and it was affected by the privateer attitudes broadcast into the city slums – by the frontiersmen with their loathing of regimentation, by the Yankee pedlars who beat around the outpost farms with their pushcarts of patent medicines, "notions" and snappy Eastern kitchenware. In the atmosphere was independence and challenge, the promise of infinite boon awaiting those with the spirit to wrest free of the East. There were additional inducements to move. In the 1828 depression the New York *Times* reported: "Thousands of industrious mechanics who have never before solicited alms were brought to the humiliating condition of applying for assistance."

The assistance was limited and harsh. Early in the colonial period workhouses were instituted, according to the puritan view that labor was an obligation of all, as houses of correction for "Beggars, Servants running away or otherwise misbehaving themselves, Trespassers, Rogues, Vagabonds, and other people refusing to work."

The early American statutes about vagabonds were derived from the English fourteenth-century remedies, after the Black Death, to restrain plague-carriers from meandering around with the virus. They were adopted by the puritan settlers similarly to check the infection of workshyness and worklessness, so that even today anyone on the road without a regular job or money in his pocket can be given the criminal rush and clapped in jail.

Indeed the American vagrancy laws in their vague omnicompetence can be utilized to arrest such a motley bunch as gipsies, jugglers, recalcitrant minors, practitioners of hoomanamana (Hawaiian black magic), fiddlers without orchestras, sleight-of-hand artists, prostitutes, fortune tellers, "persons who paint their faces," down-and-outs in general, gamblers, and, of course, eminent racketeers, who while reasonably able to murder safely are occasionally booked for vagancy.

Neurosis about people not palpably on a pay-roll somewhere became of such national obsession that in 1892 the Assistant Secretary of State asked all foreign consular officers to obtain "the manner of dispensing of public charities and of controlling and abating that class of vagrant generally designated 'tramps' in various countries."

Back came the replies from all over the world, from Warsaw and from Austria-Hungary and from Cadiz, describing how down-at-heels were scourged abroad, the symposium of which – a blood-chilling encyclopedia of ingenious persecution and punishment – was published in 1893. Branding-irons, nose-slitting, flogging and the sexual separation of paupers were never officially adopted in America, yet the actual methodology of small town vigilantes and railroad beadles was not far short.

Come what may refusal to work could never have been the

social problem which later arose through inability to work because of the absence of work. Non-workers were, *per se*, no-
account – can't work means won't work : the American faith
admits only grudgingly, and then mostly academically (not in
applied form) the notion that worklessness may be more com-
plicated than individual sloth.

It was at the height of the immigrant flood, and the change
from agrarian simplicity to industrialized complexity, that the
double attitude became chronically schizophrenic. The voice of
authority bayed sternly about the duty of diligence and the
honorable splendor of sweat, while the hand of authority cast
vast numbers of able eager men into permanent alienation.

It is interesting to see how this was vindicated, not only tol-
erated as a natural condition of an open economy but robed in
myth to stimulate the advance into the interior. It was a sort
of civilian Somme : men were shoveled through to the front,
and the banners, trumpets and odes proclaimed the glory of the
new land and its conquerors, while the casualty lists lengthened
and the walking wounded silted up in the workhouses and doss
houses.

In 1763 after the defeat of the French, and when no doubt
lingered that British sovereignty would stretch out beyond the
Mississippi Valley, the Secretary of State, Lord Egremont, urged
that fidgety Americans should be forbidden to clear off into the
interior. Instead they should be steered to Georgia or Nova Scotia,
still near the sea, "where they would be useful to their Mother
Country instead of planting themselves in the Heart of America
out of reach of Government where from the great difficulty of
procuring European commodities, they would be compelled to
commerce and manufactures to the infinite prejudice of
Britain . . ."

Then this seemed a perfectly logical proposal to those who
conceived America as (except for the coastal colonies orientated
toward the Atlantic and Europe) a lunar land beyond the scope
of sea trade.

However the opposing view was led by Benjamin Franklin,
who had the foresight to understand that no one, lawyer or
soldier, was going to dam the inevitable overspill. In 1782 in

his *Information To Those Who Would Remove To America*, Franklin expounded: "Strangers are welcome because there is room enough for them all, and therefore the old Inhabitants are not jealous of them ... Tolerably good Workmen in any of these mechanic Arts are sure to find Employ." It was endorsed by the backwoodsman's motto, that of the picaresque Simon Suggs: "It is good for a man to be shifty in a new country."

Immediately here was a conflict of interest and vision: one, of an America as part of an empire held on the old British reins of sea power, and two, the agricultural transformation of those "savage groves as yet uninvestigated by the traveller, unsung by the poet, or unmeasured by the chain of the geometrician," as *The Freeman's Journal* put it in 1782. It was the tug away from the old bonds which created the first densification of vagrants on the bum, the result of Jefferson's Embargo Act, designed to avoid embroilment in the Napoleonic Wars, which halted sea traffic with Europe. Thousands of sailors were thrown ashore. Many continued their voyaging on "the wavy waste" of the uncharted land West of the Appalachians.

It was after the Civil War, when a railroad reached its terminal point, when a canal was cut, when a new mine was sunk, when any large scale construction finished, that there began the recurrent, quickening situation of a mob of abruptly unwanted laborers being stranded 1,000 miles and more from cities. They were never savers. What money had piled up fizzed away in the local gambling-drinking-whoring caravans that followed them. To get back East or onto the next work site they panhandled – they begged grub, stake and fare. Panhandling worked for quite a time, because it implied (true or false) that they had been having a tough time out in the Texas Panhandle, which signified pioneer railroad building in the whole of the South-West.

But in fact it was not until the startlingly recent date of the 1840s that the idea of those "savage groves" becoming a manageable commercial estate was taken seriously, the time when a Connecticut senator spoke of "the creative power of a railroad," and Asa Whitney, seeking a sixty-mile wide land grant to run a rail track from Lake Michigan to the Pacific, contended that until that was done the settler in that remote fastness would remain a "demi-savage."

5: THE PHANTOM DEER ARISE

*The American intelligentsia has a deep senti-
mental attachment to barbarism and savagery,
preferably of a nomadic sort.*

Floyd Dell.

THE filling station sign says: "How's your gas? Next town
113 miles." Ahead are the 1,676,676 acres of Idaho's Clear-
water National Forest and the adjoining 1,239,840 acres of the
Selway-Bitterroot Wilderness, a terrain of granite and forest
uncrossed by roads and penetrable only along canyon paths and
elk trails.

A chunk of this – an area about twice the size of Yorkshire –
is supervised by a forester of thirty-three named Frank Fowler
who lives in a log cabin at the Powell Ranger Station, loomed
over by fir-bushy crags that only the black bear can negotiate.

Rolling a cigarette from a leather pouch and sitting on the
steps of a building marked LUMBERJACKS' HAVEN: GRUB
WANAGAN, Frank Fowler says: "I was pretty directionless
when I got out of high school in Washington DC. I'd run wild
in the streets as a kid, getting into plenty of trouble with fights
and heaving rocks. I'd worked around as an usher in a stock
car race track, dug ditches, carried shingles for roofers, toted a
hod and mixed mortar.

"It was a scout-master who'd been a forester who put me on
the right track. He said he'd get me a summer job in the woods.
This was what I needed, to get out of the city rat-race.

"I hitch-hiked up to Montana to enrol in the forestry school
at Missoula. I was so bushed when I got there that I flunked the
entrance examination but I did get in with another try. To
support myself in college I enrolled as a smoke-jumper.

"They drop you on lightning fires from Ford tri-motors and
C47s. They train you to land in trees. You have a canvas suit
with a knee-pack holding a hundred-foot rope for lowering your-

self and two days' rations. They drop a parachute cargo of radio, shovel, saw and a pulaski, a kind of hatchet tool. You go down on a steerable 'chute. Your job is to go in as soon as there's a trickle of smoke in the summer storms, before a blaze develops if you can get there in time.

"I did nine operational drops and one rescue. When I'd finished college I went on smoke-jumping to clear off some debts I'd accumulated. Then I went off down to North Carolina on a timber reserve survey, random sampling timber in the coastal swamps, until I was drafted and sent to Germany in the Army. When I was back I got fixed up at Metaline Falls in the state of Washington on timber sales and then I moved to Kettle Falls in the same forest and eventually took charge here.

"This life means everything to me. You have to feel like that about it because it isn't easy. By Christmas the snow's banked up fifteen feet and stays there till April. You've got to be self-sufficient and value what you've got.

"Historically, ideally, independence is supposed to be very important to Americans but in truth I don't think we're sustaining it. We're too ready to trade it in for goods. The pressures reach even here. I find I spend more and more time on office routine, timber sales and administration, with just an occasional helicopter patrol across the primitive area.

"But when the pressures get too much I can always saddle my horse and go up the trails. There aren't many places left in the world where a man can go and find his peace with nature."

THE practical mechanics of wiring-up the unknown with the modern world acquired unexpected allies, poets and writers who charged the Westward compulsion with destiny and drama.

It was Walt Whitman who in *Leaves of Grass* illumined rhapsodically the virgin quality of life, man's second chance, vouchsafed out there in the sunlight beyond Old Europe's stultifying gray shadow. "A free original life there ... simple diet and clean and sweet blood ... litheness, majestic faces, clear eyes and perfect physique there . . . immense spiritual results . . ."

The dichotomy here has been analyzed by Henry Nash Smith. There was Whitman's ecstatic philosophy: that from the languid, effete people of the bone pile of Europe "the youthful and sinewy pioneers take up the cosmic burden," inaugurating a new era for mankind. "We debouch upon a newer, mightier world . . ." There was Davy Crockett who, says Parrington, "had the good fortune to preempt the romance of the backwoods, to file on an unsurveyed tract of Western life" . . . Popular imagination seized upon him and endowed the mighty hunter of the canebrakes with the fugitive romance that had been gathering for years."

But Crockett was also used as a political instrument – as a weapon against President Andrew Jackson and his policies, for the 1830s were "robustious times when broadcloth in politics had suddenly gone out of style and homespun had come in. The new coonskin democracy had descended upon Washington . . . Wastefulness was in the frontier blood, and Davy was a true frontier wastrel."

Awkwardly there were these two contradictory and discordant Wests. There was the Wild West roamed by pathfinders like Kit Carson, "cougar all the way," the trappers, buffalo hunters and backwoods lone wolves, "an exhilarating region of adventure and comradeship in the open air," whose white Indian heroes were not members of the society that entrapped the majority, but "noble anarchs owning no master, free denizens of a limitless wilderness."

Remarked *The Crockett Almanac* in 1838: "The backwoodsman is a singular being, always wanting to move Westwards like a buffalo before the tide of civilization." He moved because, just as the American rape was to continue to the modern day, he pillaged as he went. He was unmarried; no tendon held him to family, parents, farm or responsibilities; land ownership neither attracted him nor occurred to him. Jefferson's prescript, "The land belongs to the living generation. They may manage it, then, and proceeds from it, as they please, during their usufruct," had no meaning for them. Usufruct? Hell, what's that? They had the whole wilderness to use. They "enjoyed a once-upon-a-continent freedom."

Then there was the other West, the domesticated arable in-between, lacking both the city's culture and sophistication and the bold, dangerous dazzle of the outpost country. This attitude is typified in *The Journals of Francis Parkman*, the account of an 1842 tour by a Harvard student who set forth to seek "a superior barbarism, a superior solitude, and the potent charm of the unknown."

Parkman – in his own words, "haunted by wilderness images day and night" – encounters a woodsman in the bosky wilds: " ... resolute and independent as the wind," compared with whom the New England farmers are "a race of boors about as uncouth, mean and stupid as the hogs they seem chiefly to delight in."

The dichotomy was apparent again in the attitude to the coon-skinned Daniel Boone character, seen by one body as the trail-blazer with bowie knife and hatchet, and by the poetical who recognized with "a delicious melancholy" that, while the cult of progress could not be gainsaid, the borderman was the one American not to be brought to heel.

There was general acquiescence with the sentiments of George C. Bingham's 1851 painting, "The Emigration of Daniel Boone," depicting him shepherding a party of settlers, with wives, children and livestock, out "into a dreamily beautiful wilderness." This was the prescribed mode of thought at that time, as expressed in Timothy Flint's unctuous biography of Boone: "The rich and boundless valleys of the great west – the garden of the earth – and the paradise of hunters, had been won from the dominion of the savage tribes, and opened as an asylum for the oppressed, the enterprising, and the free of every land."

Udall has pointed out that Boone's so-called autobiography (ghosted for him by John Filson) provides more insight into folk beliefs than into the mind of the real Boone. The "Kentucke" Filson depicted was "a halfway house between the Garden of Eden and the Big Rock Candy Mountain." It was "a moving magnet – a neck of the woods that moved a little farther West each year, always one step ahead of settlement ... The Filson-Boone autobiography is one of the early manifestations of the Myth of Superabundance that later caused us to squander our natural resources ... Implicit in his (Boone's) way of life also was the idea ... of unspoiled country where the land could sing its authentic songs, and where men could hear the call of wild things and know the precious freedom of the wilderness." Udall adds sadly: "By the time Boone died, however, his countrymen were already preparing to dismember the wilderness."

About a century later, when the shimmer had dulled, Vachel Lindsay wrote:

> When Daniel Boone goes by, at night,
> The phantom deer arise
> And all lost, wild America
> Is burning in their eyes.

While the dismemberers got to work, the pious veneration of the brawny and essentially wholesome russet open-lifer remained prevalent in the mid-1800s.

Leaves of Grass, published in 1855, carried a frontispiece of the new bard, bearded, shirt-sleeved and revealing a bark-like undervest. The preface winged straight into the inflating myth: " ... here are the roughs and beards and space and ruggedness and nonchalance that the soul loves."

Whitman's announced motive was to "write the evangel poems of comrades and love," to make "a song of These States," "a world primal again," Adam's innocence retrieved and iridescent in a pure, eternal spring.

This was felt by a few to be a "barbaric yawp," yet it was a yawp which was ringing throughout all the industrialized, or industrializing, nations of the West. It was a reaction attuned to the German summerlander bliss of *Erdlebenbild*, the image of the earth's organic life, Lenau's *Drei Zigeuner*, and the untrammeled gipsy heroes of Romantic poetry. It was an idealistic banner against the black beastliness of factory smoke and for the stunted drudges who dwelled amid it.

This was the period when Ruskin was sanctifying "rude untutored freedom," when there was ardent melting at such tremulous sentiments as Francis Lucas's 1897:

> Heigh ho! for the hedger and ditcher
> There's many wiser and many richer

But leather, all leather from top to toe
The worst weather that ever can blow
Is good enough for the hedger and ditcher,

when Thoreau, after his year in a hut just outside Concord, was rediscovering the "simplicity and nakedness" of primitive man, "still but a sojourner in nature. When refreshed with food and sleep he contemplated his journey again. He dwelt, as it were, in a tent in this world, and was either threading the valleys, or crossing the plains, or climbing the mountain tops," and Thoreau found that "the occupation of a day laborer was the most independent of any, especially as it required only thirty or forty days in a year to support one. The laborer's day ends with the going down of the sun, and he is then free to devote himself to his chosen pursuit, independent of his labor . . ."

Even after the turn of the century an American president, Theodore Roosevelt, was exalting the vision, being photographed in his North Dakota rancher role, wearing Davy Crockett cap and fringed buckskin frontiersman rig, bowie knife shoved through cartridge belt, and rifle across knee, and declaring: "I wish to preach, not the doctrine of ignoble ease, but the doctrine of the strenuous life."

The vision sought increasingly frantic forms. In 1855 General Buncombe (whose name was added to the vernacular) a great huffer and puffer, was booming at the House of Representatives: "Sir, we want elbow room – the continent – the whole continent – and nothing but the continent! Then shall Uncle Sam, placing his hat on Canada, rest his right arm on the California coast, his left leg, like a freeman, upon Cape Horn."

From the start Americans needed a frontier as a rampart to be topped and consequently the frontier concept has been applied to some pretty peculiar and dubious undertakings. The search, in its nineteenth-century form, became perversely unreal: a retreat into a limpid arbor of humbug. The actual life lived by the frontier farmer or the day laborer had not been *looked* at, only imagined, by the enthusiasts.

Ralph Chaplin's mother, a farmer's wife in Kansas, thought life on the frontier wasn't glamorous at all. It was just "hard work and lonesomeness." Cowboys were "nothing but farm hands in ten-gallon hats, Indians and Buffaloes were anything but romantic."

Few people in the East heard this point of view. There was a much wider promotion of the idealized nature boy, roughneck but radiantly virtuous, in the steam literature of the period. The popularizations in the Fenimore Cooper manner by Charles W. Webber, who produced fanciful novels about the gold mine and Redskin terrain, and the output of a host of fiction-churners such as David H. Coyner and Lewis H. Garrard, and the glamorization of Kit Carson by John Charles Fremont and Charles E. Averill, all put together did not achieve what Erastus Beadle did.

Beadle was the man who in 1858 launched the Dime Novel series, thousands of short takes aimed at mass sales to the emerging, peripherally literate, working-class readership. Therein the symbolic free-sailing figure was processed and vulgarized, but held to an amazing consistency of leathery saintliness. In the dime novel he was usually a hide hunter or fur trapper, not yet a cowboy. It was to be another decade before the plainsman and Indian-fighter of the Deadwood Dick and Buffalo Bill stripe was merged into the Tom Mix knight of the cattle ranges. But, the protagonists were invariably monadic, self-sufficient, steely loners with shoulders straight and heads high in a menacing universe, each one solitary and undeterred by an isolation awful yet sublime.

In the 1905 *Prose and Poetry of the Livestock Industry of the United States* it was recalled how, as late as the Civil War, the curious eidolon of a grim, hostile bleakness was the hob-goblin in the American fairy tale, both lure and mental barrier: " . . . attribute to this almost unknown region every conceivable horrid aspect . . . the desolate barren land of horrors that constituted the Great American Desert . . .

"According to all these fantastic tales, the water-less, windswept land of sand and stone, this howling, hopeless, worthless cactus-bearing waste inhabited by savages of extreme fierceness and cruelty, and haunted by prowling beasts of unexampled ferocity, were joined to a mountain region in the far West where towering mountain peaks tore all the clouds to tatters, where snow that fell before Columbus landed still was under snow that had fallen since, where the naked granite sides of the mountains went straight aloft until lost to view, where shrieking gales forever blew over the frozen desolation that reigned supreme, and as they drove along, wailed out the warning to rash mankind: 'Abandon hope, ye who enter here'."

It may appear puzzling that Beadle's dime novels did not exploit the roving cowboy who had entered this land of "every conceivable horrid aspect" and had found no cause to abandon hope, and that he did not crystallize as a star until long after the brief twenty-five-year span of frontier range industry and the truly phenomenal drives of longhorns from the Texas spread up the Goodnight-Loving, Chisholm and Sedalia-Badter-Springs trails.

Assuredly in 1875 Laura Winthrop Johnson, in an article in *Lippincott's*, did not recognize him as the lone hero. She responded with only nose-wrinkling distaste to the brutish crew of buckaroos she had seen at a Wyoming round-up: "Rough men with shaggy hair and wild, staring eyes."

Why after being passed over for so long was he selected for the heroes' gallery? As recently as 1952 Dobie remarked: "For every hired man on horseback there have been hundreds of plowmen in America, and tens of millions of acres of rangelands plowed under, but who can cite a single autobiography of a laborer in the fields of cotton, or corn, or wheat?"

6: THE POT OF GOLD

Part of the American heritage is the spirit that hates a cribbed confinement ... the American will not tolerate the fate of being boxed in, like a trapped rat.

Max Lerner

JACK PENROD comes limping out of the Triple T Arena at Custer, South Dakota. He has just been swiped in the thigh by the horn of Holly, the big black bull he has been riding bareback. "Now you won't be able to come to the dance tonight and polish the tarnish off your belt buckle rubbing bellies with the ladies," shouts a cowboy in a polka dot shirt and fringed green chaps with the signature "Gene" slanting across each leg, who is cantering his roan in for the team roping.

The cowpokes have ridden in from surrounding ranches or driven in auto parties up to 600 miles to compete in the afternoon's saddle bronc riding, bulldogging and buffalo riding. Some came by charter plane and used friends' horses on the spot for the events.

Jack Penrod piloted himself up in his 150 Cessna from Cheyenne, Wyoming, where there was a rodeo the day before. He runs three ranches near Ashland, Montana, and owns a herd of 1,200 head of cattle but he is also a professional rodeo bullrider. He is spectacularly good-looking man with the traditional hard-frozen Western taciturnity which offsets the feminine flamboyance of his dress: an iridescent purple silk shirt, high-heeled white boots with black curlicues, and around his Levis an embossed belt with a grapefruit-sized championship buckle in no need of polishing on a lady's belly. He is thirty-two and was born at Pinetop, Arizona.

"I compete in maybe fifty rodeos in the season, May through September, two or three a week, which means flying about 15,000 miles during the summer. I keep the plane at the ranch, just land it on a sod field. Wintertime I put it away in a hangar but in summer I just tie it up.

"This way I can cover pretty near all the rodeos in these five states, North and South Dakota, Montana, Wyoming and Nebraska. In the three years I've been bull-riding I've won about $5,000. That pays for the plane but I shall keep it for getting around the ranches even when I've finished with rodeos.

"I started bull-riding late. The world champion lives fifteen miles from me and he got me going in 1963. He put me on about twenty practice bulls. I sort of took to it and I won the championship the first year. I reckon I've got another year.

"I don't reckon I've hit my best yet but a guy starts tapering off about thirty-five. He slows down. He isn't so fast and his co-ordination isn't so good. I've been on about 200 bulls and only once been hurt bad, last year at Riverton, Wyoming, when I broke six ribs. I love riding the bulls. You get to know which are the true ones and which are unpredictable. You can look yours over before the show, talk it over with him. My wife's glad I shall be quitting soon. She's always scared I'll get hurt, but I'm going to miss like hell doing the rodeos because I got friends all over these five states and it's kinda nice running across each other all the time."

Below the snow-capped peaks of the Sangre de Cristo Mountains in New Mexico and the volcanic lava drippings, now thinly grown with juniper and squawbush, is the lushly grassed rangeland which was the hunting ground of the Kiowa and Comanche Indians. The ruts of the Cimarron Cutoff, the pioneer road through to the west, are still visible, old scar tissue in the turf. Capulin on Highway 87 is a sprinkle of buildings: the Auto Tramp Trailer Court, the Wigwam Camp Modern Motel and the Country Store. Opposite the Texaco gas station lives Orb Gossett in his first permanent home.

He is seventy-nine, a trifle bent but still tall and sinewy, and quite toothless. His jeans are held up by braces over a check shirt with pearl buttons, and he keeps on his pale fawn ten-gallon hat in his sitting room with its Victorian profusion of photographs, china bric-a-brac and embroidered table runners. He also wears brown riding boots although it is two years since he sold his horse, Tony, and was last in the saddle.

"I've been a roving cowboy all my life," he says. "My father was a rancher at Throckmorton, Texas, and I began riding when I was eight. I worked for dozens of ranches, through Texas, Wyoming, South Dakota and New Mexico, always moving on.

"I always wanted to see what was on the other side of the hill. Sometimes on long distances me and a companion would move with a covered wagon and a chuckbox but oftentimes I'd just go alone with my horse. Longest trip I ever did do by horse was 1,000 miles and when I was sixteen I rode 600 miles from Throckmorton to Dumas, with a bedroll and cooking for myself on cowchip fires.

"The ranges were bigger then. They didn't have no corral. You just rounded up the longhorns and roped 'em down by the fire for the summer branding. We'd brand 30,000 calves a year.

"I thought I was tough and I didn't wear a slicker, one of them overcoats that throws off the rain. I just toughed it out, sleeping in wet bedding or riding all night. You don't get no strays now because everywheres is fenced in but then we'd have to ride fifty miles bringing in the strays. The steers was wilder then – they weren't fed and they lived wild. A rabbit or lightning would make them stampede and it took days to round them up again, and you could get skinned real bad if you got in the way of a stampede.

"In those times you never did quit riding. I was a bronco rider, too: I broke them Spanish horses to ride to cattle. I've broke fifteen or twenty a day, just knocking the rough edge off them, enough to saddle and hobble.

"My daddy, he could crease those wild horses with a .44 Winchester when they was running, just put a bullet across the top of their necks and they'd turn somersault but soon be all right. I carried a six-shooter, everyone did. I was no expert but I carried it, trying to be tough, I guess, though if a fellow had got awkward I'd probably have thrown it down and run.

"Back in '52 in South Dakota I near froze to death. I was with my son, who was killed four months ago when a horse rolled on him, and we were driving in a jeep through the Black Hills to feed 1,250 head on a ranch ten miles away. The road got drownded out in a snow drift and we sat in the jeep for thirty hours. My teeth froze to my gums.

"My son finally got help with an airplane and got me out

72

but they thought I'd lose my hands and feet. I worked on after that but I wasn't the same. I could have went and worked that herd in a pick-up truck but that wouldn't have been right for me. I'd a heap rather be out there on the range than sitting in this room. I cried when I sold my saddle. I'd had that saddle for twenty-five years and when I sold it I figured 'I'm through now.' So I don't ride no more."

IN 1917 Hamlin Garland published his *Son of the Middle Border*, one of the few books to deal with pioneering and the Westward epopee other than in poet-pilgrim terms.

Its start is in the 1860s in a little Wisconsin coulee at the fork of a trail. "Beyond this point all is darkness and terror." Garland's father is consumed by the hunger for the West – where there is "a fairer field for conquest. He no more thought of going East than a liberated eagle dreams of returning to its narrow cage ... Beneath the sunset lay the enchanted land of opportunity."

To his father "change is alluring. Iowa was now the place of the rainbow, and the pot of gold." The family is kept on the hop, to Minnesota, on to Iowa, then across the line of the middle border, and even farther West, and Garland begins to perceive that they are actually part of a destructive agency of the very quality that "the pioneer impulse throbbing deep in my father's blood" is in quest of. He sees the swift changes, the fencing and the houses neatly fretting the wild country. "And yet with all these growing signs of prosperity I realized that something sweet and splendid was dying out of the prairie. The whistling pigeons, the wailing plover, the migrating ducks and geese, the soaring cranes, the shadowy wolves, the wary foxes, all the untamed things were passing, vanishing with the blue-joint grass, the dainty wild rose and the tiger-lily's flaming horn. Settlement was complete."

Again his father turns his face to the free lands farther West. "He became again the pioneer. Dakota was the magic word ...

Once more the spirit of the explorer flamed up . . . Once more the sunset allured."

When Garland himself reaches manhood he takes a train to Farmington, where the Dakota branch of the Milwaukee railroad crosses his line of march, in the hope of obtaining a teaching post. Here in Farmington he feels "to its full the compelling power of the swift stream of immigration surging to the West. The little village had doubled in size almost in a day. It was a junction point, a place of transfer, and its thin-walled unpainted pine hotels were packed with men, women and children laden with bags and bundles (all bound for the West) and the joyous excitement of these adventurers compelled me to change my plan. I decided to try some of the newer counties in Western Minnesota. Romance was still in the West for me." All America was "in the process of change, all hurrying to overtake the vanishing line of the middle border."

Now the train had replaced the prairie schooner and the canvas-covered wagon. "Free land was receding at railroad speed, the borderline could be overtaken only by steam and every man was in haste to arrive."

Here encapsuled is the American tragedy of disenchantment, the inability to enter the mirage. Years later Garland returns from the East to the Iowa where he grew up. He finds the young men "worn and weather beaten and some appeared both silent and sad . . . The days of the border were over." Yet the people there are still "living in pioneer discomfort, toiling like a slave."

Says one woman: "We make the best of it, but none of us are living up to our dreams." Garland looks at "the hard and bitter realities . . . the gracelessness of these homes, and the sordid quality of the mechanical daily routine of these lives . . . The essential tragedy and hopelessness of most human life under conditions into which our society was swiftly hardening embittered me . . . This wasteful method of pioneering, this desolate business of lonely settlement . . . These plowmen, these wives and daughters had been pushed out into these lonely ugly shacks by the force of landlordism behind."

In 1891 Garland published *Main Travelled Roads*. He explains: "The main travelled road in the West (as everywhere) is hot and dusty in summer and desolate and drear with mud in fall and spring, and in winter the winds sweep the snows across it . . . Mainly it is long and wearyful and has a dull little town at one end, and a home of toil at the other. Like the main travelled road of life it is traversed by many classes of people, but the poor and the weary predominate."

All about him as he traveled he "perceived the mournful side of American 'enterprise'. Sons were deserting their work-worn fathers, daughters were forgetting their tired mothers. Families were everywhere breaking up. Ambitious young men and unsuccessful old men were in restless motion, spreading, swarming, dragging their reluctant women and their helpless and wondering children into unfamiliar hardships. At times I visioned the Middle Border as a colony of ants – which was an injustice to the ants, for ants have a reason for their apparently futile and aimless striving . . ."

Garland was not the first to be disillusioned with the sanctified West. In 1871 there had appeared the irreverent *The Hoosier School-Master* by Edward Eggleston, which had a considerable impact on the young Garland, and in the next decade had appeared an out-of-step growling novel entitled *The Story of a Country Town* by Edgar W. Howe, in which a character utters the blasphemy: "Men who are prosperous . . . do not come West, but it is the unfortunate, the poor, the indigent, the sick – the lower classes, in short – who came here to grow up with the country, having failed to grow up with the country where they came from."

Even earlier, it might be noted, examination of the state of the nation, in *The Transactions of the Medical Society of the State of New York, 1836-37*, revealed a morose disharmony with the orthodox mood of ebullience and mettle: "The population of the United States is beyond that of other countries an anxious one. All classes are either striving after wealth, or endeavoring to keep up its appearance . . . We are an anxious, care-worn people."

Garland quite deliberately set out to earn his tag "The Ibsen of the West" by iconoclastically exposing the "mystic quality connected with free land" which had "always allured men into the West. I wanted to show that it is a myth."

This downbeat melancholy did not suit the determined Argonaut policy of the time. Editors, Garland found, "did not like this stark reality treatment of farming and the West." He had difficulty getting his stories accepted, and when his collection was published he was "execrated by nearly every critic as 'a bird willing to foul its own nest'," and editorials and letters denounced his "message of acrid accusation" as giving a viciously false picture of the middle border and the pioneer life.

Yet what was the fruit of the pioneer surge and the rainbow hopes? Thirty years later appeared a book which aroused a similar outcry of outrage and treachery, Sinclair Lewis's *Main Street*, which provides a direct continuity from the West Garland saw made sordid and dull.

This is Lewis's Gopher Prairie: " ... Main Street with its two-story brick shops, its story-and-a-half wooden residences, its muddy expanse from concrete walk to walk, its huddle of Fords and lumber-wagons ... The broad, straight, unenticing gashes of the streets let in the grasping prairie on every side ... Not a dozen buildings which suggested that, in the fifty years of Gopher Prairie's existence, the citizens had realized that it was either desirable or possible to make this, their common home, amusing or attractive ... Always west of Pittsburg and often east of it, there is the same lumber yard, the same railroad station, the same Ford garage, the same creamery, the same boxlike houses and two-story shops."

It is the "flimsy temporariness ... so that the towns resemble frontier camps" that so depressed Lewis, and of course this is precisely the way all America's Gopher Prairies grew and in many cases are still used. One is reminded of the girl in Tennessee Williams's *Orpheus Descending* crying: "This country used to be wild, the men and women were wild and there was a wild sort of sweetness in their hearts for each other, but now it's sick with neon, it's broken out and sick with neon ..."

Was there ever such a wild sweetness? It really does seem doubtful. Questioning the rhetoric of Turner – "the Westward marching army of individualistic liberty-loving democratic backwoodsmen" – Athearn and Riegel suggest that, if it existed, the desire for liberty was infinitesimal in comparison with the desire for wealth. The frontier was "crude, materialistic, unlettered, exuberant and lacking in artistic development." They argue further that there was nothing particularly "Western" about these traits and in fact, as the West emulated the East, they were possibly only a slightly more primitive reflection of prevailing Eastern culture.

There has of course been a generally accepted revision of the fancy that the West, "the region of revolt," was a great innovator in material progress and social ideals. Athearn and Riegel take the line that the usual Westerner was basically conservative and was striving to clean up so as to obtain what Eastern society defined as the good things of life.

So the Westerner had neither the imagination nor the energy left over for the strange and new. The truth was that in a region of great social conformity, despite its opportunities for lawlessness, the West "contained many individuals but very little individualism." The "safety valve of discontent" theory worked in the sense that the economically successful Easterner saw no attraction in the disruption and danger of moving West. It was the man who was unhappy, socially or emotionally, but vigorous enough to meet the challenge, who struck out. Lice, bedbugs, toil and privation were commoner to Western experience than acts of valor and euphoric liberation.

Where, then, was the wild sweetness? Perhaps in expectation rather than the result, yet it is that which has always been the American lure.

It is arguable that the cowboy was an exception to the conformity and dullness of the West, for it seems probable that there really was a more genuine tang to his life when set beside the farmer's drudgery. At least most retrospective musings suggest so: " ... something romantic about him. He lives on horseback as do the Bedouins; he fights on horseback as did the knights of chivalry ... he swears like a trooper, drinks like a fish, wears clothes like an actor, and fights like a devil," a 1931 view (Webb), and reasonably typical of the redolent afterglow.

Yet, as we have seen, he was not considered much cop when most available as the emblem of the unremitting, dust-stained pioneer – in his original form as "cattle hunter" when stock were grazed in the public meadows of Virginia and the Carolinas. By the time the cult of the magnificent loner was in production, the cowboy had been too long an embarrassment to a previous attitude, contemporaneously he had been an irritating inconsistency. He marred the portrait of the sinister, uninhabitable barrens beyond the Mississippi that transfixed the Eastern mind.

There were by this time sizeable numbers of advance guard, the Indian traders who had got their bearings from the earlier Mexican *comancheros* and French *voyageurs*, and rummaged into Sioux and Apache country with pack mules or with wooden carts hauled by dogs or oxen. There were also the gold-washers and the mountain men, all of whom had gone beyond the Missouri and across the Great Plains and who knew differently about the "desolate barren land."

Yet until about 1850 gentlemen essayists and letter-writers had peered fastidiously into the emptiness, like astronauts scanning the moon for soft landings, had assessed what they flinched from by their criteria of familiar, lush-wooded vales, and had elaborated the legend. Zebulon M. Pike's journal of his 1810 expedition to the upper Rio Grande Valley likened the treeless prairies to Africa's sandy deserts, and seven years later Henry M. Brackenridge, who had taken a jaunt with a trapping party up the Missouri River, related: " ... the prevailing idea, with which we have so much flattered ourselves, of these western regions being like the rest of the United States, susceptible of cultivation, and affording endless outlets to settlements, is certainly erroneous."

7 : IN GOD WE TRUSTED,
IN KANSAS WE BUSTED

We too will thither
Bend our joyful footsteps

Adeste fideles

NATURE continued to imitate bad reporting. For the next thirty years desert burning athwart the continent was described by preconditioned travelers.

As late as 1846 Edwin Bryant, who made the trek to California, pronounced Nebraska to be "uninhabitable by civilized man." Long ago when Britain was attempting to snip the wings of emigrants, Edmund Burke told the House of Commons, in 1775, that if settlement was forbidden in the trans-Allegheny, the American rebels would "wander without a possibility of restraint; they would become hordes of English Tartars."

This Asiatic metaphor was much savored. To Thomas Hart Benton, in his *Thirty Years View*, the Southern Plains Indians were the "Arabs of the New World," and Flint called the same tribes "ruthless red Tartars of the desert."

Washington Irving in his 1836 novel *Astoria* warned that on these arid flats " . . . may spring up new and mongrel races of broken and almost extinguished tribes; the descendants of wandering hunters and trappers; of fugitives from the Spanish and American frontiers; of adventurers and desperadoes of every class and country yearly ejected from the bosom of society into the wilderness." He presaged picaroon bands, Arkansas Attilas, preying on the tillers of the soil on the hem of Eastern culture.

Moreover in 1856 Jefferson Davis, an Indian Wars dragoon before becoming Secretary of War, and who had first visualized America as a Hellenistic slave-based republic, advocated a frontier policy copied from that of France in Algeria – relinquish the desert to its nomadic bands but for garrison forts – and he had seventy-five camels sent from the Near East to San Antonio for the Texas Rangers. (The camels never took.)

79

It may be seen that the cowboy only too alarmingly seemed ready-made militia for the howling mongrel guerillas, and consequently was excluded from the myth of the admirable independent. It was much later that the cowboy was enshrined in the mold of Daniel Boone. In 1955 Frantz and Choate, praising "the cowboy's civilizing influence," wrote: "Into this enormous region, larger than all of the lands east of the Mississippi, came riding the Texas cowboy ... The forbidding desert, which had withstood the Spaniards and which, with towering mountains, was threatening to withstand Anglo-American encroachments as well, turned out not to be so forbidding after all when the right type of man, the cowboy, came along."

Perhaps, up to a point. However the leverage that cracked open the obstruction was not a wandering cowpoke crooner, any more than it was Daniel Boone, or any other outrider. It was an instrument of politics.

The Republican Party's post-Civil War policy was forged by the agrarian ideal and the symbol of the idealized yeoman, and in turn the policy stamped the brand mark deeper.

To win the 1860 election, when Abraham Lincoln became president, the Republicans had to carry the hitherto Democratic North-West, and the issue that mattered most in those parts was the Homestead Bill. "Land for the landless," a young country and untrammeled opportunities for "old Europe's hapless swains," those who had congealed in a looming bulk of unemployed in the preceding slump, the tip of another impending avalanche – these were the pressures.

"Go West, young man, go forth in the Country," exhorted Horace Greeley, the Republican leader, turning a phrase picked up from an Indiana newspaper into a national rallying cry. The experience of many who responded gave it a different connotation later. "Gone West" came to mean something very different.

But then Greeley's cry was heeded and the Homestead Act provided the access of the urban masses of the East to their 160 acres each, "Uncle Sam's generous domain," a New Jerusalem where the noble savage and the sturdy plowman would fuse into the Typical American. It was an idyll of simple, self-sufficient and harmonious tilling, which abides until today in the observance of the farmer's sanctity in Federal subsidies and aid.

Just as there had been earlier men who had found out for themselves that the belly of America was not the other side of the Styx, so there were men who promptly tested the revised prospectus and, like Garland, questioned its accuracy. The early waves Westward were not long afterward followed by a steady trickle of sorry wagon trains on the way back, painted with such messages as: "In God we trusted/In Kansas we busted." Sour replies to the call-of-the-wilders came in other forms. *Greer County Bachelor* was a sardonic song which had a masochistic popularity among frontier homesteaders:

> *Hurrah for Greer County! The land of the free*
> *The land of the bedbug, grasshopper and flea.*
> *I'll sing of its praises, I'll tell of its fame,*
> *While starving to death on my government claim.*

The California-bound, too, were warned in *Crossing the Plains:*

> *When you arrive at Placerville or Sacramento City,*
> *You've nothing in the world to eat, no money – what a pity!*
> *Your striped pants are all worn out, which causes people*
> *to laugh,*
> *When they see you gaping round the town like a great big*
> *brindle calf.*

Such vulgar cynicism did not puncture the fantasy: it was too entrenched. George Washington himself, discussing the opening of Ohio "to the poor, the needy and the oppressed of the Earth," had continued: " ... anyone therefore who is heavy laden or who wants land to cultivate, may repair thither and abound, as in the Land of promise, with milk and honey ..."

It goes without saying that the Washingtonian generosity of acceptance to all has not been followed to the letter. An observer of the Chicago press in the early 1900s commented that if the unemployed were American they were tramps, bummers and loafers; if they bore foreign names they were "European scum," and continued: "Discontented working men had no real grievances, but were always dupes of foreign agitators ... Strikers and labor demonstrations were always mobs composed of foreign scum, beer-swilling Germans, ignorant Bohemians, uncouth Poles, wild-eyed Russians."

But before the bulk imports of manpower from old Europe could be foreseen, the early bugle note was constantly resounded, as by Franklin who in 1780 reinforced the idea of America's spine and vitals being "the industrious frugal Farmers inhabiting the interior Part of these American States." The young man's concept of the good life became not to carry on his father's farm or business, but to build an idealized homestead for himself in the Golden West. Poverty, loneliness, hardship were felt to be only temporary, like a Gopher Prairie house. Across the river, over the next hill range would be found that perfect valley, where the will-o'-the-wisp idyll would become true.

There is left behind the sad explanation of the wife of a farmer who in 1820 sold his Maryland plantation and went to try out Florida: "It was all for the love of moving. We have been doing so all our lives – just moving – from place to place – never resting – as soon as ever we git comfortably settled, then, it is time to be off to something new."

One Virginian pioneer who moved into Ohio in 1819, from there to Indiana six years later, and in 1835 to Wisconsin, wrote in 1849: "I reached the Pacific and yet the sun sets West of me and my wife positively refuses to go to the Sandwich Islands and the bark is starting off my rails and that is longer than I ever allowed myself to remain on one farm." Another pioneer, who saw the frontier closed in Oklahoma, reflected: "We learned that God's Country isn't in the country. It is in the mind. As we looked back we knew all the time we was hunting for God's Country we had it. We worked hard. We was loyal. Honest. We was happy. For forty-eight years we lived together in God's Country."

8 : OUT INTO THE KINDLY SUNLIGHT

We declare it a vice and a sin for a man to be poor, if he can help it.

Newspaper editorial.

BETWEEN the Painted Desert and the White Mesa, a hundred empty miles short of Flagstaff, Arizona, is the Tsegi Trading Post. The clapboard doorway is festooned with old Navajo saddles made from tree roots and leather strips. Inside the counters and floor are piled with brilliant Indian rugs, silver bracelets, barrels of oranges and water melons, bales of cloth, wooden beads and safes of frozen foods.

In front of the notice PAWN WILL BE SOLD AFTER 6 MONTHS is a barrel-shaped man with a graying ginger beard. A deputy sheriff's shield is hooked on his khaki shirt; around his neck is a tie of black lace and an enameled throat brooch; on either hand are immense turquoise rings. He introduces himself as Trader Jim. His full name is James D. Porter and he was born seventy-three years ago in Indian Territory before it was consolidated into Oklahoma. Visible through the thin hair is a long grooved dent in his skull.

"That was done when I was a boy," he says between sips from a carton of milk. "My father was ranching near Lubbock, Texas, and got in a range feud with some cattle-owners. We were a week under siege before they over-ran us. They knocked me on the head, killed the foreman and cut my father's throat. He recovered, hunted down those three men and killed them.

"My father was half Scotch and half Cherokee, and my mother was half Irish and half Cherokee. She died when I was a baby. I never went to school. I loved my father very much but by the time I was eleven I was tired of sand blowing in my face and looking up a cow's ass. I rode off. All I took with me was a hot roll – that's a snap-fastener canvas with blanket – and a frying pan, a little flour and coffee, a ·22 rifle and ·44 and ·3030

83

revolvers. I rode down to Douglas, Arizona, which was a wide open town with two or three gun fights a week.

"I fell in with four men. They were bandits but honorable thieves and nicer than many gentlemen you meet. They took me under their wing. Now and then one of these men would say to me 'We're going on a ride, want to come?' That meant they were doing a train hold-up or robbing a bank. I never did go but when they told me they were going over the Mexico line to enrol with Pancho Villa I went too. We met up with Villa's army, 150 men with pistolerros stuck round their waists and draped with bullet belts.

"I rode with Villa for nineteen and a half months. We were mostly fighting the Carranza government troops but we really did rob the rich and give to the poor and underprivileged. We were also, what shall I say, well paid. I buried 20,000 dollars and never found two-thirds of it again, it was in such wild country.

"It was an exciting life but it was also very boresome and rough. Your saddle was your pillow and for two or three days at a time you'd have nothing to eat and only bad water to drink. Then in a fight with the troops one of my friends had the side of his face laid wide open with a curved sword. We packed it with horse dung and stitched it up, and took him into a border town near Yuma, Arizona. Another of the crowd knew a robber who was in the Yuma bastille and we went to see him. I was appalled. It was a real hell hole. I looked around and thought 'Boy, this is where you're going to end up.'

"I'd never anyway enjoyed shooting someone just to see him kick so I broke away. I said 'I'm off to see the Golden Gate.' I bought a Pierce-Arrow and drove west. In San Francisco I worked in a book store. I still couldn't write or read but I identified books by their brand mark – the publisher's design on the spine. Meantimes I'd started professional boxing and I'd also broken into the movies, airplane and auto stunting, and doubling for Jack Oakie. I began buying and selling used cars and became one of the biggest dealers in Los Angeles. That went the way of all flesh in the Depression.

"I'd married this little girl who's with me now (actually I'd married six times before in Mexico and around but I told her only three) and we drove up to the North California mountains and began panning gold. I sold out a two-third share in that mine for 3,000 dollars cash, a 160-acre ranch and an old Cadillac. I started another auto business. I had ulcers, couldn't sleep, hadn't had an erection for two years, went down with a heart attack and was told I'd got cancer and couldn't live more than three months.

"I thought what the hell. We cashed in everything and started off North. It took us sixteen months to get up to Alaska. I was pretty sick. I was bald, worn out by the rat-race, and then I had another heart attack.

"We were living with the Indians up there and they brought down their shaman. He gave me something, herbs, meats, and for two days and nights I was in sweating delirium – and suddenly I was all right. Back in the United States I had a check-up. There was no trace of the ulcer, heart condition or malignancy. That was fifteen years ago. My hair grew back. I became a man again – as good as a twenty-eight-year-old my wife and doctor tell me. It's not only that. I used to be a mean man, a fighter. In my heart I've changed too.

"You know why? Because in all my roamings I've managed to get back to what matters. For two years I covered every part of America before staying here. The Indians call me grandfather. They don't like the white man because he has stolen almost everything in the world from them but they assess you by your conduct.

"I bring them into the world and bury them. I took four dollars the first year I opened this trading post. Now I do 200,000 dollars' business a year, ninety-eight per cent with the Indians. They trade with their wool and jewelry. They make their thumb prints on their bills and maybe five years later they come in and pay them off. We trust each other.

"No white Americans can figure why, after all my wanderings, I've stopped off here. It's because I've found complete happiness."

THE search for Utopia united all who felt the lure of the great continent, but migration stamped upon the American family the characteristic of casualness toward place, kinship and stock. In the charge toward gold and land social cohesion and discipline dropped away.

The dissolving pattern was stimulated by scriptural visions of millions of urban disinherited fanning out to fructify the prairies. "Make the Public Lands free in quarter-sections to Actual Settlers," Greeley expounded in an 1854 New York *Herald Tribune* editorial, "and deny them to all others and earth's landless millions will no longer be orphans and mendicants; they can work for the wealthy, relieved from the degrading terror of being turned adrift to starve. When employment fails or wages are inadequate, they may pack up and strike Westward to enter upon the possession and culture of their own lands . . ."

Greeley's compulsion to bring order and decency to the semi-industrialized masses, whose sense of direction had already been atomized, should certainly not be scoffed at for the problem was bitter. In the period Thernstrom examines – just a segment, from 1850 to 1880 in Newburyport, Massachusetts – there is revealed a ferment beneath the graceful vignettes composed by the scribes who were the mouthpieces of the business aristocracy.

Industrialization had sucked into Newburyport a swarm of floating workmen, propertyless "lack-alls" in a state of bubbling turnover. The immigrant bog Irish and the farm boys from New England streamed in, found either snatches of employment or none at all, streamed out, and were replaced by other "permanent transients," still cheaper labor.

They were "buffeted about from city to city within the New England labor market . . . helpless before the vicissitudes of a rapidly changing economy." This new influx, unable to form a stable economic connection to a community "which provided no soil in which to sink roots," were relegated by the masters to an invisibility where they could not pester the middle class sensibilities.

This was not profoundly difficult to do for personal contact was tenuous. Contemporary observers were, even then, characterizing the new working class as "floating." These hordes of impoverished, unskilled, disorientated arrivals were – like Negroes and Puerto Ricans in present-day America – the first laid off in a recession, the first forced onto relief, the first kicked out of the city. The records show that after the 1857 collapse an estimated 1,000 left Newburyport for "locations where work is more abundant" – a statement unlikely to be more than a hope common to both the floaters and the burghers.

The rhythm quickened in reverse when "abundance" seemed promising in Newburyport. When the local cotton mills re-opened during the economic recovery of 1879, 1,120 "tramps" applied for lodgings at the local jail: 381 gave their occupation as laborer and 235 others as mill operative, both groups presumably bidding to be first in when the factories began humming again.

The dichotomy between the classes – which gave scope for shifting a block of human beings about like ledger entries, in or out, wanted or not wanted, valid or void – ensued from a changing situation that had not yet been understood. The old order, disintegrating since the turn of the century, fell in a shambles with the sudden industrialization and urban explosion of the 1840s, and the resulting disruption of the old hierarchical relationship between the social groups. The arising of the factory caused a swerve into an ecology arrived at in Britain forty years earlier, the subject of Engels's examination of a "weird inhuman society," a nation riven into two classes, rich and poor.

Engels looked with horror at the new shiny satanic mills and their stews into which millions were being drawn from "merry old England," in which "no comfortable family life is possible ... only a physically degenerate race, robbed of all humanity, degraded, reduced morally and physically to bestiality."

Karl Marx decided that machinery "lays the worker low, abolishes humane relations, stultifies the masses and depopulates the countryside ..." Capital "comes into the world soiled with mire from top to toe and oozing blood from every pore."

Marx and Engels had been scrutinizing the results of a social eruption. In America the convulsion was still in action. Not all the bourgeoisie were callously and uncaringly oozing blood from every pore. In some quarters there was at least a nervous pes-

simism, even concern for the alien rabble. This concern admitt-
edly was usually expressed in ever shriller exhortations to the
"indolent class" to grasp the chances for advancement dangling
before them, ripe cherries.

"We declare it a vice and a sin for a man to be poor, if he
can help it," boomed a Newburyport editorial. Poverty was "not
a want of means, but a want of will – of real manliness and
self-control." The customary method of proving that conditions
were really splendid and healthily bustling was to label the Old
World evil, stagnant, decaying. Industrial Britain and France
were filled with "ignorance," "imbecility" and "squalid misery,"
the people generally "poor, miserable and starving."

Among the beholders of the American Shangri-La, however,
there were some anxious to ensure that a menacing, revolution-
bent proletariat such as Europe's should never gang up in
America.

It was out of this line of thought that the ideology of mobility was born. The theory behind the building of Lowell, Massachusetts, the first great textile center, was an ambiguous blend
of flyness and quixotism. The mills would be kept churning
by a steady "succession of learners," farm hands attracted in by
higher wages. After a few years they would strike out West
and buy a farm with their savings, to be replaced by the next
ripple of eager apprentices (at reasonable prices) from the surrounding rural regions.

Nathan Appleton and his fellow sponsors believed that
Europe's factory hands were "of the lowest character, for intelligence and morals," whereas because "most of our operatives
are born and bred in virtuous rural homes, and, after working
for a few years in the mills, return to agricultural pursuits, the
interests of Lowell will rest secure."

Thus there would continue a circulation of well-rounded and
contented workers, and Jefferson's early tenet that democracy
was inextricably bound up with agrarian qualities would be
substantiated.

Much of this argument was an effort to solve a situation that
had been building up for a long time, and which was now forcing itself upon the propertied classes. Many still clung to the
faith that the virus of class-hatred and rebellion, carried over

from the decayed carcass of Europe by the immigrants, would "melt before the kindly sunlight" of American freedom, that these vile social diseases would be healed by the "hidden alchemy in the air of the United States."

The average East Coast manufacturing center at this time had a turnover of more than half the local unskilled labor force every decade. On a much vaster canvas the economy was increasingly dependent – in industry, in agriculture, in the forests, in cattle rearing, in canal and rail construction – on disposable labor, on a brimming pool to be tapped for seasonal need, shut off when the need expired, and left to flow onward under its own power to the next vent.

Accordingly this volatile society had to create an ideology of the Open Road as a short cut upward in the Open Society, and the go-about began his metamorphosis into lion-heart and hero. It took numbers, and the necessity to keep those numbers high-stepping, to accomplish this revision. Until then a tramp had been a tramp.

This change of role, or rather change of guise, was not a novel enough idea to cause alarm for, as has been seen, already established as something deeply and valuably American was the hero figure of the solitary, daring man of action. Nor was the extension of this example to the urban industrial laborer entirely an imposition from above. Man is resourcefully adept at squeezing compensation, even satisfaction, out of the most arid predicament. Minute and subtle caste marks are invented to give dabs of color in the grayest circumstances; a pecking order is swiftly introduced in the pokiest farmyard. In April 1853 the Newbury-port *Daily Evening Union* explained that America was a truly natural society, a collection of millions of competing atoms held together by enlightened self-interest. Those atoms were in a state of constant motion. The never-ceasing up-and-down, "like the waves of the sea," could only "purify" society. Few of the atoms then being purified could obtain much comfort from those words, because they were mostly illiterate. But it was not only the burghers who believed that, distressing though the condition of the working class was, it was only temporary, that fixed social layers could not exist in the United States – the floating laborer believed this, too.

That is one reason why in the first place he undertook the grueling journey across the Atlantic. And ever since arriving he had been ceaselessly told that it was so. He was reluctant to believe that he could have been hoodwinked, that the promised land of milk and honey was a bread and water sentence for him. Indeed why, despite his personal misfortunes, should he believe that? For frequently the evidence was before him of someone who was breaking through, "pulling himself up by his bootstraps." When, sporadically, he did try to enhance his bargaining position by collective action, he was blocked by mercenaries, company agents and Pinkerton guards bringing in the "black sheep" and the "rats," all armed and mobilized at trouble spots by the new machinery of railroad and telegraph. If really pushed, the factory owner got rid of his entire work force, for strike-breaking replacements could be hustled in from Canada or from the contract shiploads just arrived from Europe. If areas became too militant, industry packed up and went – as did the cotton and steel companies who transferred to Carolina and Alabama to milk the meek, cheap Negro labor.

But the greatest impediment to collective action was not simply the craftsman's suspicion of the unskilled laborer, nor that of the native against the immigrant prepared to work for lower wages, nor the immigrant's ignorance and the difficulty of getting co-operation between Ukrainians and Austrians, Poles and Italians, but, as Thistlethwaite observes, "the lack of conviction among working men that they constituted a separate class. Whether skilled craftsman, Nebraska farm boy, or European peasant, the industrial worker believed his job to be only a temporary makeshift, a stepping stone to better things."

This basic faith may have wavered during bad patches but it has never really altered. Very recently a five-city survey by Wilcock and Franke among workers dismissed by the Armor meatpacking plant and a laundry-equipment firm turned up the traditional acceptance of this being the natural scheme of things. Although "anger, resentment, bitterness, frustration, bewilderment" were some of the words used by the interviewers to describe the emotions of these "blighted men," and although

90

the long-term unemployed, uprooted from a productive institutional tie and a seemingly secure place in society, felt "isolated from the work environment and a large part of their usual human associations," the report shows "surprisingly little radicalism or rejection of the social and economic system. Many accepted economic insecurity as part of the American way of life, and few had very specific ideas about what could be done to help them in the labor market." And there was, despite attachment to the home town and apprehension about the risks of moving, "a substantial degree of willingness to move under the spur of economic necessity."

So it was from the start. The newcomer found it tougher than he had expected but he'd make out, and in the way it should be done in America – on his own. Here is the basic explanation for the slow, patchy growth of unionism in America, for the absence of a strong radical political party, for the lack of solidarity and class-consciousness among the working population – and for the floating laborer's readiness at this time to adapt to the definitive part in which he was being cast.

In the event the Homestead Act did not melt away the industrial poor, for few had the money to transport themselves to the happy valleys or the agricultural skill to make them bloom if they got there. And those who did set forth mostly found themselves beaten to it by land speculators and railroad corporations.

One clue to the dearth of realistic results from Appleton's theory is that there is only one report in the Newburyport newspapers between 1850 and 1880 of a local laborer successfully settling in the West, and this single instance would hardly have delighted Horace Greeley. On June 22, 1878, the *Herald* carried news of one Michael Welch, son of a Newburyport working man and who had been treasurer of a local volunteer fire company. Welch had financed his venture forth into the land by lifting the firemen's funds and he had now written to his parents reporting that he was doing very nicely out in Nevada.

Few aspiring pioneers could so readily get their hands on capital and few of those who did were the laboring poor for whom the theory was devised. Many were artisans, school-teachers, farmers and businessmen who went to grab a fast fortune out of Illinois wheat or Californian gold. The "safety valve" purpose of the frontier never worked.

This indication that a century ago, despite much physical mobility, there was little social mobility sharply conflicts with all the claims for the American open economy. Nor was this merely a peculiarity of that time and place. The compilers of a recent report, *The Reluctant Job Changer*, find: " ... a substantial proportion of workers in American cities never leave the general skill levels of their fathers or of their own first job ... At the same time, there is evidence of considerable downward movement between generations or over a working life, perhaps even more in this country than in Europe."

Added to this somewhat devastating inversion of a myth is a not wholly convincing consolation: "Downward movement may be of little social significance to American workers, however, if other desires, especially for increased income, are satisfied in the process. Many Americans are saved from a sense of frustration by their ability to believe in an equalitarian society while drawing satisfaction from a modest position in life," but it is concluded: "The prevailing rates of vertical mobility in this country as compared with Europe do not provide much support for the belief in opportunity that is generally held to be a dominant American idea ..."

When in 1893 Turner read his paper, *The Significance of the Frontier in American History*, to a historians' meeting in Chicago, and furled across the curtain on the frontier, he set circulating an anamorphosis which was believed for a long time.

Turner declared that class war had been prevented, and democracy disseminated, by the disgruntled machine operator working off his grudges by breaking virgin ground in the West. This was simply not so. Apart from the schoolteachers and businessmen who had the little bit of capital for such an enterprise, the genuine settlers, those who became Western farmers, had been Eastern farmers. Also, a run down the years of flood migration shows that this occurred not when the unemployment pools were biggest but when they were lowest: the Westerners took off when there was prosperity in the East and capital was therefore available. The peak migrations were immediately before the panics of 1819, 1837, 1857 and 1873 and during the halcyon early 1880s.

The factory hands without factories to work in, who were willy-nilly pushed West by distress became not land-owners but a general-purpose labor gang, errant in the country. The Homestead Act did draw them out in a subsidiary capacity: to provide the transport lines to the front-line farms, so, in a far less fair and munificent way than its exponents intended, it did break up some of the log-jams of workers from the East. But those who strapped up their belongings and moved inland were still adrift.

The ousting of the five Southern Indian tribes and the Black Hawk War of 1832 when the starving, desperate Sauk and Foxes attempted to recover their corn plots, also gave temporary jobs to men anxious to escape from the city purlieus and prepared to sign on with the Army auxiliary. In 1832 a special Western force was created to man the forts and patrol the 1,500 miles of Indian border. It was a rag, tag and bobtail immigrant crew with no uniforms, few arms and less English, which was later hammered into a regiment of mounted dragoons. More drifters from the industrial belt were drawn into the wilderness when in 1837 the whole region beyond the Mississippi was constituted the Western Department, and increasing numbers of rangers were needed to establish new outposts and ride as detachments guarding the overland caravans.

In another form the casual laborer had already sashayed in many directions before the Homestead Act. He was familiar in the version of the early pack-rat miner who footslogged California with bedding and pick on his back. He was the river tramp who worked as roustabout on the Mississippi paddle steamers and hung around the landing stages at St. Louis and St. Joseph, much as the *bosyaki*, the bare-foot itinerants of Russia's rivers, later appeared in Gorky's stories of the "superfluous men" of the Lower Depths. He was the pick-and-spade ganger who scooped out the canals, when every city euphorically saw itself as the radial point of a network of waterways on which the merchandise would flow in and out – until the panic of 1837 damped the canal fever. Dozens of plans were abandoned half finished and thousands of foreign-speaking Germans and Scandinavians, as well as the Irish (and some of those spoke only Gaelic), were left broke far from family and port-of-entry, the slipstream of a vanished machine prosperity.

9 : STRICT BEAUTY OF LOCOMOTIVE

They were hikin' through the tunnels,
Holdin' on the funnels,
Ridin' on the gunnels,
On the way to Montreal.

Hobo song

IT is a slow, slithering drive from Klamath Falls, itself at an elevation of 4,105 feet, up to the crown slopes of the 8,500 feet Quarter Butte Mountain in the High Cascades. This part of Oregon has perhaps the world's thickest stand of Ponderosa pine. The fifteen-mile climb is up steep, coiling shale roads, at first beside lakes of stabbing blue fished by pelicans, then between crags where cougar and the bald-headed eagle live. It is wild country but by no means deserted, for down that ruckled track there is heavy traffic of colossal thundering articulated trucks piled with chain-buckled logs for the valley saw mills.

This timber stand is one of the summer "shows" of the Weyerhaeuser Lumber Company (the winter snows close it down and work shifts to lower, more accessible zones) whose 610,000 acres stretch 120 miles across. Logging is not the freebooting trade it was forty years ago when the companies slashed bare swathes through the United States, and when the lumberjack – inevitably a single man "batched-up" in remote and primitive camps – fought bitterly with management for better conditions and the right to unionize. Now, even though he may have to commute in a crew bus 120 miles each way daily between site and base, he can live in the community. Even so logging is still seasonal and migratory, and among the men now working on Quarter Butte are many who were drifting through the passes looking for a summer job or just a quick grub-stake.

The location of this day's operations is betrayed by a fog of dust floating through the white firs and cedars. With a grinding roar each massive trunk is being yanked by cable and winch down through the secondary growth to a clearing where the knot-bumpers trim off stubs before a caterpillar-mounted grab hoists it in iron pincers aboard the trailer. It is another twenty-minute climb on foot to the tree-fallers – they "fall" a tree – themselves. Their position is signaled by the erratic shrieking of an electric saw. They work in teams of two, each cutting three trees in turn.

Under their metal helmets the faces of J. W. Scoggins and Dallas Chalfant are masked with a paste of sweat and red dust. They squat to talk on the bole of a hundred-foot Douglas fir that has just toppled to their saw, clean, without touching another tree.

Chalfant: "I got in just today. As a matter of fact, I'm Oregon-born, at Prineville, 180 miles north of here. My father had fallen timber but I went to try out at accountancy up in Sun Valley but, well, I guess it's in the family and I went back to falling.

"After the war it was on a gyppo basis, on piece rates, and you could make more money. I floated around the Idaho woods, just speculating, seeing what there was. That's ruggeder country than here, higher and steeper. Last time I was falling near Boise but then the outfit moved away up the Payette River and that meant batching. I'm married and I didn't especially want to spend the evenings playing dominoes and poker.

"So I pulled out of there and looked around Bend, in central Oregon, then heard they were wanting hands down here.

"I suppose loggers are a pretty footloose lot, always have been, but you have to go where the timber is, you know. Now the sawdust savages down at the plant doing the pulping and milling, they're another breed of cats, but I myself like being out in the woods and maybe trying a new territory once in a while. I feel that's where I belong though it is a rough life."

"It's a rough life all right," agrees J. W. (he was christened J. W., the initials of his two grandfathers) Scoggins. "Last winter we were cutting in seven feet of snow. I came up from Arkansas. My dad was a logger, but I didn't neither go straight into it.

"I drove a truck for a time. I covered this country from coast to coast, trips from Los Angeles to Chicago or to Seattle or to Philadelphia. You drove eight hours, rested twelve – you pulled

96

off the highway and slept in the little cubicle behind the cab.

"Sometimes feel I drive nearly as much on this job. Last spring I was commuting 200 miles a day by car. It always happens – the timber's cleared around a town and the shows get farther and farther away. But I don't leave home if I can help it, you betcha, boy. It used to be come and go, you know, and the woodsmen had no anchor at all, so maybe it's a change for the betterment.

"Yet there's still a lot of loggers work just long enough to get up a grub stake and then go off on a binge. It's really true, there's a different breed of men in logging. There's less brute force now and more knowledge of machinery needed but it's still harder work than most jobs. That's okay because the way I see it, you're a freer man."

THE innovation of the railroad in the late 1820s was a loop-hole a multitude was becoming used to: the shipping out of tough labor into distances and places few could imaginatively measure or locate, living a cruelly hard, misogamic life in secular monasteries of company hutment or caboose.

As the line bored onward, the recruits got farther from what had been briefly home, with always another branch line or loop system to side-step to when the present one finished. They suffered the "growing pains" Thistlethwaite refers to when looking at the great changes between 1820 and 1850. "The unplanned haphazard expansion went ahead too fast ... Many of this literally dislocated generation, without familiar landmarks, lost the sense of identity and direction ... Many succumbed to the violence and solitude of the frontier which abounded with shiftless drifters and strange, broken characters, flotsam on the turbulent flood of change."

The canal fever was a faint flush compared to the galloping contagion that cheap steel – the basis of the railroad age – loosed. By the outbreak of the Civil War there was a skeleton gridiron East of the Alleghenies and a flimsy link with the Middle

West. By 1860 30,000 miles of track were down. The decade of 1880-90 packed in the most headlong growth in the history of American railroads: 70,300 miles were added, more than 7,000 each year. The hot pace slackened off after the 1890s, but by 1916 every state, nearly every county and every city and size-able town was served by one or more railroads, and was served by daily trains to and from all parts of the country. There was business out there. Between 1860 and 1910 the number of farms increased from two to six million, and 500 million acres were brought under cultivation – an area about the size of Western Europe.

The rail mileage had proliferated to 193,346 by the end of the century, and rose to 254,000 (its peak: the luxuriant iron vine has withered since) – all that free travel for a man with pliant bones and a readiness to take the rough without any smooth.

But long before that, by the 1860s, those names that are a plainsong of American dimensions and power – Rock Island; the Louisa; the Nashville and Chattanooga; the Chicago, Mil-waukee, St. Paul and Pacific; the North Western; the Southern; the Texas and Pacific; the Peoria and Oquawka; the Illinois Cen-tral; the Atchison and Topeka; the Hannibal and St. Joseph – emblazoned the thousands who rode into Arcadia.

Those early tracks probed into a frontier life that was decay-ing before it was callow, and the engineer was the new cavalier to supersede the horse-riders. From the start the railroads clanged with romance: they were "the links of that endless chain that was to bind the States in love together." (The love sonnet is still in the language of even the businessmen of rail-road management. In 1966, after being appointed to rehabili-tate the ailing Chicago, Burlington and Quincy Railroad, Lou Menk declared that the aim of the line was to write more of "the poetry of the railroad – a nice long freight train.") The huge soot-belching contraptions with their cowcatchers and fun-nels like mill chimneys, and their headlights striping the prairies, threw their sparks abidingly into the American imagination. For the train has remained an arrow, the line out and yet at the same time the umbilical cord coiling back across stupendous spaces to a home and kin lost from sight.

To a foreigner – to this one, at least – hearing an American locomotive sounding through the darkness of, say Nebraska or New Mexico, never fails to cause a bewildering moment of expectation that a ship is hoving up. For that hoarse bellow resembles not the reedy shrill of an English train but the sirens heard at a river mouth or through dockland fog. Yet it fits – fits on these great interior seas of earth, and perhaps the feeling in the blues,

> *I see a train coming down the railroad track*
> *Love to hear the bark of that old smokestack*

and

> *I hate to hear that freight train blow boo-hoo!*
> *'Cos every time I hear it, feel like riding too*

is probably as akin to sea fever as can be known by land-locked Vikings.

The "dream world" that the railroads created for boys of his generation has been recalled by Holbrook, quoting a boyhood friend who had set out "for that magic country to which all passing trains went" and worked for forty years on the rails.

"Boys didn't go to work on the railroad simply because their fathers did," he said. "What fetched them were the sights and sounds of moving trains, and above all the whistle of a locomotive. I've heard of the call of the wild, the call of the law, the call of the church. There is also the call of the railroad."

The whistle of a locomotive on those new lines was a signal to all within earshot, even out of sight of it across the white pine hills and the blueberry swamps, that America was all of one piece. It was a telegraph message across exciting distances to dwellers in a perfunctory loneliness. They listened and read the code of the engineer's quill and knew which train was racing by.

The whistle's call was one that millions of Americans responded to in the latter half of the nineteenth century, and the railroad immediately bloomed with an aurora of bucko deeds that the staid system in built-over Britain never acquired, despite

Kipling's attempt to whip it up with the claim that "romance brought up the nine-fifteen."

Indeed long before, when the train was still the splendor of Britain's industrial age, Matthew Arnold had seen more accurately that it merely carried its passengers from a "dismal and illiberal life" in one factory hell-hole to the same life in another factory hell-hole. Actually, a surprising number of English nineteenth-century poets – apart, that is, from Scotland's own William McGonagall and his *The Newport Railway* – did turn their attention to the snorting marvel: not only wrathfully, as Wordsworth in *The Kendal and Windermere Railway* and W. E. Henley in *Journey By Train*, but many such as Rossetti, Landor and William Cosmo Monkhouse were rapturously moved by this black and crimson dragon at large in England's tame acres. There was the determinedly "modern" attitude expressed by Charles Mackay in 1846:

> *"No poetry in Railways!" foolish thought*
> *Of a dull brain, to no fine music wrought.*

Yet, like the later "keen/Unpassioned beauty of a great machine" of Rupert Brooke and "strict beauty of locomotive" of Auden, these were poets reacting sensitively to the concussive onrush of "unconquer'd steam," and indeed the railway came to be cosily incorporated by John Betjeman in nostalgic runs on the "Early Electric" through "autumn-scented Middlesex again." But in Britain the railway was superimposed upon settled communities; in America the railroads were the ligaments of a strengthening nation, and the ordinary people felt this poetically and expressed it in their own crude poetry.

In practical terms the migrants and settlers and prospecting business men and traders and adventurers and recruited yeomen climbed aboard and saw for the first time what really did lie where either the Great Desert or the Land of Milk and Honey was supposed to be. And one man who was then coming into existence as a passenger the railroad companies hadn't foreseen and certainly didn't want, but who was going to bestow his own private legend and lore upon the railroad, was the free-rider of the steamcars later to be known as the hobo.

As far as I know the first printed report of snagging a ride – to become the *de rigueur* mode of travel for the hobo – appears in *Strikers, Communists, Tramps and Detectives*, published in 1878, a work of vibrantly pious tone by Allan Pinkerton, founder of the company private detective system, who was loathed by every working man and radical.

There was a popular song sung with savage emotionalism in every industrial town, *Father Was Killed by the Pinkerton Men*. The motto of the Pinkerton National Detective Agency was "We never sleep" and its trademark was an open left eye ("eye sinister") which gave birth to the term private eye. The word fink – meaning a scab, strike breaker, company spy or other variety of rat and stoolpigeon – is also said to derive from Pinkerton and its contraction to pink, dating from the 1892 Homestead strike.

The Pinkertons wore military-style blouses and slouch hats – that is, when they were in uniform. For the Pinkertons also operated as undercover operatives, spies infiltrating unions and strike committees.

After its founding at mid-century the agency participated in seventy major industrial disputes, always on the management side. Its 2,000 trained active men and 30,000 reserve totalled more than the standing army of the nation. They were, in truth, an army: a private army available to any corporation or individual factory offering a fee for the smashing of a union or the de-fusing of a strike.

They were armed. They killed. After the Homestead scandal, in which dozens died and hundreds were wounded, eight states enacted mild anti-Pinkerton statutes, and Populist-controlled Colorado withdrew the Pinkerton's Denver license. Yet overall little was done to curb the Pinkerton finks, and they continued to appear, predictable as blue-bottles on bad meat, wherever workers had to be taught not to be uppity.

It is therefore not excessively surprising that the Father of the Private Eyes, in his 1878 account of his own exemplary ascent from immigrant guttersnipe to four-square prosperous patriot, should see the tramp from the commanding heights of establishment service as a bit of the rubble, and rabble, at the bottom.

Here is the first recorded observation of a hobo *in situ*: "During the passage of the fast train sent from New York to San Francisco, by Jarrett and Palmer in '77, a tramp boarded the train at Cheyenne, climbed to the top of the coach and enjoyed hugely his elegant and rapid manner of making his journey until Sherman was reached. At that point the engineer got a glimpse of him and he at once began throwing a heavy shower of cinders and increased the speed to the utmost power of the engine . . . The cinders burned into his clothes, cut his arms and legs and face." After cleaving for his life to the rocketing coach, smouldering the while, "at Green River he was let down more dead than alive and his hair had turned gray and he looked more like an old man of sixty than a lad of nineteen as he was."

There is one reference to an even earlier pioneer hobo. In a 1912 broadsheet *The Curse of Tramp Life* by "A No. 1," California Dan says: "Have you heard that old 'Omaha Bill,' you know the 'Old Timer,' who back in the Sixties beat the first train the Union Pacific sent West across the plains, has found his end?" (A freight had side-swiped Omaha Bill as he dozed on a sleeper near Fargo.) Tenuous hearsay, but there is no reason to doubt that an enterprising hobo vanguard had already begun nailing rattlers by then.

Certainly during the decade following Pinkerton's incident a throng of like-minded must have decided to take the weight off their feet and risk instant gray hair, for the clandestine passenger had become a problem familiar enough to support a dramatic drawing by A. B. Frost in *The American Railway* in 1888. It shows a staunch, upright brakeman, fists raised in Queensberry mien, confronting two tramps to whom he has been giving the bum's rush. They are clearly very ugly characters, not only wearing expressions of snarling venom, but ragged clothes, too. One is pulling a knife, the other brandishing a cudgel. Fortunately for the brakie, a fellow shack is running along the catwalk on the roof of the adjacent freight train to lend a hand.

Pinkerton provided the first description in the annals of a jungle, a tramps' camp. At about the same period as that jolly anecdote about the barbecued hobo, one of his agents "in pursuance of his duty at Wilkesbarre, Pennsylvania" during an

1877 strike, when the Pinkerton squads were busily beating up troublesome pit workers "suddenly came upon a bivouac of tramps near a coal-shaft" deserted by the down-tooled miners.

The peerless Pinkerton instantly gives this camp fire soirée the sinister air of a coven celebrating Black Mass. "This grotesque company numbered thirty or forty persons," he relates. 'They were cooking their supper at the edge of the timber, among the rocky bluffs and overreaching protecting trees. The moon, rising above the lonesome scene, fell across the camp, giving its inmates a weird, witch-like appearance. They seemed to be a tired, dreary, wretched lot, and had the marks of traveling and weary wandering upon them. Most of them had fallen upon the ground for rest and in all sorts of sluggish positions were dozing in a stupid, sodden way that told of brutish instincts and experience."

Nowhere in Pinkerton's book is the word hobo used. Quite evidently at this time the hobo had been neither observed with interest not distinguished from the other tattered casualties on the industrial battlefield. The certain origins and etymology of the word seem untraceable, but plenty of explanations have been offered. Ben Benson ("The Coast Kid") in his 1942 pamphlet repeats authoritatively the dubious claim first advanced in *The Bugle*, a sheet proselytizing "Marxian Socialism" among the unemployed and spasmodically published in the early Twenties from Oklahoma City, that hobo comes from the Latin *homo bonus* meaning good man. Benson clinches this with: "A real Hobo is a migratory worker – most of the Pioneers in this country were hoboes."

Elsewhere it has been suggested that the word was a concertinaing of a standard greeting: "Ho, boy!" That might seem, in the laconic American idiom, to ring with improbable Falstaffian heartiness. Minehan passes on another idea. In his *Lonesome Road* he has one old bum give his young hero this somewhat pedantic explanation: "It's a contraction for 'Hello, Brother.' Later they shortened it to 'Lo bro.' Well, they sort of changed that to 'lo bo,' and then because 'lo bo' sounds like saying 'low' they just said 'o bo.' Most persons like to bring out their o's good and strong so somebody added an h, and it became hobo, meaning a man who travels and works."

Yet another suggestion I have seen put forward is that it comes from hoosegow (why? Hoboes weren't the only men put in jail) or from hoosier, meaning an inexperienced worker or rustic (no more convincing, I think). One more theory is that it began as the call "Hi, boy!" of railway mail-handlers in the North-West when throwing out the delivery sacks.

A possibility that does not seem previously to have been examined – and it is as good as the foregoing – is whether the alteration from its root may not have been a deliberate jocularity based on the derivation of oboe. The original sixteenth-century French term for what had been the shawm was haulx-bois or haultbois (meaning high wood). Shortened to hautbois, it was then anglicized to hautboy, hoboy, howeboie, hoeboy and howboy. The similarity might seem too close to be ignored, especially as in German the word was hoboe, and there were many Germans among those early migrant lumberjacks and farm hands.

Alternatively it could, although neither have I found this suggested, have filtered into general use from Negro usage, for "boy" (usually in mimicry of the white boss's form of address) is commonly used among Negroes, and it was in the last quarter of the nineteenth century that there began the first big swell Northward of Southern black field labor.

Perhaps the best solution advanced is that by Nicholas Klein, a one-time Hobo College president. Pointing out that the floating laborers had become an essential harvest force on the Western farms, he maintains that "the name originated from the words 'hoe-boy,' plainly derived from work on the farm.

Whichever the case, by the 1890s the word hobo was generally known. It does seem a little strange, then, that W. H. Davies's *The Autobiography of a Super-Tramp*, in the section concerned with his five years of hoboing around America from June 1893, constantly employs the words tramp or beggar. But it seems unlikely that the stilted speech Davies puts into the mouths of Brum, Philadelphia Slim and the rest has much relation to their actual style, and Davies, although undeniably a pro, is careful to underline his separation and superiority: the itinerant canal-builders at Chicago are "the riff-raff of America and the scum of Europe," the Negroes he especially loathes and despises. Perhaps Davies thought the hobo too low class and inelegantly plebian. Nevertheless the word was without much doubt in wide currency at that time – like the hobo himself, carried and spread by the railroad and the railroaders, whom lexicographers consider the first American sub-group with a nation-wide cant and jargon. Hobo was soon everywhere and in its shortened form, 'bo or bo, took on classless form and was direct, matey address up through the Thirties.

It was in the 1880s that the first discrimination began to be made, that the hobo was singled out – or, more accurately, was singling himself out – as a sub-species.

Jack London in two essays, "How I Became A Socialist" and "What Life Means To Me," published in 1903 and 1905 in *The Comrade*, a Socialist Party organ, and in an article "The Tramp" for a 1904 issue of *Wilshire's Magazine*, drawing upon his own experiences riding the rods with the bindle stiffs and road kids as an eighteen-year-old in 1894, makes the first careful differentiation between down-and-out transients and the hobo.

Feied points out that Poole's *Index* yields not a single reference to an article concerning tramps or hobos in an American magazine in 1875. "That there were homeless men tramping the roads and making use of the rail lines before the 'seventies and 'eighties can hardly be doubted," he says, "yet it seems likely that until they became a problem scant attention would be paid to them," and there puts his finger on the cause of the flood of writing about the unattached man which was released by Bret Harte's 1877 short story, *My Friend, the Tramp*, and which mounted through the 1890s.

It was the crash of 1873 and the subsequent depression which tossed three million men into vagrancy, and transformed the tramp into a burden and a threat. Before that the tramp was in any case a speck through the wrong end of a telescope, socially and geographically negligible, for his drifting circuit was through the Western mining towns and railroad construction redoubts.

Nor, even if he ever did encroach upon their consciousness, was he a fit subject for the Boston sociologist or belletrist. As long ago as 1859, Frederick Law Olmsted wrote: "Men of literary taste ... are always apt to overlook the working classes, and to confine the records they make of their own times, in great degree, to the habits and fortunes of their own associates, and to those of people of superior rank to themselves ... The dumb masses have often been so lost in this shadow of egotism, that, in later days, it has been impossible to discern the very real influence their character and condition has had on the fortune and fate of nations."

Ginzberg and Herman ran into the same fog bank when delving for material for *The American Worker in the Twentieth Century*: " ... much of history is the history of the successes and failures of those who held positions of power and influence. But a dull silence prevails when it comes to the work and lives of working men and women." Thernstrom remarks, too: "One of the most glaring gaps in our knowledge of nineteenth century America is the absence of reliable information about the social mobility of its population, particularly at the lower and middle levels of society."

This is a continuing lacuna. Laubach's *Why There Are Vagrants*, published in 1916, remarked that "at last the world of 'hoboes' has begun to attract notice in the front pages of the newspapers" – because vagrants were becoming "envious and discontented." The hundred homeless men he "studied" were sorted into various personality categories, such as "childish or silly, low ideals, stupid, false pride, repulsive face, sarcastic, treacherous, vulgar." Laubach's nostrum was: "If we can eliminate drunkenness we may therefore greatly reduce vagrancy."

In 1817 Edward Markham wondered wistfully if the literature of the future would "discover that the working man is the prince in disguise." That same year Francis Hackett commented upon the "enormous gap between literate and unliterate America."

In the Twenties Edwin Seaver in *The New Masses*, advised the critic to "take his nose out of the literary gossip columns and go to the Hoovervilles, to the Hard-Luck-on-the-East-Rivers, to the deserted mines and the impoverished fields, to the jungles outside our big cities, to the flophouses, to the charity dispensaries, to the empty warehouses where the homeless ones gather by stealth until they are chased out by the law – for it is here, and not in the library, that the strongest elements in our new literature are likely to come from. It is here that you may meet our future Gorkys, and not at your literary teas. It is here that you may meet our future poets and dramatists and novelists, not in the ranks of the cultured riffraff who no longer bother to talk about books."

A dreamy thought, but either no one did venture into thòse dives, or the poets and dramatists weren't there anyway. Looking with less Marxian fixity and a longer view, Aaron wrote in 1961: "Among the major American writers, only Walt Whitman addressed himself to the working man without inhibition or restraint, but no writer of stature in nineteenth century America had written 'the *Uncle Tom's Cabin* of Capitalism' or had ennobled the factory hand or the tenement dweller ... Most of the nineteenth and early twentieth century attempts to deal with the 'poor but honest' working man as a 'prince in disguise' failed to convince, because the writers themselves were temperamentally and culturally too far removed from the proletarian's world. Their books were more often than not merely well-intentioned slumming expeditions from which they returned exalted or depressed."

One of the sparse number of clues to what was happening outside the literary tea salons – and particularly in terms of geographical mobility, so by deduction the lack of social mobility – is the estimate of Josiah Flynt, a hobo himself, who put on record a little sketchy anthropology of the ostracized tribe he helped form.

Flynt reckons that in the Nineties there was a railroad tramp population of about 60,000 men. Information about their way of life, and familiarity with their language and credo, were slow to seep through to the general public because of that literary and journalistic primness of the time, but also because except when invading the towns on begging reconnoitres, their orbit was as separate as that of the Bedouins of North Africa.

When they rode a train it was not "on the cushions" for normally they picked a freight as it left the yards and they traveled with the boxcar merchandise. When they disembarked they dropped off before too embarrassingly near a station and its detectives. When they rested they congregated in a fleabox hotel in a section of the town few respectable citizens ever saw; or in the jungle camp which still exists close to every American rail division point, and which has become a foundation as venerable and traditional as Main Street but as unknown to most locals as the Congo.

Pinkerton, it can safely be said, positively was not hopeful that there were future Gorkys in that jungle party he describes. What is of especial interest is that after so zestfully describing the ape-life of the deserted mine site, there is an abrupt switch into complacent sentimentality.

Soddened, grotesque, brutish and so on though all the tramps were, "all seemed as contented and satisfied with their fortune as though it was all they deserved and better than they expected." And in his reference to another jungle in Philadelphia he says: "They fare well, and are apparently the happiest and jolliest dogs under the sun."

There in a couple of sentences is vivid expression of the schizophrenia about the tramp that had long been developing and which now, with the 1890s' three million unemployed and a festering class enmity bursting into strikes and armed battles, was epidemic.

Thenceforth, having been reluctantly but inescapably, accepted as an American institution, the tramp was recognizably there to be feared and romanticized, recommended for extermination and given the pet dog pat, to be seen alternately – or simultaneously – as a figure of fun and as a bird of prey.

Apprehension sounded louder than the laughs. It can be traced back to 1877, when a J. H. Morison in *The Unitarian Review* put in print the misgivings of the secure. He deplored the "sudden and fearful development of vagrancy within the last two or three years."

It was a development that had been proceeding beyond the contracted horizons of the settled citizenry since 1865 when the Civil War's end disgorged a legion of raggle-taggle demobbed soldiers, homes and background shattered, old jobs gone and in many cases health and limbs also gone, unable to relocate themselves in an altered labor market.

Land grants were made to "the boys" but without achieving a painless back-to-normality, and the pre-war dribbles of jobless mechanics and restless plowboys about the land suddenly billowed. Now that the warriors were out of uniform the beam of patriotism turned stony upon them. Mr. Morison in his article demanded "stringent laws, made as they were in England five or six centuries ago, against 'sturdy beggars'. Tramps who can give no satisfactory account of themselves," he pounded, "should be summarily condemned to hard work and coarse fare."

Well, hard work was the elusive factor, and they were getting coarse fare already. The tramp as an individual had long been an Ishmael. In Mark Twain's *Life on the Mississippi* is the "poor stranger, a harmless whiskey-sodden tramp" who wanders into Hannibal, Missouri, in the 1840s. "The tramp was wandering about the streets one chilly evening, with a pipe in his mouth, and begging for a match; he got neither matches nor courtesy; on the contrary, a troop of bad little boys followed him around and amused themselves with nagging and annoying him." Eventually, touched with shame by the tramp's "forlorn and friendless condition," young Clemens retires from the baiting. But later that evening the tramp is arrested – for what? – and locked up in the calaboose by the marshal. (He accidentally sets his straw bed alight: there is a terrifying description of the tramp burning to death, screaming, hands gripped around the cell bars, "a black object set against a sun, so white and intense was the light at his back.")

The impression left by Twain is of quick community cruelty toward one unlike themselves, and although that tramp's incineration was his own fault it would not have been considered amiss later when numbers changed suspicion to fear. Mr. Morison was, in fact, going easy on the sturdy beggars. Severer "cleaner America" campaigners urged farmers' wives not to burn them to death, merely to poison the criminal city scavengers wheedling grub at the back door.

10 : A LITTLE STRYCHNINE
OR ARSENIC

'Twas transportation brought me here,
Takes money for to carry me home.
The long steel rails that have no end
Have caused me for to roam.
They've caused me to weep, they've caused
*   me to mourn,*
They've caused me to leave my home.

To The Pines,
a nineteenth-century banjo song

CRUDE advocacy of murder – like a public health drive to exterminate a plague of rats or flies – is not easy to swallow as credible now, but in its issue of July 12, 1877, the Chicago *Tribune* printed this advice to its country readership: "The simplest plan, probably, where one is not a member of the Humane Society, is to put a little strychnine or arsenic in the meat and other supplies furnished the tramp. This produces death within a comparatively short period of time, is a warning to other tramps to keep out of the neighbourhood, keeps the Coroner in good humor, and saves one's chickens and other portable property from constant destruction."

The note of rough jollity therein does not detract from its serious intention. In the tramp scare of the late 1880s the *Tribune*'s voice was not an isolated screech of savagery. The depression of the 1870s, although of unprecedented grimness, was strange of its kind. During previous slumps and waves of worklessness, the jobless had piled up relatively locally and statically. Now there was a national railroad network and the penniless were foraging ever farther afield, either hunting work or just escaping from the stagnation of closed-down company towns.

Apart from the Yankee and Rebel infantry men who had kept on walking after the armistice, regiments of demobbed had branched away to the outpost construction jobs restarting after the wartime interruption.

The war itself had created work. It was the first in history in which troops and ordnance went on scale by rail, and accordingly the railroad itself was a military target. Bridges, track and rolling stock were shelled and blown up. The South was left with the rags of a rail system and the urgent rebuilding temporarily soaked up a fair body of ex-rankers.

There was a short hectic boom. The transcontinental link was made by the crashing hammers of Irish and ex-convicts and mule-skinners and men still in scraps of blue and gray uniforms thrusting inland from the East, and the Chinese and Mexicans thrusting inland from the West narrowed the divide until there came the epic spurt when a thousand tons of rail crossed ten miles of mountain in one day, and the final golden spike was driven in at the joining of the Central Pacific and the Union Pacific lines at Promontory Summit in Utah.

Up to 1873 there were railroad jobs anywhere for men who could swing hammers and stand the wear and tear. They lived in railcars, on Texas beef and locally shot buffalo meat. Three strokes to a spike, four rails to a minute – the graders ahead broke the soil and rock and made the bed, the ties and rails were dropped from the horse-drawn rail dolly, and the parts spiked and bolted into position. Just behind were the "hells on wheels," the terminal point "roaring towns" from which end-o'-track was fed with food and materials. These were the "semi-colons of railroad history," the short carnival pauses on the long grind forward, such burgs as Elko, Wells, Toano, Cisco, Truckee and Lakes Crossing, where the whores, faro table gypsters, land speculators and operators of six-d joints (dine-dance-drink-dice-dope-dames) swiftly sluiced in to meet the needs and whip the dollars of the gaugers and bolters and spikers.

There "Jay Cooke's Banana Special" (snide comment on the Cooke company's advertisements of the tropically luxuriant vegetation which would lap settlers in Minnesota and the Dakotas) ran out of funds. The closure set sliding one of the worst American financial subsidences and for the rest of the 1870s railroad building – and industrial enterprise at large – shuddered to a halt.

Regardless in this wintery blackness of abrupt dismissal up in the wilds and nowhere to go, the American admiration of greed and grit was not dislodged. Josephson draws the picture of September 1873: "The settlers' farms continued to fall under the hammer and hundreds of thousands of muscular, industrious laborers wandered the streets begging for bread." Yet belief endured: " . . . the laborious crowds in the cities were *free* to endure idleness or lowered wages; the digger of coal or of oil, the planter of corn and cotton, was *free* to accept such sums as were offered for his produce." The rich pillagers who had pre-empted railroads, ore fields and harbor rights were defended by the hungry jobless: "Well, sir, he is a smart man," while Jay Gould "roved through the West eyeing the ruined hulk of transcontinental railroads . . . the mighty fragments cast off, the *disjecta membra* of an industrial system's agony."

Big-spending and now spent-up construction men, firemen on strike and freight brakemen dumped by bankrupt or ailing lines, loggers with their axes hocked and miners without a market, all were heading all ways, to anywhere that rumor attributed pay packets, and for the first time these new unemployed began riding the trains they had themselves manned, or whose tracks they had laid, or whose trucks they had filled. The tramp was in a hurry, and as he began to steal his lifts on the freights he began to turn himself into the hobo.

That rhyme of Tudor England,

> *Hark, hark, the dogs do bark,*
> *The beggars are coming to town,*

was echoed in the siren of panic that reverberated through rural America. The Chicago *Tribune*'s helpful tip about how to poison off the wayfarer was not a quirky outburst.

The development of the tramp scare may be winnowed out from contemporary newspapers in all parts of the United States. On August 6, 1875, the Cincinnati *Daily Gazette* reported that: "The Legislature of New Hampshire at its last session passed a very severe law in regard to them [tramps]. For merely begging, any Justice of the Peace is authorized to put them to hard labor for six months at the county or town farm. If they cannot be profitably employed in those institutions, they are to be hired out to work for any citizen who may choose to bid for their services." The *Daily Gazette*'s evident object in carrying this item was to indicate that Ohio might learn from New Hampshire's ukase, and henceforth many states did pass similar laws.

A few months later an Ohio farmer wrote to the Cincinnati *Commercial* favoring rounding up all these vexing undesirables and sending them to the South as cotton pickers, concluding: "Some helpful hint, no doubt could be taken from Russia's Siberia business. The only remedy for the 'tramp' is occupation."

In the December 9 issue appeared a long account of a statewide "Anti-tramp Convention" held in Columbus, Ohio. Delegates from small towns and large cities all resolved "not to be gentle or generous to 'tramps'," and urged that workhouses should speedily be constructed throughout the state.

The same month the Cleveland *Leader* was invoking its readers' moral responsibility: "The people of the city at large have a duty to perform. Whenever a vagrant knocks at the side of the door for a breakfast or dinner, the answer should be that the applicant must report to the Police Station ... The thing to be done is to stop feeding the army of loafers who have taken advantage of the hard times to inflict themselves upon people not too lazy to work."

The Iron Age, the leading steel industry journal took an even harder boiled line in its issue of July 27, 1876. "We must compel the vagrant to become an industrious, useful, self-sustaining citizen," it intoned, "by making vagrancy disagreeable to him, and this can only be done by treating him as a criminal and making him earn by labor the bread he eats and the clothes he wears."

The ground tremors of America's unemployed troubles, channeled as they were into enmity and indignation toward those hit hardest by them, were registered in Britain. On October 5, 1876, the London *Times* said in its editorial: "The West, once the paradise of the working man, echoes back the lament of the East, of a superabundance of labour ... The worst feature of the hard times is, however, the appearance of a distinct class of vagabonds, called tramps, who are not in search of work ... They usually go in gangs ... The tramp is not a picturesque character like the gipsy of the English lanes, and does not awaken sympathy like the 'strapped' journeyman in search of a job. He is a low-browed, blear-eyed, dirty fellow, who has rascal stamped on every feature of his face in nature's plainest handwriting."

Here at hot bubble is the familiar chemistry employed to prepare the ground for persecution: establish that your victim is debased and barely human, thereby justifying inhuman, draconic measures.

As well as the salt mine and arsenic curatives, there was a waxing enthusiasm (which must have activated that 1892 consular circular seeking tips on vagrancy control abroad) for importing European methods. In the same year, 1877, that *The Unitarian Review* writer was clamoring for a revival of England's medieval hounding of "sturdy beggars," the Victorian English workhouse was being looked to as a meritorious model.

The extent of the tramp scare and its infection of even liberal opinion may be judged by the recommendation of Elihu Burritt, philanthropist, reformer and U.S. Consul in Birmingham, who supported anti-slavery, and organized the 1848 Brussels Congress of "Friends of Peace": "We have with us already all the classes that vice, poverty and ignorance have made 'dangerous' in the Old World, and we must have the Old World institutions to protect society against them ... We must have the English workhouse, with whatever improvements we may add to it ... With such an institution, every town and village could make a clean sweep of tramps ... We must supplement our jails, poorhouses and asylums with this English institution."

Never, among these moral uplifters, remorse for acquiescing in a system which hollowed men out and junked them. Never analysis of what made the difference between a diligent, honest workman and a low-browed rascal who must be punished and persecuted for being out of a job.

The leap in logic was repeatedly accomplished with dextrous syntax. Yet, to see this with balance, it should be remembered that the climate in which such proposals were made was one of general distress. Communities were in a state of fiscal crisis, worsened by the burden, in both cost and perhaps secret guilt, of local unemployed. Banks had closed; ranks must be closed.

The passing of years has not momentously altered this vernal concept of guilt and punishment. Still in the Twenties, as Wecter shows: "The most acute problem was relief. Traditional American ideas about relief sprang not from modern Britain, with its 'soul-destroying dole,' but from English poor laws dating back at least to Queen Elizabeth. It was commonly believed that charity corrupts those who receive it, that public relief and politics are inseparable and above all that such disbursements are 'Something for nothing.' Aid to the indigent thus tended to become a local responsibility, given as grudgingly and humiliatingly as possible in order to discourage spongers and point up the disgrace of poverty. The bleak horror of the poorhouse was thought to be salutary."

Later still the hard-mouthed attitude of Harry Carr, a Los Angeles *Times* columnist, in January 1935, crystallized the response of many Californians toward the ingress of the violated people from the Dust Bowl.

"The desert roads are streaming with hoboes," wrote Carr. "All those with any desire to work have gone to the government camps. Most of those on the road are vicious and dangerous ... Florida and Washington are both stopping indigents at their border. California should do likewise.

"The government relief boards could stop these wandering nomadic bands of tramps if they would ... From the days of Rome in its decline to Paris just before the revolution, the problem of civilization has been to compel the unemployed and unemployables to stay in one place. California is willing and able to take care of its own jobless, but the doors should be shut against the indigents of other states."

There was understandable groaning against this unbidden strain on local budgets, just as there had been half a century earlier in New England townships, and, as there, it was an easy if unjustifiable emotional step to believe that the invaders were "vicious" and "criminal."

In the economic earthquakes of the late 1800s the tramp, the foreigner in town, was a convenient scapegoat upon whom hysteria and anxiety could be sweated off. It helped also to be able to blacken him with political menace. The title of Pinkerton's book – *Strikers, Communists, Tramps and Detectives* – is a ripely pejorative portmanteau. In January 1878 the New Orleans *Picayune* was declaring: "The extreme poor are all that Louisiana can feed on account of charity. We have no surplus bread for the communists and vagabonds of other states."

Invariably as the tramp scare flamed across America, the workless man's immoral laziness and his diseased subversive thinking were indicted: not only for the community's good but for his own, he had to be reformed. What more fitting means of forcing him to overcome his sloth than to make it a matter of his own life or death?

In the Newburyport *Herald* of June 14, 1878, James D. Parton, the biographer of Andrew Jackson and a popular writer of the day, proposed as the answer to the escalation of vagrancy that paupers should be placed in cisterns, into which water was to be pumped at a rate equal to that at which a vigorous man could pump it out. "If he worked he was saved," Parton coolly observed, "and if he refused he was drowned."

This neat plan seeded, for eight years later this report, "adopted by an overwhelming vote," was published by the Supervisors of Westchester County, New York: "Hundreds of this class flock to this county from the city of New York and the adjoining State of Connecticut . . . These tramps are a source of great danger and great nuisance to our citizens . . . The expense, directly and indirectly, to the taxpayers of this city, caused by this tramp raid, has reached the enormous sum of 75,000 dollars per year . . ." The Superintendents of the poor and asylums were instructed: "to erect a building in a suitable place on the county farm, which shall be so situated and constructed that it can be flooded with water to the depth of at least six feet, and so arranged with apartments and platforms that all persons committed as tramps and vagrants can be placed therein and thereon, and when the water is turned on to be compelled to bail or be submerged thereby."

Poisoning. Drowning. And there were those who swore by guns. A writer in the New York *Herald* in 1878 said, "It is very well to relieve real distress wherever it exists, whether in city or country, but the best meal that can be given to the regular tramp is a leaden one, and it should be supplied in sufficient quantity to satisfy the most voracious appetite."

The faith in summary butchery for dealing with scroungers remained spring green in many an American breast. When in 1915 the IWW was campaigning for better conditions for itinerant mowers and shockers, vigilante committees, known as pick-handle brigades, were formed everywhere to break up the "Wobbly menace." In 1917 the South Dakota *Morning Republican* counseled "every member of the vigilante committee over twenty-one to supply himself with a reliable firearm and have it where he can secure it at a moment's notice." And when in 1920 Attorney-General A. Mitchell Palmer directed the round-up of Communist leaders for deportation to Russia on a ship tagged drolly "the Soviet Ark," Guy Empey reminded the public that the best instruments for Communism-control could be "found in any hardware store," and declared: "My motto for the Reds is SOS – ship or shoot. I believe we should place them all on a ship of stone, with sails of lead, and that their first stopping-place should be hell."

Nor is poisoning a solution that has entirely faded from the more blood-hazed imagination. In March 1966 a Californian was charged with solicitation to commit murder. Obviously a white supremacist planner of national executive stature, he had, said the police, arranged four distribution points, one in each zone of the country. From there free poisoned food samples, such as powdered gelatine desserts, would be sent to almost every Negro in the United States. Another like-minded American, exposed during 1964's House Un-American Activities Committee hearings, was the organizer of a Ku Klux Klan firing squad and of classes on how to exterminate Negroes with poisonous snakes.

Whether any individual householders really rid their neighborhood of visiting vermin by means of strychnine and bullet cannot now be ascertained, but at least on an official level the wilder penalties were not enforced. That drowning trap was never built in Westchester County. Instead the officials urged only the removal of the tramps "from a condition of demoralizing idleness and degrading associations to a situation where they can be permitted and compelled to work at some laborious occupation."

The change of mind was made under heat of protest for all the foregoing venom and vengeance was not without opposition. Also making themselves heard were those who defended the tramp. In the same period that deportation, imprisonment without trial, forced labor and execution were being commended, the progressive press was insisting upon deeper investigation of the tramp situation.

The National Labor Tribune on August 14, 1875: "Who are the tramps and who made them? A tramp is a man, an unfortunate man, because he can find no work. He starts out and travels because he wants to work, and on, on he goes . . . They are products of recent times . . . Society itself has created every tramp who is compelled to beg . . . Beware ye money bags; beware ye political leeches; beware ye cormorants of society. The tramps you now despise will some day become tigers, and wise, rise like an army and suddenly wrest your ill-gotten gains from your grasp, appropriate them to their rightful owners."

A more considered piece appeared in *The Weekly Worker* on the same date: "It is said 'the devil is not so black as he is painted.' May this not be true of the tramp? No doubt there are naturally bad men who assume this character . . . But does it follow that every tired, ragged, foot-sore, dirty and hungry wretch who comes to the door to ask for something to eat is a vicious fellow? By no means.

"There are thousands, even hundreds of thousands of working men in the country who have no work, can get none and 'know not where to lay their heads' . . . How easy for the wicked to lay chicken-stealing and worse crimes to the tramp. He thus becomes the natural scapegoat of the whole criminal tribe, and on him, as he wanders forth in a world that is a wilderness to him, are heaped the sins of society. About the only consolation left the truly unfortunate tramp is the thought that Christ was a tramping vagabond whom the world crucified to get rid of, and all honest men suffer for the sins of the world . . ."

Most revealing of less well organized, or at least less ventilated, humanitarian opinion of the day was the Executive Proclamation by Governor of Kansas, Lorenzo D. Lewelling, which became known as the "Tramps' Circular." Ever since the business slump following the Civil War, the cry had been heard that the sparse city relief services, the charity soup kitchens and mission shelters, were being preyed upon by greedy, cunning "vagrants, bummers and revolvers." But it was in this year of the "Tramps' Circular" that the pattern of future depression oscillation formed, for this was the first severe coast-to-coast slump, the first economic drought to settle upon the whole nation. Now there began the transcontinental pendulation. Now there began the shutting of doors and the eviction from towns, counties and states of any roamer. It was this intensified, increasingly official policy against which Lewelling's proclamation protested. It appeared in the Topeka *Daily Capital* on December 5, 1893.

"The monopoly of labor saving machinery and its devotion to selfish instead of social use," it ran in part, "have rendered more and more human beings superfluous, until we have a standing army of the unemployed numbering even in the most prosperous times not less than one million able-bodied men; yet, until recently it was the prevailing notion, as it is yet the notion of all, but the work-people themselves and those of other classes given over to thinking, that whosoever, being able-bodied and willing to work can always find work to do, and Section 571 of the General Statutes of 1889 is a disgraceful reminder of how savage even in Kansas has been our treatment of the most unhappy of our human brothers.

"The man out of work and penniless is, by this legislation classed with 'confidence men.' Under this statute and city ordinances of similar import, thousands of men, guilty of no crime but poverty, intent upon no crime but that of seeking employment, have languished in the city prisons of Kansas or performed unrequited toil on 'rock piles' as municipal slaves, because ignorance of economic conditions had made us cruel.

"The victims have been the poor and humble for whom police courts are courts of last resort – they cannot give bond and appeal ... They have been too poor to litigate with their oppressors, and thus no voices from this underworld of human woe

119

has ever reached the ear of the Appellate Court, because it was nobody's business to be his brother's keeper . . .

"And who needs to be told that equal protection of the law does not prevail when this inhuman vagrancy law is enforced? It separates men into two distinct classes, differentiated as those who are penniless and those who are not, and declares the former criminals . . . To be found in a city without some visible means of support or 'some legitimate business' is the involuntary condition of some millions at this moment, and we proceed to punish them for being victims of conditions which we, as a people, have forced upon them.

"I have noticed in police court reports that 'sleeping in a box car' is among the varieties of this heinous crime of being poor. Some police judges have usurped a sovereign power not permitted the highest functionaries of the states of the nation, and victims of the industrial conditions have been peremptorily 'ordered to leave town.' The right to go freely from place to place in search of employment, or even in obedience of a mere whim, is part of the personal liberty guaranteed by the Constitution of the United States to every human being on American soil. If voluntary idleness is not forbidden; if a Diogenes prefer poverty; if a Columbus choose hunger and the discovery of a new race, rather than seek personal comfort by engaging in 'some legitimate business,' I am aware of no power in the legislature or in city councils to deny him the right to seek happiness in his own way, so long as he harms no other, rich or poor; but let simple poverty cease to be a crime."

It was a brave, and original, statement – to remind Americans that Americans had the right of way over American soil. There was a great rush of response to the "Tramps' Circular," from a body of opinion hitherto unheard behind the tally-hos of the hunters.

A Denver police magistrate wrote: "I know of no laws which have been so universally abused and used as engine of oppression against the unfortunate poor." One newly-made tramp, a regularly employed cook before the depression, related his own experiences after requesting permission to sleep the night in Kewanee jail, "treatment as that would soon make a criminal of me, and I really believe that many criminals are made in this manner." A North Wichita man wrote: "The tendency of the times is to force the masses into a propertyless condition, then persecute them for vagabondage." Another correspondent saw the tramp as a natural outcome of a society in which "the dollar, instead of humanity, is the object of the supremest regard and protection . . . *Who* does *not* bear constantly with him the dark spectre that by another year perhaps he and his may be *vagrants*; and does not each succeeding year give to the word a deeper and more damning dye."

The "Tramps' Circular" was also praised by Eugene Debs, then editor of *The Locomotive Firemen's Magazine*: "Governor Lewelling is the first and only man in authority to brand the cruel, savage, heartless wrongs in fitting terms . . . his letter ought to arouse everywhere the inquiry in this country: why are there so many tramps?" A Texas lawyer, named Andrew Jackson, wrote condemning the system under which local officials "are paid fees in criminal cases only in case of conviction." This, he said, "has fostered a slave trade" through "the selling of honest and innocent men for the fees of office."

The phrase "slave trade" was no melodramatic exaggeration. Four years before the governor's proclamation, this report appeared in the Chicago *Tribune*, datelined Moberly, Missouri: "Four vagrants, Samuel Rankin, John Smith, Frank Joes and Thomas Clark, were offered at public sale here today under an old Missouri law that is virtually a reinstatement of slavery. All the offerings were able-bodied men. The sale had been duly advertised according to law, and the men were auctioned off in front of the court-house to the highest bidder for a term of six months each. Two of the men brought two dollars apiece and were at once released by their purchasers. The third was bought for seventy-five cents by a farmer who meant business, and he took his man out to put him to work. There was no bidder for the fourth and he was taken back to the county jail."

It is worth side-stepping for a moment to look at the stance from which Governor Lewelling spoke. He was a crusader and a Populist, and in a curious way the Mid-West farmer felt more on terms and more in a shared economic position with the shunned, ragged floater beating his way through his county than he did with his socially opposite number in the East.

The Populist movement called for reform and a new standard of social justice, but based on agrarian radicalism and not on city criteria. Essentially it was the last stage of a struggle to save agricultural America from the manacles of industrial America. Later it became seen as a hotbed of reactionary Luddites fighting to put back the clock, and of proto-fascist groups, McCarthyism, anti-Semitism, anti-Intellectualism and xenophobia in general: a theory recently revised since Norman Pollack's first-hand researches into Populist journals of the late 1800s.

Pollack, refuting the charge that Populism was "a Ruskinesque lament for an outmoded handicraft existence," shows the Granger movement, founded in 1867 to regenerate farming, did not want to abolish the railroads, as often alleged, but to subject them to public control. What the Populists did, at a period when most eyes could descry only glory and glut ahead, was to sense that "man was becoming dehumanized in psychological as well as economic terms;" they recognized "the trend toward what we today call alienation."

It follows that the alienated men all around them, the sad offshoot of the new industrialism, should become an emblem of their protest. Industrial America, they accused, was creating not only poverty but a new man in whom an awful personality injury was being wrought.

Unexpected though these attitudes might appear in this rural and not deeply educated quarter, they are better understood when it is remembered to what they were responding. This was the time when a man could hold the credo, and expect it to be received with the solemn ardor in which it was smelted, that: "Upon the sacredness of property civilization itself depends – the right of the laborer to his hundred dollars in the savings bank and equally the legal right of the millionaire to his millions." That was Andrew Carnegie's cracker motto in *The North American Review* in 1889. It was the period in which a father – John D. Rockefeller's – encapsuled the skin-and-win spirit thus: "I cheat my boys every time I get a chance ... I trade with the boys and skin 'em and just beat 'em every time I can.

I want to make 'em smart." It was the period when Rockefeller himself, the perfect horticultural bloom of the economy could preach: "The American Beauty rose is only brought to flower by sacrificing the early buds."

Men like these both created the high-octane atmosphere of ambitious drive and themselves used it as fuel. They saw nought but good in the rapacious energy on all sides. Carnegie wrote to a Scottish friend: "Our dense forests are falling under the ax of the hardy woodsman. The Wolf and the Buffalo are startled by the shrill scream of the Iron Horse where a few years ago they roamed undisturbed. Towns and cities spring up as if by magic ... This country is completely cut up with Railroad Tracks, Telegraphs and Canals ... Pauperism is unknown ... Everything around us is in motion."

What Carnegie probably meant by that penultimate phrase is that pauperism, as subtly distinct from poverty, was too contemptible to be considered, for this was high noon of the self-made man cult. Everyone had a whetted appetite, and, as the Puritan clergy had from the outset assured their congregation, secular success was blessed in God's eyes.

The essays of Cotton Mather teaching that wealth was God's gift, were invaluable to the success ethic. Franklin, himself a disciple of Mather, published *The Way to Wealth*, and became the idol of the rags-to-riches movement. When his statue was unveiled in Boston, Robert C. Winthrop delivered an address designed to spur the poor to greater efforts.

"Behold him, Mechanics and Mechanics' Apprentices," he said, "holding out to you an example of diligence, economy and virtue ... Behold him, ye that are humblest and poorest in present condition or in future prospect, lift up your heads and look at the image of a man who rose from nothing."

Poverty was a disgrace if it was allowed to continue; it was, on the other hand, glorified as of inestimable value in purifying and strengthening the character, especially if it was rural poverty, for there its corollaries were fresh air and no temptations of city sin.

Carnegie venerated poverty for, as he never wearied of reiterating, he and the great men of the time had all been disciplined by this rigorous experience. "They appear on the stage," he said, "athletes trained for the contest, with sinews braced, indomitable wills, resolved to do or die . . . Abolish luxury if you please, but leave us the soil, upon which alone the virtues and all that is precious in human character grow; poverty – honest poverty."

Although the bare-foot newsboy was appointed the hallowed exemplar of self-help, Lewis E. Lawe, the Warden of Sing Sing, has mentioned that seven out of ten of his inmates sold papers in their youth. Indifferent to such practical tests, the self-help handbook literature – while short on practical information – slogged away relentlessly at character-building leading to the building of a bank balance, and religious approval chanted piously in the background.

"Adam was created and placed in the Garden of Eden for business purposes," asserted Matthew H. Smith in *Hunt's Merchants' Magazine* in 1854; "it would have been better for the race if he had attended closely to the occupation for which he was made." In 1836 the Reverend Thomas P. Hunt had published *The Book of Wealth*, "in which it is Proved from the Bible that it is the Duty of Every Man to Become Rich." In *Acres of Diamonds* Russell Conwell pronounced it to be man's "Christian and Godly duty" to make money. In *Young Man's Counsellor*, Daniel Wise, a Methodist minister, said, partly in capitals, "Religion will teach you that industry is a SOLEMN DUTY you owe to God, whose command is 'BE DILIGENT IN BUSINESS'."

The Episcopal Bishop of Massachusetts, William Lawrence, explained that although sometimes the wicked prospered it was only occasionally for "in the long run it is only to the man of morality that wealth comes . . . Godliness is in league with riches."

The poor young man who could read was, around the turn of the century, strafed from every point on high with these golden bullets, aimed at driving him from his squalor and lethargy. For a continuing theme through these pep sermons was the necessity for the lad to sever the apron strings and stride off in pursuit of fortune. "A boy at home seldom has a chance," declared one manual. "Nobody believes in him – least of all his relations."

Out then into the commercial jungle of social Darwinism to

prove himself the stronger in tooth and claw. So it may be seen that the opposing view, that unbridled big business was wreaking appalling hurt upon its servant – "Degradation was destroying his sense of being human" – did not make itself widely heard against those thunderous homilies.

(Not that this vein of inspirational literature is out of business. In 1926 Elbert Hubbard in that work beloved of Babbitts, *A Message to Garcia*, wrote: "We have recently been hearing much maudlin sympathy expressed for 'the downtrodden denizens of the sweatshop' and the 'homeless wanderer searching for honest employment,' and with it all too often go many hard words for the men in power. Nothing is said about the employer who grows old before his time in a vain attempt to get frowsy ne'er do wells to do intelligent work ... When all the world has gone a-slumming I wish to speak a word of sympathy for the man who succeeds." And at this very time the market hums with best-sellers putting a shine on the shibboleths of the "folk-lore of capitalism" with the old but welcome news that "God always pays off.")

The tramp, then, needed friends in the 1890s. Yet it is startling to find in rural newspapers, in a traditionally insular region, and in a period when socialism was still spores in the wind, such as this in the Lincoln, Nebraska, *Farmers' Alliance* in 1892: "It is in the interest of the capitalist class to have as many men as possible out of work and seeking it in order to keep and force wages down by making competition fierce between those seeking work and those employed," or this from the Topeka *Advocate* in 1894: 'Has society, as a whole, derived the benefits from the use of labor-saving machinery that it might have done under a different system? We think not. Under the prevailing system the capitalist has been the chief beneficiary. Instead of using the machine to displace men, it should have been used to reduce the hours of labor."

The same journal wrote directly of the tramp: " ... they are entirely unnecessary, given the country's unlimited resources ... the result of our vicious social and economic system ... Are the poor of America poor from choice any more than were those in the reign of Queen Elizabeth, or in France under a 'dissolute monarch'? Is a dissolute monarchy any worse than a dissolute republic?" In a later issue the Topeka *Advocate* declared: "Remember that tramps are men, and that they are a natural product of our social system."

For Populism the tramp was the drummer boy of the approaching crisis. Industrial America had reached a juncture in social development: it could continue on disaster course or make the decision to return to democratic ideals. So it was that, oddly, the farmer felt at one with the worker, in or out of a job: because the Populist recognized that solidarity was the only basis for a radical policy.

On March 25, 1894, a throng of unemployed gathered at Massillon, Ohio, and, enlisting under the banner of the "Commonweal of Christ," were led by Jacob S. Coxey, a contractor, on a march to Washington to demand that the President and Congress should launch a programme of public works. As Coxey's Army marched East they were joined by increasing battalions of workless, and from California came two more armies of "industrials" led by "General" Charles T. Kelly and "General" Lewis C. Fry, all the time supplemented by migrant workers riding on freight trains to catch up. Townships watched them approach with alarm. Had the marauders come for them? Some states tried to drop the bar at the frontier. In Utah the railroads called for police and military help when bands of hundreds swarmed like boarding parties onto possession of freight trains.

But the "petition in boots," the muster of men from pits and timber camps and railroad sites on a mass job hunt, moved massively onward to Washington, and among the thousands were many Populists.

The public press was antagonistic – the Pittsburgh *Press* printed under a cartoon:

> *Hark, hark! Hear the dogs bark!*
> *Coxey is coming to town*
> *In his ranks are scamps*
> *And growler-fed tramps*
> *On all of whom workingmen frown.*

But the Populist papers and spokesmen loudly supported the hunger march.

Five months after issuing his "Tramps' Circular," Governor Lewelling said: "The Coxey movement is a spontaneous uprising of the people. It is more than a petition, it is an earnest and vigorous protest against the injustice and tyranny of the age." The Topeka *Advocate* was in there rooting for them. Stressing that all "reference to the causes which have produced the Coxeyites is studiously avoided," it continued: "When forced into idleness and compelled to take to the road in the fruitless effort to find employment it requires but a short time to make a vagabond of the man who under other and more favorable circumstances would be numbered among our best citizens."

During the 1890s the rural press of the Mid-West – the Lincoln, Nebraska, *Farmers' Alliance*, the fiery *Advocate* in Topeka, the *Custer County Beacon* of Broken Bow, the *Platte County Argus* at Colums, the *Saunders County New Era* from Wahoo, the *Representative* from St. Paul, Minnesota – seethed with anger and protest at the damaged men being thrown out on to the road, and it may appear that the hobo was in sympathetic territory, passed along a cordon of helping hands.

For all that, potent force though the Granger movement was on paper, the average hobo was probably lucky if he ever came into physical contact with a Populist brakie, farmer or hick town sheriff. The boot was always likelier for him than the helping hand.

The Populist faith certainly hadn't percolated into Clinton. Iowa, only a state way, to judge by Tully's reminiscences. He describes meeting outside Clinton a hobo who had just been pulped by the whole township.

"I comes a whistlin' in there like a cattle train," says this hobo, nursing his bruises. "Well, sir, they ketches four of us and makes us run the ga'ntlet ... The natives stands on each side for a quarter of a mile or more. They hit us wit' stones and whips ... Some guy caught me wit' a rock here where you see this bump ... I'll bet there was 200 men there, an' a dozen women."

Elsewhere Tully is told by a railroad detective who has arrested him: "Ye guys are the ruin of the country, a bummin' honest people, an' a stealin' money, an' a breakin' into cars, an' a burnin' barns," and Chaplin, recalling his first experience as a migratory harvest hand in the early 1900s, says: "To all good citizens we were 'pesky go-abouts.' We were indeed as sad a lot of unskilled, unorganized, overworked, and underpaid undesirables as could be imagined ... everlastingly out of luck."

Justice was a joke: "If a stiff had as little as twelve dollars on him when arrested, the judge would fine him ten of that. Rather than go to jail for thirty, sixty, or ninety days on a trumped-up charge of vagrancy or disorderly conduct, the helpless culprit would cough up. If he refused to pay the fine, he was jailed.

"The real punishment consisted of being released in the middle of winter without warm clothing to keep the frost from his bones as he 'rode the rods' back to his native 'skid road.' We were expected to 'keep moving,' yet we couldn't move at all without breaking the law ... Our farmer bosses, rich and poor alike, were inclined to treat us as human outcasts beyond the law."

Occasionally there are to be found flickers of self-knowledge, a half angry, half repentant realization that the tramp was not merely either offscourings of city industry or a workshy on the fiddle, but a curse brought upon country people themselves. For industry could not be solely blamed. The commitment of almost all the Middle West to wheat during the second half of the nineteenth century killed the American tradition of the small, compact, diversified family farm, and set in motion the process toward the huge agribusiness prairie tract. It also created the short-term harvest hand, the man for whom the need was urgent but brief, a beautiful person in the sight of God when the wheat ears hung heavy but whose absence was required, in short order, as soon as the single stupendous crop was in.

One big South-Western land owner encouraged hobos to cross his territory (about 11,000 square miles) so that they could be pulled in for harvest work. His instruction to his ranch foremen was: "Never refuse a tramp a meal, but never give him more than one meal. A tramp should be a tramp and keep on tramping. Never let the tramps eat with the other men. Make them wait until the men are through, and then make them eat off the same plates." That neck of the country was known to hobos as the Dirty Plate Route.

Thus the hobo's constitution and function were completed, as if all those wheat and timber and oil and mining regions were each, individually, supplying a characteristic feature for the identikit creation of the new laborer. They had to have him, and they lamented the truth of it. He was a harvest hand when the fields were golden and a tramp as soon as they were stubble. He was profit and loss, guilt and redemption. One of the most direct expressions of this muddle of feeling, which reflects Tully's experience on the receiving end and the sense of blame on the other, came from a Mrs. E. T. Curtiss, a farmer's wife, who in 1902 addressed the North Dakota Farmers' Institute on "Our Farm Life, How to Decrease its Evils and Increase its Blessings."

Mrs. Curtiss castigated the abandonment of the principle by which her own settler ancestors had abided, that which allotted to each man "so much land as he could well and faithfully till." "Not a thousand-acre farm," she repeated, "but 'only so much land as he could well and faithfully till.'"

She told her audience that of all evils, "the one most destructive of happy family life is the attempted farming of too much land for the capital wherewith to do it well, resulting in exclusive wheat raising with its long periods of comparative idleness alternating with weeks of spasmodic labor when all the family work to exhaustion," and she added, "taking into their midst as help travelling transients or 'Hobos,' four-fifths of whom are moral lepers."

She saw the hobo as a maleficent germ-carrier infecting the purity of the farming family. "What makes possible," she demanded, "the many slum saloons and houses of ill fame that cluster so thickly in the Minnesota border towns, their long fingers reaching greedily over into Fargo and other parts of North Dakota that they may gather into their slimy clutches your boys as well as ours? Hobos. Who make up four-fifths of the inmates of our jails and alms-houses for honest taxpayers to support them? Hobos. What brings the hobo here? Wheat farms. So there you are."

Leaving out compassion, such standards of self-criticism did not then and have not since ameliorated the four-square Plainville detestation of the tramp, and when a later depression swept yet another cataract of discarded men across the continent the relaxation of penalties that had come with the good, or better, times stiffened once more with the fear and genuine shortage on every doorstep.

California reacted to the Dust Bowl refugees of the Thirties with the "bum blockade" and the "hobo express," in the spirit in which the Los Angeles *Times* columnist demanded that the door be slammed on the "vicious" and "criminal" invaders. Because some of the towns hit by the removers in their coughing old cars on their way over from Oklahoma and Arkansas often had to bear the cost of food, clothing, medical care and sometimes petrol to hump them on, local communities "felt impelled to discourage the coming of the migrants."

They were given temporary care and told to move on: the "passing on" principle of relief. Or if single men they were detained in jail, usually a one-night cool-off in the cell, then directed to scram in the morning, perhaps embarked at gun-point on an outgoing freight. Or in some cases towns adopted the "hobo express" system: of packing a collection of hobos into trucks and hauling them to the county or state line, where they were dumped and told not to come back.

Or if a town was under particularly heavy bombardment from migrants, a posse met every incoming train, rounded up the tramps as they jumped off and put them back on as it pulled out – not a custom that pleased the railroads but their complaints were countered with the reply that if the railroad brought them in the railroad should ship them out, the belief being that a tough reception committee at every stop would sharpen the railroad's vigilance against free riders.

Or in towns where it was seriously believed that the highways and railroads were conduits of a new breed of cut-throat and thief, all arriving migrants were arrested, finger-printed and held until a check had been made with the files of the Federal Bureau of Investigation – a method which, if producing few sensational captures of wanted men, was thought guaranteed to frighten off strangers with criminal records.

Governor Lewelling's reminder of the personal liberty guaranteed by the Constitution to every citizen on American soil was, forty years later, in even more decrepit neglect. The tightening barricades had the immediate effect of shifting men off the railroads and on to the highways, where there was a slightly better chance of getting through. But the "cracker" refugees from the Dust Bowl states were not freight riders; all their families and boxes were stacked on the steaming, shuddering wrecks that crawled along the roads to the "object" state of California. So California, netting few at the railroad depots, decided to stop the migrants at the road state line, and the border blockade, or "bum blockade" as it was more generally known, was carried on from November 1935 to April 1936.

The blockade was initiated not by the state but by the city of Los Angeles. When the Federal Transient Service, which had been taking some of the load of the destitute travelers, decided to liquidate there was consternation. California was then in the Thirties receiving thirteen per cent of all transients in America and, it was bewailed, local communities and Los Angeles in particular would be overrun by packs of vagrants. The Los Angeles police, according to McWilliams, went "wildly hysterical." The first step was the creation of an emergency body with the roundly biased title of the Los Angeles Committee on Indigent Alien Transients, headed by James E. Davis, Chief of Police, which "proceeded to establish some sixteen border patrols located in counties hundreds of miles removed from Los Angeles . . .

"Some 125 policemen stationed at these various points of entry stopped all cars that looked as though they might contain 'unemployables' and turned them back. When a court action was brought in the U.S. District Court by the American Civil Liberties Union, to test the constitutionality of this procedure the Chief of Police detailed the head of his celebrated 'Intelligence Squad' to 'work over' the plaintiff in whose name the action had been commenced. Not only was the plaintiff himself intimidated, but his wife and child were threatened and browbeaten by police officers . . . and ultimately the plaintiff was 'induced' to drop the action."

Los Angeles police justified the "bum blockade," irregular and unconstitutional though it was, as protecting women and children in the city from forays of criminals or potential criminals –

and they added the imaginative blood-curdler that they might also be carriers of disease.

The move appears to have enjoyed popular support, from of course transients of the previous generation who were dropping the bar on transients of this generation. This was a particularly monstrous illogicality even in a nation that has based its success formula on getting there first, and awarding the prizes to the fleet and the strong.

Decidedly there were many who did not approve of these illegal and callously strong-arm methods of staving off the desperate poor and, apart from the civil rights campaigners, there were objections in the press. In a *Survey Graphic* article, "Rolling Stones Gather No Sympathy," January 1939 – eight months, incidentally, before Steinbeck's *The Grapes of Wrath* aroused national shame and anger – Victory Weybright addressed attention to the point that California had been made by migrants: conquistadores, forty-niners, Chinese coolies, hobo field hands and, finally, the drought refugees. If the American pioneer tradition still counted for anything, he submitted: "Localities with defensive barriers cannot be allowed unwittingly to 'Balkanize' a nation that ·has built its cities and peopled its farms by the greatest mobility of population any nation has ever known … Or else, our vital American system will decay."

The blockades lost in the end and the migrants moved in but this came about less from public revulsion against such police state "walls" than by the blockades themselves. They did not fail from want of trying.

Governor Floyd Olson, testifying in December 1939 before the Senate Civil Liberties Committee, reported that twenty-seven Californian counties had taken steps to "regulate" the inter-county movement of workers – the attempt by the association of Californian land owners and agriculturists to control migrants in and out of the crop zones.

This was an authoritarian extreme not reached in any other state but in 1936 Colorado also, briefly and unsuccessfully, set up a border blockade, the pretext being that it was to ward off alien Mexicans making for the beet fields but which quite certainly was aimed at hard-up drought families.

Apart from this during the meager years of the Thirties state after state hardened its restrictions to ensure that it was not going to be the one to take up the slack of the population. Sumptuary legislation – if not by the state, by counties or municipalities – was enacted to disqualify border-crossers from the benefit of public relief, and the period of legal settlement, whereunder a man was eligible for public work, was raised in a number of states.

This multipartition of the United States, with border patrols and cash tests for residence, was a curious and distant divergence from Washington's Land of Promise, where "the poor, the needy and the oppressed of the Earth" could "repair thither and abound ... with milk and honey." The milk and honey route was laced with tank traps and dragons' teeth, and, as the repetition monotonously displays itself, was then found not to provide holy security for those so hemmed around. As Brown and Cassmore showed in their WPA research in 1939 on migratory cotton pickers in Arizona, having made the migratory worker as unwelcome and uncomfortable as possible, the local farmers then panicked because of shortage of seasonal field hands.

"Arizona residents, with normal short-sightedness in this respect," the report says, "dislike the cotton workers because of their poverty characteristics for which Arizona is itself at least partly responsible. Though Arizona's most valuable crop cannot be harvested without them, the migratory cotton pickers are everywhere regarded as pariahs."

McWilliams understands this when he attributes the "roundabout and delayed" general recognition of the industrial revolution in agriculture, and its terrible havoc upon the millions of little people made redundant, to the invisibility of the migrant. (And Michael Harrington, twenty-five years later, drew attention to this continuing invisibility, both geographical and social, of the poor of the Great Society.)

In previous periods, McWilliams observes, when the bulk of America's migrants were single men, they occasionally made themselves conspicuous: as when they descended in droves from boxcars to harvest the Middle West wheat, when they huddled in long lines outside the winter soup kitchens, when as in California in 1914 they marched to Sacramento as part of Kelley's Army of the Unemployed.

"In moments of acute crisis the tramp became an ominous symbol: the shadows merged to form clouds. But the clouds always dissolved, somehow, and we forgot about the shadowy figures along the roads and in the jungle camps."

The invisibility of the early Dust Bowl refugee was partly the nature of the migration, partly shame, partly self-protection. The Okies and the whipped families from the other Great Plains states did not cluster on freights, nor converge upon soup kitchens, nor amass in protest demonstrations. They could be seen, flittingly, limping in their Tin Lizzies and trucks along the highways. But at nightfall they vanished: into some squatter's bivouac in the wayside thickets out of sight of the local harness bulls and property-jealous citizens, around the bend of a river, in a patch of woodland.

If they had any money at all for slightly better stop-over accommodation it was in the cheapest auto courts and tourist camp sites, again where they misted away. Even today when present in force in a township or district for the fruit picking season, the migrants' hut compounds are at the edge of the parish where their poverty and foreign ways cannot cause offence to the civic delicacy of the residents.

Even if the harvest force for that bailiwick is trawled in from the local skid row, the farmers' lorries have been through, loaded up with their human cargo and dropped them for all the daylight hours in distant fields long before the businessman and his family have finished breakfast and emerged into the morning air.

11 : THE CURSE OF OUR YANKEE NATION

What did hobo say to tramp?
"Night's a-comin' an' leaves gettin' damp."
What did hobo say to bum?
"Git any cornbread, save me some."

American children's chant

THE tramp has remained an ominous symbol, always solidifying blackly when times are bad. The Joads and their kind could have wandered for ever along the pit galleries of American life, never identified as a particular and altered phenomenon, had it not been that the compass needle flickered inside them toward the West as the direction-finder always had in the American promise, and they had gone like migrant birds to the illusory summer.

The pariahs themselves, even in the Thirties, had not many channels of communication to the public at large, but here and there have occurred men on the road with the ability to get down onto paper the situation of the mudsill and outcast, and the average countryman's reflex action as he came across the skyline.

A John McIntosh of Rochester, New York, published two poems in the *Labor Standard* in 1876 and 1877 which have rarity value as a direct despatch from the hopeless job-hunting hundreds of thousands who were then silently enduring. The first is a dialogue between an Old Farmer and a Tramp:

> OLD FARMER:
> *A tramp! a tramp! sic! Ponto! seize him!*
> *Call out folks, Jim, it will please 'em ...*
> *I guess he's a vile Communist, Jim!*
> *The squire, I vum, must take car of hum ...*
> *What in thunder do you fellers mean?*
> *To think that we are so plaguy green,*

135

As stand to be robbed by you durned tramps:
A lot of poor, ragged, mean city scamps.

TRAMP:
Poor and ragged, I think you said,
Right; and we come for a little bread,
To help us along our weary way,
Asking for labor from day to day,
That is the reason we're here, you see,
Forced from the city by poverty ...
We canvassed the city through and through,
Nothing to work at, nothing to do;
The wheels of the engines go no more,
Bolted and barred is the old shop door ...

FARMER:
What! rob us? hear the old villain, Jim,
We'll be murdered, too, by the likes of him.
And yet they will ask for food and drink,
Guess you ain't quite so bad off's you think.
I say to you as I allus say:
No man need starve in Ameriky.

The second, The Tramp — The Scamp, appeared nine months
later:
Oh! what will be done with the tramp — the scamp!
The curse of our Yankee nation
A nuisance is he,
And a mystery,
Defying interrogation ...
Oh, what shall be done with the tramp — the scamp!
Our national poor relation?
A riddle is he,
And perplexity
Defiant of legislation ...

Elsewhere, in Garland's A Son of the Middle Border is reflected
the anti-tramp feeling that was growing, with particular vehemence in the Eastern states where the industrial flotsam washed

thickest out from the city limits, and where on the small family farms there was no need for the transient harvest crews of the West.

In 1881 Garland is tramping penniless in rain without glint of a job. He is refused shelter at a farmhouse: "A sudden realization of the natural antagonism of the well-to-do toward the tramp appalled me." At a cottage he is repulsed by an old woman who says sharply: "We don't feed tramps."

He joins up with his brother. They find the residents "suspicious and inhospitable .. hostile contempt. No doubt these farmers, much beset with tramps, had reasonable excuse for their inhospitable ways, but to us it was bitter and uncalled for."

That is an understandable reaction, the feeling of the "loss of identity" invariably referred to by any middle-class writer or social scientist experimenting with plumbing Jack London's abyss; it is more sympathetic than the slightly irritating description by Tully of "the systematic unkindness" with which he is greeted by seven housewives as he goes begging down a "dingy block." Having thrown bricks at one back door and at the woman's dog, he manages to scrounge some food at his next call, and this, he says, "made up for the harsh treatment accorded me, and my sensitive spirit was appeased." It does not seem to have occurred to his sensitive spirit that during this depression the working-class families he was panhandling were probably almost as hard-up as he was.

But in reasonable times as well as bad there has always been a cold harshness shown by small town America to the wayfaring stranger. Stephen Graham, an Englishman who crossed with a shipload of Russian emigrants in 1913, found that the hospitality extended him as a writer with credentials vanished when he "put pack on back and sallied forth merely as a man ... Little is given anonymously in the United States."

Indifferent to the hardships of a tramp, "they do not look on the stranger as a fellow-man but as a loose wheel, a utility lying rusting in a field ... No one is good enough for the American till he has 'made good.'" Refused lodging by farmer after farmer between Williamsport and Scranton, he tells a storekeeper that he considers the harboring of travelers a Christian duty. "They don't feel it so about here," is the reply.

Graham continues: "America has more tramps than any other country except Russia" – but whereas the Russian tramp is "a gentle creature" the American is "often a foul-mouthed hooligan . . . an enemy of society."

Out West, he is told, it is different. There, as in former times, every farm-house has open door and free table to the tramp, and no one is more welcome for he brings news and stories of personal adventure; he might even be persuaded to work in the fields. But the tramp in the East has suffered "in the heartless commercial machine, he got out of it only by luck, and his hand is against every man. He has cast over honor, principle and conscience."

According to Graham the farmer's experience is of being "robbed, assaulted and insulted, his property damaged, barns set on fire, crops in part destroyed by wilfully malicious vagabonds." So all strangers are turned away. In Russia a pilgrim-tramp had told him: "When we leave this world to get to Heaven we all have to go on the tramp, and those find shelter there who sheltered wanderers here." Graham continues: "But Americans will not be judged by that standard. The early Christians received strangers and often entertained angels unawares, but the modern American is afraid that in taking in a strange tramp he may be sheltering an outcast spirit. Once tramps were angels; now they are rebel-angels."

Graham's personal nibble at tramping was too perfunctory to provide dependable evidence of overall conditions, yet without realizing it (one suspects) he hit a striking truth in speaking of the American's fear of "sheltering an outcast spirit." For this is indeed how the tramp was seen: an anarchic pagan interloper threatening by his example a precarious existence sustained only by its containment within a rigid frame of discipline and duty.

Chaplin illuminates further the woebegone and impossibly ambiguous position of the outcast spirit. He describes how he and a friend booked up with one of Chicago's "slave market" employment agencies for a construction project at East St. Louis, free transportation laid on. From there they went on to Amarillo, Texas, to find field work, "two raw recruits in a vast army of harvest workers," and flitted from job to job from the Texas

Panhandle through Oklahoma, Kansas, Nebraska, Minnesota and the Dakotas, learning "how the underdog was forced to live." He continues: "Throughout the entire trip we were compelled by poverty to steal rides on freight cars. Nothing we could do about that. Between jobs we would sleep in haystacks or nearby boxcars. That was illegal also ... During spells of bad weather, the farmer would stop feeding us or fire us outright. Most of the stiffs were working for a winter stake without which they would be 'on the bum' all winter. With the going wage at a dollar-and-a-half or two dollars a day, it was not easy to acquire a stake."

Between the harvest workers themselves the relationship was one of suspicion and distrust. "We shared the policy of dog-eat-dog with the human pack who preyed upon us, the 'shack' and the judge who shook us down for stealing rides, and the farmers who haggled pennies when it came time to pay off and sometimes refused to pay at all."

Even if the harvest hand managed to nurse his dollars and end the season with a winter stake his troubles were not over. "There was still the gauntlet of bootleggers and 'tin-horn gamblers' to run. If the stiff managed to escape this parasitic army of harvest camp followers, he was still, in danger of being 'hijacked' or 'rolled' by professional thieves who made a practice of 'harvesting the harvesters.' If he made this hurdle, and his stake was intact, he still faced the danger of riding boxcars and of being shot, killed, wounded, or arrested by railroad detectives for stealing rides and encroaching on railway property."

To be sure it might reasonably be suggested that with money in his pocket the stiff could have avoided the danger of the boxcars by buying a ticket for his destination and traveling as a legal passenger. Apart from the slenderness of his savings, and a reluctance to part from any of those hard-grafted dollars so tamely, the psychology of the stiff was not such. Tully has a splendid passage where he and a bunch of hobos are riding a mail train from Cedar Rapids toward Omaha.

At the end of a viaduct the train stops and the entire crew, carrying guns, surround the boxcar and demand money from the hobos. "Pay us, or hit the gravel," snarls the conductor. "We ain't haulin' livestock," puts in the brakeman. The reply of Bill sums up the anti-activist pride of the hobo: "I wouldn't give you a cent if you hauled me cheap as a letter. It's against my principles."

All the scattered hobo reminiscence still in existence is threaded with this uncertainty. The attitude of train crews varied from company to company, from state to state, from time to time. The experienced hobo carried his own mental inventory of hard-core "horstile" towns and lines; also of the areas, particularly in the Pacific North-West, where crews were likely to be sympathetic to the hobo with an IWW card, perhaps were even Wobs themselves, or sufficiently fellow traveler to help a red card carrier.

But the crews changed, a new detective would begin a zealous onslaught of discipline, or the company itself would temporarily turn on the heat after a case of flagrant theft from a freight, and for a while and on that run the hobo would be given a rough time. He could never be sure: one conductor might amiably let him ride, the next try to squeeze out of him a token fare for his own pocket or toss him overboard or bring in the cops.

Objectively it can hardly astonish that the railroad companies detested the hobo. They saw him not as a reinless privateer giving their prosaic mercantile steaming a dash of Spanish Main flamboyance, nor as a lame dog to be aided on his way, but as bilker, robber and spoiler. He was also a potential legal bane, for claims by injured men handled by specialist shyster lawyers began to rain in on them. Often the brakeman, out of ferocious sense of duty or because he had failed to extort the standardised private-deal ten cents a hundred miles (twenty for an all-night run), would throw the hobo out under the moving wheels. Apart from this death was met and many a limb lopped off while voluntarily leaving or boarding a train.

The case of W. H. Davies, the Welsh poet, is of course well known from his account of it in *The Autobiography of a Super-Tramp*. Davies spent five years zig-zagging about the goods yards, work camps and jails of the Eastern states and the South, until in March 1899, heading for the Klondyke, he stumbled when snagging a Canadian Pacific train in Ontario and had his right foot severed.

It was a routine hazard that claimed thousands of men – 23,964 trespassers killed and 25,236 injured on America's railroads between 1901 and 1905, "largely tramps and hoboes" – It was those who were merely crippled who bothered the railroad companies. Feeling themselves to be legal suckers, and also to stamp out boxcar burglary, the companies began appointing armed watchmen. The guard system was pioneered by the redoubtable Pinkerton, who organized for the Rock Island the first exclusive railroad police force.

Apart from injury claims and theft the railroads had more general reason for abhorring hobos, for they were not too considerate of the property they made use of. If there was anything edible in the boxcar they ate it, anything combustible they burned it.

Tully describes how on a nippy night a gang of them breaks up some loose bits of wood and proceeds to get warm: "Soon a fire was blazing in the car ... The men talked in animated fashion while the fire ate its way through the floor and fell on the track below. Another fire was built in an oily spot. It burned slowly at first, while we huddled around it ... The blaze spread and crept over the floor and up the sides of the car to the roof." Well toasted, they swing off and watch from a safe distance as the train pulls up.

A great many illicit train riders were working men getting from A to B, or right though the alphabet, the only way they could and without causing trouble; but, understandably perhaps the crews and bulls had no sure means of distinguishing between the harmless and the harmful. The safest, or easiest, principle was to be consistent by treating them all as criminals. Pinkerton's grand grouping – "confirmed tramps, disgusting drunkards, miserable communistic outcasts" – has remained pretty untrammeled as the railroad detective's view of the hobo.

12 : THE DREAM CINDER DICK

An overland limited
Chalks a streak of gold
Across the blackboard of night ...
Prosperity lounges in pullman coaches ...
While American jobless
Ride the decks, the rods of coaches
And nurse a great hunger with dreams
Of wheat cakes and coffee steaming
On the counter of a coffee-an' joint
Somewhere in Omaha, Denver, Colorado Springs.

Jim Waters: *Prosperity*

H. W. DEWHURST's bulging compendium for "cinder dicks" (the author's own phrase) describes the railroads of the 1890s as "the prime prey of flourishing, well-organized bands of outlaws. Pilferage was rampant. The losses of freight, parcels and luggage were soon to amount to a million dollars. Bridges, tunnels, stations and tracks were dynamited in daring holdups."

There might seem here to be a confusion between the career train robber and the nomadic harvest hand, but the author says flatly: "The sizeable hobo population, particularly following the Civil War, took to the railroad yards for transportation and loot."

This book, intended for the education and delectation of downy-cheeked cinder dicks, contains some rousing, red-blooded yarns, such as that about the sergeant on a routine seal-inspection of merchandise shot through the head at Fayetteville, North Carolina, by a man in an empty gondola, and about another patrolman slain in a boxcar battle at Petersburg, Virginia – both killers were hobos.

An even more explicit identification of the hobo as both homicidal thug and fanatical political assassin is contained in the Henty-ish code of J. C. Harper, police superintendent of the

Pennsylvania Railroad, whose 1925 pandect of the dream cinder dick was: "He must be such a man among men as a thoroughbred is among horses. He should be taller than average folk so that he can see over the heads of the crowd. He should be fit and limber as the athlete, have no surplus fat, have good feet, perfect eyes and ears, and be ready any minute to spring after a yeggman, or climb upon a moving freight or passenger train.

"He is to be always neatly dressed, his home life must be above reproach, his wife must not talk too much; he must not take a drink on or off duty; he must have a care in conversation with women; and to cap all, he should possess sufficient strength of character, will power, and moral courage to resist successfully any temptation to do wrong . . .

"He must be a good shot. He must be able to pick out the trespasser from the brakeman riding the top or bumpers of box cars in the dead of night . . . He must be able to pick out the 'deaf and dumb panhandler' who is 'working' the train before he begins to pass his cards . . .

"He must be ready at all times to walk into a band of car thieves and get the stuffing knocked out of him with a piece of gas pipe, or have some apostle of liberty shoot him from the top of a box car . . ."

In practice, the function of the railroad bull seems to have been less lofty and noble than their written manifestos imply. Holbrook summarizes it as "to put fear into the hearts of all migrants who rode rods, blinds, bumpers, and decks. They accomplished this in various ways, by tossing tramps off moving trains, by shooting at and sometimes hitting them, by beating them up with fists or saps."

He quotes a detective named Hotchkiss, who had a roving commission out of the yards at Portland and Eugene, Oregon, and Oakland, California.

"The best way to keep tramps off trains or other railroad property," Hotchkiss explains with radiant simplicity, "is to beat up any unauthorized person you find in the yards. I might see a couple of men hanging around. They looked as if they were waiting for a freight to be made up.

"I'd go directly up to them and ask one of them a question. No matter what he answered, I'd cuff him across the face with a good slap. I'd ask the other guy a question. He'd start to back off. I'd follow him up and really hit him.

"Then I'd turn back to the first bo. If he wasn't already getting the hell out of there, I'd give him the billy – not hard enough to break anything. but hard enough to remember.

"On the trains, I might talk a while with tramps riding the boxcars, and I'd never throw them off if we were highballing. I'd wait until we were down to twenty miles or so an hour, then force them to jump, or push them off."

Hobo jungles "made Hotchkiss see red." He enjoyed nothing more than "to devastate a jungle." His tactics were "to drive all the bums out of camp, not giving them time to pick up their bindles and suitcases, or even the food they were preparing. Then the bulls would shoot every cooking utensil full of holes and tear down any small shelter such as a homemade tent or shack. If there was washing hanging on a line, as was often the case, Hotchkiss tore it off and threw it on the jungle fire."

This seems to be a candid précis of the policeman's hobo policy, and indeed toward anyone during depression times without visible means of support.

But Hotchkiss was Dimples beside Jeff Carr, notorious hobo-stalker and exterminator of Cheyenne, Wyoming, whose name brought the hush of half-admiring awe in jungles throughout the United States. A self-appointed Mountie, Carr's method was to intercept a slow-moving freight, and gallop beside it on his white horse shooting with his six-gun at hobos on the blinds, decks or in open boxcars, or yanking them off under the wheels. Any who survived were unlikely to last through the manhandling he gave them in the cells. Carr died on duty – killed by a coupling-pin in a fight with hobos.

In the Thirties the guardians of poverty were everywhere trigger-twitchy. Kromer, a breadline drifter of that time, is staring in a restaurant window one night; he has not eaten for two days: "A hand slaps down on my shoulder. It is a heavy hand. It spins me around in my tracks. 'What the hell are you doin' here?' It is a cop. 'Me? Nothing,' I say. 'Nothing, only watching a guy eat chicken. Can't a guy watch another guy eat chicken?' 'Wise guy,' he says. 'Well, I know what to do with wise guys.' He slaps me across the face with his hand, hard. I fall back against the building. His hands are on the holster by his side. What can I do? Take it is all I can do. He will plug me if I do anything.

"'Put up your hands,' he says. I put up my hands. 'Where's your gat?' he says. 'I have no gat,' I say. 'I never had a gat in my life.' 'That's what they all say,' he says. He pats my pockets. He don't find anything. There is a crowd around here now. Everybody wants to see what is going on. They watch him go through my pockets. They think I am a stick-up guy. A hungry stiff stands and watches a guy eat a chicken, and they think he is a stick-up guy. That is a hell of a note.

"'All right,' he says, 'get down the street before I run you in. If I ever catch you stemming this beat, I will sap the living hell out of you. Beat it.'"

However hard the knocks the detectives dealt out, on the railroads themselves they were defeated by numbers. By the railroads' own estimate around the turn of the century there were at any one time 500,000 hobos beating their way but this, believes Parker, was "a fraction of the migratory millions actually in transit."

By then the economic impetus was so great behind them, and the habit so infixed, that all the Hotchkisses and Carrs armed with pistols and billies could not keep the hordes off the trains and out of the jungles. The weight of numbers was having another effect, too, which was the accentuating of the double attitude toward the tramp, at one time "pesky go-about" and free man, cadging parasite and romantic reminder of the old boundless horizons officially closed in 1890 by the Census Bureau, when it declared that there was no longer a land frontier. There were few in authority in the cast of Governor Lewelling and not all that many defenders of the tramp even in the Populist farming area – defenders, that is, in humanist and economic terms.

13 : WEARY WILLY AND TIRED TIM

*Once a bum always a bum ... When the virus of
restlessness begins to take possession of a wayward
man, and the road from Here seems broad and
straight and sweet ...*

John Steinbeck

ON Columbus Day 1892 every school child in the land sang
a special song:

*Humanity's home! thy sheltering breast
Gives welcome and room to strangers oppress'd
Pale children of Hunger and Hatred and Wrong
Find life in thy freedom and joy in thy song.*

It went without saying that "strangers" in this ambrosial
abstraction did not include that everyday reality, the tramp.
Yet at the very same time that the tramp was being short-listed
for poisoning as communistic vermin, and being smashed off
the trains with blackjacks and bullets, the Pinkertonesque "happy
dog" myth was waddling off the drawing board.

The bewildered ex-squaddie, the evicted farmer, the migratory logger, the miner on his uppers, the construction worker
hunting his next hiring, the boomer railroad man, the refugee
factory hand – all this sinister mob of throw-outs who looked
like the *canaille* advance guard of the Revolution when they
came trudging into the town outskirts – were being mingled
into a fictional-pictorial composite.

In his Tired Tim guise he was a harmless, daffy, ne'er-do-well,
exasperating but pathetic, whom the citizenry could laugh at
and feel comfortably superior to. He began to appear in quality
periodicals in his folk robes drawn by Frost, as the hoosier cartoon character Weary Willie drawn by Zim in the popular
newspapers, and as Happy Hooligan in Opper's nationally syn-
dicated comic strip.

He also stepped out of the funnies and into three-dimensional caricature on the stage in the person of the actor Nat Wills, in the by then ceremonial robes of burst hat, shapeless duds, black scrub on jaw and – the signal light of his dissolute booziness, the mark of the beast – the crimson nose. His miserable chattels were in a red bandanna bundle on the end of the stick over his shoulder.

Perhaps the most powerful popularizer of this comforting image was Norman Rockwell, who for fifty years illustrated the front cover of *The Saturday Evening Post* (continuing, says his biographer, throughout changes of fashion, to "dip his brush into the honey-pot of lovableness and zest in living.") Rockwell introduced his tramp on the front of the October 18, 1924, issue: there he was, complete, straw hat with crown apparently gone round with a can-opener, and corncob pipe jutting through walrus moustache, cooking a couple of sausages impaled on a stick, while from between his legs a lovable mongrel leans forward sniffing hungrily. "I always enjoyed doing these tramp pictures," Rockwell has said. In the mid-Twenties he produced his famous Fisk Tire advertisement, an oil painting of a beatific bum (dented Derby, patched trousers, flapping boots, daisy jauntily in buttonhole) snoring under a billboard upon which a bird is chirruping. Another ad in 1927 for Interwoven Socks showed the same tramp figure (with the same merry pup as companion) pulling some socks out of a garbage can; it had the title *Still Good*.

This whimsical local-colour view, comprised of both mawkishness and contempt, served the purpose of depersonalizing the hobo, of conveniently disqualifying him from concern and contact. It marked him off as a social curio, as absurd and stylized as Harlequin, and, in human terms, in his grotesque mask just as invisible.

Hobo numbers continued to fluctuate but in troughs of depression there were by the early 1900s probably more than a million men riding the trains by unorthodox means around the United States. The impact of them upon any one place may be judged by the fact that 500,000 homeless workers steadily billowed through Chicago, America's railroad axis, from which forty railroads radiated and with 3,000 miles of track within its city limits.

Now it can seem only to be astonishing legerdemain that numbers of this size could be deleted from society. The incidental literature of the time reveals how it was done: by never looking at the tramp as a person or a social malady, but always side on as a lesson in something or other, either as an example of wayfaring chirrupiness, a commendable means of making the best of your rotten lot, or as the wages of sin and inertia.

The beginning of this pollyanna perkiness may be found in such exhalations as *Winter Sunshine*, published in the 1880s, by John Burroughs, an earnest nature lover. In a piece entitled "Exhilarations of the Road," Burroughs takes the theme of the charm of the noble urchin. "Occasionally on sidewalks," he confides with fetishist relish, "mid dapper, swiftly-moving, high-heeled boots and gaiters, I catch a glimpse of the naked human foot ... How primitive and uncivil it looks in such company, a real barbarian in the parlour ... Though it be a black foot and an unwashed foot, it shall be exalted. It is a symbol of my order – the Order of the Walkers."

It is a trifle surprising to come upon similar sentiments in the reflections of the wrathful Pinkerton. Yet nowhere else is the two-facedness of that age of the "tramp menace" so nakedly revealed. Pinkerton begins by asserting his right to "say plain things to the countless toilers" involved in the Great Strikes of '77: "I say I have *earned* this right. I have been all my lifetime a working man. I know what it is to strive and grope along, with paltry remuneration and no encouragement save that of the hope and ambition implanted in every human heart.

"I know what it is, from personal experience to be the tramp journeyman; to carry the stick and bundle; to seek work and not get it; and to get it, and receive but a pittance for it, or suddenly lose it altogether and be compelled to resume the weary search."

Having established his first-hand knowledge of bottom-doggery, he plunges into panegyric of "the careless, happy-hearted order, richer, and more satisfied, than some men worth their millions." He describes the miseries of overcrowded transport, and proceeds: "No person can ever get a taste of the genuine pleasure of the road and not feel in some feckless way ... that he would

148

like to become some sort of tramp . . . an irrepressible impulse to go a-tramping."

There is the "physical and mental elevation of spirit which comes to the walker." To "the better class of tramp . . . what a perfect panorama of beauty is opened, what miles of smooth road, or crisp, half-trod grass-paths, are covered, what dallyings by moss-grown bridges where the sunlit waters ripple along with soft murmurs below, what meetings there are with sturdy old farmers on hay-ricks, in ramshackle buggies, on horseback, or afoot . . . What sly flirtations with blooming country lasses, arguments with cautious housewives, explanations to vigilant constables, and chattings with Rip Van Winkles at roadside inns, what quaint villages are reached."

Alas, there is a seamy side to the idyll. "But oftener you get the vagabond. Shiftlessness, discontent, restlessness, all creep in and take possession of him . . . from this stage it is but a step to a bullying mendicant; and from that condition to one of becoming a criminal . . ."

Nevertheless, says Pinkerton, he disagrees with a certain Professor Wayland "as to the universal villainy and ferocity of the tramp." He continues: "I feel that they have been somewhat misunderstood and always scorned and vilified. While wishing it thoroughly known that I deplore and condemn the vicious features of the fraternity, I am quite willing to have it known that I have a kind word to say for thousands of them who have become homeless wretches and wandering outcasts."

Pinkerton particularizes. He has a kind word to say for Walter Scott, for Dr. Johnson, for John Bunyan and, indeed, for Jesus Christ. He points out – "with no levity or sense or irreverence" – that Christ was himself a tramp; moreover, the Bible is "full of illustrious instances of tramping."

The fact is, "the tramp has always existed in some form or other, and he will continue on his wanderings until the end of time." In Switzerland and France there are tramp tailors, tramp cobblers, tramp tinkers, all carrying their awls and hammers and soldering irons about the countryside. Even dressmakers and midwives, he amplifies, have been part of that careless, happy-hearted order, wending their way from bust to bust, pregnancy to pregnancy.

There are, too, tramp printers such as "the noted tramp-printer," Peter B. Lee, who "met his death by attempting to board a train and steal a ride. He had been a man of a good deal of independence of character, and had never before made an effort of this kind. Nearly his last words were 'Served me right for goin' back on principle!'"

Pinkerton clearly agrees that it served him right but presents Peter B. Lee as the kind of unobtrusive, untroublesome tramp who would never have tangled with Pinkerton's "extensive and perfected" force. Grieving for the passing of Lee's breed, Pinkerton examines the decline in tramp standards: " ... the severe and unprecedented hard times that have lately been experienced, and which still seem to girdle the entire globe, have manufactured tramps with an alarming rapidity. Where they previously existed as single wandering vagabonds, they now have increased until they travel in herds, and through the dire necessity of their pitiable condition, justly create some anxiety and alarm ...

"The conditions which have always existed in our country, and which still exist, have made it imperative on the part of a large portion of our population to tramp it. Men leaving Eastern cities for Western towns, desiring to economize, have pushed their way along afoot ... Farmers of great wealth with a view to changing their residence, have walked hundreds of miles to see the country and make personal enquiries and investigations; but the hard times which we have experienced have so depressed our own industries that thousands of mechanics, clerks and laboring men have been thrown out of employment here."

"Our late war created thousands of tramps. This fact seems to be generally overlooked." Why did the war do this? Because "hundreds upon hundreds became demoralized by the lazy habits of camp-life, and were suddenly turned loose upon society without any regular employment, or desire for any."

Here Pinkerton relapses into tender ruminations about "old knights of the road" he has met and the "Freemasonry of tramping ... When brighter days return to our industries, people will see tramps disappear ... the thousands among them who have trades and professions will gradually but surely return to them. But during this period, when the hard hand of necessity bears down so heavily alike upon businessman and workingman ...

there should be a more general leniency toward a class who are made up of people often as good as we; and some charity should be exercised, rather than a relentless war inaugurated, and result of which will only be to reclaim no one of them, and rapidly increase crime and criminals."

Enough, Pinkerton apparently decided at this point, just as one might have begun to suspect a Lady Bountiful behind the unblinking private eye mask. He seems to realize that he has gone almost too scandalously far toward siding with the knights of the road, for then comes that familiar schizoid swerve away from sympathetic analysis into obeisance to the *laissez faire* open economy, from the Homeric to the plain man.

First he wants it known that it is his conviction "as certain as life itself, that the workingman is never the gainer" from being corrupted by unionism and strike action. He is always the loser.

"These trades-unions of every name and nature are but a relic of the old despotic days. The necessities for their creation, if they ever existed, have passed away. In American citizens there exists all the essentials to make success in the life of every man not only possible but probable."

In "the big scare at Louisville" Pinkerton's hawk eye perceived, "there was not a railroad man, or a respectable mechanic. Its members were merely Negroes, half-grown boys, tramps and cowardly thieves . . . vile rabble." On another occasion of industrial unrest, although this time there was a "small percentage of thoughtless and inconsiderate workmen," among the mob were "howling communists, vicious tramps, mischievous boys and idle city riff-raff." The Trainmen's Union had been broken up by Pinkerton men armed with guns and clubs – for it was well known that the troublemakers "are confirmed tramps, disgusting drunkards, miserable communistic outcasts or are now occupying the gloomy cell of some jail."

Stating proudly that "my agencies have been busily employed by the great railway, manufacturing and other corporations, for the purposes of bringing the leaders and instigators of the dark deeds of those days to the punishment they so richly deserve," Pinkerton vows juicily: "Hundreds have been punished. Hundreds more will be punished."

It may be seen how simply, how positively, the tramp could at one and the same time be the happy, jolly dog and the disgusting, drunken, miserable communistic outcast. In fact what precisely was the man behind the apoplexy and the clichés?

14 : FATHER, FIX THE BLINDS
SO THE BUMS CAN'T RIDE

Do you know how a hobo feels?
Life is a series of dirty deals.
This is the song of the wheels.

Hobo song

A FREIGHT train comes rumbling into the Rock Island yards at Little Rock. The boxcars and gondolas and flatcars are emblazoned with a litany of distance and random possibility: ROUTE OF THE EAGLES; TEXAS-PACIFIC; BURLINGTON ROUTE – EVERYWHERE WEST; FRUIT GROWERS' EXPRESS; NICKEL PLATE ROAD; EERIE LACKAWANNA; SOO LINE; SANTE FE ALL THE WAY.

Four men who have vaulted out of a boxcar as the train slowed into the approach walk down the track beside the water tank tower and out of the road crossing on to Confederate Street, where there is the Pig Stand Bar-B-Q drive-in and Lucille's Coffee House. An electric arrow indicates LIQUOR on one side of the street; opposite an even bigger sign declares JESUS SAVES.

The four men, on this occasion, choose salvation and book in at the Rescue Mission, and they carry their bundles down to the bull-pen, a basement made of cinder blocks with wood bunks divided by wire netting to prevent after-dark fraternization or filching.

There is a central space with benches; a group is playing dominoes; one man is having his hair machined down to bristles with an electric clipper. Most wear striped engineer caps or track layers' canvas caps with tie-up ear muffs and one has on a silver crash helmet, badges of artisan respectability and status otherwise lost. They are middle-aged to elderly, most of them ex-railroad men, now contraband passengers on the lines they used to operate.

"I used to be a freight loader up in Chicago. There used to

be two million men working for the railroads, now there're 700,000. Now I just kinda odd-job around. Guess I've traveled 50,000 miles in the last three years."

"I was born in Bauxite, Arkansas, and my father was a brakeman on the Rock Island Line. All I wanted to do was move way off like him, I wanted to be a railroad man like my daddy, and I was. I became a fireman and went all over Missouri and the South. Man, that was a good job."

"Well, it's all manner of things that gets you into this life. With some it's cocaine or marijuana or just wine. With me it was women and now I'm too old for that even."

"One reason a lot of guys travel so much is that they roll into a boxcar drunk in Philadelphia and wake up in Portland and find they've rode right across the United States."

"I'm sixty-two now. Used to be a welder, mostly on construction sites and oilfields. But mostly all I get to do now is follow the crops. I just been picking soya beans. Reckon by now I must've made forty-six states."

"I just got in from Nebraska. I was up there with a steel gang on the railroad. We laid a quarter-mile of steel at one time. Now I've heard they're going to start laying and repairing track up in Wyoming in September so I may as well head up there."

"The men who ride the trains don't bum. They're looking for work. There are more men on the road than ever. I was in Denver and there were hundreds walking the streets. Me, I've just been working a combine in Texas. I'm from North Carolina, but I haven't been back there in years. Why did I leave? I couldn't tell you that to save my life."

"I ride because I have to. There's no kicks in it. I'm too old to work and not old enough for the pension. I was in Illinois picking strawberries in May, but I didn't stay because the peaches was all froze out. I can't figure out the next move."

"Well, it's kinda funny but I like riding them freight trains. Yes sir, it's just in some people. You want to travel on. Some people just got that roamin' blood in them."

———————

LET us look more closely at the hobo and his manner of life, when still geared absolutely to the railroad and the outpost work areas it served up to the Twenties.

The floating proletarian of the West of this period usually had a basic trade. He was a transient trackman, the railroad section hand who laid the lines and was called a gandy dancer from the incongruous ballet movements he made as he levered the sections into position and smoothed the gravel, a choreography exquisitely formalized by Southern Negro gangs into a group effort timed to work chants and hollers.

He was a sheep shearer, furiously busy – and highly paid – for four months as the wool harvest shifted from curve to curve through the South-West. He was a sewer hog who dug ditches, roadbeds and construction excavations. He was a timber beast, a saw mill worker or a logger who could traverse a river-borne raft of trunks and who followed the clear-felling through the North borderland to the Puget Sound.

He was a harvest stiff who threshed his way from the "headed wheat country" of Southern Kansas to the "bundle country" of Nebraska. He was a metal miner or a coal miner or a rock-breaking dynoe or a fence erector or a fruit canner.

But no matter what his original trade or training had been, to sustain himself he had to be a jack-of-all-works, a handyman able, according to season and province, to drive a mule team, fall a pine, shock wheat, dam a river, grade a railroad embankment, chop cotton, brand a calf, spike a rail, rope a steer, glaum soft fruit and knock apples, flick a gandy dancer's crowbar, use a banjo shovel and a tamping pick, harvest ice for the reefers or refrigerator cars on the fruit trains, and, of course, to panhandle for food and money between times.

Essentially, too, he had to have a polymathic knowledge of the railroad, the lay-out and interlockings of the systems, and the anatomy of the train itself. Many of them had this knowledge professionally, for yet another category of hobo was the boomer, a word originally loosely applied to the nesters, squatters, homesteaders and Western land-rush settlers in the 1880s, but which narrowed down to a railroad term, meaning most often a free-lance brakeman or fireman, cast off in the bloody labor clashes of the 1880s and 1890s, and who, blacklisted, boomed around under assumed names.

A million railroaders were thus set afloat in the last quarter of the nineteenth century and slid into nomadism. There was another huge retrenchment in the Thirties: in 1936 the American railroads employed 1,066,000 workers, 57·4 per cent of a decade earlier. The boomer developed into what was probably the nearest equivalent to the British tramping artisan, for, like him, the boomer's precious passport to the working world was his paid-up union membership. "What ya ridin' on?" was a shack's routine greeting to a freighting hobo, meaning Railway Union or IWW card – if neither, the trip was likely to end at that point, overboard.

Wherever he wandered his card, flashed to an engineer or conductor, his employed brothers, was his season ticket for a free lift; it was also his "pie card," his meal ticket, for it could be counted on to produce a roof to sleep under and shared grub from the clan. It did not necessarily get him a job if he had been involved in a strike or sacked for drunkenness.

If drunkenness was on his record (and it was the custom for railroaders to kit-up with a bottle of red-eye hooch until Rule G forbade consumption of liquor on duty) some unions circulated the name in their monthly journals, a practice which perhaps ought to be approved in the interests of public safety (one thinks of the old silent movie caption: "Through the night roars the overland express, a crazed engineer in the cab.") Blacklisting meant for the tippler a one-way ticket to Palookaville and little hope of getting his mitts on the controls of any train better than a crackerbarrel short-line.

But drink was far from the only reason for blackballing. If a man had been prominent in the 1894 Pullman strike the letter of reference with which the General Managers' Association had in law to furnish him was likely to be (although this was not discovered for nearly a year after the strike) on a sheet of paper with the watermark of a broken-necked crane. Rank and file strikers, or men shifting ground for other reasons, got a reference bearing the watermark with the crane's head erect and were eligible for consideration up the line; but if the head drooped – no job.

Boycotting drove boomers high up the tracks to "the Indian Valley line," the railroaders' Shangri La where was said to be the fabled "pike" (short coal or fish line) offering superlative pay. In fact, Indian Valley was likely to be in comfortless country on the railhead frontier, up in Montana, the feeder branches in the Dakotas, the Sevier Valley line through the hostile Ute Indian territory of Colorado on its way to San Francisco, or the drive across the flatlands of Nebraska where competing companies fought with thugs and guns to be in first. More often than not he found himself able to get employment only on the "jawbone" lines serving the Montana mining camps – named so because up there all the shantymen, dynoes, muckers and teamoes got was jawbone pay: tobacco, food and scrip for the company store, but no hard cash.

Or the boomer rolled around in the thick of the seasonal scrambles, when no one had time to check papers, and the urgency was to rush the wheat and vegetables Eastward. If there was no time to follow up references, or a man said he had "lost" them, the yardmaster's test was to tell him to hold up his hands. Fingers missing, he got the job – few seasoned railroaders kept all ten when freight cars were manually coupled with link-and-pin.

Between harvests and the short-lived races to mesh new tracks, the boomer hoboed. He was, anyway, an artefact of the railroad, both his host and his enemy, and his reckless, choppy, violent personality was forged by those very same qualities in railroading itself. With the railroad he stayed, as a semi-outlawed supernumerary, hopelessly attached in an unrequited love affair.

The boomer carried a roll, or "bindle" or "balloon," of usually, inevitably, lousy blankets; but then so did bindle stiffs at large. Every logger and reaper and construction man was, in Ashleigh's words, "compelled to follow literally the advice of the founder of Christianity and 'take up his bed and walk.'"

157

The drawing of a stiff pouring petrol on his flaming cord-bound pack – "All 'bindles' will be burned on May the First 1918" – was the emotional focus of the IWW's poster campaign for better bunkhouse conditions.

While being miles short of uniformed, the hobo worker tended assertively to hallmark himself: the harvester's corduroy breeches and high-crowned J. B. hat, the lumberjack's gaudy mackinaw, tan tarpaulin overalls and spike-soled corks, the hop-picker's high-front climb-ins, the ranch hand's riveted Levi Strauss pants, the carpenter's white bibbed overalls, the ironworker's brown overalls, the boomer's thousand-mile shirt of black sateen, subject to no whiteness window-test in those pre-drip dry days. And among them, in any old scarecrow rig, was the general purpose hobo, navvy or ganger for any job going.

In his boomer form he was often, says Holroyd, "actuated by a restless desire to see what lay beyond the next hill or to follow the wild ducks northward in the spring and southward in the fall. Others had an irresistible urge to punch some train-master on the jaw for a real or fancied insult and then collect their pay. Still others hit the bottle too much, or carelessly let a boxcar fall off the dock, or perhaps caused a wreck by failing to deliver a train order, and flew the coop ...

"Boomers were generous, worldly-wise, self-assured often to the point of insolence, humorous, resourceful and given to braggadocio, and withal a likable lot. They knew railroad operations better, perhaps, than the home guard did, because they circulated widely and were continually picking up new kinks ... It required plenty of red-eye to make some fellows even want to railroad in the rowdy wooden-axle days when the industry was young, hard as steel, and sprinkled with blood."

So a million nomads were moving in intricate cross currents about the spaces of America, some purposefully, most desultorily, on the cord lines of the huge net flung over the new country. Some had "pulled the pin" (resigned) and most had "got the gate" (dismissed), and all believed, or tried to believe, that they were taking the primrose path to another job.

They had learned to ride a train the way an Indian brave could ride a horse: they could hang onto belly, back, neck or rump, and get there. From preference, the hobo rode in boxcar. Even this was always hard traveling, unless there was comfortably upholstered freight for a makeshift bed, but there were risks with most merchandise. Machinery or other heavy consignments could shift and sway on a manifest, or cannonball – a fast through train – and kill or mutilate. Nor was any veteran hobo lured by fine weather to sun himself in the doorway, for a lurch on a bend could hurl the huge sliding door shut and amputate both legs like a bacon slicer.

To the general public the term most familiarly equated with hobo travel is riding the rods. Certainly the rods were ridden, when there were rods, but then not from choice, not if there was an open boxcar to climb in, for this was just about the most perilous and hideously uncomfortable nook of a train's exterior. Beneath the old boxcar – not on today's streamlined models – the iron frame was underbraced by gunnels, or iron bars, running lengthwise eighteen inches below the belly of the car, leaving a space into which a reasonably slim hobo (and they were seldom fat) could sidle and so be borne, stretched flat on his back like a kipper on a grill, cradled between the thundering wheels and a few inches above the sleepers and spraying cinders.

The indefatigable who were ever willing to truck it the hard way also often carried in the side pocket a piece of board about ten inches long and grooved down the center. This was slotted on to the yard-long slender lateral strut parallel with the cross section and the axles of a passenger coach, thus forming an improvised, and very painful, seat.

The ingenuity of the practised train limpet was impressive. He could use almost every excrescence to render himself portable. He rode on the iron plate, yet another toehold in the "guts," or lower berth, of a steamcar. He rode the "death woods," the narrow plank above the couplings of a boxcar. He rode the couplings themselves – the whipple trees or swingletrees – and the bumpers. He burrowed in the coal of the engine tender. He rode among the sheep and cattle of the livestock cars. He rode in open gondolas piled with granite.

He rode on the top deck, the boardwalk along the center of boxcars, and, if that was loaded as at harvest time, he rode on the grab irons and ladder on the side. He rode 'possum belly on the tool or supply box under a car. He rode the toe path, the narrow loading platform bolted on the walls of some rattlers. He rode the footrail at the rear end of tankcars.

He rode the steps, the cramped compartment formed by the closed doors of a passenger car vestibule. He rode on the blind, or blind baggage, the space between the locomotive tender and the baggage car, "blind" because the forward end door is locked – the place incidentally for which W. H. Davies was jumping when he fell and had his foot slashed off. He even rode, if desperate to be on his way, under the headlight on the pilot or cowcatcher, the grilled scoop that projected afore the front wheels to clear obstructions from the line.

He rode on the water tank and in the empty ice boxes of refrigerator cars. There was even one obsessional hobo who perfected a method of stowing away in the battery box, an oblong container suspended under a passenger coach for spare lighting system storage batteries. Frisco was his name and, according to Mullin, he cased the battery boxes in the depot yards until, finding an empty, he crawled in, jack-knifed with knees under chin, pulled up the flap door and secured the screw-eye with a hook of wire, letting himself out in the same way at the end of the run.

Frisco had heard it rumored that somewhere under the boiler of a certain make of locomotive there was a crevice which had been used as a nacelle by a few exceptionally audacious hobos; but he never, he grieved, located it himself. Perhaps it was but a camp fire boast. (I know of only two attempts to adapt this machinery parasitism to the newer potentials. In April 1966 a Spaniard secreted himself in the undercarriage bay of an Air France Caravelle: his corpse was found at Orly Airport after the aircraft had returned from a round trip to Moscow. In October the same year a seventeen-year-old Mexican rode in a jet's landing gear assembly from Colombia to Mexico City, a five-hour flight at 35,000 feet and 600 mph – theoretically "biologically, technically and humanly impossible" – and survived.)

All these places, inside and out, were at the least comfortless and at worst hair-raisingly dangerous. Most of the open ledges could be used only under cover of darkness, because of the likelihood of being spotted, which meant that nodding off to sleep for a second could cause the hobo to lose his grip, and hence his life, by rolling off.

He always had to decide whether or not to lash himself to a brake beam with his trouser belt, thereby being safer from injury but an easier snatch for a detective. On the deck he was even more exposed to discovery – he could be seen by the brakeman from his caboose cupola and was open to attack from gun, sap or pick-handle; he was safer from surprise on the slanted roof of a mail or passenger train, which no official would walk when the train was highballing, but there again it was a more precarious ride.

On the blind baggage there was always the risk of being pelted with coal lumps or hot ash by a hostile fireman. Even inside, and if riding without interference or accident, it was a villainously cold and grueling journey.

On top of the bow end, the outside rider bound a rag around his eyes and pulled coat collar over his head as shield against cinders from the smoke stack, and tied string around his trousers to keep out the draughts. He also had to watch for deliberate booby traps: one trick employed by brakemen to discourage rod-riders was to lower a rail spike or coupling on a wire through the floorboards so that it bounced on each tie, whipping like a javelin at the hobo's head and body.

The degrees of predilection were fine but when the daughter of Jay Gould, the railroad baron's daughter, was making her deathbed bequest, the dirtiest turn she could think of was, according to the hobo song:

> *Father, fix the blinds so the bums can't ride.*
> *If ride they must, let 'em ride the rod,*
> *Let 'em put their trust in the hands of God.*

The hobo trusted to his own quick wits and self-sufficiency. For his improvised landlouping along the cinder right-of-way he evolved a one-man band equipment. All traveled light, but the bindle stiff, with his quilt or blankets, was less spry, limited by his snail-load impedimenta mostly to boxcars. The do-anything-go-anywhere casual laborer carried his necessities economically distributed about his person.

His benny, or overcoat, served also as pillow or bedcover, with sidepockets enlarged into pouches for razor (or a substitute sharp sliver of glass), soap, needle and thread and patches, bag of coffee, knots of sugar, salt and pepper, a couple of onions for the next jungle mulligan stew, a bottle of sugared water if nothing stronger could be paid for, newspaper as additional underwear and shoe-lining, a grain sack with three holes cut out as a windcheater, if he could afford it a slicker or macintosh cape, and a "frogsticker" knife for both peeling potatoes and self-defense. When he slept he tied his boots around his neck, for these were the one possession he could on no account have stolen, and, if he ever had any to put by, he sewed a few dollar bills into the bottom of his necktie or in the lining of his jacket.

He was in business and henceforth able to cultivate an epicurean taste for the available varieties of transport. There were those, the "scenery tramps," who frankly owned to an aesthetic pleasure in the country they sailed through free. "I think that's one of the reasons we kept on moving as much as we did," Dick Brazier, the Wobbly poet, told the labor folklorist Archie Green. "In addition to searching for the job, we were also searching for something to satisfy our emotional desire for grandeur and beauty. After all, we have a concept of beauty, too, although we were only migratory workers."

This type of hobo – more exactly the "primitive American tourist" than the whole drifting population Lomax applies the phrase to – beat his way at a leisurely jog, lounging on a load of sand in an open gondola, a pioneer vistadome trip, in a mixed train (a freight with linked passenger coaches) or a jerkwater switch or a peddler freight or a mechanics' special, which chug from station to station with many a halt. Those in a hurry, or who just enjoyed the sensation of 500 mile overnight leaps, took the *gran turismo* Big Four mails, or a red-tagged highliner freight or a yellow meat manifest or a scarlet cannonball express or even a crack cross-continental Pullman.

Those are the bare bones of the operation, and a good deal of the technique is still in use, but there is needed the flesh of actual experience to understand what it took of a man. Just here and there, in the few exercises in autobiography that have come from hobos' pens, there are vivid snapshots of this impossibly arcane undertaking. They jump out from what is often a stodge of stilted moralizing – the sudden sweat of fear, a reek of smoke, the sense of being dwarfed by monstrous machinery, and the wet, cold darkness flickering with headlights and lanterns in the yards of some remote Western anthracite town.

"The bells of the switching engineers were clanging; the car inspectors were calling out orders and numbers ... The shouts of the mail, baggage and express handlers ... The exhaust valves of the engines sent steam-plumes hissing into the air, shrill peals ... The station bell-signal for the Limited to leave. Conductors shout 'All aboard.' The engineer, after looking at his watch, climbed into the cab, released the air-brakes, opened the throttle, and with the bright electric headlight showing the way, the ponderous machine's drive wheels gripped the steel rails ... Here in the darkness, hanging under the Pullman betwixt life and death, I watched those wheels ahead and in the rear of me slowly revolve, squeaking as they passed the many cross-overs and switches, and I at last felt that I had given up everything but life itself to please the bane of my existence ... Soon we were rushing at top speed, onward." (Leon Ray Livingston.)

"The train curled like an immense dark snake before it straightened itself on the main track. As it rumbled along the rails, the engine whistle shrieking for crossings, I stood on the bumpers between two cars and dreamed of many things. I gripped the iron brake-beams until my wrists ached and tiny particles of rust worked their way into the palms of my hands ... The roaring train lashed through the air. The wind blew viciously between the cars. It nearly blew the torn shirt from my body. My hair was wind-tangled and full of cinders ... Perhaps the grueling grind of the road, the lashing of the wind, the rain, and cinders combined with the smoke and gaseous grime of tunnels, gave me the courage to endure the keener mental tests that met me at the yearly stations ahead." (Jim Tully.)

"It is so dark you can hardly see your hand in front of you ... We ease up as close as we can without being seen by the bulls. We scrape our knees and our hands on the sharp pebbles in the tracks and stumble over the ties ... You can judge how fast a drag is coming by listening to the puff. This one is picking up fast ... I judge my distance. I start running along this track. I hold my hand up to the side of these cars. They brush my fingers as they fly by. I feel this step hit my fingers, and dive. Christ, but I am lucky ... I slam against the side of the car. I think my arms will be jerked out of their sockets. My ribs feel like they are smashed, they ache so much. I am bruised and sore, but I made it. I climb to the tops. The wind rushes by and cools the sweat on my face. I cannot believe I made this drag, she is high-balling it down the tracks so fast. I am shaking all over. My hands tremble like a leaf. My heart pounds against my ribs ... If you make it, you are lucky. If you don't make it, well what the hell? What difference does it make if a stiff is dead? ... But just the same I am glad I am here on the tops and not smashed all to hell underneath those wheels that sing beneath me." (Tom Kromer.)

Those testimonies span about thirty years of hoboing, from the 1900s to the 1930s. In this period, and indeed before and since, when a stiff was not riding a drag or in an upcountry work camp or house car, his alternatives were a jungle or skid row.

A jungle can be any hollow or windbreak, only intermittently occupied, where a fire may be lit in comparative security and relaxation, much as every frontiersman has done on the trail. But on the main hobo routes, and outside any big rail junction or work center, the jungle is quite a complex unit of society. It can be, as Benson writes, a "small one-tomato-can affair with a lone hobo, perhaps two, boiling java" right up to "those of California and the North-West, where one jungle was a mile long." At Dunsmuir, California, there was a fire and a group of hobos under almost every tree – it looked "like an Army camp." A huge one at Jacksonville was Camp Busted.

The jungle's siting is based on exactly similar factors which decide the siting of any human community: access to water, food, fuel and transportation. So the jungle is usually abutting on a river or a railhead water tower or perhaps on the edge of a city rubbish dump, which provides useful pickings. The site has to be dry enough for sleeping out on the ground, sheltered from winds and for preference coolly shaded from the midday sun. There must be water for cooking and washing, and kindling for the fire. It must be convenient to the track so that new arrivals can find it after dark and so that an eye can be kept on the making up of freights in a division point yard, where locomotives and crews are changed after their hundred miles' shift, or stops made for taking on coal and water, and where the departing trains can be snagged before picking up high speed.

The jungle though must not be too near either depot or town, where it would be glaringly exposed to the company detectives and the local citizens. Of course the officials know the local hang-out of the hobos. If there is a tramp scare on, or if there has been boxcar pilfering or any other trouble for which the transients are rightly or wrongly blamed, the bulls and town clowns are hotfoot on the scene to arrest or beat up the lodgers of the moment, and, Hotchkiss manner, to tear down their shelters and riddle their cooking pots with bullet holes.

For this reason, and because all concerned are ephemeral, the jungle is a makeshift home. Its accommodation and furniture are extemporized out of any oddments and materials within snaffling distance. A boxcar door set on two piles of ties may serve as a table. If enough ties are to be had some low cabins may be built of them, three sides and a roof.

They are seldom so solid. A rag of tarpaulin, some cardboard cartons, orange boxes – anything wind- or rain-deflecting can be converted, and is. A billboard smartly snapped off after dark keeps the damp from the bones, and burlap sacks stuffed with straw make reasonable mattresses.

Similarly almost anything that can be is used as a receptacle or cooking utensil. The two central domestic articles are the wash pot in which men lousy from bad bunk huts and begrimed from long rides in coal trains can boil up their clothing, and the container for the mulligan, the stew which is kept perpetually replenished by contributions from all, hoppins, or vegetables, and gumps – meat of any description, butchers' scraps, bacon rinds, the occasional rustled chicken. All render down into a mess which may vary in savoriness but which is always hot. A fireman's broken shovel or discarded tie plates are substitute frying pans; meat is kebabbed on bent wire; potatoes are baked in the hot ash; tomato cans or sardine cans are plates for the stew.

It is all a bit like a seedy Boy Scout camp, a picnic that never packed up and went home. There is little that cannot be made over for use in the hobo jungle, the bag held out under the theory of conspicuous consumption, the public level at which built-in obsolescence is a boon. Here, in Anderson's words, "absolute democracy reigns." Few – outside the South – draw a color line and in this ground floor social gathering perhaps the American melting pot really does work, rather like the federative action of the mulligan pot upon its miscellaneous ingredients. Whites, Negroes, Mexicans, Indians and their combinations live and mix in mutual support. No credentials are required and no questions are asked about a man's past. The jungle is the communications center of tramps where practical information and tips are exchanged about the whereabouts of other hobos, about work possibilities, about wage rates, about changes in train schedules, about towns that have gone hostile and divisions where the crews are tolerant to free riders. All that is expected of a man is that he collects a share of sticks, washes up the utensils he has used, dries them and leaves them turned bottom up so that they will not rust with rain water, and pitches in to keep the camp clean. In return he gets a place at the fire and a share of what food there is, if he has not got his own lump with him.

Most old hobos, at all events those with literary airs, give the impression that talk around the jungle fire sparkles with philosophical epigrams and political wisdom, a conversazione of gipsy scholars, with late evenings of concerts and recitation. This gilding of the dandelion has been given another coating by such folklorists as Milburn, with his "hobo poesy and balladry," and the fancy that hobos are "imbued with the spirit of the medieval troubadours."

In truth hobo poesy – and one can judge only by that which has found publication in the subterranean hobo newspapers and broadsides – is puerile, although it almost always has a throb of genuine indignation or derision; but when composing for print the didactic tramp strains for an august and bookish style. This is missing from his songs, usually cynical, caustic parodies of the hymns forced upon him when left no choice but a mission's bleak charity.

A crowd of calloused men conditioned by enmity, molestation and harsh treatment into cunning, bitterness and violent retaliation, do not go in much for poesy. Theirs is not quite the jollity of Robert Burns's *The Jolly Beggars*;

> *See the smoking bowl before us,*
> *Mark our jovial ragged ring,*
> *Round and round take up the chorus,*
> *And in raptures let us sing.*

Sometimes lachrymose but oftener cockily proclaiming the hobo's status as the man of the open road and the big country, the womanless rover occasionally rueing his loneliness but also proud of his skill at staying whole and separate by means of wits and hands and feet, spikily conscious of his cowboy reputation and his wild, runagate legend – the hobo's songs are bawdy, tart and, when not slushily sentimental, as hard-hearted about themselves as about others. In *The Dying Hobo*, as his head falls back in the cold, bare boxcar after bidding his chum a tender farewell, in the last line, with utterly practical adjustment: *His pardner swiped his shirt and coat and hopped the eastbound train.*

The mood in which they are sung is usually enkindled by hooch of some kind, wine or whisky if it can be bought, otherwise derail or dehorn – alcohol ingeniously derived from some other source, such as that favored by "gas hounds" of the Sterno Club. Sterno, a heating liquid, has carried large numbers of hobos through the privations of fourteen years of national Prohibition and through many a dry state and county. The wood alcohol can, after a style, be separated from the paraffin by emptying the contents into a handkerchief and wringing it into a cup. Topped up with a Coke, soda pop or water, it is a short cut to drunkenness, a slightly longer one to brain damage and poisoning. With a squeeze of lemon and a drop of iodine added, it is known as smoke: the impact and the repercussions are similar.

The jungle also is the kindergarten for the road kid and the academy for all. Here are learned the techniques of survival and even enjoyment. There is, at the simplest stage, the two-times table of tramping: the shorthand code of symbols which the floater's eye picks up on a town's signboard or gatepost, the half-moons and triangles and interlinked circles and crossed lines that indicate in hieroglyphic detail the reception a hobo can expect and the potentials for working or bumming.

He learns how to use the hobo's *poste restante*, the division point or fueling-stop water tank, where everyone passing through by boxcar who wants to keep in touch with buddies dispersed elsewhere writes or carves up his name, destination and date. The water tank is to the hobo what the Rotary Club is to a traveling businessman, grapevine and life-line linking him with his particular brotherhood. (The one-time Hobo Fellowship Union of America called its branches "tanks".)

The water tank works like a bush telegraph and an answering service combined; even if a trailer is not himself trying to join up with a friend, he keeps a mental note of the latest monikers chalked up where he caught his freight, and can pass on the information in the next jungle he hits to men who have come in from other directions. One song collected by Milburn relates how a hobo leaves the Coast for Chicago and is ditched from the freight in "a burg the other side of Fargo." Naturally he goes down to the water tank to see who's around, and

> there were stiffs from every state
> From Frisco to New York,

among them Houston Bahney, Big Mike Devanney, Denver Flip and Baltimore Tip, Mush Fake Tom and Big Sim Long, Snow-bird and York Skew Hip, K. C. Jack and Mobile Mac, Spokane Slim and Biff 'n' Bim, Wingey Ed and young Chi Red, Porkey Tim, Poison Face Sim and Toledo Slim, and a highbrown boogie called Jap Tokey, old Shervoo and Kalamazoo, and a kid called Hokey Pokey, Wino Bill and Burly Hil, Printer Ted and Painter Red, Pete Shellaber and Dick the Stabber and a bo called Winne-peg Ed. And others.

He must have felt at home.

With the fall and the end of open air summer work some hobos decide to cross the Rockies, over The Hump, into the Californian sunshine. Others, like Florida-bound vacationers, scoot South – but not many for the vagrant is given few inches of toleration below the Mason-Dixon line, where rigidity of class, color and station in life has always been closely observed, and the hobo's winter quarters down there are likely to be on the county farm or in a road-maintenance chain gang, in the turpentine swamps or down the coal mines.

Hence the hobo is likelier to head for a Northern city, to blue his wad on real drink and real food, to sleep again in a bed for a short break, and to cast around for the next job. His center is the main stem. The Bowery in New York, West Madison Street in Chicago, Pratt Street in Baltimore, Twelfth Street in Kansas City, South Main Street in Los Angeles, Third Street in San Francisco, Scollay Square in Boston – wherever it happens to be it has the same rancid smell and the same sleazy carousel air, and it makes little difference. They are all skid row, the honkytonk farrow of Seattle's old Skid Road, where in the early days the Yesler Company's log-slide came down the hill, through the town and to the waterfront. Oxen hauled the timber across pole "skids," and it was there, on the original skid road, that there congregated the boardwalk bars, dance-halls, brothels, employment agencies and cubicle hotels for the itinerant foresters, miners and railroaders.

In any skid row there is the "slave market," the rows of commission shops where chalked notices advertise out-of-town jobs for unskilled labor – "free transportation, bunkhouse provided" – the clearing houses for the nation's unorganized manpower. The "sharks" who collect high fees, the saloon keepers with job lists who charge a percentage of the first pay packet as commission, and the public labor exchanges – all, although responding to the economy's peculiar demands, stimulate the casualization of labor.

All operate on a three-scale assumption: those at work on a job, those quitting, those filtering in as replacements, for there is no expectation that many of the men will be "long-stake" candidates. A random list of fifteen men taken from the Chicago Federal Labor Exchange for less than six months in the Twenties shows that the fewest number of jobs worked by any of them in that period was ten, that one had twenty-one jobs, two twenty and most of the others nearly that number.

Says Lescohier: "The casual . . . has acquired a standard or scale of work and life that makes it almost impossible for him to restore himself to steady employment. He lacks the desire, the will power, self-control, ambition and habits of industry which are essential to it."

Those habits, however, have never been cultivated in the migratory worker. He has been given a role and he has fostered his own beau idéal, the properties that give a certain mien as well as logic to a person who has had to break off diplomatic relations with polite, pensionable society.

So the hobo who has hit town strolls the main stem, his Piccadilly or Fifth Avenue of rooming houses and burlesques; tattoo-booths and cinemas that advertise "Stay as long as you like" trading on an audience which knows it cannot find warmth and shelter, and even some entertainment, so cheaply anywhere else; the second-hand clothes shops and the missions; the barbers' schools and the liquor stores; the barrelhouse saloons and the whorehouses.

The food in the myriad of never-close eating joints, chop sueys and chili parlors is not exactly Escoffier, but it is better than he has been getting in the jungles or in the sawmill chuck-wagon. At least he can choose between liver and onions, hamburger with Spanish sauce, baked macaroni, kidney stew, pigs' snouts and kraut, pigs' brains, ham shank and cabbage, and eggs in a dozen disguises.

He window shops: casting a judicious eye across the gaudy posters and the blackboard postscripts of the latest shipments, and listening to the "man-catcher" touts who stroll the sidewalks soliciting thousand-mile tickets, keeping up the volume of 250,000 homeless nomads who passed through Chicago's employment agencies alone in one year in the Twenties.

Chicago was at this time (and still qualifies) the down-and-outs' capital, the center of hobohemia, the temporary port of vagabonds and fugitives and hands for hire, the driftwood – the moochers, stewbums and dingbats – as well as the job-hunters and the working stiffs. West Madison Street is the slave market area, Clark Street is the Rialto of the slum – In Zorbaugh's description the "Zone of instability and change – the tidelands of city life ... an all-night street which harbors the criminal, the radical, the bohemian, the migratory worker, the immigrant, the unsuccessful, the queer and the unadjusted."

This dumping ground, with accelerated change, has prolonged in Chicago the atmosphere of the frontier town it had so recently been. This leads to an atomization of social relationships, the swill of the shipwrecked and unadjusted through their half-life, their world apart: that quality of the adventitious that they seek yet which makes despair and detachment easier, but which also gives the life its element of chance and adventure, and stimulates behavior that is like "the attraction of the flame for the moth, a sort of tropism."

This is the scene that meets Chaplin's eyes when he hits Chicago's slave market in the slump of 1914: " ... the streets swarming with migratory workers resting up between jobs or ready to ship out – loggers, gandy dancers, lake seamen, harvest hands ... 'barrel-house stiffs' and human derelicts ... 'No Shipments' signs. Every freight train that reached Chicago dumped jobless odd-job workers on the already crowded 'skid road.' The huge immigrant population of the foreign sections and the 'ghetto' slopped over into the industrial and downtown districts ... Unemployed men and women were begging shelter at the police stations or sleeping on park benches. The police were busy with their clubs driving what the newspapers called 'wharf rats' from lumber and freight yards along the river front ... Hunger riots ... in Halstead Street, plain-clothesmen charged with upraised 'billies,' smashing right and left through the crowd."

Tired Tim, Weary Willie, Happy Hooligan, the moss-grown bridges and sunlit water, and the chats with Rip Van Winkles at roadside inns enjoyed by the happy Order of the Walkers – deceptive though appearances are, they and Chicago's skid row are one and the same.

15: THE WAND'RING BOYS

It's the railroad for my pillow,
This jungle for my happy home

Brother Son Bonds: *Old Bachelor Blues*

BARILAN SA PUGAO LANIN is on at the Linda Lea Cinema, "Home of Filipino and Japanese Films." The jukebox music blaring out of the bars is Latin-American. The strippers in the photographs outside the Girly-Go-Round Follies Theatre are racially unidentifiable but unarguably girls. The food is everything, from shrimp chili and Roger's Gigantic Submarine Sandwich to the pungent Mexican reek from El Progresso and the Lopez Café. The pawnbrokers – "Money To Loan on Everything," "WE LOAN THE MOST" – also cater for all.

So does the Union Rescue Mission, standing aggressively white-washed among the sleazy clutter of South Main Street, Los Angeles's skid row, a few blocks out of the financial district and the Civic Center. About 850 transients a week float into the Mission for food, bed and the obligatory religious service, from as far as the East coast, and there are still, says the superintendent, a few like the sixteen-year-old who just hitch-hiked in from Tennessee to crash Hollywood and star in the movies.

Samuel Taylor has no such ambition. He is twenty-five, and plump, and a rolypoly jollity is thinly spread over a sulphurous contempt. He arrived three weeks ago after a month picking plums in the San Joaquin Valley, where he happened to be dropped off flat broke from a lift. Since then he has been "on vacation."

"I wanted to be a hobo and that's what I am. I don't panhandle: I work, when I have to. I've been a bellhop in Columbus, Ohio, I've hauled lumber in Chicago, I've been a barman in Amarillo, Texas; I've taken jobs as a plumber, electrician and carpenter. Actually, I'm a communications engineer. I was six months in Alaska with Operation White Alice, and I worked in Cape Canaveral on tracking equipment, and in New Orleans for a missile plant. I'm a tramp but I work my way.

172

"I was born in the Philippine Islands of American parents. I don't know who they were – as far as I know they were killed. I was in a Japanese prisoner-of-war camp. We were taken over by the Marines and evacuated. I was in Boys' Town in Nebraska until I was eight, and then raised by a Mormon family in Salt Lake City. What were they like, my foster parents? Oh, they thought I was God. Yes, every time I went in it was 'God, you're ugly!' or 'God, you're stupid!'

"I kept running off. At fourteen I got a lift out here to Los Angeles, and was working for a hot dog stall when the cops grabbed me and sent me back. Three months later I hopped a freight train for Augusta, Georgia, and was put in the cooler. Next time I set off for New York and got as far as Dayton, Ohio, before I was picked up. I was sent to a house of detention. But every time I was returned to Salt Lake City. Once I'd finished school I got out for good.

"I always go by road now. I have an air bag and a brown suit and a pair of Pan-American wings I pin on. That gives a vague impression of being a serviceman and motorists come across with lifts. My story's always the same: my father's dying in Michigan or wherever I'm heading. Beautiful!

"I have no friends and don't want any. I don't want people to depend on me and I don't want to depend on anyone else. Everyone I've ever tried to have a close relationship with has either hurt me or I've hurt them. My emotional problem is that I can't stay put. I get bored, restless.

"Of course I regard myself as a failure. I must be, mustn't I? I don't owe the bank 3,000 dollars for a car and I'm not killing myself to meet 300 dollars a month repayments on a house so naturally I'm a failure. Beautiful!

"When I was eighteen I made up my mind never to put down roots, to spend the rest of my life just traveling around. Well, that won't take too long. In the next five years the world will destroy itself anyway, so I might just as well see it while I can. Sooner or later someone's going to push the button. Until then I live from day to day. Name anything better."

IN 1877 the pastor of Plainfield, New Jersey, the Reverend Robert Lowry, already a successful producer of hit hymns (*I Need Thee Every Hour*, with Annie S. Hawks, and *Something for Jesus*, with the Reverend Sylvanus D. Phelps) wrote both the words and the music of a song that impaled America.

It was entitled *Where Is My Wand'ring Boy Tonight?* and dealt with a prodigal son not yet repentant and returned, but which was wistfully hopeful that rectitude and temperance would prevail in his absent heart. The song was eventually enshrined as the climax of Denman Thompson's *The Old Homestead*. This was a Victorian sobbie, first staged in 1896, which became a perennial repertory piece of the touring river-boat and tent-show troupes, along with other dependable box-office melodramas such as *Uncle Tom's Cabin*, *Ten Nights In A Bar Room* and Lottie Blair Parker's *Way Down East*.

The Old Homestead has been crowned "the world's hokiest play," and Denman Thompson made a career from the part of Josh Whitcomb – twenty years without interruption. In 1908 when "mellers" had given ground to dollar-top farce and comedy, *The Old Homestead* was being promoted with the assurance "not a thing in the play has been changed or brought up to date," which indicates that, however straight the cast still treated it, an element of sardonic irreverence had entered the audience attitude.

Even so the reason for the imperishability of both the play and its crescendo song is because both, however hammed up, had a genuine poignant reality for a huge number of families in America, where this plaint of a mother whose son has gone into oblivion has had much greater application than the sinister ballads and nursery jingles about kidnapping gipsies ever had in Britain.

From the start the pop song about far-away hearths and nostalgic day-mooning about the old folks at home has been central to American music, going back as far as William Billings, the Colonial psalm-singer, to the touring musical families and parties, and to the minstrel shows.

Always homelessness and distance have most quickly and

sharply touched American emotions. *My Lodging Is On the Cold Ground* in 1775 was one of the first indigenous American popular songs. The lyrics of *Home, Sweet Home* were set by John Howard Payne, a New Yorker, to a Sicilian air, and later he wrote it into the libretto for the opera *Clari*. "It is the song of my native village," exclaims the heroine, "the hymn of the lowly heart, which dwells on every lip there and like a spell word brings back to its home the affection which e'er has been betrayed to wander from it. It is the first word heard by infancy in its cradle; and our cottagers, blending it with all their earliest and tenderest recollections, never cease to live." Not too easily understood, but the general message got through. Not only did *Home, Sweet Home* become the most famous of pre-Civil War sentimental ballads, but its title entered the language as a phrase guaranteed to prick an eye with tears.

Whar Did You Cum From?, *Poor Wayfaring Stranger*, *Railroad Chorus* (*Singing through the mountains, buzzing o'er the vale, Bless me, this is pleasure, a-riding on a rail*), *Lament of the Irish Emigrant*, *My Old Kentucky Home*, *Do They Miss Me at Home?*, *The Arkansas Traveler*, *Dixie*, *Maryland my Maryland*, *My Southern Home*, *California Gold*, *Carry Me Back To Old Virginny*, *Traveling Back to Alabam'*, *Way Up Yonder*, *There's A Mother Waiting For you at Home Sweet Home*, *My Dad's The Engineer*, *You're Going Far Away, Lad*, *On the Banks of the Wabash, Far Away*, *Way Down in Old Indiana*, *In Dear Old Illinois*, *Put Me Off At Buffalo*, *My Old New Hampshire Home*, *Mid The Green Fields of Virginia*, and *I'm the Ghost of the Troupe That Was Stranded in Peoria* – all these, and scores more, comic and tragic, but all about somewhere distant or a sad parting, came out between the mid 1800s and the early 1900s.

It was *Where Is My Wand'ring Boy Tonight?* that jabbed the nerve most tellingly: which, as pop songs often do, stated a commonplace truth at precisely the emotional pitch at which it is felt by us all.

Mothers really did put lights in windows. Chaplin recalls his mother at the organ – "I don't know any fine songs," she apologizes, "only the kind sung by farmers' wives," and renders

Where Is My Wand'ring Boy Tonight? to the hushed family circle. One day when Chaplin and a young friend returned late from the wild country, where they had caught sunfish and roasted in wet clay a guinea hen, killed Indian-fashion with a slingshot, there is a light in the window. "I lit the lamp and left it for welcome," his mother says, "I'll keep a light in the window for you always. You'll remember that, won't you?"

Tully, once knocking at a door for food, is told grievingly by the housewife, "I don't understand why boys knock about so": her own son went off in a freight train.

The motto of the period, worked in colored wools and printed in gold, and which hung framed in saloons, and also in brothels where sentiment did not impinge upon trade, was "There's No Place Like Home" – if only, as the last resort, Robert Frost's definition: "the place where, when you have to go there, they have to take you in."

Where Is My Wand'ring Boy Tonight? was a song that became specifically identified with the hobo, and who himself identified with it, and which was sung, with varying degrees of seriousness and sobriety, at jungle soirées:

> Oh, where is my wand'ring boy tonight,
> The joy of his mother's pride?
> He's treading the ties with his bed on his back,
> Or else he's bumming a ride . . .
> He's on the head-end of an overland train,
> That's where your boy is tonight.

The authentic sorrow the song reflected may be gauged, but only roughly, by the dubious statistics given by "A No. 1" in his luridly moral *The Curse of Tramp Life* that "annually 350,000 boys run away from home, 35,000 become confirmed tramps, 7,000 are crippled by accidents, and 3,000 killed by the cars and through exposure."

Although it is unwise to trust those figures, at the peaks of the big railroad movements this was a murky social problem which little was done to tackle. The floater was hard to trace and there was next to no liaison between one police force and another, and there is no evidence that local records were kept

176

of boys who upped and went down the track, away from their homes probably for ever.

Yet that there was this social spur, a kind of initiation into manhood ceremony, exerting itself upon the young rural American of the late 1800s and onward – those steel blades cutting through the skyline beyond the Mid-West corn strip or Southern cotton field – is clear from a body of literature either of that time or reminiscence written later.

It can also be glimpsed in pulp magazines of the hobo flood tides. *The Detective Story Magazine* and *The Western Story Magazine*, to be found in the racks of skid row news stands and in radical book stores along with Jack London, *The Industrial Standard*, *The Hobo News* and *The Masses*, carried "Missing" columns, trysting places for those who had disappeared without trace.

Messages of the Twenties from these columns read: "Zookie, Agnes. Still love you, Roaming around the country, making no headway without you. Write to A. G., Klavicord, Denborough, New Mexico."; "Reese, Harry S. Your mother is very sick. Please communicate with her at once. I will not interfere with your plans. Daddy"; "S. L. No word from you since June 1914. I am heartbroken. Please write to Mother."

In December 1922 *The Hobo News* printed a letter which somehow is more eloquent than it intends to be about the deserted woman in these shifting sands of migrant industry. The letter was from Mrs. Nellie Miles, of 1412 First Avenue, Dallas, appealing for news of Walter, her former husband. "He was a knight of the open road," wrote Mrs. Miles, "and I am sure he has cooked 'mulligan' for some of you in some of the camps of the West. Won't you help me find him? His little daughter, Katie Lorene, asks me every few days, 'Mother, where is Daddy and why don't he come back?' and she prays at night, 'God, please send my daddy back to Mother and me – we love him and we need him so.'" The Editor's note was: "We gladly print this appeal and hope the boys will do their best to trace the missing brother."

This theme has not lost its meaning, both somber and comic, in present-day America. Last year, 1966, *Time* Magazine reported a double teenage murder in Tucson, Arizona, and commented that missing girls did not exactly galvanize the city police because in this "boom town with an unusually high proportion of transient residents, more than fifty runaway minors are reported each month." Most, it was stated, vanished from the drive-ins and juke joints along the East Speedway Boulevard: "Propelled by the same aimless itch, unrestrained by permissive parents, hundreds of teenagers haunt the Speedway." At about the same time in *The Saturday Review* there appeared a cartoon depicting a mink-clad mother, executive father in background, imploring a Beatle-haired guitar-playing youth, who is serenading a girl in dark glasses outside a Greenwich Village espresso: "Son, dear son, come back to Scarsdale with us!"

The implicit facts that make that funny are horrifying. As recently as the Thirties packs of feral youth roamed America's roads and rights-of-way. They attracted much worried discussion in educational and sociological journals, but little action out there in the no-man's-land they had entered.

There were publications such as Sullenger's, which lists as one of the five reasons for boys leaving home "the desire to escape school difficulties," and Armstrong's which estimated that school conflicts accounted for about sixteen per cent of the runaway cases before the New York Juvenile Court. Such were the surface euphemisms, for, as Minehan pointed up in an article in *The Clearing House* in November 1936, the "difficulties" and "conflicts" which were being escaped were simply that many were "economically unable to attend school." It was the Depression which had "brought out in stark relief the plight of many of these youngsters who often lacked shoes or clothing to attend school, to say nothing of the money to purchase textbooks."

There seems no cause to believe that most of the juvenile hobos, caught up in "the wave of youth-wandering which swept the country" – as Outland describes it – were sub-standard unteachables. In an article in *School and Society* in October 1934 Outland published some conclusions drawn from interviews with 5,000 transient boys between fifteen and twenty who had registered with the Federal Transient Service in Los Angeles between December 1933 and July 1934. There he wrote: "The statement has frequently been made that all transient boys included are 'bums' and 'hoboes', and the Federal Government has been often condemned for attempting to care for them ... Whereas there are a few transients who might properly fall in one of the above listed undesirable categories, the great majority of them are individuals who have lost their jobs on account of economic difficulties over which they had no control, and who are extremely anxious to rehabilitate themselves.

"Especially is this true of the army of minor transients ... How eager they are to find work and to help the folks back home ... The general average of 4,970 boys was found to be 9·09, or slightly better than a ninth grade education. This figure might be quoted to those individuals who insist on calling our transient youths 'young bums' and 'wild boys of the road.' It might prove to be that the average education of these 'bums' would be better than that of the persons making such statements!"

Three years later in another article discussing school dropouts Outland gives examples of "boys, evidently average or above in scholastic attainment, dropping out of high school, and eventually drifting onto the freight train." But he found "most of the boys did not go onto the road until being out of school for several months, and, in most cases, a year or more" – that is, when the icy truth was undeniable: that there was no work for him around there.

In a May 1933 article in *Scribner's Magazine* Lowell Ames Norris, in "America's Homeless Army," wrote: "The traditional hobo is not to be found in these ranks of starving youth. The majority come from substantial American homes. A goodly number are college trained, an even higher percentage are high school graduates, and most of the others have had an eighth-grade schooling."

The ordinary, uncomplicated fact was that the young boy shuttling about, as if before gusts, on the trains of this time was either in flight from actual starvation or had taken a Captain Scott decision to relieve the pressure on a family in extremity by removing one stomach.

Los Angeles alone in 1932 gave asylum to more than 200,000

adolescents in its free flophouses and midnight missions. Two-thirds said they had left home for economic reasons – "one less mouth to feed" – and only one-seventh admitted to a pre-dicative wanderlust. More detailed examination reveals that over thirty-five per cent of the families represented were on relief at the time the boy left home; over fifty-five per cent came from homes broken by death, divorce or separation – and, of course, it can be only speculation as to how frequently those two last categories themselves were due to economic stress.

It is significant that in the late Thirties there could still be debate about whether a young man became a runaway because of "wanderlust," and "inner urge" or not. Anderson was then reporting "a trend" toward explaining transiency in terms of social or economic duress upon the individual. There should not be overlooked the diagnosis of Dr. Robert C. Van Riggle, a psy-chiatrist working with the Florida Transient Service, who in 1935 explained the myriads on the road as the result of "a deep inner need to escape from a known condition into an unknown condition, to remove the old and discover the new, to break restraining bonds and find freedom, to renounce the too obvious 'real' for the more glitteringly 'unreal.' Stability in life has al-ways meant sacrifice." Doubtless all Dr. Van Riggle's elaborate deductions could be found occurring as rationalizations, means of making the best case out to oneself, but the "real" was mass unemployment and hunger, and the flight – the futile flight – was from these. "Wanderlust" – the medical mysteries of dromo-mania and drapetomania – offered a more comfortable vagueness to the burgher than the realities of starvation and despair.

Out of the 466 youngsters Minehan talked to, twenty-eight of them said just that they "liked to travel"; 387 gave their reasons as "hard times." At least in these young people the rea-sons were still raw. In the older man the stages become intricately layered. Sutherland and Locke worked out from their talks with homeless transients in Chicago's public shelters during 1934 and 1935 that they had hit that depth in the course of "roads to dependency," a series of related experiences, sexual and marital problems, illness, alcoholism and economic transitions. Many chronically wavered back and forth across the "line of depend-ency."

The point was did Americans have to start out on those roads at quite such an early age?

"America's wandering youths are back home again," ran an Associated Press despatch in May 1937 with excessive cheeriness. To be sure Outland did in that year find "indications ... that the great wave of youth transiency which swept over America during the years 1931-1936 is abating somewhat, but signs also point to a continuation of the high degree of mobility among the American people as a whole."

Although there had during that decade been sporadic flutters of disquiet about the horde of young Americans snapped loose from their moorings, that Associated Press story, filing away the bothersome business as tidied up and done with, is symptomatic. The handful of social workers and bodies attempting first aid treatment were up against encrusted dogma. When, in 1936, a recreational program was launched in the Boys' Welfare Department camps and lodges in Southern California, the leaders were astonished and not a little piqued that the young hobos responded with "listlessness and indifference" to group games. "They don't know how to play," was the way this resentment at such un-American non-activity was expressed.* Outland remarks: "When an adolescent has been kicked from one town to another, and has been jailed and beaten for no reason other than trying to get a job, or to obtain something to eat, baseball and scouting must of necessity take a back seat."

Even then, when the Wall Street volcano of 1929 was still spraying human slag across the landscape, there were those who saw boon in the desperate wanderings of young America. "Wishing to apologize for the present mess and justify the ways of mammon to man," writes Minehan, "they assert that the boys are learning independence, self-reliance and the whole gamut of ancient virtues which made this country what it is today. One social worker executive has asserted that they are carrying on the glorious tradition of American life and extending the frontier. Another relief official has asserted that road life may be good for a lad. It toughens him."

(In a similar spirit of hearty pragmatism did Wilbert L. Hind-

* See page 394 for modern equivalent.

man, Los Angeles Welfare Planning Council chairman, a quarter of a century later speak up for skid row. "Skid Row is a very healthy institution," declared Mr. Hindman. "It has sprung up spontaneously to meet the demands of the homeless ones – the men who have resigned from society. It is not something that was dreamed up by a group of arm-chair planners without any real notions of the needs. It has resisted change for more than a century. It is meeting certain needs and meeting them well.")

Throughout the Thirties at scattered points there were a few anxious, determined people trying to mitigate the affliction, but it is notable that as late as summer 1935, when Outland published some of his findings in *Sociology and Social Research*, there was still a fumbling around to chart the origins and motives of the juvenile vagrants.

Outland had found in his examination of 100,000 cases in Los Angeles during 1934 that every state in the union was logged, Texas top with the "astounding total" of 1,051 boys, or more than ten per cent, and with Delaware and Vermont – nine and ten boys respectively – bottom. Territories and overseas countries also contributed to California's intake of young hobos – there were boys from Alaska, Hawaii, Puerto Rico, the Philippines, Brazil, Canada, China, England, Ireland, Italy and, of course, Mexico. Most of these boys could yet be rehabilitated, Outland insisted, for many making their first road trip had not "acquired that cynical outlook which frequently characterizes the experienced old transient. The immature young wanderer still believes in his home and his country, and his religion, and he is trying desperately hard to maintain this faith."

(Those Minehan talked to had stopped trying: "Casual association with the child tramps indicates that they have no more religious life than a healthy young colt ... But if religion is a search for values the boys are religious. There is in their lives a vague quest for something beyond the present, a hope of union with the beautiful and the good, with the purpose and cause of life.")

Outland warned: "Mix him for a prolonged period with the old 'regular' and this faith commences to wane ... The next step will be the acquiring of one of two viewpoints of life; either one of bitterness and cynicism, or one of dullness and apathy. Either is bad for the boy, and a danger to our social order.

"Neither philosophy is so apt to be acquired if the young transient is maintained apart from the older man . . . The warped social outlook which frequently results when transient boys and men are mingled over a long period is often accompanied by definite physical dangers. Sex perversion is the worst of these, with cases frequently found where a boy has been bought, or forced, or led into degeneracy."

16 : ROOSEVELT ROOSTS

*What chance have I got? Less chance than a man
with two wooden legs in a forest fire.*

American teenager of the Thirties

IN April 1933 the Civilian Conservation Corps of the New
Deal began operating. Its purpose was to round up the discarded children into work camps. Promptly nicknamed "Roosevelt Roosts," their occupants wore a green uniform and each
youth received a monthly wage of thirty dollars, part as family
allotment. Peak enrolment was in autumn 1935 when the CCC
had half a million members, including 50,000 Negroes.

Of the 2,750,000 recruits who passed through CCC camps
up to 1942 the great majority were in their teens. Wecter, while
conceding that the "Depression's full toll upon susceptible youth
was hard to assess because in large measure it resembled a pay-
ment deferred," believes that its sum would have been greater
but for the creation of the CCC, "to keep idle youngsters from
riding the rods, living off soup kitchens and sleeping in hobo
jungles."

Yet although the figures are impressive, and it cannot be
doubted that the CCC did check many from slithering irrevoc-
ably down into destitution, its catchment area was midget. First,
the age of eligibility was eighteen, and the entrant had to have
dependents, a residence and a reference. This was a case of two
index fingers missing connection in the dark for, according to
Minehan, fully half of the boys and girls on the road in the
Thirties were under eighteen, many lacked traceable relatives,
the only reference they could offer was a police record, and they
had been drifting so long that they could claim no place of
residence – so the opinion was that the CCC did little effectively
to check the child exodus.

There was, too, collective unease about the militaristic tinge
of the camps. Perhaps some boys saw disagreeable similarities
to the uniformed, drilled, trainee Nazis of the German Youth

184

movement; perhaps it was erosion of patriotism by the privations undergone, the loss of faith Outland predicted. Minehan's findings among the more battered, ingrained road kids were that "of service to state, duty to nation, the boys knew nothing and are willing to render less." Objections to the CCC by the boy tramps he encountered were that "in the event of trouble the Corps would have to fight." In March 1933, he says, all rootless boys would have enlisted with enthusiasm but when the first fine glow subsided the Corps' lists began increasingly to be marked "deserter"; within three months the camps were being called "prison" by the renegades, within five months "Army chain gangs."

It was certainly mole-building with mudpies against the size of the torrent but there were other hands at work. The policy of the Federal Transient Service in almost every state was to return minors to their legal residence (if they still had one). If the fare money could not be raised from relatives, and the Service bureau in the "object" state decided that there was reasonable hope of reinstatement in the home town, the boy was provided with train ticket and meal money.

Ninety-nine per cent of the boys so despatched arrived back home and, it was claimed, eighty-two per cent had not become migrants again (although there is vagueness about the period over which this contentedly settled state was judged). Seventy per cent, stated a report, "had found the home town to be a pretty good place after all ... throughout the replies on the boys that were working there runs an optimistic note of gratification at renewed independence and security in the home community. Frequently this is coupled with the expressed desire on the part of the boys to remain at home and not take to the road again."

Presumably that was a reliable enough conclusion to draw if the truant could be found a job, but since most of the wanderers derived from stagnant regions, this could not invariably have been the happy outcome.

To be fair it is reported that some boys, upon landing back on a Service ticket, "have searched five months for something to do and the patience of some of them is nearly exhausted, and the thought of the open road is becoming more and more attractive."

How many children were abroad, dust in the wind, on the American continent in that period? Webb, in a 1935 Works Progress Administration monograph states with what might seem to be staggering complacency: "The emphasis on the number of boys on the road was a compound of sentiment and propaganda ... Judging from the number of transients who received care under the transient program, the number never exceeded one half million."

Oh, one half million: that's all right, then. Outland, with qualifications, supports the view that "all estimates made on the number of transients in the period from 1930 to 1933 were unusually high." However let that figure, put forward apparently with sober satisfaction, be accepted: one half million.

It may become more concrete and real if split up into smaller segments of experience. In 1932 a Chicago University research team reported for the Children's Bureau that there were probably 200,000 juvenile hobos then in movement on America's highways and railroads – and then apologetically adjusted their estimate to that appalling sum of half a million, all aimlessly wandering the face of the country, begging, stealing and often in thrall to adult exploiters. How strange is this quibble over precise figures, how strong the feeling received now that once packaged up in a report the problem was docketed and dealt with.

The majority of the wanderers were not city dead-end kids but farm boys for whom there was no space in the great field tracts of the United States. Woofter and Winston point out: "Coming of age in the farm depression of the 1930s involved unprecedented dilemmas ... Entry into agriculture has been growing more difficult, the Depression made entry into industry almost impossible, and during the period of contracting agriculture and stagnant industry there was an increase of more than 200,000 in the farm males of working age. On the threshold of productive life, at the age of readiest adaptation to work and to family and community life, youth of this generation faced an economy which, at least temporarily, did not need them."

Of course they had to find that out for themselves – by scouring the states for the phantom job, then just slouching on, phantoms themselves in the factory graveyard. The shocking truth about the youth of so many rootless migrants had already been cataloged in occasional departmental reports, but they stopped a long way short of general public awareness.

In 1932 McMillen took samples in South-Eastern and Western states. He found that there were 10,000 homeless transients being given shelter in Phoenix, Arizona, and 1,529 of them were under twenty-one; in El Paso 45,150, twenty-five per cent under twenty-one; in Oklahoma City 13,047, eighteen per cent under twenty-one; in Ogden, Utah, 919, eighteen per cent under twenty-one; and in Memphis, Tennessee, 10,870, twenty-seven per cent under twenty-one. In 1932 the Central Bureau for Transient Men in Washington DC recorded that twenty per cent of the men aided were under twenty-one, and added: "A small proportion inevitably will join the ranks of the permanent wanderers because of low mentality, lack of education and training, and unfortunate backgrounds. The majority however were those who are ready for the world, but find the world has no place for them."

One example of the rush to the railroads can be taken as reasonably typical: on the Missouri Pacific the number of freight car migrants (including repeaters) leaped from 13,000 in 1929 to nearly 200,000 in 1931 – and they, needless to say, were the ones observed. Railroad detectives in general agreed with social workers that most of this new generation of nomads were neither criminals nor voluntary vagrants, and but for the Depression would have been at work or in school.

This – not Scott Fitzgerald's jazz age whoopee crowd – was America's true Lost Generation. Minehan, when at the University of Minnesota, traveled in six states as a transient, collecting in boxcars, jungles and missions more than 500 case histories of homeless boys and girls. He began his study of the unemployed with the transients who had gone down with the "Big Bust" of 1929. It was as he hung around with the down-and-outs of the slave market employment offices and free meal counters that he noticed the bands of youths "too proud to be seen lingering in the sunlight with the old bums" who sneaked in "for a bowl of beans and a flop" after dark.

He realized – and this was only thirty-odd years ago, it should be noted – that "here was the possibility of a new, strange field of investigation." In other words for certainly forty years America had managed to relegate the problem of the exiled industrial worker to invisibility.

Minehan investigated this "new, strange" sociological field and became increasingly perturbed by the numbers of young. "As I left the mission district to live in hobo railroad yard camps or jungles and river shanty-towns, I found more and more youths and not a few girls. In the railroad yards I waited near a block signal where freights from Chicago and the South stopped.

"Mobs of men got off every train. Many were not youths, but boys, and some were girls – children, really – dressed in overalls or Army breeches and boys' coats or sweaters – looking, except for their dirt and rags, like a Girl Scout club on an outing.

"Where were their homes? Where were they going? How long had they been on the road? Why did they leave home? What did they expect to do in the future? I began to ask questions."

Minehan came back with his dossier. "They were boys and girls, flesh and blood youngsters who would be in high schools and home and were in boxcars and jungles. I had seen pictures of the Wild Children of revolution-racked Russia. I had read of the free youth of Germany after the world war. I knew that in every nation, following a plague, an invasion, or a revolution, children left without parents and homes became vagrants. Before my own experiences I had always believed that in America we managed things better. And yet in the face of economic disorganization and social change our own youth took to the highroad."

According to his researches, 387 out of 466 boys and girls stated that hard times had driven them away from home, flimsy and directionless as tufts or prairie tumbleweed. Even at this distance there is the unmistakable voice of the Thirties, of a people "hit by the economic whirlwind" in those snatches of biography.

"I lammed," "I skipped," "I hit the road," "I beat it" . . . the phrases constantly recur; they refer to "When the big trouble came." Texas, a youth whose front teeth have been kicked out by a cinder dick in Sante Fe, who has half an ear frozen off, who walks with an "odd irregular stiffness from too much sleeping in boxcars on zero nights and too much walking and too little food," tells Minehan that he has a broken hand from a fight with a Nashville shack wearing brass knuckles.

"I've been ducking cops and chain gangs all winter in the South," he says. "What now? Oh, anything. I can't get a job anywhere. I can't get in the CCC because I have no dependents. I can't remain in any state unless I go to a slave camp, and that's that.

"What chance have I got? Less chance than a man with two wooden legs in a forest fire. I've seen a lot of the country in the last year, and I'm glad I've seen it, but if a guy travels too much he becomes a bum, and I don't want to be a bum."

Jenny, a dumpy Hungarian girl from Pennsylvania, says: "My old man was crippled in the Lackawanna shops. I just sort of scrammed." Carl: "I don't care how I go as long as I'm going. Any place, I think, is going to be better than the last place, but it usually turns out to be worse."

Another boy hobo: "God is guts. What makes a guy keep pushing on, doing things when he's all in, walking when he's so tired he can sleep standing up, going without food when he's hungry? . . . If he loses his guts, he's all washed up." Another: "The big trouble came. I went up to Fort Worth where mother used to know a man who she thought maybe he could help me get a job, but he was as hard up as anybody else . . . Since then I just been traveling."

Here are two extracts from diaries of boy tramps, scrolls from that economic dead sea, which – perhaps uniquely – convey the day-to-day life, the fly agility of leaping from one life-saver opportunity to the other which pretty totally occupied the boy on the move.

One was kept by Blink from Pennsylvania who had lost an eye when a live cinder blew into it on a Santa Fe freight: "August 24, 1932. Fight with the old man. He can't boss me. Packed clothes and left. Got a ride on truck full of furniture going to Louisville. Two men driving. Good guys. Bought me my meals. Slept in truck. We stole some melons and apples from a farmer.

"August 27: Truck burned out bearing near Covington. Picked

ride to Cinci. August 30: Chicago. Picked ride with salesman. September 2: Momence. Slept in farmer's barn last night. September 6: St. Anne. Got pants from priest and ten cents. Slept in corn crib. September 7: Walked Paineau, hitting farmers on way. Plenty to eat.

"September 8: Woodland. Tough town. Marshal boots me soon as I hits the main drag. September 9: Walked part way from Cessna. Took freight Hooperton. Good town. Picked forty cents from doorsteps and swell meals. Stayed down in jungle near river with four other guys for four days.

"September 10: Slept in paper box. Rode freight Rossville. Small burg, but got dinner. Walked Bronson. September 11: Villa Grove, rode with truck. September 12: Shelbyville. Cop picked me up. Sent to jail. September 16: St. Elmo. Good. Twenty cents and new pair of socks. September 20: City. Slept under loading platform. Rain. Got wet. Hit woman for breakfast and dry shirt. September 22: Cop caught me with pocket full of apples. One hour to scram. Took freight. Going East St. Louis."

The other extract is from the diary of Simple Sam from New York. "April 6: Marshalltown, Iowa. Good. Made 85 cents hitting back doors and all I want to eat. April 7: Hit small towns today. Albion, Union, Gifford and Abbott. April 8: Slept Hampton back of station. Got hitch to Livermore. Tough bull. Hit guy for dime in front of barber shop. Three women sic dogs.

"April 9: Fort Dodge. Stem too tough. Ride to Algona in truck. April 12: Estherville. Hit country for chicken. April 14: Ride to St. James, Minnesota. Good town. April 15: Mankato. Swell town. Hit main drag thirty cents in half hour. Lady gave me nine pancakes, four eggs and 5 cups of coffee and two pieces of pie.

"April 16: Sleepy Eye. NG. April 17: New Ulm. Farmers want you to work. All I want to eat. Hit stem for meals, cinch. April 20: Hit small towns, Manchester, Hartland, New Richland. All little burgs. Slept in farmers' barns. April 25: Montgomery. NG. Women too tough. April 26: Jordan. Got breakfast 5c. April 27: Shakopee. NG. Tough cop. Can't hit the stem. Pick up truck to Mpls. Good town."

Why did they, why do they still, stop for little more than food, usually not even for sleep? Minehan begins his book as he is among a load of men and boys riding into a small division point town. "The freight jerks wheezily to a stop in the early autumn twilight. Southbound, the majority of the transients remain in the cars.

"Fifty or sixty, transferring for Chicago and points East, drop off, skirt the station, and head for the main stem . . . Two autos shoot out into the middle of the street, effectively blocking the first intersection.

"Five men alight, four carrying ominous looking pick-handles . . . The stout man without a club and with the cigar steps forward, flashes a sheriff's badge and speaks, 'You're under arrest, boys, come along . . . We aren't going to be tough on you unless you make us tough. But you can't panhandle this town, boys . . . How would you like a nice supper, a good warm bed, a nice breakfast and be out of here in time to catch the morning train?'

"Without great margin of choice, they troupe to jail. They get a slice of sour bread, tomatoes and one cold boiled potato, and a bare cell to sleep in. They talk : 'Why do they have to have jails?' 'Or sheriffs?' 'Or hard times?' 'Or bums?' 'God, I don't believe that anybody knows what it's all about.' 'We come and we go,' says an old man. 'Where the hell we come from and why and where the hell we're going nobody cares and nobody knows.' "

It is later at a limestone quarry near the jerkwater town where he has disembarked that Minehan meets his first group of road kids, five boys and two girls who have dropped off a Big Four freight.

One of the girls has black hair cut like a man's, face tanned as an Indian's, and is wearing overalls, an O.D. shirt open at the neck and heavy Army shoes. The other is a curly-haired blonde in riding breeches, cloth puttees, tennis shoes and a dirty sweat shirt. They are on the circuit.

The majority, says Minehan, then remained within five hundred miles of the place they once called home. Within a circle, after many experiments, they laid their route, moving from city to city, making the rounds of different relief stations, returning to ticked off shops and houses, panhandling the same towns, streets and lunchcarts.

They linger nowhere. "Relief policies force them to move ... It was in truth impossible for the transient boy or girl to stay anywhere. Relief authorities gave a meal – and an invitation to move on. No matter how tired, how willing to work, how weary and disgusted with the road and its aimless wandering, he had to take it.

"Police did not trouble transients so long as they kept moving. As soon as they attempted to halt, however, police acted. Jungles were raided, soup and bread lines searched for non-residents, mission lists combed.

"The child tramp was out again on the road ... Strange as it may seem, the boys walk as much or more than they ride. ... While hitting the stem and begging meals at back doors, he must walk. He must walk, too, from the yards to the relief stations – often several miles. In small towns, the freights usually stop at water towers or sidings some distance beyond the business section. To board a train, in many cities, the child tramp must walk several miles in or beyond the yards. When he drops from the freight, he must drop off some miles before it reaches town. Walk, walk, walk, the child tramp's existence seems, at times, to be a dreary march never ending ..."

City relief stations were as a rule then much more stringent toward youthful vagrants than toward older ones. Where an adult was given six meals and two nights' lodging, the boy tramp got one of each. (A girl tramp was sent to jail.) By forcing the youngsters out of town and onward, the relief men argued, they were forcing them back home. In reality, because few had homes, they were being forced into beggary and theft.

In a clumsy attempt to co-operate with the government policy to reduce vagrancy by establishing vagrancy camps – actually to corral vagrancy – the police became more hard-boiled.

In the early Depression years the child tramps hitch-hiked. As their numbers grew motorists' sympathy shriveled. Unable to travel in gangs by car the hitch-hiker on the highway "was alone among enemies," easily picked up by the police. So they transferred to the traditional American chariot for elsewhere, the open boxcar, moving about in groups to protect themselves

– but, as ever, never knowing (or rather being fairly sure) how a town would receive and treat them.

Some cities and railroad systems maintained the dualism of not permitting hobos to ride openly: if the hobo circumspectly sneaked on he could ride. In other places the railroad police insisted that no hobo should approach a train until it was in motion, so departing from their jurisdiction.

Minehan describes such a scene, several hundred men and boys lined up along the railroad fence. "A train is being made up a track or two away. The intervening space is patrolled by railroad police. 'Get back there, I tell you, get back,' shouts an officer, swinging a club, to a pair of boys nipping over the tracks. 'Don't let me catch a one of you putting a foot on railroad property until that train gets in motion.'

"The transients are silent. Boxcars buckle and bump. A brakie connects the last air hose. From a station near the caboose the conductor gives the highball. Imperceptibly the train moves as the fireman rings the bell.

"Like a group of race horses springing the barrier, or football players surging forward when the ball is snapped, the boys and girls surge en masse across the tracks. They alight and swarm all over the train as a cloud of locusts alight and swarm over an orchard. Some climb ladders to the roofs. Others pile in the gondolas. The majority choose boxcar doors."

It is clear that wanderlust had little to do with the vagrancy of the young, that it was basically poverty or a home broken by poverty that catapulted the child out on to the road. When the mission preacher "tries to account for unemployment as being the will of God, they do not believe him. Nor do they believe him when he relies upon stereotype sentimental pictures of home and mother to convince his congregation of a point.

"Five or ten years ago, the mission preacher could appeal to the wandering boy to return to his sorrowing mother and his ageing father. Today the wandering boy knows he will help his parents more by remaining away than by returning." The young boy tramp "has no background of sinful experience and dissipation to which the preacher may appeal as justification for his present need, none of his money was squandered upon harlots and riotous living. Unlike the older man, he knows little of gambling joints and houses of booze and sin. Nor of bonanza wages and foolish sprees. For him life has merely been progressively difficult as month after month, at home, he saw more worry lines on his mother's face, less bread on the table and increasing distress in the house."

The boy tramp soon learned to sing with anti-religious fervor with the lumberjacks and out-of-town bindle stiffs refused mission beds:

> I don't care if it rains or freezes
> I'll be safe in the arms of Jesus
> I can lose my shirt and britches
> He'll still love us sons-of-bitches
> Am I Jesus's little lamb?
> Yes, you goddam right I am.

Then, Minehan found, there was bitter political militancy among the young. Whereas the older transients remained impervious to Communism (" . . . a mental hold-over of war psychology, the anti-Red drives of Palmer, and a belief in the American success story, which will not let them accept the new doctrines"), he interpreted Communism as being seen to offer "school, hope and adventure" to the youth on the road.

"I'd rather be a Red than starving and dead," he quotes them as saying, using a phrase later subject to many an adaptation. Of patriotism "the boys appear to have not a shred. They do not have any more feeling of loyalty to America than they have to the South Pole" – a disaffiliation that has certainly held solid down to the present day among the kind of rubber tire tramp and train riders I talked to around the United States.

"Practically all boys and the girls on the road, whether Communists or not, believe America is going to have a revolution soon if things do not improve. They are vague as to who is going to lead it and how it is to be brought about, but almost all agree that trouble is imminent. 'We can't stand this forever.' 'Hell is going to pop some day now.' 'The workers could do it, but they won't. They're too damn dumb. You never saw a working stiff who wouldn't cut another working stiff's throat for a nickel.'"

The future? American cities might be "overrun with groups of hoodlums and depredators as London was in the eighteenth century and Paris in the seventeenth century, forcing the honest citizen to remain in his domicile after dark ... Today's child tramps will supply many recruits for the new army. Street beggars, hideous, deformed and depressing, may swarm our land and deface our cities and again many of them will be graduate child tramps."

That may be a somewhat empurpled prediction, yet Minehan's anger at the indifference, callousness, cruelty and stupid wastage he searchlit is understandable. "We prided ourselves upon the mobility of our labor," he says. "Economists told us that it was a source of natural wealth not unlike water power or mines. Labor traveled in day coaches, in flivvers, on work tickets, on its own money, but labor traveled.

"And in traveling labor dissipated much of its earnings, lost home-making habits and acquired the mental outlook of vagabondia. Today we are paying for the mobility of labor during the last decade, and we may continue to pay for years to come."

From having lived with these young people whom some social workers saw as "learning independence" and "carrying on the glorious tradition," he concluded that there is in it "little that is wholesome and nothing that is permanently good ... It is not encouraging to see the youth of our land spend their days in idleness and acquiring habits definitely anti-social."

The discrepancy in the above is of course that America, the cloudy Uncle Sam collective, did not "see" what was happening to its youth. Even in that time of extremity, of breakdown and bread lines, of the Fall from innocence in almost every individual's personal experience, the racial faith in self-help and self-sufficiency hung on blindly.

America has always been saved by the citizen's guilt. In no other nation in the world and in history has the ordinary taxpayer been so eager to acquit his government of criminal negligence, so unwilling to convict industrial barons of robbery with violence, of murder by evisceration. With the sacrificial alacrity of a fundamental Bolshevik, the beaten American has elected his own treason trial and confessed to the commission of failure and the omission of prosperity. He has continued to believe that he deserves all he gets, boom or slump. He has never lost the capacity for surprise at repeated revelations of corruption and perfidy in his own community or state. Essentially the Americans still sing in unison that newspaper editorial of a century ago: "It is a vice and a sin for a man to be poor," and the accusatory passion with which it is caroled by the rich is echoed by the abject passion of the disowned.

There is no other way of explaining what happened when in January 1939 (ten corrosive years after the Depression began) a group of evicted sharecropper families staged a silent protest by camping along Highway 60 in New Madrid County, Missouri, a tragic mardi gras of decrepit mattresses, bedsteads, rocking chairs and stoves. The published Farm Security Administration photograph (one of the great mural of the American disaster by such new wave photographers as Walker Evans, Dorothy Lange, Margaret Bourke-White, Ben Shahn and Carl Mydans) "caused nation-wide discussion."

The eye had blinked and momentarily widened with dismay before being again nervously averted; the community heart performed its ritual diastole and systole. The photograph was, it was stated, "very embarrassing to local residents" and one official cried indignantly: "The trouble with them is they was organized."

In the first flush of the Roosevelt administration, the Federal Emergency Relief Administration was permitted by law to allocate funds for the care of "resident, transient or homeless persons" – a whole-hog departure in American public welfare. During 1934 FTP was operating in about three hundred towns and cities, providing transients' shelters, known as Uncle Sam's Hotels, where food, lodging and some medical care was available. By October 1934 all the states in the Union except Vermont were participating, and hard-up wanderers were encouraged to seek work locally or were given tickets for return to base if they were willing to go.

It did not last. Why? Because, quite simply, says Anderson, "it was not popular mainly because migrants are not popular." As a palliative a work program was started and relief passed back to individual states, and in 1936 the Farm Security Administration began setting up its own hostels for migratory field workers to lift them out of the ditch bank and jungle camps. Again there is the weary jolt of amazement when one comes upon Harry L. Hopkins, administrator of FERA, writing in 1936: "To move into such a program meant to move into uncharted and hazardous territory. No one knew exactly how many transients there were. Little experience was available on methods of assisting them. Even advocates of their cause were confused whether transiency should be treated as an evil to be suppressed, or a necessary function of our economy to be rendered as painless as possible."

By now there was actually some debate; but the simon-pure tenet came up trumps: it was, when all was said and little done, an evil to be suppressed. Writes Hopkins: "Transient camps under WPA came to an end because of a strong conviction that their psychology was not consistent with the aims of a work program. The final victory for the transients is only won when, working side by side with the local man, he is known simply as a workman worthy of his hire."

This splendid, rigorous bibliolatry was undermined by a change in many state relief laws which excluded non-residents almost entirely, meaning that a workless migrant's name on project assignments was likely to be written in minuscule. In fact, Anderson's investigations show that "they cannot get on WPA unless they are first accepted for relief by the local public agencies. Cases of migrants who are assigned this are so rare as to be conspicuous."

To look at the statistics, these snippets from a time when concerted, businesslike and humanitarian action aborted out of misgivings or defeat, is to put one's head down into a mist of bewildered loss. It is like reading a guess-work estimate about stray dogs. The Bureau of Agricultural Economics reporting on 1930-1934 puts baffled emphasis on this point.

It announced that of 6,578,000 persons who *migrated to farms* (their italics) in that period fewer than two million were still on farms at the beginning of 1935. Of 7,176,000 persons who *migrated from farms* in that period, 2,593,000 had failed to return up to the beginning of 1935. There are more than seven million human beings unaccounted for in those tables – seven million unharbored people, dissolving away like ghosts into America's economic twilight. This is the common denominator of most attempts to make sense out of this ectoplasmic swirl of human population: an anxious perplexity merging into the unreality that the luckier, more stable, or even just the more unbudgeably loyalist Americans, felt toward the phenomenon. Anderson confirms that it was "owing to bewilderment" about the migratory problem that the research foundations in 1934 and 1935 financed a study supervised by Professor Carter Goodrich then of Columbia University.

What did this survey, *Migration and Economic Opportunity*, unearth? That "the study of migration led to some very profound queries about 'population redistribution,' an expression which carries the implications of control. But the contemplation of control raises equally profound queries about the possibilities and difficulties that would attend a controlled or 'managed' migration of people."

The matter was left in this quodlibetical form. Drop it, then, was the implicit outcome.

It may be seen that such a picture as Minehan's of young America was not one that had much likelihood of breaking through into public consciousness, which was being supplied with a somewhat cosmeticized version, the co-ed campus movies of the day or the Mickey Rooney suburban actings-out of *Saturday Evening Post* covers. Grim and outlandish in its truth about this invisible teenage America, nevertheless Minehan's economic equation never captures, or even admits as a factor, the accretion of ritual in the roving life of the young.

Even in the spreading climate of radical dissension of the early Thirties, Minehan does retain some of the older whimsy of the tramping syndrome. He notes the camp fire myth of "the child tramp who is a cross between Huckleberry Finn, the English Puck and the German *Eulenspiegel*. A mischievous lad, he is always playing tricks." But while in broad terms he accurately saw the wandering youth of that decade as scrapped people, destroyed by the "economic whirlwind," and warned that "hunger and cold and death ride the green light of every train the child tramp flips," his litmus paper seemed not to soak up the yearning that has always pulsed in the younger American – which may most often have been ignited into action by economic compulsion but which was none the less there, a hot spot in the imagination, a dare in the air.

17 : THE ABSSY,
THE CHARNEL-HOUSE

I inhale great draughts of space;
The east and the west are mine, and the north and
the south are mine.

Walt Whitman: *Song of the Open Road*

BREAKFAST is being served in the long narrow room in the Loop side street. This is Chicago's "slave market" district where small agencies display hand-printed cards and notices chalked on blackboards, and sign up shipments of homeless men and casual laborers for out-of-town construction jobs. Johnson Scott, like the rest of the men sitting on high stools along the bar, isn't planning to go anywhere at the moment.

These are the ones with a few cents to start the day with a shot of liquor or some beer. Some shout quarrelsomely, some slump broodingly, but all are detached in the windowless twilight from the city's business life roaring by where the sun blazes in the open doorway.

Johnson Scott is conspicuous among the ragged clothes, greasy mechanic's caps, whiskery chins and wrecked bodies, either gaunt or shambling. He is a lithe Negro of thirty-three from Birmingham, Alabama, clean shaven and quite spruce in a red button-down shirt. He is drinking a glass of straw-colored brew named Golden Port, the cheapest kick-administering drink in the house.

"I got out of the South in 1951," he says. "In a hurry you might say. There was this white girl in the store where I was working. One morning I hadn't felt in the mood to be nice to her and she put it around that I'd tried something with her, which I hadn't.

"It seemed healthy to get out of town. Another fellow told me about riding the trains, about how to get aboard and avoid the railroad dicks, how to check the marker on the side to see which state it was going to. Well, all I knew was that it was going North, a long way from out of Alabama, and in fact it landed me up in California.

"Since then I've been generally speaking on the move. I do jobs here and there. Picked cucumbers and oranges in California, worked in the shipyards at San Pedro until they started laying off, washed cars and things in Berkeley. As a matter of fact I *flew* up to Seattle and I *flew* from Denver here to Chicago – a few women helped out on this. But on average I ride the trains.

"You get to know the score. I always carry bread and a plastic jug of water, and a blanket because you can get aboard in ninety degrees and during the night go over the hump into mountain zero, and brown paper to pack my shoes. In winter you get a bucket half filled with sand and some kerosene oil and you can have some heat in the boxcar.

"I carry a knife, an open knife, too. It's important on those trains to travel with a buddy, not alone, because you can get killed by some of those guys. On a slow-traveling train at night if I've been alone I've kicked a guy off who was trying to jump on. But you daren't close the door behind you. No, you have to spike that door open. If it slides shut it may be ten days before they open it in the yards, and you can be dead.

"It's nice down in the jungles where the hobos camp near the freight yards; it's like one big happy family. Five or six guys go out different ways and put all they bring back into the pot. You eat, and you smoke, and you drink, and you talk: real companionable.

"I'd rather be in the jungle than these missions. They're *nerve-racking*. Monotonous. You hear the same old stuff every day. Blackmail. It really bores me.

"I don't head nowhere in particular. I just decide to get off a train at a stop to see what's doing in that town. You just bum along. I go down to the vegetable market – always something to pick up. And often other guys who've got a stake will help you. If I'm really busted and there's no work I stop someone in the street and tell him. They can always tell if you're telling the truth. When I feel a place getting under my skin I know it's time to be moving on.

"I don't see this ending. It's habit-forming. It's like trying to give up smoking. It takes a lot of will power to stop moving.

But I'm thinking seriously of going back to Birmingham. A Negro really can live better there now than up here in the North. You can walk down the street like a man. Chicago's the most prejudiced city I've known. It destroys your will power and self-confidence.

"I've started drinking since I've been here. Most days I raise enough to buy a bottle of whisky or wine, and I take it into the park ... You happen to have fifty cents?"

———————

IN *The Road* Jack London, the first American writer of stature to write about hobo life from the inside, describes how he was first drawn into it. His words have ever since skirled like the pied piper's whistle to thousands of American boys.

It was in the 1890s that he became hooked: "On the sandbar above the railroad bridge we fell in with a bunch of boys likewise in swimming. They talked differently from the fellows I had been used to herding with. It was a new vernacular. They were road kids, and with every word they uttered the lure of The Road laid hold of me more imperiously.

" 'When I was down in Alabam,' one kid would begin; or, another, 'Coming up on the C & A from KC'; whereat, a third kid. 'On the C & A there ain't no steps to the "blinds." ' And I would lie silently in the sand and listen.

" 'It was at a little town in Ohio on the Lake Shore and Michigan Southern,' a kid would start; and another, 'Ever ride the Cannonball on the Wabash?' and yet another, 'Nope, but I've been on the White Mail out of Chicago.' 'Talk about railroadin' – wait til you hit the Pennsylvania, four tracks, no water tanks, take water on the fly, that's goin' some.'

"A new world was calling to me in every word that was spoken – a world of rods and gunnels, blind baggages and 'side-door Pullmans,' 'bulls' and 'shacks,' 'floppin's' and 'chewin's,' 'pinches' and 'get-aways,' 'strong arms' and 'bindle-stiffs,' 'punks' and 'profesh.'

"And it all spelled Adventure. Very well; I would tackle this new world ... I was first a road-kid and then a profesh ... the profesh are the aristocracy of The Road. They are the lords and masters, the aggressive men, the primordial noblemen, the *blond-beasts* so beloved of Nietzsche."

Later in "What Life Means To Me" in *The Comrade*, a Socialist Party publication, in 1905, London stresses the hardship and horror of tramp life: "I became a tramp, begging my way from door to door, wandering over the United States and sweating bloody sweats in slums and prisons ... I was down in the cellar of society, down in the subterranean depths of misery about which it is neither nice nor proper to speak. I was in the pit, the abyss, the human cesspool, the shambles and charnel-house of our civilization. This is the part of the edifice of society that society chooses to ignore."

Abyss, cesspool, charnel-house withal, predominant in all London's stuff about his time on the road is a swagger, an exuberance, a coruscation of adventure. It is this Melvillean spirit – never fully realized, considers Feied, who believes there could have been a *Moby Dick* of the boxcars, given a writer of its author's genius "pursuing his elusive dream across the thousands of miles of heartland track, linking up with all the lost places at the terminus points of trunk lines, riding possum-belly across the Rockies, being ditched in Florida cane brakes or at the end of a logging line and then going home to write a symbolic epic of hobo existence" – which, *diminuendo*, has continued to beguile young Americans.

It is striking how often a similar start has been narrated by those putting their hobo years down on paper, how the railroads' hatchments branded themselves hotly on the imagination, much as did the navigational charts brand St. Exupery's: " ... the green and brown and yellow lands promised by the maps; the rosary of resounding names that make up the pilot's beads." Chaplin recalls: "There was always activity in the yards even when the gates were up. There were slow-moving, ever-puffing switch engines, the continuous bumper-together of uncoupled cars. There were block after block of 'empties' along the tracks with names of strange cities and far-off places." Tully's *Beggars of Life* has the classical opening: as a boy he loitered near the marshalling grounds of Van Wert County, Ohio. He "met hoboes there, who nonchalantly told me strange tales of far places." One day, near the trestle outside St. Mary's, he gets into conversation with a one-eyed youth on his way through from California who urges Tully to chuck in his factory job and take to the road.

"All you're doin' here's eatin'," he says. "You kin git that anywhere. A stray cat gits that. Besides, you're learnin' somethin' on the road. What the devil kin you learn here?"

Tully snags his first ride on a freight to Muncie, Indiana, and shelters from a snow-storm in a sand-shed where a flock of hobos are heating coffee on a stove and eating their "lumps." One says: "It takes a lotta guts for green kids to beat it on a day like this. I'd beat it back home if I was you till the bluebirds whistle in the spring."

But Tully cannot wait for the bluebirds' call because to him, as in the case of London, the talk of the ragged young rovers is more bewitching by far. "I came in over the Big Four today from Saint Louie. I wanta make it to Cincy an' beat it South." "It ain't bad in New Orleans. A guy kin allus git by there."

So Tully goes on, hoboing around Kentucky and Indiana, through to Chicago, and then out on a mail train to Omaha — the beginning of twenty years of jungles, jails and a thousand American towns passed through on manifests, in coke cars, through rain and frost spreadeagled flat on the top of passenger coaches. At length, Tully concludes: "Tramping in wild and windy places, without money, food or shelter, was better for me than supinely bowing to any conventional decree of fate. The road gave me one jewel beyond price, the leisure to read and dream ... voices calling in the night from far-away places ..."

The nimbus of glamor had not receded when Anderson was investigating the hobo more than twenty years later: "A visit to the 'jungles' reveals the extent to which the tramp is consciously and enthusiastically imitated. Around the camp fire watching the coffee pot boil or the 'mulligan' cook, the boys are often found mingling with the tramps and listening in on their stories of adventure. To boys the tramp is not a problem, but a human being and an interesting one at that.

"He has no cares nor burdens to hold him down. All he is

concerned with is to live and seek adventure, and in this he personifies the heroes in the stories the boys have read. Tramp life is an invitation to a career of varied experiences and adventures. All this is a promise and a challenge."

Anderson has his definition of wanderlust: " ... a longing for new experiences. Its expression in the form of tramping, 'making' the harvest field, roughing it, pioneering, is a social pattern of American life."

He cites two cases personally encountered: "S. who is nineteen years old has been a wanderer for nearly four years. He does not know why he travels except that he gets thrills out of it ... When he can outwit the 'bulls' he gets a 'kick' out of it. He would rather ride the passenger trains than the freights because he can 'get there' quicker, and then, they are watched closer. He likes to tell of making 'big jumps' on passenger trains as from the Coast to Chicago in five days, or from Chicago to Kansas City or Omaha in one day. He only works long enough in one place to get a 'grubstake,' or enough money to live on for a few days. He says that he knows that he would be better off if he would settle down at some steady job. He has tried it a few times but the monotony of it made him so restless that he had to leave.

"In the case of W., who left home at sixteen, he was the oldest of a family of five boys and three girls ... Most of his letters were boastful. He told of prospering and he moved from place to place often to show the other children at home that he could go and come as he pleased. He traveled in different parts of the country and from each part he would write painting his experiences in a rosy hue. He succeeded in stirring up unrest in the hearts of the other boys ... All five boys left home before they were sixteen. Only one returned home. The others roamed the country following migratory work. The father always blamed W. for leading the boys away ... He was the idol of the rest of the children and they left home to follow in his footsteps."

Long before the government began its feeble and half-hearted efforts to recapture those unknown divagating numbers there were many admonitions to young people. Often written by reformed hobos they exhorted the tempted to ignore the voices calling in the night.

In the early 1900s there was a considerable volume of subterranean news-stand literature, smudgy little booklets in wavery type printed by back street jobbing firms in Seattle or Oklahoma City or Butte, whose tone was that of Temperance holy horror but which in fact were an early version of lid-off journalism. Always here was an inverted glorification of the hobo's vocation or fate effected by "exposing" its vileness and degeneracy, much as the more stridently edifying Victorian tracts against loose-living could hardly have failed to stimulate the appetite of the normally lusty.

Typical of this idiom is Benson's *Hoboes of America* pamphlet in which he loudly warns boys – and "hoboettes" too – not to "satisfy your travel urge by beating your way" and he alerts them: "STOP, LOOK AND LISTEN! Among the millions or so of men and boys on the road every summer can be found parasites, defectives, imbeciles, jail-birds, perverts, morons and such of every description.

"But – your pride is apt to keep you at it – until it is too late, and you eventually become a chronic tramp or hobo. Wait until you can PAY your way – and travel like a man – with your head up – chest out and so you will enjoy travel life without the dangers and the risks I have truthfully enumerated."

He appends this somber poem:

> *The Road today has lost its charm –*
> *It's a road that's filled with pain!*
> *It's to be feared with real alarm,*
> *With misfortunes in its train!*
> *For a while – it may thrill you –*
> *And you'll follow it with a smile –*
> *But the end of the road may lead you to*
> *Untold regrets – at its "Last Mile."*

Even more bloodcurdling are the writings of Livingston (or "A No. 1," as he signed himself) and who claimed to have been on the road with Jack London. In 1910 appeared the first of his hobo paperbacks, *Adventures of "A No. 1,"* and this was followed a year later by *Hobo-Camp-Fire-Tales*, with the sub-heading (which must straight off have eliminated an entire potential jungle readership) STRICTLY MORAL NO STALE JOKES NO LOVE AFFAIRS. In 1912 he produced the most enthralling of all his works, a booklet with a rancid orange cover bearing the sketch of a gigantic locomotive hurtling down upon a tattered gadabout with a stick and bundle, and a famished looking vulture on an adjacent signpost marked DEATH. This sold for twenty-five cents, and was entitled *The Curse of Tramp Life* by "A No. 1, The King of the Hoboes, Who Traveled 500,000 Miles for Only $7.61."

The sixty-one cents must alone have been enough to prick the reader's curiosity to the extent of forking out twenty-five cents yet it is difficult to stifle one's disappointment upon finding inside a full-page photograph of a gentleman of ramrod respectability, looking rather like a retired cavalry colonel, with sensitive cow-lick hair-do and a brisk parade ground moustache.

"In presenting this, my third tramp story, to the public," begins the author of *The Curse of Tramp Life*, "I do so with the assurance that this book is absolutely suited to be read by the most delicate child as well as the most dainty lady, has not a single objectionable word or phrase written here. It tears to shreds the glamor thrown over his miserable existence by romancing writers. Primarily its object is to prove to boys and men of restless dispositions that by their heeding the 'Lure of the Wanderlust' they not only wreck their own futures but very often the lives and happiness of their parents."

In a further prefatory address, A No. 1 addresses the reader: "Will you please do your share to assist humanity at large and the railroad companies especially to solve the tramp problem by explaining to every boy you find at your door asking for a lunch what a fool he is, trying to lead all his days, the life I am attacking in this book, from my personal experience as a tramp. Can you not take the time and patience and do by him the same as you would pray some other person to do by your own son, brother or relative, should he run away from home, leaving behind him a broken hearted mother to mourn while waiting perchance for a return of that ever same wandering, wayward boy, who had knocked at your door? THE AUTHOR."

Yet more preamble. "TO EVERY YOUNG MAN AND BOY," begins the next page, "who reads this book the author has led for over a quarter of a century a pitiful and dangerous life of the tramp gives this well meant advice. DO NOT jump on moving trains or street cars if only to ride to the next street crossing because this may arouse 'wanderlust' besides endangering undoubtedly your life and limb."

How deadly is this streptococcus, poised to worm into the bloodstream of every lad who as much as lifts his boots from the neighborhood sidewalk? Lethal. "Wandering once it becomes a habit is incurable so NEVER RUN AWAY. STAY AT HOME. As a roving lad there is a dark side to a tramp's life.

"A tramp is constantly hounded by the minions of the law; is shunned by all humanity and never knows the meaning of home and friends. To tell the truth, it is a pitiful existence . . . And what is the end? It is an even ninety-nine chances of a hundred that the end will be a miserable one – an accident, an alms house, but surely an unmarked pauper's grave."

The actual story, up to which all this has been leading, is magnificent melodrama, up among the McGonagall and Amanda Ros summits of banality.

"But look!" it opens. "There upon the hill amongst the majestic oaks, in the upper story in the left wing of the Manor, a lighted lamp was moving from room to room." The lady of the manor, Mrs. Braxton, enters the library and holds the lamp up to a painting of a "handsome, manly boy of about seventeen . . . her runaway son, Buford." She spends some time sobbing, then "suddenly with a loud thud she falls heavily in a dead faint upon the floor." In a drawing Mr. Braxton crouches praying at her bedside: "Oh God! Bring back our wandering boy before his mother loses her mind."

The author introduces himself in Chapter Two. He is leaning against a lamp-post in Cleveland, listening to a nagging inner voice: "Get out of this, A No. 1, this is no place for you . . . Go where you hear real noises, the pounding of the wheels, the clicking of the rails." The author continues: "Thus the voice whispered, implored, then threatened. I, too, like so many others, had become ensnared by this strange something, the 'Wanderlust,' so subtle and yet so strong, that whosoever follows its call more than once, always stays its victim."

Wanderlust wins. Later he is huddled on a train ledge in the gale of wind and smoke. "I fully realized the pitiful existence I was leading ... hiding like a hounded criminal risking every moment, my liberty, limbs and life – a slave of the 'Wanderlust'!"

All the tramps A No. 1 encounters are with extraordinary unanimity also writhing anguishedly in the grip of the 'Wanderlust,' and all with the barest excuse deliver confessions of a turgidity one suspects seldom reverberated within a boxcar. One, the Kentucky Kid, slides off at the end of a run from Cincinnati, saying: "Good-bye, Bo, Good-bye the 'Road,' and the cursed 'Wanderlust,' it's 'Home sweet Home' and mother after this for me."

Another, California Dan, repining for the death of a comrade who has "greased the rails" – been squashed into extinction – says: "In the cars, under the cars, even upon this 'Path of Blasted Hopes,' this cursed 'Wanderlust' collects its uncanny dues from our ranks" and he plods off whistling *Home, Sweet Home*.

Toward the end of his rambling reminiscences the narrative is unexpectedly wrenched back to its original motif. By an amazing coincidence he finds himself the fellow casualty of a train wreck in hospital with a bandaged lad – yes, Buford Braxton.

A No. 1 tells him: "Buford Braxton, your darling mother is waiting with open arms for you this moment ... old Aunt Dinah and all the other faithful darkies are yearning for your return ... tell her that you do not wish to end your days an outcast, despised hobo, but instead will take your place again in the world as Buford Braxton of Braxton Manor?"

A No. 1's eloquence works. "Hardly had I spoken the last syllable than he threw his arms around my neck and amid loud sobs begged me to bring him back to his mother. I asked him to join me in a silent prayer to God for Him to help us to reach Kentucky in safety."

Someone was double-crossing someone. After the interlude of a year or two following his delivery of Buford back to mother and the faithful darkies A No. 1 drops in at the manor, but Buford isn't there: he is up in the cemetery.

Says his mother: "Buford could not resist that monster he has so often called in our presence the 'Wanderlust.' Every so often he would almost rave, until he had another fling at the road ... Our pleadings were in vain. Once too often he went, as they brought him back to us in a pine box – killed under the cars by the 'Curse of Tramp Life' – the 'Wanderlust.' "

One cannot doubt the sincerity, nor the basic truth, of A No. 1's grisly and harrowing tale, yet somehow his text is anti-climactic. Although Buford from his hospital cot hints at some unpleasant experience with a jocker named Railroad Jack, he does not admit to having done worse than beg for him. And either A No. 1 managed by miraculous rectitude to remain sterling and chaste during his twenty-five years on the bum or he is holding back, for he admits to corruption no more heinous than submission to a bit of light-fingered snitching, an implied oath or two uttered within his hearing, and suffering five days in the county chain-gang in a "zebra-striped suit of shame" for trespass.

Preposterous though A No. 1 succeeds in making it sound, perhaps wanderlust is the aptest condensed term for the compulsion that has been disturbingly active in American life and which cannot be explained by a moving streetcar, nor by hearing other boys boast of their travels, nor by economic straits alone. It is the restlessness of that pioneer who saw with agony that the bark was peeling off his fence-rails and there he was still in the same place – the search in the mind for God's Country.

The spirit had already entered literature long before London and Tully and A No. 1 hit the road, even before the railroads were accessible to absentees. It was there in *Huckleberry Finn*, Mark Twain's "Odyssey of Adventure on the Mississippi" published in 1884, "the symbol of a little boy who ran away from home because he did not want to be civilized."

Parkes sees *Huckleberry Finn* as a profoundly melancholy book because it marks the point at which American individualism began to succumb to defeat. It was written as the old uninhibited freedom of the frontier was rapidly vanishing and the outrider American was being overtaken by all that he had spurned, and implies that "civilization, with all its restraints and its hypocrisies, is an inevitable process to which the individual must finally conform; to assert oneself against it is impossible, and to attempt to run away from it is infantile .. It represents the transition between the folk hero of agrarian and frontier America, who believes in self-reliance and seeks to assert his will against his environment, and the folk hero of industrial America, who is the victim of social forces he cannot hope to control. Mike Fink is in the process of being transformed into Charlie Chaplin."

18 : SEX AND THE SINGLE MAN

I've hiked and hiked till my feet are sore
I'll be God-damned if I hike any more

punk to jocker in *The Big Rock Candy Mountains*

MANY Americans have, as we have seen, attempted the "infantile" solution: they ran away from "civilization" and often when not much more than infants. And the particular function that these child tramps fulfilled in the hobo netherworld is one which has seldom been examined frankly and directly, the role of the punk.

Punk in tramp terminology is a catamite or young male "wife" of a sodomite, also known as a lamb or "preshun," a shortening of apprentice. It cannot be doubted that the call of the illusory wild, together with the thrust of home hardship from behind, drove a large number of juveniles on to the road, but nor can it be doubted that many were victims of a basement white slave traffic, deliberately lured away by hobo homosexual hunters.

Avoidance of a confrontation with this common alliance in the hobo's womanless, tentative life has usually been accomplished by either totally ignoring its existence, or by glancing references in remote Athenian terms, or by presenting it as a rather touching example of the gruffly kind of wayfarer taking the greenhorn under his scrawny wing.

London, while describing the savagery of the jackal-packs of road kids, who roll drunks, goldbrick, steal and lie, never includes in his recollections male prostitution or pairing off with adult homosexuals. Perhaps London never brushed with it but it is likelier that he thought it inadmissible when writing in 1907.

Nor does Tully give more than an ambiguous hint of this side of jungle recreation. At the start, when the one-eyed boy is coming on with the lowdown on the craft, he says: "If you ever go on the road, Kid, don't you never let no old tramp play you for a sucker. You know, them old birds're too lazy to scratch themselves when they're crummy. So they gits young kids and teaches 'em to beg. They know people'll feed kids quicker'n they will them. There's a lot of punkgrafters on the road." And the matter is left with the vague pendant: "Lota things I could tell you."

Tully says elsewhere that "a vast army of men in hoboland and jails are recruited from orphanages and reform schools." An equally large number, it can be inferred, were drawn from the yards and sidings which have been the playgrounds of poor white, Negro and Indian children since the railroads snaked out to the rural townships of America, and the water tank where the train riders stopped off for rest and refreshment was the enlistment office for infatuated punks.

The seasoned jocker or wolf, as the homosexual hobo with a lad in tow was, and still is, called, developed a Pied Piper art. It may be disconcerting to those accustomed to hear that apparent nonsense song *The Big Rock Candy Mountains* played on Children's Favorites radio programmes, to learn that this is a homosexual tramp serenade or at least a parody of what are known as the "ghost stories" the accomplished seducer spins to entice a child away with him on the next train out. For general consumption the verse has been changed:

> *One sunny day in the month of May*
> *A jocker he come hiking,*
> *He come to a tree and "Ah!" says he,*
> *"This is just to my liking."*
> *In the very same month on the very same day*
> *A hoosier's son came hiking.*
> *Said the bum to the son, "O, will you come*
> *To the Big Rock Candy Mountains?"*

Then follows the lip-wetting catalogue of what the hoosier kid will be introduced to under the jocker's protection and guidance: hand-outs that grow on bushes, empty boxcars, cigarette trees, whisky springs, lakes of stew, a land of eternal sunshine where the cops have wooden legs, the bulldogs rubber teeth, the hens lay soft-boiled eggs, and where "they boiled in oil the inventor of toil."

The jungle version continues, less equivocally:

> The punk rolled up his big blue eyes
> And said to the jocker, "Sandy,
> I've hiked and hiked and wandered, too,
> But I ain't seen any candy.
> I've hiked and hiked till my feet are sore
> I'll be God-damned if I hike any more . . ."

Or, he adds, be carnally used in the Big Rock Candy Mountains.

The hyperbole itself is not all that immoderate when set against the prose in which the West promoted itself to prospective settlers, and indeed *The Big Rock Candy Mountains* may have started out as a parody within a parody. "Sunshine and green salads all the year will promote cheerfulness. Where there are not bitter winds, no sleet or hail"; "It is so healthy we had to shoot a man in order to start a graveyard"; "Where there are no aristocrats and people do not have to work hard to have plenty and go in the best society, where ten acres, judiciously planted in fruits, will soon make one independent, all varieties being wonderfully successful and profitable" – these are actual Big Rock Candy Mountain phrases with which the states advertised themselves.

There are a good many variations of the tramp's Cockaigne, perhaps the next best known being *The Sweet Potato Mountains*, about a floater who settles down among the cigarette vines and ham 'n' egg trees, where whiteline springs squirt booze to your knees. Less well known outside the jungle circuit but which speaks more candidly of the turn up for many young boys is *The Road Kid's Song*:

> Oh, when I was a little boy I started for the West –
> I hadn't got no farther than Cheyenne,
> When I met a husky burly taking of his rest
> And he flagged me with a big lump and a can
> When I saw that can of coffee how it made me think
> of home

"Won't you let me have some," said I, "Good Mr. Bum?
Remember you was once a kid yourself."
He asked me how old I was, I told him just fourteen,
That Muncie was where I come from.
In his eyes appeared a stare.
"I think you I will snare,
For you ought to have the makings of a bum."

Harry "Mac" McClintock, one of the early song buskers for the IWW and who played the clarinet in the first Wobbly street band and edited the first edition of "The Little Red Songbook," claimed to be the author of not only *Hallelujah, I'm a Bum* but also the original *The Big Rock Candy Mountains.* McClintock had himself been a road kid. He ran away from his Knoxville, Tennessee, home at fourteen to join a circus. When the Gentry Brothers' Dog and Pony Show played its last date of the 1896 season at Anniston, Alabama, about half the fifty canvasmen and razorbacks collected their pay off and grabbed the first rattler out of town.

"I traveled alone," he says. "I was only a kid and looked even younger than I was. So the brakemen and the coppers in the towns ignored me and let me go my way unmolested." He found that instead of being "a moocher of pokeouts at back doors" he could collect pocketfuls of coins in Bourbon Street in New Orleans by singing in the grog shops and can joints where a table of sailors was provided with glasses and a gallon tin of beer for two bits.

But he also found that his success as a troubador made him a prize catch for the type of hobo who would indubitably have been a pop group's agent in other times and circumstances.

"Most of the vagrants were mechanics or laborers, uprooted and set adrift by hard times and they were decent men. But there were others, 'blowed-in-the-glass-stiffs,' who boasted that they had never worked and never would, who soaked themselves in booze when they could get it and who were always out to snare a kid to do their begging and pander to their perversions.

"The luckless punk who fell into the clutches of one of these gents was treated with unbelievable brutality, and I wanted no part of such a life. As a 'producer' I was a shining mark; a kid who could not only beg handouts but who could bring in money for alcohol was a valuable piece of property for any jocker who could snare him.

"The decent hoboes were protective as long as they were around, but there were times when I fought like a wildcat or ran like a deer to preserve my independence and my virginity. I whittled my way out of two or three jams with a big barlow knife, and on one occasion I jumped into the darkness from a boxcar door – from a train that must have been doing better than thirty miles an hour."

Hallelulia, On The Bum (as it originally was) became widely popular, the anthem of the Wobblies and a set-piece anywhere for migrant workers, but *The Big Rock Candy Mountains* on the other hand remained for a long time significant to only a limited and specialized audience. McClintock obviously wrote this out of keen inside knowledge of the jocker's methods and spiel.

Lomax shrewdly draws connecting threads between *The Big Rock Candy Mountains* and *Oleana*, a satirical ballad still sung in the Norwegian communities of the Northern states. *Oleana* was based on the German legends of Schlaraffenland, where roast pigs trotted about with knives and forks stuck at the ready in their back inviting you to help yourself to some ham, where cakes rained from the skies and the rivers ran with beer. Originally ridiculing the fantasies of Norwegian émigrés about the life of effortless luxury awaiting across the Atlantic, it is conceivable that it may have germinated Ibsen's *Peer Gynt* and *Gyntiana*. What is quite probable is that it was a Norwegian bindle stiff singing *Oleana* around a jungle fire who gave the start to *The Big Rock Candy Mountains*, the ancient Utopian fancy converted to the day dreams of the rod-rider.

The cynical spoof of the original *The Big Rock Candy Mountains* speaks more truly of a routine road relationship than the interpretations of later writers. Milburn saw in this partnership a rosy similarity to "that which once existed between the knight and his squire." Indeed, Milburn hails in the jungles and the hobo assemblies in jails and flophouses a revival of

216

"games that once flourished around the wassail bowl," including "extemporaneous rhyming" which was a favorite form of parlor entertainment in Georgian England.

The song of these landloping Homers that make the closest approach to epic proportions is the one the jocker sings to justify himself before his fellow and the other tramp kids for his exploitation of his own 'preshun: the song sometimes tells of the hardships the jocker has to undergo in protecting and training his kid. At other times a mythical jocker, whose kid has been taken from him by the dicks, is the hero of the song. It tells of the Odyssean exploits of the jocker in following the detectives back across the continent and his ultimate reunion with his faithful kid.

It was this manner of romanticization which deodorized the man-boy relationship and made it edible to the public at large, so that it eventually, at many removes from the reality of the jocker and his punk, took on the entirely innocent sentimentality of Charles Chaplin's 1921 *The Kid*.

In *The Kid* Chaplin the tramp picks up an abandoned waif, played by Jackie Coogan, and the story is of his ingenuity at eluding the police and officials who are trying to snatch the boy away for proper institutionalization.

In his autobiography Chaplin describes his negotiations to sign up Jackie Coogan. "Can you imagine the tramp a window-mender, and the little kid going around the streets breaking windows, and the tramp coming by and mending them?" he enthused to the cast while it was still uncertain if Coogan could be lured from a Fatty Arbuckle contract. "The charm of the kid and the tramp living together, having all sorts of adventures!"

When Chaplin got to Coogan Senior, he said: "This story will give your son the opportunity of his life if you will let me have him for this one picture." Replied Coogan Senior: "Why, of course you can have the little punk."

Clearly, punk had by then passed into the general cheery vernacular, just as the British working man will refer fondly to his child as "the little bugger." It is also quite obvious from Chaplin's guileless excitement about the "charm of the kid and

217

the tramp living together, having all sorts of adventures" that he was utterly unaware of the griminess of the relationship he was idealizing, for it had passed through a filtering process before it reached him as an idea invested with comedy and pathos. *The Kid* reflected the unconscious sanctions the American public had to exercise upon the underground partnership of a man and a boy, and its actuality of squalor, buggery and semi-slavery.

Female prostitution of course was an acceptable condition of life. Minehan found it prevalent and orthodox among the freight train travellers: "... regarded as a normal occupation ... They say she is a whore just as others might say she is a school teacher. The term is descriptive. That is all. Some girls pride themselves on the fact that they 'either got cash or liked him'." His estimate was that at this period one child tramp in twenty was a girl. "Never does a freight pull out of a large city without carrying some girls, disguised usually in overalls or Army breeches, but just as certainly and appallingly homeless as the boys ... Girls go from jungle to jungle and from box car to box car without discrimination. Any place where there are men or boys, they know they will be welcome. They enter a box car or a jungle – and without more ado the line forms to the right."

His report on homosexuality is more perfunctory. It does occur, he admits, and in fact: "Whenever you see a trainload of transients, there is always a wolf on the tender and a fruiter on the green light. Like the vultures following a caravan, the perverts trail boys, waiting with bribes and force to ensnare them. One of the first lessons that a boy learns on the road is to beware of certain older men. These men become friendly with a lonely boy and attempt to seduce him. It is to protect himself from the approaches of such men, as well as for other reasons, that boys travel in pairs or in gangs."

But to a degree he supports the theory of Platonic tenderness: "I have seen wolves and their little 'lambs' or 'fairies,' and their relationship seemed to be one of mutual satisfaction. The man and boy were pals.

"Far from being miserable, the boy did not want to be separated from his friend. He resented and refused all efforts at his 'rescue'. In a mission older men give boys some bananas, candy or tobacco, and take them into the toilet or a dark corner and love them up." Still, Minehan believes, "The boys have a healthy aversion to it."

Doubtless many keep their aversion whole, as did Tully, who recounts being cased by an old hobo. "Ever have a jocker?" he asks. "You're a purty smart-lookin' boy." Tully continues: "I had heard of boys who were called 'punks', who were loaned, traded, and even sold to other tramps. The boys who became slaves to 'jockers' are of the weaker and more degenerate type.

"Bill told me a case where the boy was whipped by his 'jocker' for the most trivial offense, and every day of the year he was forced to bring a dollar to him – which he begged. The tramp always ruled the 'punk' by fear, the same crude and brutal psychology that the pimp practiced over the weak woman of the underworld. And always, the boy obeyed with dog-like affection.

"Perhaps it was because he had nothing else in life, as, false sentimental reports to the contrary, hobo boys always come from the swollen ranks of poverty and degradation."

After these reflections Tully replies to his suitor: " 'Nope, I'd bust a jocker on the nose that 'ud try to make me out a sucker' . . . The hobo looked sideways at me . . . 'Course it's all right. Some kids like a jocker,' he stammered after a moment. 'What becomes o' the punk kids when they big?' I asked. 'Oh, they turn out to be perfessional 'jockers' themselves, an' then they gits kids to be their 'punks'."

Nevertheless Minehan's reading of a general aversion seems a little sanguine. The real surprise would be if homosexuality was not commonplace, just as it is in prisons, boarding schools and ships, in the barren and segregated loneliness of the hobo life.

A Federal Transient Program survey in the mid-Thirties showed that of 26,306 migrants interviewed, only six per cent were married; the others were single, widowed, divorced or separated; and of course even that six per cent were "temporarily" apart from their wives. An earlier investigation by Solenberger of one thousand men in Chicago in the Twenties showed seventy-four per cent as single.

In 1914 in California, "widespread practice of homosexuality among the migratory laborers" was noted, and it was stated that in the up-state lumber camps "sex perversion within the entire group is as developed and recognized as the well known similar practice in prisons and reformatories." In fact the lumber camps provided stimulation even stronger than prison for it was pointed out, "often the men sent out from the employment agencies are without blankets, even sufficient clothing and they are forced to sleep packed together for the sake of warmth."

Anderson's study of the hobo of the Twenties differed strikingly from Minehan's about the number of women on the road and therefore about the amount of heterosexual prostitution. "Women do wander from city to city," he says, "but convention forbids them to ride the rods and move about as men do." He quotes a tramp who had covered eight thousand miles in six months: "I even saw two women on the road, and last summer I saw a woman beating her way in a box car." This is not confirmed by the first-hand evidence of Box-Car Bertha – Bertha Thompson – who described herself in her autobiography ("as told to" Ben L. Reitman) as "a sister of the road, one of the strange and motley sorority which has increased its membership so greatly during the depression."

The illegitimate child of a section gang cook on the North-Western railroad, her first play house was a boxcar and she learned to spell by reading out the names on the freight trains. "There were always wandering men," she recalls, "and even then" – this is around 1915 – "a few women travelling on the railroad and the highway." Box-Car Bertha hoboed around for fifteen years like a man and met plenty of other women riding the trains, socialist organizers, prostitutes, college girls and drifters.

Anderson states flatly but inaccurately: "Tramping is a man's game." It was much more so up to 1929 but the Depression that followed was more total than any previous one and the newly emancipated woman was in the boxcars as well as in the speakeasies.

The plaint that vibrated throughout America, *Where is my Wand'ring Boy Tonight?* was supplemented by a notice that has always been conspicuous in missions' demands: "When Did You Write to Mother Last?"

Although it has frequently been conflict with and rebellion against the stability of home and community that has set the hobo's feet on the road, mothers are regarded with reverent if unapplied love.

The older mother-figure used to be a familiar mission character: "Mother" Greenstein who kept a cheap restaurant on South State Street, Chicago, and who would never turn away a penniless hungry man, and "Aunt" Nina who ran a rooming house in the same area and who would always find space for a working stiff stranded in winter.

But where the hobo worked – and, in the period Anderson was dealing with, even within the closed frontier – were galactically remote areas, with seldom women of any kind, either mother-figures or those of sexual potential. He might spend six months in a lumber camp and not see a woman during all that time. His visits to town were, like those of the soldier or sailor, for quick connections with no strings. But these were city pleasures.

"The tramp is not often interested in small town or country associations, because they generally tend to terminate seriously and he does not want to be taken seriously. The tramp is not a marrying man, though he does enter into transient free unions with women when the occasion offers.

"A certain class of detached men makes a practice of getting into the good graces of some prostitute for the winter. The panderer is not a characteristic tramp type, but certain homeless men are not averse to becoming pimps for a season. . . .

"Most hoboes and tramps because of drink, unpresentable appearance, or unattractive personality, do not succeed in establishing permanent, or even quasi-permanent, relationships with women. For them the only accessible women are prostitutes and the prostitutes who solicit the patronage of the homeless man are usually forlorn and bedraggled creatures."

These live adjacent to the main stem, a poxy lot. Most committed hobos have been venereally diseased from time to time. One Twenties check by the Chicago Health Department calculated that one-third of the homeless men in the city were constantly spreading infection.

Obviously when heterosexual outlet is available, most hobos, however ambidextrously adjustable, will take it. The show girls who sing and dance in the cheap burlesque theaters on South State and West Madison Streets in Chicago have always been famously ready to help a returned lumberjack or harvest hand burn through a fat bill roll.

The bump-and-grind round-the-clock theatres, the blue-ish cinemas and the strip tease slot-machine arcades which cluster round any American city skid row or rail junction would not be in business if girls did not interest the hobo. Nor would the cat wagon – the horse-drawn and later motorized vehicle containing two or three whores and a procurer (or a dingfob, a blow-up life-size rubber woman, Japanese-made, an emergency substitute if the real flesh and blood failed to come through) which for a century has traditionally followed the travelling wheat harvester through the Middle West corn belt – have become such an established and prosperous enterprise.

But not amazingly in an existence which is womanless apart from the fleeting scuffle in a brothel, and with long monastic periods in forest bunk houses and construction camps, homosexuality has always been popular.

Dean Stiff makes partial admission of this but chiefly to make light of it. "It is so generally assumed to be true among hoboes," he says, "that whenever a man travels around with a lad he is apt to be labeled a jocker or a wolf ... It has become so that it is very difficult for a good hobo to enjoy the services of an apprentice. It may be that he has the boy along only to wash his clothes or bum his lumps. It is hard for people with morbid minds to understand this. In some states they will even arrest a hobo merely for travelling with a lad. Such diseased minds have the Christian law-makers and man-catchers!"

The fact remains that the man-catchers never neared in numbers and skill the boy-catchers among the hobos. Anderson's opinion is that a boy "does not need to remain long in hobo society to learn of homosexual practices. The average boy on the road is invariably approached by men who get into his good graces. Some 'homos' claim that every boy is a potential homosexual."

But he does not agree that the relationship often amounts to "a sort of slavery" in the sense that a boy is often held in

222

bondage and compelled to steal and join in sex. "This condition may exist in isolated instances but is not general," he says. "It is even suggested by some authorities that there exists some sort of organization among tramps through which boys have been 'caught' and kept in servitude." He thinks this has never been the case for "perverted sex practices are frowned upon by the tramps themselves."

Yet he admits that "court records show that not infrequently boys are held in rooms, or taken to lonely buildings or out on the lake front, or in parks ... If there is a slavery in these latter cases it is slavery to their passions, or to a state of mind growing out of their habits and their isolation.

"The duration of an intimacy of this kind in the city is seldom more than a few days. On the road however the 'partnership' may last four weeks. Whereas out of town the pair can travel as companions aiding each other, in the city they can get along better alone.

"Tramp perverts argue that homosexual intercourse is 'clean' and that homosexuals are less liable to become infected with venereal disease ... It is also urged by perverts that in the homosexual relation there is the absence of the eternal complications in which one becomes involved with women. They want to avoid intimacies that complicate the free life to which they are by temperament and habit committed."

And he summarizes: "In his sex life, as in his whole existence, the homeless man moves in a vicious circle. Industrially inadequate, his migratory habits render him the more economically inefficient. A social outcast, he still wants the companionship which his mode of life denies him. Debarred from family life, he hungers for intimate associations and affection. The women that he knows, with few exceptions, are repulsive to him. Attractive women live in social worlds infinitely remote from his. With him the fundamental wishes of the person for response and status have been denied expression."

From sociological reports and the hints of vague sinful dangers in the soft-cover hobo publications, the almost standardized homosexuality of a large group of industrial laborers has reached the larger public in a curiously ambiguous form.

The misty, imperfectly understood relationship as transmuted and transmitted by *The Kid* is interestingly present in the case of Britt, Iowa.

In 1899 two Britt businessmen, Thomas A. Way and T. A. Potter, read of the third annual convention of the Tourists' Union No. 63 held in Illinois, at which the newly elected President and Vice-President were Onion Cotton and Grand Head Pipe Charles F. Noe.

In the developing rootin'-tootin' spirit of middle-town America (later to be made definitive by Sinclair Lewis in George Babbitt and Zenith, with its Rotary Club puffers and stunted sky-scrapers), Messrs. Way and Potter espied a novel – cute, they probably chortled – way of putting Britt on the convention and vacation map. They wrote to Noe, offering hospitality and August 22, 1900, was set for the first Britt Hobo Convention.

Britt's action reflects again the dualism in the American view of the tramp – now as a joke oddity, a kind of national clown to be exploited. Feature-writers and wire service reporters were pulled in from as far afield as Chicago, Minneapolis, St. Louis, Des Moines, St. Paul and Philadelphia. A delegation from Chicago and "men of dignity and influence" from many other cities were taken on a horse-and-carriage tour of "the round elevator at the Missouri and St. Louis, the arch over the cemetery gate, the town pump, the race track, the Salvation Army barracks, and Ed Bailey's spittoons."

Britt had even greater riches to unveil. Main Street had been arrayed with banners. The Way-Healey building was placarded HOBO HEADQUARTERS; The *News-Tribune* decorated its office opposite HOBO HINDQUARTERS. A fife and drum corps "all dolled up like hobos and playing the latest rag time tunes" preceded the speech making, after which there was a barbecued ox feast and sports. Fred Corey, of Algona, rode a horse in a five-mile race with two hobos on a tandem: the horse won. That evening at the hobo camp fire assembly "Admiral" Dewey was elected the new president and "Philippine Red" vice-president. After the "slumgullion" supper, the King was crowned – and provided with a local young man for his queen.

In later years there were some genuinely female queens such as Polly Ellen Pep, Boxcar Myrtle French, Hitch-Hiker Sylvia

New York's "slave market", 1912, an agency for railroad construction, coal mining and iron mining.

The forerunners: the men who went out to the Northern woods. A log train of the 1880s.

Hobo riding the bumpers between jobs, his travelling technique established. Illustration for article "The Tramp At Home" in *The Century*, February 1894.

RIDING THE RODS—ON THE IRON BARS THAT UNDERBRACED THE BOXCAR FRAME.
Fiction
and
fact.

END OF THE LINE: THE WORK AWAITING THEM.
Extending the Illinois Central line through Indian country.

The work goes on: track-raising gang on the Santa Fe Railway near Flagstaff, Arizona.

Part of the "great black shadow", the 200,000 harvest hands who annually worked the wheat belt from Texas to Canada, 1880s–1920s.

Hobos of the 1930s, issued with bed-rolls at a Federal Work Camp.

In prototype: Western labourer acclaimed in the *Industrial Worker*.

CAREER HOBOS

The "Blanket Stiff"

He built the ROAD—
With others of his CLASS, he built the road,
Now o'er it, many a weary mile, he packs his load,
Chasing a JOB. spurred on by HUNGERS good.
He walks and walks, and wonders why
In H——L, he built the road.

In person: boarding at Minneapolis, veteran freight train rider wearing two hats, two overcoats, all possessions in burlap bag and underarm bundle.

Bindle stiff on the road, Napa Valley, California, 1938. For twenty-five
years he had worked the circuit of copper mines, farms and lumber
forests.

Workless fruit tramps beside railroad track, Berrien County, Michigan,
1940, waiting for a train out.

The "Little Red Song Book", the IWW treasury of revolutionary songs which every Wobbly carried.

Where the songs were sung: a hobo jungle, or wayside camp, in the 1930s.

Turtle soup on the rock bottom menu; hobo cutting up turtle for the jungle stewpot.

City jungle: a Hooverville, or unemployeds' shantytown, on the St. Louis riverfront.

Big Bill Haywood, IWW leader: "We are going down into the gutter to get at the mass of workers."

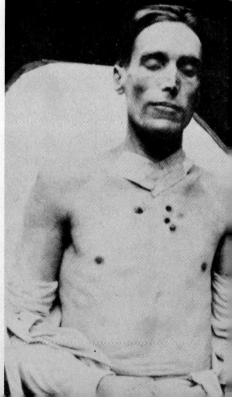

Joe Hill, Wobbly poet and martyr, after his execution by the State of Utah, 1915. Note wounds caused by dum-dum bullets.

HOBOS EN ROUTE
Game of cards in a boxcar.

Taking the sun on the "top deck".

Missouri family, "broke, baby sick, car trouble". But: "We're not tramps; we hold ourselves to be white folks."

DUST BOWL REFUGEES

Still moving: Okie family travelling by freight train through the Yakima Valley, Washington State, 1939.

What they fled: the Great Blow of 1934, when the topsoil blew off the Dust Bowl farms.

How they went: "tractored-out", a family placing a two-way bet beside road and rail, hoping to get West somehow.

The symbol: "This train is a hundred coaches long."

The reality: "hard travellin'".

"You've been to that town a thousand times." An American rolling stone.

Leaving town again: hobo fruit-pickers heading for the freight yards.

Stoop labor: Mexican *braceros* in position for their twelve-hour, seven-day week harvesting strawberries, Salinas, California, 1963.

Child labor: cotton-pickers in America's "blue-sky sweatshop".

Davis and Boxcar Betty Link; but the King's partner was usually "a local lad, chosen for his youthful beauty to wear the queenly garments." So Britt and its Rotarians and Kiwanis and summer visitors innocently supplied the facilities for a drag ball and a queasy charade of jungle homosexuality.

Naturally the press milked it. It was a Beggar's Opera, a circus of grotesques and buffoons, good for a giggle, and the tone of those contemporary reports was a there-you-are, see what hedonistic ragamuffins the unemployed are.

The type of hobo prepared to hire himself out for an advertising gag in return for free beer and stew can never have been markedly representative of the body of men riding the trains around the wilder states, assuredly not of the bindle stiffs and the Wobblies, engrossed in guerilla warfare with capitalism and who would rather have had their fingernails pulled out with pincers than be found putting on a fund-raising cabaret turn for the system.

But there were not a few who found hamming up themselves as vagabond "cards" an agreeable and even a moderately paying proposition.

19 : HOBO-TREKKERS
THAT FOREVER SEARCH

A tightening net
traps all creatures
even the wildest

Too late
the young cry out,
and the innocent
who were not wild enough.

Peter Levi: *The Gravel Ponds*

T HE virtuoso booster hobo was perhaps Ben Benson, "Official King of the Hoboes" (twice elected at the Britt ceremony) and President of the Hobo Fellowship Union of America. A printer by trade, he travelled with squares of cardboard in his knapsack, poised to dash off a portrait or a cartoon for a dime; he was also "road editor" for the *Hobo News* and he described himself without visible justification as a poet. Benson is revealed in the few extant photographs as a tiny goblin with white curly locks and a doorknocker face. There seems no reason to doubt that he had hoboed hard.

He jumped his first freight when he ran away from home in New York City at fifteen in 1898, and remained in perpetual motion for the next forty-five years around the rail merry-go-round of the Union. He wore this experience like a heraldic coat-of-arms: enchased by tattoo needle on his left forearm was a map of the United States, COAST KID underneath, and the initials SP, standing for Southern Pacific, a railroad which enjoyed his especial affection and, presumably, patronage.

A lifetime of riding the trains, either just above or in between the wheels, had by his sixties virtually destroyed his hearing, but his volubility remained unblunted and was oftener than not directed against other hobo lions whom he regarded as unentitled to attention from public and press. During his career on the road Benson had good coverage – that is, a prolific one, for he obviously always had a keen instinct for selling himself as "entertaining" copy and listed "a few who have reported me favourably," *Time* Magazine, the Columbia Broadcasting System and the Los Angeles *Times* being mentioned together with fifteen other newspapers and radio stations.

His zeal for self-projection did not temper an incandescent contempt for others with a similar aim. "Fakirs [*sic*] of all kinds besiege Newspaper Offices and Magazine Editors," he writes in the preface to one of his autobiographical miscellanies, "claiming to be an authority on Hoboes and the road . . . cushion armchair and thumb-lifting would-be hoboes . . . hobo exploiters, cheap publicity hounds and conventional home-guards or town bums . . . Hoboing, like every other profession requires experience, and a 'correspondence course' of a few months or a year or even years does not entitle one to a diploma, or right to be called King of the Hoboes."

This particular booklet carries a full-page photograph of him in baggy white pants (there is another of him, regal in cardboard crown) with the announcement: "Hobo Benson is at liberty for talks, radio and movies." He also addressed this Open Letter to the public: "A few hoboes and would-be-hoboes are roaming the country posing as duly elected King of the Hoboes. Press, radio and the public are warned against the imposters, Hoboically yours, Ben (Hobo) Benson."

When I first got my hands on some of this tramp broadsheet literature I could not at first nail down the recollection it stirred. Its determined cockiness overlaying a forlorn sadness has of course a lot in common with pavement poetry and street ballads of England's early urban proletariat, strong liquor brewed from violent misfortune, but also saucy with a battered vigor and gift for survival. "The brains trusts have discovered how to solve the unemployment problem," wrote a correspondent in a 1922 issue of *Hobo News* with sarcasm typical of the genre. "The best thing to keep the unemployed busy is to have the cops chase them around the block. They are experimenting already." Alexander E. Freeman, the white-bearded author of a

1945 booklet, *Hobo Jungle Talk*, draws a bitter little scene. The Hobo, hitting his last door – described as the Gate to the HEAVENLY PARADISE – is asked by St. Peter how much money he's got. None? Okay, says St. Peter, and kicks him swiftly down to Hell, leaping with flames and demons.

Then I remembered. Hobo literature has exactly the general complexion of pre-war schoolboy comics, with their galumphing jokes, secret society clubs, advertisements for recondite badges and stink bombs, and gory gothic adventures of penny-dreadful immortals.

Benson's odds-and-bobs autobiography for instance offers a Membership Card with this oath: "I solemnly swear never to be unjust to 'others' or take advantage of my fellowmen, and to do all in my power for the betterment of myself, my organization and America. So help me God."

Throughout there are cartoons involving the knockabout hobo Tired Tim cipher, forever facing hatchet-faced housewives and brutal judges with indestructible, sly, squiffy amiability. There are instructive sections on "What is a Hobo?" and "How Hoboes Travel," and glossaries of Hobo Terms and Hobo Monikers. There are "True Stories" and a list of "Railroads I Have Rode," and a chapter headed "Hobo Adventures and Thrills," which goes from Thrill Number One to Thrill Number Five. There are little items entitled Important Things to Know When On The Road ("Be careful whom you mix with on trains or in jungles") and numerous poems and mottoes.

Benson staunchly wags the hobo flag. He perceives at the time he was recording the lore, in the 1940s, that "after years of persistent propaganda, through the efforts of myself and others, the word 'Hobo' is becoming to be rather respected throughout the country. Especially is this true in Press reports, in spite of a few Reporters who still regard the Hobo as a tramp, bum, or parasite."

He puts forward the *homo bonus* theory of the origin of the word and adds: "A real hobo is a migratory worker – most of the Pioneers in the country were hoboes. Many leaders in all the professions and crafts, and in commercial activities, were men who left their homes, when young, years ago. They 'hoboed' to some part of the country they liked. Opportunities, twenty, thirty and forty years ago, were more plentiful than they are today.

"Many of these pioneering hoboes made good. Many of them are not ashamed of their hobo days ... hoboes – being single men – are the REAL backbone of the Nation: the first to be called upon in time of war – and the last to be helped, as they should be, in times of depression! ... The hoboes ARE a respectable and necessary part of our population. THEY helped to MAKE this country! They helped to make it GREAT!"

The tramp had the occasional outside philanthropic sympathizer, perhaps the most consistent and the most generous having been James Eads How, known as the millionaire hobo. For many years – very actively from the early 1900s up through the Twenties – How used his family fortune, derived from a St. Louis railroad company, to shore up the "hobo colleges" of Chicago and other cities, to organize hobo conventions and to sponsor his own lecture tours on economic theories, based (declared *The Bugle* during How's Oklahoma City teach-in in 1923) on the proposition that "life is a flower of which love is the honey."

How's International Brotherhood Welfare Association was but one of many bodies which sought to band together the unemployed and the migrant for both political and educational purposes. The IBWA had as a later offshoot the Migratory Workers' Union, in serious competition with the IWW. But most of the hobo fraternities – like Michael Walsh's Society of Vagabonds and John X. Kelly's Benevolent and Protective Order of Ramblers, with its anthem "Hail! Hail! You Ought To Be A Rambler" – have the strong redolence of those schoolboy secret societies, and were the inventions of individuals with a weakness for self-invested grand titles and emperor's robes. The difficulty all, businesslike and nonsensical, faced was an unreliable and non-residential membership. Even the successful Hobo College of Chicago, open to all "migrant and casual workers" on South Green Street, could operate only in winter when the hobos were back from their summer trips; and the IWW, whose membership reached impressive heights, had a high lapse rate and turnover.

Benson's patchy and none too logical memoirs are of interest because they span roughly the trajectory of the hobo's development from vermin through his high romance period to his present-day oblivion except as minor folk hero. Benson's primitive publicity sense gave him a megaphone mouth but he was definitely not peculiar or even rare in his narcissistic view of what a hobo was or should be.

There are difficulties here of distinguishing the image from the search, in the sense that recognition of an entity or meaning is often retrospective. Dorothy Parker observed upon reading the tag the Lost Generation applied to her circle of the Twenties: "Whew, we're lost!" Tom Wolfe has pointed out to me that whereas motor cycle gangs already existed in California it wasn't until Marlon Brando appeared in *The Wild One* as the leather-swathed, neo-Nazi road-rider on a plura-headlight phosphorescent two-wheel juggernaut, that the teenage tearaways on whom the picture was based identified themselves and crystallized into the Hell's Angels cult.

Similarly it is now impossible to reconstruct how much of the hobo was self-made and how much was absorbed from popularized and mythological versions of him. There are, however, certain guides.

Unquestionably Charles Chaplin importantly furthered the process already in action of de-fusing the tramp as an explosively dangerous element by either scorning or sentimentalizing him.

Enrolled in 1914 by Keystone Studio, Chaplin wandered around the sets where three companies were at work on the unscripted comedies (perhaps the first real "happenings"). Mack Sennett, chewing a cigar, said: "We need some gags here. Put on a comedy make-up. Anything will do."

Chaplin continues: "I had no idea what make-up to put on ... However, on the way to the wardrobe I thought I would dress in baggy pants, big shoes, a cane and a derby hat ... I had no idea of the character. But the moment I was dressed, the clothes and the make-up made me feel the person he was."

By the time he arrived on the stage the character "was fully born" and Chaplin explained to Sennett: "You know this fellow is many-sided, a tramp, a gentleman, a poet, a dreamer, a lonely fellow, always hopeful of romance and adventure."

Patently Chaplin's conception of the tramp – his pathos, his dignity a spot absurd but unscathed, his wiliness learned from being the butt of every man's boot, that side of him that was "a poet, a dreamer," and his exit at the end of a movie ambling into the sunset, a colophon twirl to his cane, a solitary but at one with himself – was not divined out of thin air.

Without being aware of it he was drawing from the public notions about the hobo, breathing the kiss of life into the bundle of rags. Beautifully evolved though the character was, with his swagger and flyblown genteelism, his sweetness and meekness marking him the loser in a cruelly competitive environment, it was a pathetic cartoon.

The outcast, the itinerant without home or shelter, first appeared fully fledged in *The Tramp*, a two-reeler made in 1915. The mood was hit in the opening scene, a long-shot of an interminable scorched highway bordered by scrubby bushes, up which is paddling the preposterous, skimpy figure, repeatedly being flipped over into the dust by cars roaring on regardless.

In *The Bank*, *The Vagabond*, *Easy Street*, *The Pawnshop*, and *The Immigrant* the tramp continued to wander in and out, his steps surer into their inconsequential blunders as Chaplin worked on his emotional signals without deliberate thought about the reality of the character he was intuitively feeling his way toward. The spores of "the poet, the dreamer" had been abroad in the air for some time before Chaplin hatched them into living tissue.

The moony, ruminative hobo, the "stand and stare" Edwardian model, materialized strongly in the poems of Henry Herbert Knibbs, who peeped through here and there in the columns of *The American*, or *The Smart Set* or the Los Angeles *Graphic*. In 1914 these were published as *Songs of the Outlands: Ballads of the Hoboes and Other Verse*.

Out There Somewhere was typical of the genre, with its hazy yearnings and Kiplingesque jog-trot:

> As I was hiking past the woods
> The cool and sleepy summer woods
> I saw a guy a-talking to the sunshine in the air . . .

> *And though he was a Bo like me*
> *He'd been a gent once, I could see*
> *I ain't much strong on poetry, but this is what*
> > *I heard*

Then follows the refrain: *We'll dance a merry saraband from here to drowsy Samarcand*, the central reference point being a lady named Penelope, waiting with roses in her hair and kisses on her mouth. This soliloquy to the sun arouses the restlessness of the narrator, who cries:

> *Then let's be on the float; you certainly have got*
> > *my goat*
> *You make me hungry in my throat for seeing things*
> > *that's new*
> *Out there somewhere we'll ride the range a-looking*
> > *for the new and strange*
> *My feet are tired and need a change*
> *Come on! It's up to you ...*
> *We kept a-rambling all the time*
> *I rustled grub, he rustled rhyme*
> *Blind-baggage, hoof it, ride or climb ...*

Overland's Delight goes:

> *When we quit the road at night,*
> *And the birds were folding up their music-bars,*
> *Just to smoke a little bit; rub his chin awhile, and sit,*
> *Like a Hobo statue, looking at the stars.*

It is doubtful if these verses of Henry Herbert Knibbs had much currency among the jungle clan, or indeed if Knibbs himself had. Their interest is that this slim volume, with its sickly Indian ink sketches of sunsets and camp fires, was very much of its period, a romantic anodyne for city book stores where idealistic young ladies and mildly radical young men might browse on Saturday afternoons.

Along with the lonely ruefulness was the call of the wild and winsome revolutionary preaching. *The Sheep and the Goats* begins:

Say, mate have you ever seen the mills,
Where the kids at the looms spit blood?

dilates on the dangers and suffering in steel mill, desert, railroad engineering, and oil field, and denounces the bondage of the company store.

The solution? Freedom as enjoyed by "a traveling man":

With a quilt and a rope and a kind of plan
Of hitting no one place twice . . .
I keep my shoes for the road
The long gray road – and I love it mate . . .

Contempt is there for the sanctimonious hand-out and religiosity in *Hash* where in "one of them 'Come in, Stranger' joints" a gang of hobos whose "hands were raw and stomachs flat" are sawing wood and having to listen to a lecture on the Infinite:

I reckon I got too rash
And I says, "Nix Bo, on the Infinite,
What we're needin' most is hash!"

The moral here is that they throw down the saws, spurn the pi-talk and go down the road where they are fed by a rough but kindly saloon keeper. A similar note of slightly joshing grumbling is in *Bread*.

Oh, my heart it is just achin'
For a little bit of bacon
A hunk of bread, a little mug of brew
I'm tired of seein' scenery
Just lead me to a beanery
Where there's something more than only
> *air to chew*

The sublime and the mundane mix in *My Heart's Desire*: (log cabin, solitude, rubber boots) and *The Grand Old Privilege* is

> *to chuck our luck and choose,*
> *Any road at any time for anywhere.*

On The Range underlines the hobo's growing hubris at being a different, distinct class. There is the "rich man ridin' his limousine" and there are the unemployed, "the guy that is hit by the big machine" – but there are also the thousands who stand apart from both, "a Bo like me," freer than anyone.

Nothing To Do But Go more expansively celebrates the whistling rover's philosophy:

> *I'm the ramblin' man with the nervous feet*
> *That never were made for a steady beat*
> *I had many a job – for a little while*
> *And nothing to do but go*
> *So it's beat it, Bo, while your feet are mates*
> *Take a look at the whole United States*
> *Oh, the fire and a pal and a smoke at night*
> *And up again in the mornin' bright*
> *With nothing but road and sky in sight!*
> *And nothing to do but go . . .*

This after-dinner recitation style is developed with even greater archaicness in *Ballad of the Bos*, hobo romanticism at high spiral:

> *We are the true nobility!*
> *Sons of rest and the outdoor air!*
> *Knights of the tie and rail are we,*
> *Lightly meandering everywhere . . .*

It ranges across the hurts and the ecstasies of the unattached, finding shade under the boxcars and musing contentedly upon the meaning of life. It ends with a light laugh of pity for the rich and well bred, caged birds behind golden bars:

> *Prince, our vulgarity, you declare,*
> *Shocks your soul and disgust you so,*
> *Your pardon, Sire, but accept your share,*
> *Take your bundle and beat it, Bo!*

234

Similarly a Shavian strenuity – vegetarianism and Harris tweed knickerbockers – was exuded by Roger Payne, a Cambridge scientist who spent twenty-five years militantly striding about America preaching simple, severe living. "The world today is work crazy" was his message, which urged the reduction of working hours and the reduction of wants, the examples before work-obsessed drudges being hermits and hobos.

Did all the hobos of the first great wave see themselves as "knights of the ties," as poets of poverty? The evidence to be sifted from the few literate and the larger number of semi-literate rambler scribes does indicate that – even when they were rebutting it in fierce terms of good citizenship – this atmosphere pulsed quite strongly among the fantasts of the jungles and the boxcars. It can hardly have been deliberately traditional yet amid the industrialization of an emerging leviathan nation there is the ictus of Villon, the poet who lived with roving brigands, and with the later fashion for gipsy yearnings, those of Gautier, and Baudelaire, of Nodier, Richpin, Hugo, Nerval and Merimée, when the literature of the Romantic movement was espying a way out on a wheeled wagon through the closing fences of organized society.

Did the hobo himself – the actual working stiff – feel to be a left-over pioneer? Or did he absorb the thought from the nostalgic glories almost gone which saturated the incidental writing after the official shutting of the frontier? Hart Crane in the Twenties was maintaining the admiration for the vestigial hobo, the landless pioneer, as he explained about his ambitious poem *The Bridge*, whose fifteen parts attempted to clench the size and sense of the nation. The section *The River* opens in "a world of whistles, wires and steam," where are three hungry men on the tracks:

> *Caboose-like they go ruminating through*
> *Ohio, Indiana – blind baggage –*
> *To Cheyenne tagging . . . Maybe Kalamazoo*

And Crane recalls seeing behind his father's cannery:

Rail-squatters ranged in nomad raillery
The ancient men – wifeless or runaway
Hobo-trekkers that forever search
An empire wilderness of freight and rails.

If there is an invented glorification there it is a genuine poetical response to a corpus of attitudes which Crane identified in these "ancient men," and which is still to be found in those to whom an engine's whistle is a Lorelei song.

20 : VOICES CALLING IN THE NIGHT

These are the untamable. America has always been fecund in the production of roughs.

Bernard De Voto

LIBERAL in Kansas has a street named, with exalted banality, Pancake Boulevard, thus proclaiming that it is one of the world's only two competitors in the International Pancake Race, the other, the pacesetter, being Olney, in Buckinghamshire, England. Liberal's western approaches are reflected in the commercial motif of the Short Horn Coffee Shop and the Tumbleweed Motel and the Ranch Wagon Steaks offered at the B & G Diner ("Short Orders, run by Goldie F. Cartzdafner"), and by the U-Rollit stetsons and Bulldogger Hats in the prairiewear shops. Its truer flavor is, not altogether expectedly, to be found on the dowdy northern fringe.

The suburbs here are far from blue chip: in the baking heat lawn-sprinklers twirl on cramped tufty lawns that lack the power-mower patina; the white wooden houses are not immersed in the cool of big shade trees; the gravel roads are pot-holed and rutted. On a plot at Tenth Street and Oklahoma is an assembly of house trailers, ranging from humpy Airstream caravans to immense oblongs of corrugated silver aluminium looking as long as jet liners.

This is the Hi-Klass Mobile Home Park which is kept in business because Liberal stands on the eastern edge of the vast Hugoton natural gasfield, stretching from Garden City to the North down through the Oklahoma Panhandle to Amarillo in Texas, and is the Great Plains gas and oil hub of South-Western Kansas. It is a transients' town. The specialist artisans needed during the progressive phases of development in the oilfields and gasfields come in, complete their tasks and pass on.

Helen, the wife of Wilbur "Shorty" Kneedler, a bulldozer operator with Hall Construction Company, has made a pugnacious gesture against impermanence. Along the cement strip,

237

advertised as the "patio," she has shoehorned in a tiny garden. There is a ribbon of lawn and a few wilting flowers and she has planted a walnut sapling in one corner; she has also entwined red and white plastic roses across the chain-link fencing.

She is a spry, wizened woman in her fifties who, despite the wrench of leaving her improvised gardens, declares theirs to be a great life. Her husband is sleeping late this Sunday morning.

"We've had thirty years of it, following the lines wherever they lay 'em, through Colorado, Iowa and Kansas, Nebraska and Missouri and Texas. Yet – funny – I don't really think of myself as a transit. Shorty's working at Elkhart, sixty miles west of here, but they're moving him next week to Alva, Oklahoma, to clear the trees and rubbish for putting in the helium plant and main distributing line.

"Having this trailer is just wonderful, it surely is; you always have your home with you. It's like a turtle. Always a home on your back. I like to park on a farm because there you've got God's good earth to work on and you're not always too welcome in towns. They get to call us pipeliner trash. Our downfall is that some trailer people get credit from the local stores and then skip without paying their bills which hurts the rest of us. But I think most people know that we help the city when we arrive. We bring them the gas they need and we bring money into the town.

"Shorty's always in the higher pay bracket on the 'dozer, even though he don't read or write. He's never been able to do any studying about his work because he didn't take enough schooling, but he knows how to put together and maintain all that machinery and heavy equipment.

"He says it just takes a strong back and a weak mind, but he's a good 'dozer man. I like seeing the country this way with him but you never know when you're going to sit still. And I do wish, yes, I do wish I could roll up my garden and take it with me."

Robert Odell Mitchell, a stocky, wind-burned man of forty-eight, pushes blue goggles back on to his brown steel helmet, takes off his Big Mac heat-proof gloves and tucks them into a belt slung with canvas tool satchels: "I had a little problem here.

The radius angles weren't set straight, and there was a crack in there." He indicates the twin iron pods, like great rusty boilers perched on platforms sixty feet down in a ramped pit in the flat Montana cornland. They are the brain capsules for the launch control center of a cluster of Minutemen inter-continental ballistic missiles, the last fifty of one thousand tucked in deep concrete silos in these northern states, cocked for two-second take-off to their Soviet Union targets.

The site is just outside the small township of Conrad and the Blackfeet Indian reservation, and sixty miles north of the copper and zinc base of Great Falls. There, too, at Great Falls is the nuclear delivery system's construction headquarters, at the Malmstrom Air Force station, with its motto PEACE IS OUR PROFESSION at the cenotaph-like shrine of a white-painted up-ended Minuteman rocket.

Mitchell is an iron worker, a welder. "I was born at Swearingen, in middle-west Texas, my daddy was an oilfield worker and I was raised up in the oilfield. Since then I guess I've worked for more than fifty contractors in my lifetime.

"I've built airplane hangars in Oklahoma and Texas, the Civic Center in Chicago, the University of Louisiana, a fifty-two storey building in Dallas, a structure at the Shepherd Air Force Base in Wichita Falls. I was eight months in Madrid drilling wells for the Spanish government, and I've built furnaces and factories. I've worked through California and New Mexico and Nebraska and Indiana and Oklahoma and Alabama; I never did like the east too awful much. I started on missile sites in 1946 at Roswell, New Mexico.

"That was an Atlas site and I went on to another Atlas site at Tulsa. I went on to Minutemen in Minot, North Dakota, and from there to Huntsville, Alabama, on the moon-shot rocket stand.

"Round about then I got kind of tired running around. These jobs are so strung out. You wear your car out, driving over the bad roads. I went up into the steel mills in Gary, Indiana, for one-and-a-half years. My buddies there decided to move on to Grand Rapids. I didn't want to move, but I should've went – they were getting four hundred dollars and I was getting two hundred.

"But anyway I pretty soon wanted to get out of the dust of that ole mill, so my wife and me we loaded up the little ole Pontiac with all the dishes and linens and flower pots and ironing boards wives have to take with them, and we lit out here. Well, I like to fish and hunt, and I like iron, and it's the kind of life I enjoy.

"It's something you been raised up to. It's not that I've ever found the pastures any greener the other side of the hill, but I got itchy feet; always cared for moving around."

IT is difficult to find a hobo, ex or extant, who will commend the life; but it is equally difficult to find one completely inoculated against it. There seems to be at some point a merging of a man hunting for a job into a man for whom the manoeuvres of hunting become more important than the objective.

Occasionally there is the outright warning to be found, not only the terrors and homilies of the hobo broadsheets, but such considered advice as that given by Cisco Houston, the folksinger and union organizer, who was on the road with Woody Guthrie and Leadbelly, and who just before he died in 1961 told a young guitar-happy student who wanted to cut loose from school and bum around America: "Sure, see the country. But put first things first. You don't have to go on the road just because Woody and I and Pete and Lee did it. We had to. Everybody wants to live well. That's what we're fighting for. Fight for education, clean clothes, and stay away from railroads."

The double beat of compulsion and repulsion is almost always embedded in writings about America's overland adventures. A book published in 1937 entitled *We Turned Hobo* is of interest because, uniquely in the decade, the author seems not to have had economic motives for moving.

Carl S. Shockman describes how he and his younger brother Clarence had in 1931 departed from their father's farm at Coldwater, Ohio. "The lure of far places had entered our blood and we had to obey its call."

They buy old Army uniforms, stuff blankets in shoulder packs and are ready. When their mother realizes that they shall not be gainsaid, she tells them: "Any time you find you can't get any farther by hitch-hiking, turn back for you'll always be welcome here, and last of all, please don't ride the freight trains."

Carl and Clarence got as far as Indianapolis by car but then, forgetful of their mother's pleas, switch to the freights and ride toward "the sunny land of our dreams, California." It is a singularly uneventful journey, yet the author quite genuinely conveys the poignancy of the American venture from home.

The brothers have barely reached California when Tex, a grizzled hobo, exhorts them to turn back. Tears streaking his cheeks, he tells them that six months after he likewise had hightailed from home he had returned but "my mother wasn't there to greet me. She had died several months before." Don't ever ride a train again. Go home and stay there. When the old fever grips ya, fight and just remember what happened to me."

Clarence and Carl look at each other: they board an Eastbound train. Carl concludes: "At twelve-thirty on December 20, 1931 we entered the portals of our 'Home, Sweet Home' ... I'll never, never ride another freight. I still shudder to think of what might have happened to us, and I sincerely believe there was Someone above who protected us ... Thus I'll end my story by saying simply: 'HOME, SWEET HOME, BE IT EVER SO HUMBLE, THERE'S NO PLACE LIKE HOME.'"

Then in 1941 Minehan produced a book for children, *Lonesome Road*. It's hero is Joe, a fifteen-year-old orphan living with an aunt in Tulsa. In the traditional form Joe encounters a fully-fledged road kid of eighteen, named Bill Greene, who spins the travel dream stuff, and says: "Shucks, there ain't nothing to it. All you need is a tongue and a thumb."

Joe and Bill sleep rough in jungles and equally rough in jail, but they get to California and gradually push North. Bindle on shoulder, they drift onward to the apple farms of Washington, and then East to Colorado where they pack peaches one summer and herd sheep during the winter. They arrive in Seattle where they try to ship out to the salmon canneries of Alaska, but find that they are but two among hundreds trying without a hope to get beyond the lash of the depression.

There is a muzzy socialistic flavor to *Lonesome Road*. Joe learns a poem which goes:

> *The bum on the rods is a social flea, who gets an*
> > *occasional bite*
> *The bum on the plush is a social leech, bloodsucking day*
> > *and night*
> *The bum on the rods is a load so light*
> *That his weight we scarcely feel*
> *But it takes the labour of a dozen men*
> *To furnish the other a meal.*
> *As long as you sanction the bum on the plush the other*
> > *will always be there*
> *But rid yourself of the bum on the plush and the other*
> > *will disappear*
> *Then make an intelligent organized kick, get rid of the*
> > *weights that crush*
> *Don't worry about the bum on the rods – get rid of the*
> > *bum on the plush.*

After strongly underscoring the attractions of being free agent in the United States, Minehan at the end corrects these blandishments with a swift change of tack, for eventually Joe and Bill weary of the Salvation Army homes and government Transients' Camps – "living on Sally and Sam."

They meet an old whiskery bum who says: "I've ruined my stomach with poor food and worse whisky. I've ruined my body with neglect and abuse. It's hard for me to feel at home any place except in a box car. It's hard for me to look people in the face because I'm always expecting a kick ... Get off the road while the getting's good."

After the traditional opening of the hobo morality play, the traditional close with the warning of the ancient mariner. And indeed Joe and Bill decide to quit the road.

Joe returns from the wide, wandering way to the straight and narrow, and gets a job as a truck driver, and "never again did he tramp the country ... for he knew that nobody could remain on the road too long without becoming a bum, and Joe had seen too many bums to want to be one himself."

For all that the poignant tug is there on the last page: "At night he sometimes awoke to imagine the bed under him was a swaying box car, or the rumble of a distant bus the sound of a freight engine pulling a load uphill."

Almost always when the repentance has been formally supplicated the syrup seeps through again. There is a splendid purple-heroic passage in Ashleigh's autobiographical novel where Joe Crane, his Wobbly hero is once more on the road.

"Thunder, thunder on smoothly, you long sinuous steel thing of speed," Joe exulted, standing in the blind baggage on the last lap of the ride. He had caught the Shasta Limited, the fast devil from Portland ... "Shriek, you devil," thought Joe, clinging with gloved hand to the steel hand-grip. The train swayed and heaved, sensitive, swift and beautiful, merciless.

"The wind roared past him. He loved the train as a horseman loves his horse . . . This was one of the things that kept men hobos for life: the ecstasy of the end of the journey. Meeting the others, and boasting; the relaxation of nerves which one never realized were so tensed."

Rambling Kid, culminating, as did many up-lift Marxist novels of its time, on rapturous wing to the new socialist heaven of Comrade Lenin, is yet one of the more valuable sources of information about the amorphous American proletariat of the First World War. The romantic pang is strong throughout. "Die Sache der Arme, In Gottes und Teufels Name" ("The cause of the poor, in spite of God and the Devil!"), murmurs an intellectual jungle stiff. Joe, still in his teens, forks off to the city, and to the slave market section of saloons and employment agents. "There was an atmosphere of recklessness and daring about these fellows who strolled along the streets in their blue overalls, or khaki trousers, with grey or blue shirts, open at the throat, and their black slouch hats. They knew the Western states from British Columbia to the Mexican border, from Chicago to Portland, Oregon.

"In all the vast territory where great railroads are still being built, or giant reservoirs; where wheat and other harvests are gathered where forests are felled, they roamed from job to job ..."

In a saloon called Black Davis's, where Joe is temporarily helping at the lunch counter, "by evening the air would be thick with tobacco, the odors of drink and the exudations of human bodies. They stood at the long bar thickly clustered – for men were pouring into Minneapolis to ship out to the harvests which were just commencing. Here was a bunch of "gandy-dancers." With fingers dipped in beer they traced upon the bar the diagrams of new railway branches . . .

"Near them were other men from construction camps . . . a superior breed which looked contemptuously upon those who sweated with pick and shovel. They were 'teamios,' these reckless rascals, with their great broad-brimmed black hats – the men who drove the mule carts which carried the dirt away from the excavation to the dump.

"And even among the teamsters, or 'skinners' as they were called, there was an aristocracy consisting of the men who drove the carts which were drawn by six to a dozen mules – these were the kings of the craft, the 'long-line skinners.' Nobody bothered the 'teamios' much, for these men were feared. They carried razors with them, and would use them as weapons, if necessary. They were great fighters, and an insult to one of them would be the signal for a gang attack, such was their clannishness.

"Near them would be perhaps a group of lumberjacks, men from the forests of spruce and pine along the Puget Sound, or from Eastern Washington, Montana or Michigan. These were usually big fellows with many Scandinavians and Finns among them, as well as old Saxon-American stock. Joe could pick them out by their heavy, knee-high boots about which hung their overall trousers, raggedly cut short. They wore heavy flannel shirts or blouses which hung outside their belts; and some wore the short Mackinaw coat of brightly-patterned blanket material."

The evening streets are thronged. "Rough greetings were shouted as wanderers met whose paths had not crossed for a year or more. Genial groups poured out of saloons to enter other ones. On the corner the portable rostrum of the Industrial Workers of the World was being set up, and in a moment the voice of the 'Wobblies,' singing their revolutionary songs, added yet another note to the strong symphony of the Slave Market."

Joe falls in with a particular group of Wobs, Gold-Tooth Carey, a teamster, The Terrible Swede, Boston White and Cincinnati Red, and he is permitted to join their drinking party. They begin singing Wobbly songs. The Terrible Swede "led them in a melancholy chant: 'Oh, where is my wandering boy tonight?' The lumber-jack looked at them with a tender wistfulness while he sang, droning the notes with drawn-out pathos. The tears came to their eyes as they considered the sorrows of a hobo's life. And as they joined in the chorus, they looked gratefully at the red-hot stove, thinking of the bitter night-rides when the poor hobo, frozen and cramped, must cling to the unfriendly metal of the engine-tender or car."

Next day Joe buys overalls and a pair of working gauntlets and then takes out a Red Card.

"Joe began to feel that here was a new baptism. Last night he had been received into the wide fraternity of the floaters, the migratory workers. And now he was initiated into the interior fellowship of the rebels ... Joe walked down the street, a slight swagger in his gait. His hat was cocked to one side of his head. His hands were deep in the pockets of his new overalls. He eyed impudently the respectable citizens passing by.

"He was a hobo and a Wobbly, one of the reckless rambling boys who despised the soft security and comfort of a dull-spaced city existence."

One hears the same garish pride, and contempt for the home-guard and spittoon philosophers, coming from the loud mouth of Spud Murphy, an IWW migrant described by Chaplin. At a meeting addressed by a University of Chicago economics professor, Murphy tells the gathering: "No kiddin', I pity you poor scissorbill kids sittin' down there with your little pencils and notebooks. No wonder you never know nuthin' when you go out into the big world ... I'll tell ya, why don't you go out and grab a rattler and find out things for yourself ... Three months in the harvest fields and a thirty-day stretch in the hoosegow – that's the way to get smarted up."

Braggart cock-sureness, wistful hedonism, secret misery and the canonization of the outcast bravo – all these sound a constant theme through the underclass literature of this period.

Among the bleakest pictures of a hobo's trials is Dahlberg's *Bottom Dogs*, a gloomy piece of Thirties proletarian nationalism. Young Lorry's story is unremittingly dejected. He hauls himself into a boxcar: "He huddled up in a corner. There was no straw around, and the bottom boards were splintered, with a stiff, desolate-feeling air coming up through the cracks. He kept fidgeting about, not seeming able to get fitted in right against some corner; there was a smell of human excreta coming from somewhere. He went off for an hour or so, and jarred up by some bump or other, it was hard to doze off again. The cold kept getting into him, tightening up his joints. Some time early in the morning he stood up, stiff as a nail, kicking one foot out after the other to get the ache out of his knees, which felt as hollow to him as a bone chewed raw by an alley dog."

And yet when some other hobos are planning to get themselves pinched near Ogden, Utah, to feed up in prison Lorry rejects the idea. "He didn't care if he never saw any grub, he wanted his freedom, he wanted to knock about, hit the road whenever he felt like it, bum around the country. He would get through somehow."

Later he has a moment when he almost longs to be "domesticated, cooped up in straw like poultry for the winter," for being on the bum "did appear to be a purple-fingered, desolate affair, leaving one out in the cold," but when he sees another locomotive, "its headlights drawn out like batwings" as it looms nearer, "he became all nerves and couldn't wait to hop her; he was going on, beatin' the bulls ..."

At length: "Perhaps he would go east, get out of it all, he could run away; but he couldn't go side-door Pullman again, that was finished. Boing, sleeping in coal cars, riding those railroad broncos, going to strange hotel rooms, the ghastly plaster inside those empty clothes closets, walking the streets – all that was done, but then, how did he know?"

A social-realism novel which preceded both *Bottom Dogs* and *Rambling Kid* was Edge's *The Main Stem* published in 1927 whose hero Blondey, is found in 1918 working in a Cleveland stove factory with a labor force of first generation Pollacks. In the boarding house he meets Slim whom he immediately perceives to be different: "There was something big and fresh about him ... he always brought in with him a little of the clean outdoors."

This "novel" is a college boy's dalliance with Marxist ideas, with the pre-Orwellian desire to sink into the warmth of an imagined proletariat, and Slim is the introducer – but vaporously inept, it turns out, for all his smiling, tanned sophistication.

He takes Blondey hoboing and initiates him into the craft, as they board a freight, in this language: "We are now on a gondola. This is an open car, and, when empty, can comfortably accommodate ever so many bums, provided the shacks are friendly, and the yard dicks not too hostile. Nailing a rattler, where you choose a gondola or the side-door Pullman, calls for a concatenation of skills not acquired in a day." and so, relentlessly, on.

Slim in fact is slumming. He is actually educated and played full back "for one of the greatest Pacific coast teams three years ago." Rather feebly the first ride they take together is "on the cushions": they pay for their tickets to Pittsburg. There Slim explains as is his pedagogue wont: "We are now on the 'stem' or 'main stem' or 'main drag,' as you have just heard that worthy say."

On a building project Blondey begins to get the measure of the laborer's life in America. "The personnel of our gang changed daily ... Few men lasted on one job longer than three weeks. Intermittent employment breeds the habit of wandering around for other jobs ... Also workers left because poor food or lousy beds drove them away. Employers refused to improve living conditions, because, after all the men were restless, footloose, floaters. And so it went; and nothing was done about it; and it took perhaps twenty men to fill one job annually."

Journeying on, Slim reads to him from *Ghosts* and *A Doll's House*, and after a night in a field rouses Blondey thus: "Wake up, my dusky beauty, for jocund morn stands tiptoe on the misty mountain tops, and your face is as black as a shine's." While not displaying much inclination to turn words into acts Slim characteristically declaims: "Migratoriness is, perhaps, satisfactory to only a few temperaments. Some people love the formalities and insincerity of bourgeois life; others tolerate it. I

247

don't. I have on important occasions made my escape from the hollowness and chicaneries of bourgeois environment. I doubt that I shall ever return to it." Blondey, like a girl hovering agonizedly on the brink of surrendering her virginity, fluctuates between the attraction and the dangers of the traveling adventure. On their way into Chicago they pass through sidings of cars studded with the names which he had "come to associate with romance ... 'The Pennsy,' 'The Big Four,' 'The B & O,' 'The Santey Fay,' one hears these names over and over again in dosshouses, at meals, just as one hears the words Chevrolet, Buick, Studebaker at dinner receptions and the theatre ... I was a little afraid, too, of those words. On these trains with epic names, I was to plunge into lands unknown to me."

Also in Chicago he detects a difference in the men. In the Eastern cities the hobo had been "an adventitious migratory. He went dumbly from job to job, impelled by the relentless forces of modern capitalism. He was simply a man beaten by the economic system." But here in Chicago "the hobo seemed to be a hobo by choice."

"The men were large, strong, conscious of their disinheritance. They seemed not to be the victims of circumstances; they had definite standards. They did not allow themselves to be kicked about from job to job."

He looks at this different breed of American and is frightened for so far he had been "only flirting with the forces that drag men down for good. But this was in earnest ..."

It was a serious matter, this hobo business. Elsewhere he ponders anxiously: "Will I ever again be able to take my place as a citizen in the world of the middle class? Will I be a lawyer, or doctor, or a teacher, or a realtor, or a mortician? ... Where am I going? Will I always be a stiff?"

The answer was No. Because after less than a year of laboring and a little zig-zagging around the author caught 'flu, was admitted into hospital, and then shipped home, and presumably was severed from that nympholepsy that might have prevented him becoming a realtor or mortician. Slim, one takes it, continued his pantomime of rogue intellectual and mocker of the middle classes, dazzling apprentices with Ibsen, the scourge of the passenger coach bourgeoisie.

Similarly Glen H. Mullin whose *Adventures of a Scholar Tramp* appeared in 1925, was a middle-class amateur – a university graduate who hit the road for a few months with a golden-hearted ragamuffin ("Wherever you are, old-timer, I salute you – hobo rex, tramp royal!") and who got the infection: "To the genuine hobo a train is a thing compounded of magic and beauty, just as a bravely trimmed vessel is to the mariner. It arouses within him a latent mysticism. The rattle and swank of a long freight pulling out of the yards, the locomotive black and eager, shoving hard a snorting muzzle along the rails ... an enchanted caravan moving into the mysterious beyond, hailing with poems and song blue distance ... As the hobo sits on a tie-pile, perhaps, and watches her go by, there is a lure in the cars themselves individually. He moves his lips unconsciously repeating the sonorous names that lilt past."

But at the end of his truncated "smoky trail" Mullin states candidly: "In truth I was sick of the Road, and ready to admit it. The freedom of the Road is certainly specious: it is too uncomfortable, compromised everywhere by laws ... One wearies after a while of the sordid outlawry of the Road."

At least Edge and Mullin tried it, or dipped their toes in. But there was another category of hobo literature emerging which, in the period when the refugee with family became more typical than the individual rambler, sought to glamorize what was then believed to be a dying if not already extinct species.

Anderson deserted his earlier objective sociological work on the homeless to produce, under the assumed personality of "Dean Stiff," *The Milk and Honey Route: A Handbook for Hoboes* in 1931. The paradigm Dean Stiff is met in a municipal lodging house queue in Chicago and he addresses Anderson: "There's too much hocum on the hobo subject. What with professors like you doing researches and the novelists with their human interest stuff, the rest of the world is getting to think of the hobo game as a lot of cheap comedy. I say it's a grand art and it's about time somebody stepped in and saved it from the hitch-hiker," whereupon he, the onlie begetter, hands over the manuscript of the text which follows.

Although in the preface Anderson remarks truly that "the hobo for all his simplicity, is still a phantom man, and Hobohemia still remains a realm too obscure to be interpreted vividly by any casual or occasional visitor," *The Milk and Honey Route* does not solidify the ghost.

"No fictionist can explore the hobo's province by riding across it as Stevenson traversed Europe on a donkey," declares Anderson, making doubtful extrapolations and also undermining his own case with them. "The true reporter must be of the blood, and they of the blood are few. He knows the truth because he lives it ... he becomes identified with the spirit of the wanderman, the Homer of ancient times, the *Meistersinger* of the Dark Ages, the roadside magic vendors and vagrant story tellers of every century and every clime."

What follows is precisely what Dean Stiff was railing against: a highly seasoned pudding of fact and fancy, anecdote and fable, history and taradiddle. This is not to say that Anderson did not know his stuff. Probably more assiduously than any other American sociologist, he turned an enquiring and sympathetic eye upon the homeless man, yet he uses Dean Stiff as a sounding board for a colorfully whimsy *opéra bouffe*.

"The hobo is always born a hobo," the book begins. "The American hobo is born to the caste and finds his niche in it as the actor born to the stage finds Broadway or as the naturally endowed plutocrat finds Wall Street." From this series of breathtakingly disputable premises, it prances on: "If you have this hobo's instinct, all you need to do is follow your nose and your feet will do the rest. Without this innate quality no amount of training will help you. Hobohemia will be nothing less than *omnium gatherum*, chaos and confusion. Possessing this prized instinct of the wanderman, you will find this realm as orderly as a psychological maze ...

"The hobo really floats ... Because he floats and flows away you thought him a mystery, and perhaps you thought his a purposeless way of life ... Hobohemia is American. It is a kingdom of he-men and hard men ... that is why it remains the only earthly reminder of the Garden of Eden."

At the start Anderson in a waggishly jocular tone promises that he has advice to offer the "young man ambitious to become a hobo; it is an important calling and not to be entered upon too lightly. The arch vein is maintained: "The good life

that the hobo leads must not be married to insidious toil . .
The conditions he puts on work are the same as those of the
aristocrat: which is quite logical, since he is the peer of the
aristocrat. He lives the same simple self-satisfying life. He has
the same aversion to pretension."

Anderson was speaking for those who rather disliked being
told that the hobo worker had a trying time, which is why
Anderson charged that Jim Tully "capitalizes the misery of his
hobo days" and wrote accusingly that "Tully's hoboes are not
philosophers; they are a cross between a Gorki tramp and Tarzan
of the Apes."

In fact even Tully was captive to an allure that is somewhat
elusive in his drab catalogue of arrests and hunger and violence
and cold. "I heard an old tramp say that once a tramp always
a tramp," he writes, "and I wondered just how many ever left
the road for good. In spite of all the hardships through which
I had recently passed, I found a charm about the road that I had
not known elsewhere."

There is in Tully – because the near-criminal degradation is
baldly related – a greater conviction than in all of Dean Stiff's
roundelays, so a genuine emotion is conveyed. After a stay in
hospital with fever this is Tully's reverie: "The winter passed,
and the warm winds of May made me long to wander again.
The whistling of a locomotive on a still night had a lure, un-
explainable, yet strong, like the light which leads a moth to
destruction."

He hops the blind baggage of a Big Four mail from Illinois
Central, then onward toward Washington: "The great headlight
of the Fast Flyer Virginia swept over the rails. Aroused from
the lethargy of dream, I was the rider to far places again, and
my great iron horse was snorting on its way."

There are more frozen, empty-bellied rides; more arrests. One
policeman, discovering that he is only fifteen, lets him go with
the observation: "Well, well, indade. I have a lad yere age, an'
I'd hate to see him driftin' 'round the country like a lost
sparrow."

At Cairo, a tri-state town on the borders of Missouri, Kentucky
and Illinois, snow is falling and thirty lost sparrows are hud-

dled around the water tank, some carving their monikers on the red-painted pine boards, others talking of the road, "always the road." They are "the disheveled of the earth."

Again Tully reflects upon himself as outcast and rover: "At times I cursed the wanderlust that held me in its grip. While cursing, I loved it. For it gave me freedom undreamed of in factories, where I would have been forced to labor."

In a whistle-stop town he looks at the unpainted houses, the scruffy lawns, the ugly streets, and again feels "glad that I was a hobo on the long free trail." Farther down the line, wild rain is falling upon a jungle, whipping through the shack built of railroad ties. "The clothes of the shivering tramps dripped with water.

"Miserable men they were, the shabby tricksters of life. But they endured, like stoics, with a smile. They took what life, or the elements, sent them. They fought and they drank; they begged and they robbed. But this can be written to their everlasting credit above the stars in the farthest sky – they did not whine."

In his final chapter Tully performs the familiar cartwheel of producing an eleventh-hour epilogue of condemnation of the roving life, but with more qualifications than is customary. At least "some great pugilists have been developed on the road. Jack Dempsey, Kid McCoy and Stanley Ketchell, three of the greatest bruisers that ever lived, were youthful hoboes for several years." And he reminds the reader: "Always he hears voices calling in the night from far away places where blue waters lap strange shores. He hears birds singing and crickets chirping a luring roundelay ... Traveling a brutal road, his moral code becomes heavy, and he often throws it away. Civilization never quite restores all of it to him, which, of course, may not be as tragic as it sounds.

"Gorky, the brilliant ex-tramp, returned to the road again for a year. Few people understood the reason. I did. It was the caged eagle returning to the mountains of its youth for a last look at the carefree life it had known. It remained a year, and found that the vast and lonely places were the same, but the blood had slowed around the eagle heart, and it flew back to the valley again, wearier than before – the last illusion gone . . .

"All of the philosophical stuff written about tramps should be taken lightly. The non-producers of the nation are tramps in one sense or another.

"The prattling parasitic club woman, the obese gambler in bonds, the minister in a fashionable church, all are tramps who happen to have beds and bath, and the economic security that men go mad to obtain. In fact, the tramp is merely a parasite who has not been admitted to society."

21 : MEN WITHOUT ALLEGIANCES

There is no revolutionary situation in America. Factory girls wear silk stockings but have no class consciousness – capitalism is in blacker and more complete control than anywhere else on earth.

Robert Wolf, of *The New Masses*, to the Communist Academy, Moscow, 1927.

ANDERSON'S comparison of the hobos Tully knew to a Gorky tramp, and Tully's own reference to the "brilliant extramp," are quite strikingly apt when examined. The parallel between America and Russia, these two nations so distant geographically and in spirit, does reward examination because they are the only two countries to have produced a distinct and large tribal society of detached workers – and they did it simultaneously with economic patterns which were dissimilar in origin but which converged in result.

In America capitalism had filled a vacuum, air empty of commerce and mass population; in Russia, modern capital development and nascent industry crashed in through the old agrarian-feudal system.

But Russia's new financial houses and manufacturing companies were of a mushroomy brittleness, and bankruptcies and failed enterprises went in chain detonations through the 1870s and 1880s. Peasants released from serfdom in 1861 had swarmed into the towns to form an industrial proletariat, and were promptly cast off in the series of slumps spreading unemployment into an already distressed countryside. Workless artisans fled back to the deserted farmlands, while rural paupers migrated from their villages to try their luck in the cities; a crisscrossing futility becoming institutionalized across the other side of the world.

There was another ludicrous resemblance. In 1881, when the infestation of homeless vagabonds throughout Russia had reached five millions, the authorities set up The Society for the Improvement of Public Work, the code of which was circulated to municipalities thus: "The bitter experience of other countries has convincingly demonstrated that the lack of protection, poverty and ignorance of the masses make them readily receptive to every kind of Utopian doctrine ... Therefore it is essential to teach them now the right kind of productive labor ... to encourage their moral and religious development on the basis of reasonable and honest work."

The moral and religious development urged in that Russian McGuffy's *Reader* was however inaccessible to those such as Maxim Gorky, at the age of eleven pitched into "the back-alleys of life." His companions and heroes, as described in *Makar Chudra, Old Izergil* and *Malva*, were the Black Sea coastal boat nomads and uprooted farmhands. He isolated something these implacable turbulences were creating, a new man, individually doomed but collectively puissant, whose contempt for the society that had cast them adrift was an expression of Pushkin's early poetry, was Byronic in its hauteur and was revolutionary in its political intuition.

Gorky's stories began, just as did Jack London's in America, to place the new man. The *bossiak*, meaning literally barefoot tramp, was in Gorky's usage a word as charged with philosophical and political meaning as hobo or Wobbly. These were "men without allegiances but also without fetters." Failed students, displaced peasants, outsider nihilists, outlawed unionists, pariah poets, workless teachers, rebel soldiers, footloose peasants, declasse drifters – these were the "superfluous men" in the twilight zone of the cellars, dosshouses and ruined buildings of Odessa, the readymade cast of *The Lower Depths*, produced in 1901. It was the first kitchen sink drama, the fountain-head of Beckett's dustbins and O'Neill's Bowery purgatory. It was a sensation and a triumph.

His *bossiaks*, like his petrel, the small black bird that is the rider of the storms, presaged the coming revolution: they had stepped out of the old life to prospect for a new. With personal experience as errand boy, ragpicker, bird-catcher, bricklayer, railway man, stevedore and as cadger of rides on Moscow goods trains, Gorky wrote: " ... living among the lower middle class and seeing around me people whose only object was to turn other people's blood and sweat into kopeks, I came to hate fiercely the parasitic life of those commonplace people.

"Tramps for me were 'uncommon people' ... 'declassed' men who had cut loose from their class or had been repudiated by it and had lost the most characteristic traits of their class."

As Jack London in America was just a little later to do, Gorky held up a looking-glass in which a multitude of intellectuals without bearings and workmen without outlets could recognize themselves and their constellation. It is doubtful that, as Richard Hare says, "the spreading swarm of hungry tramps threatened the whole structure of Russian society," although it is perfectly believable that the Russian bourgeoisie, like their American counterparts, feared that they did.

In his own apartness from organized society he distilled the spirit of the destitute and desperate, "strong-willed moral men, impetuous and unreflective, yet proud and self-reliant, masters of their own fate." What he admired in them, what chimed with his own revolutionary drive, was "their anger with life, their mocking hostility to everything and everybody, and their carefree attitude to themselves."

Contemporary critics denounced Gorky's writings as a menace to decency and sound citizenship: "Hooligans are his only heroes, and most of them are psychopaths ... and so long as a beast is young, vigorous and insensitive, all Gorky's sympathies are on the side of the beast." His portrait-gallery made the first distinction between the new-type vagabond and the old nomadic Asiatic Russians, and not all heroes were "hardened men of action, reckless dreamers or tough guys," but *In The Steppe* examines the very blurred hair line between the *bossiak* and the professional criminal. Gorky's attitude was not all that different from London's reverence for the "blond-beast," and indeed in *My Universities*, he says: "Among the longshoremen, hoboes and drifters I felt like a piece of iron thrown into the midst of redhot coals ... My past life drew me towards these men, arousing a desire to immerse myself in their corroding depths."

Augier's *La nostalgie de la Boue* was strong in Gorky but it does not surprise at all that in that passage he should continue:

"Bret Harte and other fiction of adventurers and outcasts helped to arouse further my sympathies for this life."

Here is the two-way traffic in action: Gorky, the estranged Russian bourgeois infected by an American's luridly dramatic sketches of the lawless, gold-crazed frontier rabble, drifters with Raphael faces, college graduates gone off the rails, sullenly tense gunmen and gamblers "with the melancholy air and intellectual abstraction of a Hamlet," all pitched into an overheated closeness against the aloof and terrible loneliness of the Sierras, and so again to recur and echo back in London's writing about Gorky's 1900 *Foma Gordyeeff*.

De Crevecoeur's observation toward the end of the eighteenth century was: "The rich stay in Europe, it is only the middling and the poor that emigrate." This had continued to be so. Either poor and desperate or poor and ambitious, the "crucial image" in the American mind has been that of a vast continent "to be discovered, explored, cleared, built up, populated, energized; which has not excluded the image of a continent to be rifled, despoiled, much of it wasted." Nor has it excluded the capacity to rue what was being done to the continent even in those participating.

The men who despoiled and discovered at the same time wrung those hands of destruction. During his first trip as a harvest worker in the early 1900s, a decade after the frontier had been declared closed, Chaplin lamented in this poem:

> The 'blanket-stiff' now packs his bed
> Along the trails of yesteryear –
> What path is left for you to tread?
>
> Your fathers' golden sunsets led
> To virgin prairies wide and clear –
> Do you not know the West is dead?
>
> Your fathers' world, for which they bled,
> Is fenced and settled far and near –
> Do you not know the West is dead?

> *Your fathers gained a crust of bread,*
> *Their bones bleach on the lost frontier;*
> *What path is left for you to tread —*
> *Do you not know the West is dead?*

Hundreds of thousands of johnny-come-latelys, catching at the hem of the dream, found that the farmland was behind rails, the timber stands razed, the minerals tapped and expropriated. So they became not the rich rancher or gold-shipper they had imagined but other people's helots – but, also, always renegades from an unendurable status.

"The freeborn American working man had become surplus labor for giant industrial combines," Lomax writes. "Viewed from a bed in the cinders along the railroad tracks, the American system was not working any more."

That was not entirely the case. The tough and frugal life that their predecessors had accepted as a temporary stage on the way up had for the rearguard hardened into permanence. Yet the illusion of having his own sweet way could be sustained if the casual laborer who would not answer to that title went on roving from job to job, and wrote an individual Declaration of Independence to go with it. That the West was dead may have been physically true but it was not metaphysically. The root-and-branch hobo contrived to survive beyond the frontier, at least outside the pale of standardized life. If Gorky was the catalyst in Russia, his exact opposite number in America was London. He not only made the written definition of the new man but himself became the symbol of, in Arthur Calder-Marshall's words, "The emergent twentieth-century man, romantic, tough, courageous, ranging the continents of the earth, the freeman of all classes – and yet the champion of the underdog: a Robin Hood of letters, the man who put heart back into the exploited earth and hope into the hearts of the exploited workers." London always believed that man had the choice: he could be either "felon or tramp," he could "learn a trade" or "roister and frolic over the world," he could take his decision "between money and men, between niggardliness and romance."

The choice London made, and continued to flaunt even when making the blackest theater out of its grim necessities, gave expression to an entire mode of American thought and feeling. London may have failed to produce "a Moby Dick of the box-cars" but his effect by being more diffuse has also been more powerful. When London made up his mind that "the thought of work was repulsive" and "headed out on the adventure-path again," naturally it was to the railroad he went, his own pathway in his "search for the lost epic virtues of America" and that of millions of humble men.

PART THREE

THE GREAT HARP

Oh, babes,
Oh, no-home babes.

22 : FEET GOT TO ROLLING LIKE A WHEEL, YEAH, LIKE A WHEEL

My sister wrote a letter, my mother wrote a card –
"If you want to come an' see us, you'll have to ride
the rods."

Leadbelly : *The Midnight Special*

ACROSS the cotton fields beyond a hamlet named England a pool seventeen miles long and seven miles wide is being built. This is Lock and Dam No. 6 in the Arkansas River and Tributaries Project, a 1·2 billion dollar flood-control scheme which will also provide a navigable waterway from Oklahoma through to the Mississippi. On these baygalls South-East of Little Rock the pile-driving gangs in yellow casques and Mae Wests are building the spillway. Cranes grind through the slush holding steel stakes like straws in their serrated mandibles; tug crews manipulate the ninety-foot sheet steel walls of the cofferdam cells; draglines, earth-shifters and tractor-mounted backhoes scoop out the connecting channels.

Jay Halverson, a crew-cut man of twenty-nine in knee-high lace-up boots, is chief engineer for Dravo, the Pittsburgh contractor, but only two of the men on the job come from Pittsburgh. They come from Tennessee, from West Virginia, from Oklahoma, from New York. Jay Halverson himself was born in South Dakota and graduated from Iowa State University.

Leaning on a red heavy duty truck among the phalanx of trailer offices beside a notice THIS IS A HARD HAT JOB. POSITIVELY! he says: "This is my seventeenth move in ten years. I've worked mostly on river and levee projects, in Georgia, in Iowa, up in Oregon, three places in South Dakota, on the Big Bend Dam on the Missouri River.

"I built a one million dollar parking lot at Mount Rushmore and before this I was excavating on a missile site in Nebraska.

263

That's how it is with most of the men in this field, the reinforced steel men and the structure steel men. They're pretty
much of a clan. They follow the jobs through the country.

"I would hate to think of settling down. There are too many
places to go. Too many new sights to see. There's a sense of
adventure about this. You never know where it'll be next.

"I'm married, with three young children, but my wife feels
the same as I do. She'd never moved out of Council Bluffs until
we got married. Then we just went *zzzzsssst*: started moving.
It sure broadens your friendships out. Everywhere we go we
find new friends, through the church organizations, the neighbors, the suppliers, the PTA.

"Usually when I start a new job I go ahead and find a house
to rent, which may take one day or four weeks, then Karen
joins me with the kids. We've always rented in the past but
this job will take until 1968 and we feel that times are good so
we've bought a 19,500 dollar home in North Little Rock. We
figure we should be able to sell for as much as we paid or even
make a profit on it.

"We buy our furniture from Sears Roebuck. It's cheap and it
looks nice enough but it's nothing we need get attached to. It's
expendable. If a leg gets broken off or something gets scratched
up it's no great loss. We don't find there's anything to hold us to
a house or a town. We're always ready for the next change."

On a July day I drove out of Arkansas, West across the Ozark
Mountains and along Route 33. This is a narrow, frayed ribbon
of poorly-maintained tarmac which jitters on flatly through the
Oklahoma savannah between pepperings of unpainted Negro
and white 'cropper huts, and little seesawing oil pumps nodding
to themselves like idiot heads in the roasting sun.

I passed many churches, as ramshackle as the melon patch
hovels, and advertisements of divine rescue were one of the
many lures: Church of the God of Prophecy and Tastee-Freez
Thick Shakes, Church of Christ Fully Air Conditioned and Ritz
Hi-Hat Restaurant, Sacred Church of Nazarene and Madame Ree
Palm Reader, First Free Will Baptist Church and a traveling
roller skating tent rink, Immanuel Baptist Church and the Cove
Motel for Colored, Twin Assembly of God Church and Clabber

Girl Baking Powder, Missionary Baptist Church and Wesleyan-Methodist Church and Episcopal Church and Free Christian Church, and Love That Delegate and Mister Donut and Micro-Midget Go Kart Racing and Dixie Comfort Peach Wine; on the car radio, a girl harmony trio with a jingle weather forecast "What is the weather like today? Are the neighborhood skies blue or grey?" and a Back To God program sponsored by the "great new way to carry home cans of beer. Each top twists off real easy" and the invitation to visit "The Book of Job, a Unique Outdoor Drama" and the drone of hog and heifer prices.

The sun dipped. The buzzards wheeled down to their woods. I ran through short bursts of neon morse code on the wayside chickenjukes and sugar shacks and at eleven-thirty entered the main street of a place named Stillwater, past the closed hardware stores, the closed business blocks, the closed five-and-ten, the closed churches. The Rio Restaurant was open, dilating with tingling lights.

I sat in one of the yellow and Cambridge blue plastic booths. The room busily sizzled with cooking hamburgers and clanged with the cash register keys. A state Trooper in fawn shirt and pants, with a pearl-handled revolver hanging from his bullet belt, was playing the Thoro-Bred pintable. Every counter stool was overhung like an icecream cone by a pair of enormous buttocks bulging inside Levis or putty ducks.

They were all fearsomely large men, some with black side-boards, some with hair skived down to an angry stubble, some wearing felt and straw hats or green forage caps tipped back, most in bronco boots. They could easily have walked in from their new land claims on Oklahoma Territory, just thrown open to its 1889 white settlement: nesters and grangers arrived in Murphy freight wagons and the big Osnaburg-topped wagons, cattle drovers passing through, or hide hunters and gold washers from beyond the new spreads.

While I ate my hickory smoked ham and hush puppies, a sort of corn meal rissole, I studied the remote-control nickel odeon panel in my booth. The musical menu displayed total indifference to the Top Ten fever charts of current metropolitan hits. Even if the churches were shuttered for the night, there was what

265

sounded like a rousing come-forward-holy hymn throbbing through the amplifier, except that the words were about the mortification of secular love: *Please don't wait for me, darling – I'll always be an ex-convict and branded wherever I go.*

It was replaced by a three-year-old recording, Gale Garnett's *We'll Sing in the Sunshine* – she'll lend him her love for a year, then she'll have to move on, a tender fatalism.

It was all country music and almost all of it to do with getting out of town or being given the go-by by a girl who had got out of town. There were familiar names there, Roy Orbison and Chet Atkins and the Everley Brothers and Floyd Cramer, but the music was as out-of-time as the oil drillers and grain milling hands around me. The titles were *Midnight Special* and *Memphis* and *Willie was a Gamblin' Man* and *Truck Drivin' Son-of-a-Gun* and *A Sharecropper's Life* and *Out of a Honky Tonk*.

I put in a dime and pressed the button for a song entitled *The Hobo and the Rose* by Webb Pierce, hitherto unknown to me. It turned out to be a plangent requiem about a young man who could not win the hand of a particular home town girl; so pinning on the white rose she gave him he snagged a freight out. Years later the girl pushes through a crowd beside the tracks at the whistle stop and she instantly recognizes the cadaver being unloaded by the rose (presumably mummified) pinned to his ragged jacket. He is buried in a poor man's grave, still wearing the rose.

One of the customers at the counter, in high filigreed boots and a scarlet shirt with a brass ring and jewel at the neck, slumped listening intently to the words. He appeared much affected by them; his face was broody.

Perhaps he had a rose among his belongings? Perhaps at least he had a home town and a home town girl somewhere down the track where earlier I had driven beside a black locomotive throwing its grunting cry, crestfallen, into the twilight as it pulled a line of rumbling trucks marked SOO LINE, EERIE LACKAWANNA, ROUTE OF THE EAGLES, THE ROUTE OF PHOEBE SNOW and TEXAS-PACIFIC LINE.

Since the first Irish navvies – canallers they had been called when they were digging the canals – sang about building the railroads in *Pat Works on the Railway* and *Drill Ye Tarriers*,

Drill, the train as a symbol of opportunity and removal, rough going though it might be, has been the dominant image in American music.

Even now that the suburbs spill out and tangle into linear "Big Streets," the megalopolis of the future, and that nowhere is more than an hour or two away by air, the train and its signatures of great distances keep their potency of enticement.

From the beginning the train's whistle wailed like a summons, or a taunt, fanning through a thousand remote, meager farming regions: *Down in the valley . . . hear that train blow* and *Lord, I hate to hear that lonesome whistle blow.* The Southern Negro, believing that there was freedom up in the fabled North, saw the train's smokestack shine like gold: that was its value to him. But in another blues: *Every time a freight train makes up in the yard, Some po' woman got an aching heart,* because taking off in it would be a man she was unlikely ever to see again.

I T is difficult to over-emphasize the significance with which the train is charged in the lives of the American poor and the American nomadic worker. Its insistent hammer of steel wheels is the bass note in the fugue of the American struggle; it is the vehicle of sadness and separation in uncountable blues and folk ballads; it has shaped and colored the music itself, the train rhythm boogie of wandering saw mill and turpentine camp pianists, the desolate rasp of a hillbilly harmonica blowing like a whistle; and it has given the metrical pattern to a vast body of country-and-Western music whose composers and singers have been brakemen or hobos or who played as children around a rail-head cattle yard.

Barrelhouse bars and honky tonks have always pressed up close to a division point or water tank stop where construction workers, argonauts in overalls, swing off the freights to spend their money on liquor and company, and where the improvised music soaks up the thumping chords of the boxcar wheels outside the door and the bitter-sweet sense of immense emptiness ahead and behind. The train, spelling distance and departure, became a keynote of the poetry and dialect imagery of blue-collar America.

Lomax credits the railroad with being the source and inspiration of the greatest body of good American music: the best ballads, *John Henry* and *Casey Jones*; powerful work-chants for every aspect of railroad building; spirituals like *This Train* and *All Night Long;* love songs like *Down in the Valley* and *Careless Love*; blues verses by the stack – "indeed the blues might be said to be half-African and half-locomotive rhythm ... What a ship on the sea is to an Englishman, a droshky on the snow to a Russian, a horse on the desert to an Arab, the iron horse became to the men of North America." *She'll be Coming 'Round the Mountain*, an early anonymous Western railroad ditty, displaced the original hymn tune, *The Old Ship of Zion*, because it caught "the jubilation of that halcyon day when the first steam engine came whistling and snorting into a horse-and-buggy town on the prairies."

And the train whistled and snorted on into jazz and pop music. The *dramatis personae* of the chart-toppers in any regional café juke box – consistently lachrymose or hearts-and-flowers Victorian in mode, and given an extra keening quality by the hard, twangy, mountain nasalness – are railroad boomers and truck drivers, moonshiners and rambling men, and perennially the theme, treated with either repining sadness or love-'em-and-leave-'em comedy, is that of restlessness and the out yonder.

It is a crude lyricism about the man who is moving out of town, sometimes because "winter's coming on" and work has to be chased elsewhere, oftener an expression of an accepted norm of edginess, the need to ensure that not a spore of moss gathers on the rolling stone; it is about a girl drawn away by the city lights and who on her way back home (wings burned or possibly burnished) stops short of her love *Twenty-Four Hours from Tulsa*, that romance broken in a highway roadhouse that could have been set nowhere but in the United States. Britain? Twenty-four hours from Truro or Tunbridge Wells, you'd be in the middle of the Atlantic Ocean or among other tongues. Even in a larger country the atmosphere would not fit the sentiment. America has it in the bloodstream.

The motif of footlooseness and estrangement is at the core of all American popular music, and nowhere more hauntingly than in the doggerel of the itinerant Negro bluesmen who traveled most arduously yet who still kept the jab in the nerve about places five or ten states away, and who sang of Chicago or Shreveport or Texakarna. Down there in his second-class citizenship the Negro has shared in the troublesome and stirring element in the *zeitgeist* of American life : that continuing wonderment, the almost baffled sense of the unreachable, that the American feels about his enormous nation. The sky's the limit, has always been the going rule – but how is the way there to be found?

The "foreignness" that the American receives from his own land has impregnated American song, for the most part quite artificially, a Tin Pan Alley aerosol squirt of nostalgia. Nevertheless, however sham is the yearning of a Manhattan lyric writer for his cabin in Alabam', what starts out as a concoction on a Union Square electric typewriter frequently takes on a true denotation.

What the lyric writer is accurately responding to is the tug between roots and rootlessness in the American inheritance. To drive through America is to have the sense of riffling through an index of sheet music : Noel Coward's quip ("Nasty insistent little tune. Extraordinary how potent cheap music is.") is naggingly borne out. As you flash past a town's welcome plaque or register half unconsciously a highway's turn-off list, uncountable scraps of by-gone and believed forgotten tunes flit into the mind. You remember the girl from Kalamazoo and that stars fell on Alabama; you mentally do the Charleston and the Jersey bounce. You remember that you are nine little miles from Ten-Ten-Tennessee and you're coming Virginia; you're shuffling off to Buffalo and deep in the heart of Texas. You have the Beale Street blues and Georgia's on your mind or you're being carried back to Peoria. You see a Chattanooga choo-choo and you realize that you're on the Alamo. Moonlight in Vermont may shine upon you and you find that you are instinctively on the look out for the big noise from Winnetka.

Although there remains a rich trove of "funny" small town names for lyricists to plug, as the eye sweeps the map it seems that there are few areas which have not had at least a brief and passing enscrollment in tonic sol-fa, and I doubt if there is any state in the Union that has not been so enshrined – there are even *Arkansas Blues* and *Montana Call* and *Florida Blues*. I do not actually know of a song dealing with Oregon or Rhode Island or New Hampshire but I would be surprised if someone at some time in the past hundred years had not worked them in. Certainly songs celebrating specific music-oriented cities or districts are too multitudinous to count. New Orleans could support a song biography to itself, and I have quickly jotted down twenty-odd jazz and pop tunes (mostly from the thirties when it was voguey with whites) about Harlem, from Ellington's *Drop Me Off At Harlem* to the improbable *Harlem Chapel Chimes*.

It does not lessen. One of Peggy Lee's best albums of recent years was *Blues Cross Country* with the Quincy Jones band. It included such standards as *Basin Street Blues* and *St. Louis Blues* but there was a lot of original material mostly composed by Miss Lee herself, including *The Grain Belt Blues* (*way out on the plains where the air is sweet*, in between the aircraft insecticide sweeps presumably) and blues about San Francisco and Los Angeles. There also – written, may it be noted, by a sophisticated cabaret singer of the 1960s who is doubtless whisked to her engagements by jet plane – is *The Train Blues*:

> Love to see those big wheels roll
> Roll over the country – it's so good for my soul.

One of America's first million sale gramophone records – the ninth, after Caruso, in the industry's history – was a train drama: Vernon Dalhart's 1924 Victor version of *The Wreck of the Old '98*, a barnstorming narrative, done very hillbilly and with lavish rumbling-and-wailing sound effects, of an actual disaster when in 1903 the Southern's No. 97 fast mail between Washington and Atlanta swerved off a mountain bridge near Danville, Virginia, killing the crew. The freight-riding rambling man especially really does "love to see those big wheels roll,"

270

and loves the lore that has been spun by them, and he sings about it in the boxcars.

That has been the manner in which the American has addressed the train ever since, in Lomax's vivid metaphor: "From the Catskills to the Cascades the continent was strung with steel like a great harp." For the railroad barons the harp's diapason was of money and power but it made a different music for the poor: "The mule-skinner in the Mississippi bottoms timed his long days by the whistle of the passing trains. The mountaineer, penned up by his Southern hills, heard the trains blowing down in the valley and dreamed of the big world 'out yonder.' The blue-noted whistles made a man miss a pretty woman he'd never seen. Boys in hick towns, lost on the prairie, heard the loco-motives snorting and screaming in the night and knew they were bound to small town stagnation only for the lack of a railroad ticket.

"Americans had always had an itching heel. When the railroads came along, they began to travel so far and so often that, in the words of the old blues, 'their feet got to rolling like a wheel, yeah, like a wheel.' "

The train whistle is still a siren call and a dart to the heart of the wanderer: the invitation away or the reminder that a thousand miles down the cinders is the town for which he may have no particular love but which is extricably bound up in his boyhood or in some years of marriage. The sound of the train and its pervasive symbolism are contained with the strongest and most obsessionally imaginative use in the blues.

23 : THE FREEZIN' GROUND
WAS MY FOLDIN' BED
LAST NIGHT

Wonderin' can I get a foot-race and a restin' place,
I likes a good race and a good restin' place,
I likes a close shave and a powdered face,
Close shave and a shallow grave.

Jealous James Stanchell:
Anything from a Foot-Race to a Resting Place

THE blues – an extremely stylized dilution from earlier "ditties," field hollers, back-country "ballits," mandolin rags, revivalist shapenote hymns and spirituals – formed and developed its subtle variations between 1885 and 1930, a period of massive upheaval in the South.

Slavery was over but so also was the power and pre-eminence of cotton. A society which had been as proud as it had been rigid crumbled into landslide and Negro laborers, free now in the most ominous sense, were adrift in legions.

By 1910 one and three-quarter million Negroes had left their native states, severed from the plantation and its enforced stability. They, the dislodged, scavenged for work anywhere, in the turpentine camps, in mines and sawmills, on railroad and levee construction and in city factories, but there was seldom continuity or security. The Negro had begun his traipsing from job to job (or from no job to no job), from town to town, from woman to woman.

The railroad's right of way was the life-line, the thin carpet of urbanism through huge expanses of wild and foreign parts, because the peasant – black and white – of early twentieth-century America was as ignorant of what kind of conditions and expectations there might be across the Mason-Dixon line as was Columbus sailing beyond the rim of Europe.

Bewilderment and misery went into the transients' blues:

> *I was standing at my window, saw a poor boy walking*
> > *in the rain*
> *I heard him saying, "It's a lowdown dirty shame."*

They had the Memphis Blues, the Fort Worth Blues and Dallas Blues, the East St. Louis Blues, the Chicago Blues, the Southern Blues, the Going North Blues – the blues which gathered in the great termini and junctions of water and overland travel, where the paddleboats could be worked and the long-stretch trains jumped, and where a man could feel irremediably lost.

Even when the Negro did not have to evacuate because of times impossibly out of joint, however, it was inevitable that he was infected by the urge to follow that red lantern on the caboose of the eight-wheel drivers and midnight mails which had already carried away so many of his family and friends. The chance was taken – a million and three-quarter times in those few years – yet it never took the Negro long to feel the draught of cold hostility. In his home country he had at least sensitively understood the local guises and forms of prejudice and the terms of toleration, and there he was known as someone's workman, so-and-so's son. Gone from there he was just another black face without a frame, open to arrest and easy to bully.

> *I'm a poor boy, a long way from home . . .*
> *The freezing ground was my foldin' bed last night.*
> *If you ever been down, know just how I feel.*
> *Feel like an engine ain't got no drivin' wheel.*

A savor of the neurotic movement in this period, and of the irresistible necessity to change ground despite its wearying pointlessness, can be conveyed in fragments from country supper guitarists and blues entertainers who floated about the land in minstrel and medicine shows, and played in wharf billets and barber shops, whom Oliver taped.

Percy Thomas: "We played at the juke at Rome down there on the 49 Highway; played at the juke at Louise – all over. Played for those Sat'd'y night fish-fries. We played blues, break-

273

downs, such as that." Whistling Alex Moore: "Oh, they were tough joints ... I'd play them all, from North Dallas to the East side ... Froggy Bottom ... Central Tracks." Blind Arvella Gray: "I did levee camp work; I worked in factories and things ... Just jumped from job to job. I did railroad; I was workin' for the B and O Road.

> *Well I got a letter from Hagerstown*
> *Saying East St. Louis is burnin' down*
> *Workin' on the railroad, hammerin' steel*
> *Hotter the sunshine, Lord, the better I feel."*

Edwin Buster Pickens: "You know I heard the Santa Fe blow one mornin' ... It cried like a child – that engine was shootin' up steam ... and I talked with the conductor, the brakeman, in the caboose – and he said, 'Where ya goin' boy?' I said, 'I'm goin' to Cowswitch.' He said, 'I don't 'llow nobody to ride this train.' I said, 'Boss, I'm hungry.' 'What can you do?' I said, 'I can fiddle a li'l bit.' He said, 'All right, go on ... I'll let you ride' ... I rode freight trains practically all over the country ... I might go to Tomball an' I might stay there until things dull down. I leave there and probably go to Racoon Bend – oil field. Then I leave there and probably go to Longview ... Kilgore ... Silsbee ... Just wherever it was booming ... Freight train, truck sometimes, even walk a while, ride a while."

Lightnin' Hopkins: "Well sometimes we jump on top of freight trains, run over there from Buffalo to Palestine. Get off there, play there, ketch the freight back to Buffalo ... Otherwise I used to ride buses – yeah, free. They'd see me goin' down the street with my git-tar. They'd say, 'Hurry on boy! Jump on there! Let's go!' I'd jump up there, riding down on that ole git-tar there, make me a little piece of change between Dowling Street and West Dallas."

Speckled Red: "I hoboed on trains – I'd catch a train right now, if I feel like it, go anywhere I want to go ... Well, I got put off so many times – run like a rabbit! I remember one time I was going down from Memphis, Tennessee. Caught a train, caught the Illinois Central going down to Cairo ... The brakeman sees a gang of 'bout twelve of us there. They got light, searchlights by the fireman's bell or something. And you could hear them bullets going ping-ping-ping-ping."

These were the entertainment men, the street singer, the dispossessed tenant farmer turned minstrel guitarist, the traveling blind beggar guided by a young boy who shook the tambourine and passed around the tin cup, the freight train picking up band of guitar, washboard, broom-handle bass, jug and mouth organ – relatively they had it good for their music was always worth some coins. But they too went through the experiences, the story of so very many more, which they condensed in their verse:

> *I'm a stranger here, just blowed in your town*
> *Just because I'm a stranger everybody wants to dog me*
> > *'round.*

For the minstrels too it has always been a gaunt and unpredictable life, with hope barely maintained. Blind Lemon Jefferson's end was commonplace enough: found frozen to death on a Chicago sidewalk in a 1930 blizzard. Pneumonia, tuberculosis and sickness from exposure all get dealt with in the blues of the men on the road, not with especial drama but as condition of life. Victoria Spivey sang in 1929:

> *Yes, I run around for months and months*
> *From gin-mill to gin-mill to honky-tonk*
> *Now I've got the dirty T.B.*

In 1936 Bumble Bee Slim recorded:

> *Doctor, please give me something just to ease these awful*
> > *pains*
> *I'm having bronchitis*
> *Give me Oil of Ninety-Nine, Three-Six – anything!*
> *. . . Well, I been wading in deep water an' I been sleepin'*
> > *on the ground*

Oliver makes the point that in the late 1920s, at the height of the pellagra outbreaks, seven times more Negroes died from

275

pneumonia: "Migrant Negroes, homeless men, those that are obliged to sleep over the gratings of basement kitchens, on the marble shelves above the station radiators, or on the park benches, cannot withstand the rigors of a Mid-West winter. Shuffling through the streets with feet wrapped in sacking and with tattered clothes offering little protection against the rain and snow . . ."

Big Boy Crudup sang:

> Went down Death Valley, nothin' but the tombstones
> and dry bones
> That's where a poor man be, Lord, when he's dead and
> gone
> . . . They goin' on 61 Highway, that's where the poor boy
> fell dead.

And another drifter, Robert Johnson, wanted to ensure that his departing soul got a last hitch.

> Bury my body down by the highway side
> So my ole evil spirit can get a Greyhound bus and ride.

Johnson, who was poisoned in 1938 also sang:

> I gotta keep movin'
> Blues fallin' down like hail
> Can't keep no money, hellhound on my trail,

and elsewhere:

> Got up this morning', all I had was gone
> Well, leavin' this mornin' if I have to, gonna
> ride the blinds.

There is the blues of the man who takes off for the lumber site: *Workin' on the saw mill, sleepin' in a shack six feet wide,* and there is the blues of the man who tries the long ride to the Northern steel works:

> Today, mama, today, tomorrow, I might be 'way
> Goin' back to Gary, that's where I intend to stay,

276

and

> *Used to have a woman that lived up on a hill*
> *She was crazy 'bout me 'cause I worked at the*
> *Chicago Mill*

– where the money was if you could get in. Again:

> *Goin' to Detroit, get myself a real good job*
> *Tired stayin' 'round here with the starvation mob.*

Thereafter, when they had dropped off the rattler in the strange and clanging cities of the North, the adventure in tow of that smokestack that shone like gold ended most usually in not only loneliness with no recourse to kinship but in worse hunger and poverty. Blind Lemon Jefferson's *Tin Cup Blues* totted up the score:

> *I stood on the corner and almost bust my head*
> *I couldn't earn enough to buy me a loaf of bread*
> *... The tough luck has struck me and the rats is sleepin'*
> *in my hat.*

That was Chicago for some Negroes. In the bitter Northern winters a new nostalgia developed – for the abandoned oppressive South:

> *Chicago and Detroit folks, have you heard the news?*
> *Old Dixieland is jumping – I've got the Southern blues,*

and:

> *I'm going back to the lowlands and roll up my jumper*
> *sleeves*
> *Then I'll be sitting pretty, baby – long as I kill grass and*
> *weeds.*

Yet for every one who came back a hundred more went North. For the black American it continued to be mainly a traffic out. In 1890 eight of every ten Negroes were residentially rural; by 1950 fewer than one-fifth lived in the pastoral South.

The man who could make his getaway received perhaps an intenser hero-worship among American Negroes than did the romanticized bindle stiff of the North-West among the white homeguard. In Negro folk lore the mysteriously flitting free man appears in many guises. He is "Joe Turner," a sort of anti-white Robin Hood, who "done been here and gone." He is Blue Jim (with blue gums, ruby eyes and diamond-set teeth) who strolls in his stripes out of the chain gang, laughing as the guards' bullets fly at him and calling: "White folks, so long, I'm going up town." He is Railroad Bill, an Alabama turpentine worker, real name Morris Slater, who shot a sheriff, took to the tall timber and lived by robbing freight trains and selling the swag cheap to the poor Negroes of the piney woods. From Tennessee through to Texas he is Long John, bad man and sport the whites can never capture, and in the Mississippi Delta he is the Travelin' Man, who is shot through the head by a police Winchester but when

They sent down South where his mother had gone . . .
They opened up the coffin for to see her son.
And the fool had disappeared!
He was a travelin' man, he certainly was a travelin'
man.

That was the ideal, the prance onward with a jeer. The dusty truth was stated in Peetie Wheastraw's *Road Tramp Blues, The Grapes of Wrath* at an economic level even more sunken than the Okies' flight by flivver, the statement of the family and village bands of destitute Negroes who trudged the dirt roads:

I have walked a lonesome road till my feet is too sore
to walk
I beg scraps from the people, oh, well, till my tongue
is too stiff to talk
Anybody can tell you people that I ain't no lazy man
But I guess I'll have to go to the poorhouse and do the
best I can.

Broken Down Man, sung by Buster Bennett, told a similar bedrock story:

Now I'm roamin' the highways and pickin' up cigarette
butts and everything I can find
... sure got evil on my mind
Now I'm eatin' wild berries and I'm sleepin' on the
ground
I'm broken down and disgusted, and I'm tired of trampin'
around.

The buses and through motor traffic were watched hungrily
by the Negro in motion but neither ticket money nor free hitch
was often available. So the railroad continued to be the mainstream of his conscious discontent and dreams of departure. It
was, and still is in both white and Negro country church music,
a religious emblem and there is at least one legitimate ride for a
man, into the Promised Land on the Gospel Train.

The fare is cheap an' all can go,
The rich and poor are there,
No second class aboard this train
No difference in the fare.

For the rustic Negro Christian the track in the sky ran both
ways. It carried not only the White Flyer to Heaven, a special
for the righteous with no seats for sinners, gamblers, jazz dancers and whisky drinkers, but also the black train, a fast run to
perdition and no return ticket, so often seized by Negro mini-
sters such as the Reverend A. W. Nix on the Library of Congress
recording:
"This train is known as the Black Diamond Express train to
hell," chants the Reverend Nix, with beautiful interwoven chant
and response from his congregation. "Sin is the engineer, pleasure is the headlight, and the devil is the conductor. I see the
Black Diamond as she starts off for hell. Her bell is ringing 'Hell-
bound, hell-bound.' First station is Drunkardville. Stop there
and let all the drunkards get aboard. I have a big crowd down
there drinking Jump Steady, some drinking Sheneg, some drinking moonshine, some drinking White Mule and Red Horse ...
Next station is Liars' Avenue ... big crowd of liars down there,
have some smooth liars, some unreasonable liars, some profes-

sional liars, some bare-faced liars, some ungodly liars, some big liars, some little liars . . .

"Ooooooooh, gambler! Git off the Black Diamond train. Ooooooooh, midnight rambler! Git off the Black Diamond train. Ooooooooh, backsliders! Git off the Black Diamond train. Chillun, aren't you glad you got off the Black Diamond train a long time ago?"

The train presented itself as dramatically good object for anagoge, and so was widely and frequently seized upon, and it is not without interest that lines which could easily be from a Negro spiritual are to be found on a tombstone in Ely Cathedral, commemorating the victims of a Norfolk railway smash in 1845:

> *The Line to heaven by Christ was made*
> *With heavenly truth the Rails are laid . . .*
> *God's Love the Fire, his Truth the Steam,*
> *Which drives the Engine and the Train . . .*
> *In First and Second, and Third Class,*
> *Repentance, Faith and Holiness . . .*
> *If you'll repent and turn from sin*
> *The Train will stop and take you in.*

In his sacred music and his secular, in his sexual imagery and his escape fantasies, for the Negro more than for all other land-locked Americans the train, rolling like gun caissons, had a mellifluous magic.

During slavery the stepping-stone network of secret hiding places in barns and cellars and woodland huts, organized by abolitionist whites and along which the runaway dodged his way Northward, was known as the Underground Railroad, so the significance was strong from the start. When the real overland railroad could be reached it was a hard and dangerous ride, but it got you out.

Dreamed last night that the whole round world was mine, sang David Alexander,

> *Woke up this morning, didn't have one lousy dime*
> *So I'm leaving here tonight if I have to ride the blinds*
> *Catch a freight train, special – engineer, lose no time.*

The importuning lover's *Let me be your side-track till your mainline comes* is a familiar blues allegory, with the bonus boast: *I can do more switching than your mainline ever done.* Brother John Seller's *Railroad Man Blues* contains copulatory imagery of steamroller subtlety:

> *That's why I'm a railroad man and I got so much energy*
> *That woman I got can't understand where it comes from*
> *Railroad work is hard, any man will tell you*
> *But when I'm drivin' steel it gives me such a thrill.*

Another point:

> *If you don't like me, Thelma, you don't have to stall*
> *I can get me more babes than a passenger train can haul.*

These are the blues of the rambling man.
Sometimes, occasionally, it is the woman who rides away:

> *Baby caught the Katy, she left me a mule to ride*
> *When that train pulled out, ole mule laid down and died*
> *Looked down the track just as far as I could see*
> *And a little bitty hand kept a-waving back at me.*

Johnny Temple recounted that experience:

> *Well, the Bob Lee Junior passed me with my baby all on*
> *the inside*
> *And the conductor said, "Sorry, buddy, but your baby she*
> *got to ride"*

and there was Leroy Carr's rebuke for the Cincinnati, Indianapolis, St. Louis and Chicago railroad for taking his girl away from him:

> *Big Four, Big Four, why are you so mean*
> *Why, you the meanest old train that I ever seen.*

The Kansas City Southern-Louisiana and Arkansas, known as the Flying Crow, is accused by Washboard Sam of snatching away the last woman he had, but all the same there's this to be said for the Flying Crow:

Flying Crow leaves Port Arthur, calls at Shreveport to
change her crew
She'll take water at Texakarna, yes, boys and keep on
through.

In other blues the Sunshine Special, the Panama Limited, the Shorty George and dozens of other personified route trains are blamed for carrying women away, but as many more are extolled for offering transportation out:

Green Diamond's blowin' her whistle, train's coming round
the trail
Can't ride the Pullman, guess I'll ride the rail,

and:

I'm a railroad man and I love that M and O
And when I leave this town I ain't coming back no mo'.

Perhaps the most famous transient's track is the Yellow Dog, the Mississippi line whose nickname was adopted from the Yazoo Delta logging railroad which had primrose cars. W. C. Handy's *Yellow Dog Blues* just about sums up the unpredictability of the here today gone tomorrow Negro experience in the supposed message sent by one train rider (who knows "every cross-tie, bayou, burg and bog" on that route) up from Tennessee to a girl whose lover has lit out:

Your easy rider struck this burg today
On a South-bound rattler, side-door Pullman car
Seen him here and he was on the hog
... He's gone where the Southern cross the
Yellow Dog.

24 : IF THEY HAD MET GOD THEY WOULD HAVE ASKED HIM FOR A BONE

White man was born with a veil over his face,
He seen the trouble 'fore it taken place;
Nigger was born with rag in his ass,
Never seen trouble till it done pass'd.

The Dirty Dozens

A 1964 United States Department of Commerce report for the Area Redevelopment Administration on *Negro-White Differences in Geographic Mobility* arrived at conclusions which may seem surprising in the light of the generally accepted notion that the Negro is, if not by nature, as the result of conditioning, rootless, casually wanton and shallow in family and emotional ties.

The report shows the exact opposite: "Negroes on the whole seem to have stronger emotional and family ties to their current place of residence than the white population" and the graphs show almost twice as much movement by white family heads between labor market areas as among Negroes. "Negroes with steady jobs," it is added, "are considerably less likely to move than white workers who are continuously employed." Patently the 700,000 Negroes who left the South between 1920 and 1930 were taking that giant step with reluctance, with little of the entrancement by the hobo life that took so many white boys on to the road. "Long lonesome roads I have been down," says Odum's "black Ulysses." " ... hobo always havin' hard time ... Sometimes I goes as a road hustler, from job to job, doing 'most anything. I am just a man gettin' over the world."

> *I'm a natural born ram'ler an' it ain't no lie*
> *... My foot in my han'.*
> *I'm de out-derndest traveller of any man.*

The distinctions are thin at this existence level but the Negro hobo had the tougher time: the scope for jobs was smaller, the black face was a more obvious target for the firemen who turned their hoses on the riders on boxcar roofs, and for small town police watchful for vagrants. Gellert writes: "The migratory Negro 'just a-lookin' for work' suffers most. A 'vag.' No white folks to intercede for him. He falls as easily as small change into the pocket of the constable ... It is based on the law of supply and demand for convict labor."

> *Railroad look so pretty*
> *Boxcar on the track*
> *Here come two hoboes,*
> *Grip sack on their back.*
> > *Oh, babes,*
> > *Oh, no-home babes.*
> *Clothes are all torn to pieces,*
> *Shoes are all worn out,*
> *Rolling 'round an unfriendly world,*
> *Always roaming about.*
> *Where you gwine, you hoboes?*
> *Where you gwine to stay?*
> *Chain gang link is waiting –*
> *Can't make your getaway.*

A natural sequel to that is Langston Hughes' cuttingly sarcastic *Florida Road Workers*:

> *I'm making a road*
> *For the cars*
> *To fly on.*
> *Makin' a road*
> *Through the palmetto thicket*
> *For light and civilization*
> *To travel on ...*
> *Sure,*
> *A road helps all of us!*
> *White folks ride –*
> *An' I gets to see 'em ride.*
> *I ain't never seen nobody*
> *Ride so fine before.*

In the South even the Negro's jungle camp might be segregated, in whatever spot was left on a garbage tip flank after the white hobos had picked over the more salubrious spots. The gulf of antagonism between black and white drifters – not much feeling of being bottom dog brothers – is pointed up again and again in W. H. Davies's *The Autobiography of a Super-Tramp* and in his novel *Dancing Mad*: the internecine robbery and killing on the duneland jungle at St. Louis, the razor fight between white hobos and a gang of Negro river rats on a Twain-like boat voyage down the Mississippi.

The weight of total defeat, of indecision approaching stasis, is in the blues. Bumble Bee Slim's

I had so much trouble, swear my nerves is weakening down
I would swing on a freight train but I'm afraid to leave the
ground,

and Son Bond's

I'm a broken-hearted bachelor, travellin' through this wide
world all alone
It's the railroad for my pillow, this jungle for my happy home

both contain a desolation not encountered in white hobos' songs.

The Negro desire to keep his boots in the dust he knows is substantiated by the findings of Frederic Ramsey Jr. in his journeys during the 1950s through Alabama and Mississippi "following the trace of wandering blues singers." Ramsey salvaged information about a remote and dying class of serf Negroes whose pattern of life was little different from their forebears in bondage, and with an only slightly increased fluidity.

He found scattered hamlets, sharecroppers' strips and cane-brake shacks where the home-made entertainment was religious chants, reels and jump-ups for dancing, country brass bands playing tunes remembered from traveling coon and tent shows of a century before, and the most rudimentary blues – all the rapidly drying tributaries that had confluxed into the formation of jazz and the blues as they are known today.

Tom Huff, born in 1871, the son of two slaves, whom Ramsey discovered farming in the Oakmulgee district of Alabama, knew many hoeing and brush-cutting call-and-response songs. He was a rooted country dweller and his conception of travel was the last pilgrimage to the Holy City:

That's when-a we walk, walk this milky white road . . .
I'm goin' to meet my livin' mother . . .
Tell her how I made it over my highway . . .

Necessarily many of these Negroes in isolated, semi-wild country, far from the "black-top" highway, the tarred road that marked civilization, had had to be drifters.

They had "cut out and banished away" under the whip of starvation. They had wandered around working when they could in barrel-stave mills, in packing plants, on the docks at Mobile Bay, in the Mississippi pecan groves, in Louisiana's sugar fields. Their paths had been through the pine barrens toward the grid of the black-top highways.

"Their hopelessness," writes Ramsey, "began at home, when they tired of cotton-chopping and plowing, day after day, from sunup to sundown. So they left and went to work along the rails with the gandy crews, in sawmill gangs, in backwater levee camps with mule skinners, and mud and sand movers. Pay was low, and the hours were long . . . they lived on beans and rice. They took it for a while, then moved on. Between camps they stole and begged. If they had met God, they would have asked Him for a bone . . . the road, which offered adventure, was better than their homes, which offered nothing. Some left with regret, but they left just the same."

These early drifters carried the blues about and spread the idiom for many toted an instrument or sang, their survival kit. They carried "the devil on their back" – the guitar as seen by the deeply religious – or a banjo to pick, a fiddle, a jug to blow in. "The vagrants, easy riders and drifters of a period just past," says Ramsey, "are hardly ever to be encountered along Southern highways today."

Yet he did encounter some musical nomads, not so skilled or confident or knowledgeable about city ways of show business as many who made their one or twenty records, and vanished, who sang about their floating life: *It's a long lane that's got no*

286

end or *Lord, I'm standin' here wonderin' will a matchbox hold my clothes.*

They were rural tramps who saw little of the legendary railroad other than the small depots scattered about the Mississippi countryside, where the drowse was shattered by a shock of blackness as a manifest ripped through blaring and thundering, but deserted for most hours of the day.

For all that, even in the emptiest alluvial lands served by feeder lines to the main cotton road – the "streaks of rust" – the railroad touched most, however impersonally, and cut into the imagination: "At the edge of wire-grass prairie on the outskirts of Uniontown, Alabama, they could sit on porches and wait for cattle cars to go through and hear the braying of steers riding to markets and slaughterhouses at Demopolis; and at night they could lie in their beds and hear the long, lonesome whistle of the freight as it came pounding across the prairie from the cotton depots at Selma. From the crossing outside their windows, the whistle blew louder ...

"The people who lived alongside tracks, in the towns and in the fields, could also ride them, walk them, work for them. The railroad touched them all; it created impressions that became part of song and music. Trains were nearly everything ... glory trains, little black trains, good morning trains, good-bye trains, midnight specials and South-bound rattlers ...

"Trains took people home, if they had a home; they took people down a long road, if they were looking for a home. Engines and drive-wheels and whistles, traveling through dark miles in the wakeful hours just before day, created impressions of sound that pulled and twisted at people's hearts. The roar of a fast freight, high-balling from no known point of departure to no known destination, struck a music in the ears of those who heard it and were left behind.

"Musicianers played with the rise and fall of sound, mimicking the far-to-near-then-far-again shuffle of the train winding through hills and valleys. They blew its whistles through harmonicas and horns and reed flutes; they thrashed out its coughing and scurrying rhythms across the sound boxes of their guitars."

There were, as well the songs not created out of the railroads but created for them, those which were an accompaniment to work. Now machines do most of the maintenance work and less track is laid. But for sixty years no tie was tamped, no bed graded, no rail laid or gauged up, no plug engine and rawhide freight train coupled on a peg-leg, or one-track, railway, without songs to bind together the boomer crews into the harmonic beat of the operation. As the gandy dancers bent to gain united leverage with their crows they grunted:

> *A sack of flour, a bucket of lard*
> *Wonder what makes these sons work so hard*
> *I been on the Morgan, I been on the Branch*
> *I would I had a section, but they wouldn't 'llow*
> *me no chance.*

Part-time railroad coal-heaver or points man, or full-time railroad rider, the Negro who got involved with the trains was unlikely ever again to have a permanent home:

> *Homeless, yes I'm homeless, might as well be dead*
> *Hungry and disgusted, no place to lay my head.*

There was a place, the final commitment to the railroad, the bluesman's valediction:

> *I'm all alone at midnight and the lamps are burning low*
> *I'm gonna lay my head on some lonesome railroad line*
> *Let that two-nineteen train pacify my min'.*

25 : AIN'T IT HARD TO STUMBLE WHEN YOU GOT NO PLACE TO FALL?

... we must write about our own mud-puddle.

Michael Gold

THE Negro wanderer, frightened at the strangeness around him, longing secretly and ambivalently for the prison cell safety of the Southern birthplace he hated, had his situation summed up, with a stoicism and grace beyond bitterness, by some illiterate anonymous poet: *Ain't it hard to stumble when you've got no place to fall?*

The frustrations of being trapped economically, of being castrated of dignity and worth as a human being, produced this vacillation between optimism and pessimism: the hope that something better could be found up the track inevitably to be punctured by the realization that there was nothing there either.

Yet, although the experience probably differed only in degrees according to the color of skin, the wraith of the adventurer with a bedroll hitting the cinder trail to elsewhere remains the *doppelganger* of the American who lives a steady and relatively anchored life. The orphic awe and pull is bottled in its most acrid distillation in the blues, and not only the railroad blues.

The blues has always been the Negro's escape clause in the white man's coercive agreement with him and has been used to the full. There have been the blues composers whose fantasies vaulted across the steel rails, who sang of how they would "get in my airplane, ride all over the world," or take a trip "in my submarine, ride under the deep blue sea." There has also grown a body of blues about the roads for during the mass migration North in the twenties, and its lessening waves in the Thirties, the highway became an alternative loophole.

The interstate systems were linking, the bus tickets were cheaper than the rail, and there was the occasional possibility of clubbing together for a clapped-out old barouche that might wheeze on as far as the Yankee factory belt. The man so busted that he had to tramp it was, at least, on public property on the roads, out of firing range of the rail constabulary, and now and then a motorist would respond to the jerked thumb.

The geography of many evicted peasant Negroes extended no farther than the unmetalled mule roads through the stump lands and cotton fields of Georgia and Alabama. The railroad tracks and the interstate turnpikes were in themselves an attainment, the steerings toward that imagined viable life across the firmament. Oliver writes: "For the migrant Negro with his eyes focused on the far horizon the long ribbons of the 'odd' numbered highways have a magnetic fascination. Harsh edges unsoftened by wayside vegetation, their stark concrete whiteness causing them to glare cruelly in the unrelenting sun, they guide his steps to the North," hard causeways on which "countless thousands of flapping soles and bare black feet have made no indentation."

Tommy McClennan, who lived on Jackson's outskirts, sang of watching the Greyhound buses lickspittin' away up Highway 51:

Now here comes that Greyhound, with his tongue stickin'
out on the side
If you buy your ticket, swear 'fore God and they'll let you
ride

and Lee Brown declared:

Baby, ain't you ever been to the Greyhound bus depot
Baby, that's the fastest bus running on Highway 51.

In 1961 an album of the road blues of Big Joe Williams was issued, *Blues on Highway 49*, a dossier of routing information of the Delta country. Although *Highway 45* Blues is about walking "with my suitcase in my hand" on the tall vertical road from Mobile through Mississippi into Tennessee at Corinth, into Illinois at Paducah, and through to Chicago, most of Williams's blues are not scored for the main roads. *13 Highway* and *Highway 49* are about back country roads, the first South-East from St. Louis through Marion and Harrisburg in Kentucky and into Tennessee, the other from the Northern border of Tennessee down to Nashville. In *13 Highway* Williams says "I went down in my V8 Ford," but it is a walking script mostly, as in *Poor Beggar*: "Please don't turn me from your door" – he just hopes "some crumbs fall from your table." Still, his summation is the boast: *Yes, I been travellin', boy, I been to the four corners of the world.*

The Negro experience has not fundamentally changed. As John A. Williams, a Negro journalist, recently showed in his account of touring America on magazine assignments, the very same roads which for a white motorist may be dreary or entrancing, according to objective scenery and subjective mood, are for the Negro, however respectably dressed and however smart his car, a tense venture: any stop, at a motel, a restaurant, a lavatory, can be loaded with rebuff or worse. Perhaps Bob Dylan's *Highway 61*, about that road which runs from Lake Superior down to the Gulf of Mexico, is not as surrealistic as it sounds:

> *Well, God said to Abraham 'Kill me a son'*
> *Abe said 'Man, you must be putting me on . . .*
> *Where do you want this killing done?'*
> *God said 'Out on Highway 61.'*

Carl Sandburg in his *American Songbag* sees the escutcheons on the sides of trains as giving "cruel desert spaces a friendly look" but the Negro vagabond especially was unlikely to have his loneliness and loss of bearings eased by those messages from afar; to him:

> *There's three trains ready but none ain't going my way*
> *Well, maybe the sun'll shine in my back door some day.*

Despite the mere shadow of difference between the black and white American rail nomad, the difference has always held, and it is reflected in the songs. The white has had a slightly larger latitude. The Negro blues regarded the railroad with variable emotions, with longing or loathing or admiration, but although he might have swung a hammer on the right-of-way and even in small numbers have been employed on the locomotives, the stance of the bluesman toward the railroad is from a distance: it is just one factor in his plight.

White railroad songs have a stronger bond with the trains. Usually plaintively mournful, it is a mournfulness often brazenly enacted, without the grief that is deep in the bowels of the blues. They are, unfailingly, about being stranded or exiled far from home. They are also dramatized with hobo hyperbole. A rover trudging down the track with tears in his eyes and a letter from home in his pocket, at last snags a ride:

> *Well, this train I ride on*
> *Is a hundred coaches long*
> *You can hear her whistle blow a million*
> *miles*

Railroadin' Man declares:

> *I rode ten thousand miles of rusted rails*
> *Because my pappy was a railroadin' man*
> *And I never had no home 'cept a county jail*
> *... Well, I stole a locomotive just to take*
> *a ride*
> *Now there's a price on my head alive or*
> *dead.*

For much of its lifetime the blues has been a shut-in racial music, a discussion among a clan of racially and economically separated people, but the blues filtered across the color line into such white music as this and it found this different outlet through white men on much the same beat but with those few degrees better opportunities. "Discovered" Negro blues singers and musicians may be the idols of the informed white *afficianados* but, rather as Elvis Presley performed the function of making the raw alcohol of Negro rhythm-and-blues drinkable to a mass public in its rock-and-roll dilution, so at an earlier period was the country blues given pop form by a white man. This shade of the railroad roving life came through most individualistically in the songs of Jimmy Rodgers, a white brakeman from Meridian, Mississippi, who died in 1933.

Rodgers had wide popularity on the country circuit. Probably more than anyone he stimulated the spread of folksy music into the developing radio and wind-up phonograph prologue to mass electronic entertainment. He had a pleasant rich voice employed for the pleasure of millions in the more maudlin rural plaints and yodels.

Yet the rhythm and roll of the trains he worked on stamped themselves upon his plunketty guitar style and upon his subject matter. There is the same feeling, lighter textured, here as in the Negro blues, about life in the landscape of cotton gins, about Hobo Bill's last ride, about building "me a shanty and settle down, gonna quit this runn' aroun'," about Ben Dewberry, "a brave engineer on the old North Eastern and A & B" who died fearless with the throttle wide open, about

some likes Chicago, some love Memphis, Tennessee
It's sweet down in Texas where the women think the
world of me.

Jimmy Rodgers's work was a polite devitalization – nothing more disturbing than wistful sentimentality – of the harsh, despairing blues he must have heard on his trips through the black South, and most of it sounds wishy-washy and pasty. Yet in itself the "white blues" he wrote (many of them old-timey tear-jerkers with titles like *Old Pal of my Heart* and *Daddy and Home*) were authentically homespun out of regional life on the hillbilly side of the color line and carried the conviction that he had been where he said he'd been and done the things he sang about.

At his best Rodgers put into his stanzas the brininess of that infatuation with the railroad: pensive but with that old crab-apple flavor:

Every time I see that lonesome railroad train
Makes me wish that I was back home again,

and:

Now I can see a train coming down the railroad track
And I love to hear the bark of that old smoke stack.

The loss of his mother, and his father's enforced absences down the line, perhaps later colored Rodgers's languishing yodel. Left on his own, the locomotive sheds became his center – "the great, rushing, clanging, hissing machine . . . the symbol of his life," writes Silverman. "He would spend hours in the yards, absorbing the lingo, the yarns, and the songs of the railroaders, those wonderful wandering men who had been everywhere, seen and done everything."

From the Negroes in the yards he learned the rudiments of guitar and banjo and also their pentatonic blue notes. He became a railroad man on the New Orleans and North Eastern and for fourteen years was "the Singing Brakeman." He was never robust. Tuberculosis developed. He left the railroad and became a street corner singer with a collecting cup, then joined a touring medicine show. He tried railroading again but it defeated him physically and he returned to a thin living from his guitar, until in 1927 he cut some audition records in Tennessee.

"America's Blue Yodeler" became the rage, the Presley of his day. His first record royalty was twenty-seven dollars; when he died, he was making 100,000 dollars a year. His body was, appropriately, freighted back by funeral train from New York to the Southland.

It is, though, questionable if the Jimmy Rodgers story is quite the "epic" it has since been proclaimed. What it does illustrate yet again is America's narcissistic devotion to its own concurrent romance.

In 1953, twenty years after his death, his home town established itself as a shrine by staging a Jimmy Rodgers Memorial Day, at which were present Carrie Rodgers, Congressmen, governors of surrounding states, the widow of the famous Casey Jones, and a host of hillbilly singers and disc jockeys from neighboring radio stations. The ceremonial focal point was in the park, a locomotive and a marble monument bearing an inscription of a fulsomeness which, while not being entirely persuasive that immortality is here, is informative of the American need for legend:

> His is the music of America.
> He sang the songs of the people he loved,
> Of a young nation growing strong.
> His was an America of glistening rails,
> Thundering boxcars and rain-swept nights;
> Of lonesome prairies, great mountains
> And a high blue sky.

He sang of the bayous and the cotton fields,
The wheated plains, of the little towns,
The cities, and of the winding rivers of America.
We listened, we understood.
JIMMY RODGERS
The singing brakeman – America's blue yodeler
HIS MUSIC WILL LIVE FOREVER

Since Jimmy Rodgers brought the blues into the white parlor, many more young whites have tried to cross the color line to the blues proper. Fairly typical of the contemporary folk-rover type are Spider John Koerner, Dave Snaker Ray and Little Sun Glover who made a limited edition album in 1963 entitled *Blues, Rags and Hollers*. They are all of college boy beat cast and the sleeve note pullulates with references to Bunuel, "Ingmar Bergman imagery," "Existentialistic Hit Parade," J. P. Donleavy's "The Ginger Man," Truffaut movies, and with protocol genuflexions to Muddy Waters, Bukka White and bottleneck style. The music is deliberately primitive, in the manner of chaingang chants and surge-songs, and hoarse with harmonica wailings. The cover shows Spider, Snaker and Little Sun in windcheaters, jeans and sweaters, scuffed instrument cases in hand, apparently waiting for the next freight to smudge the skyline, the ghost train that can't be exorcised.

Tom Paxton is another young white folk singer who keeps the old fables fresh and, if his listeners know that Olympus is covered with gas stations, he helps to people their imagination with the dryads and fauns of the American Pantheon. His songs are not autobiographical but legend of the American proletarian tide-wrack. *Standing on the Edge of Town* is about a man cast off the factory line by automation. Now, misput,

> *he is standing on the edge of town,*
> *Gonna get chilly when the sun goes down*
> *Cardboard suitcase full of my clothes*
> *Where I'm heading just the good Lord knows.*

Rambling Boy is a sentimental ballad about a buddy who "stuck with me in my hard old days." They rambled around together in rain and snow, and when once

hunting work in Tulsa town the boss said he had room for one
Says my old pal 'We'd rather bum.'

Then in a jungle camp in winter his pal catches "the chills"
and dies:

Here's to you, my rambling boy, and may your rambling
                                                    bring you joy,
in the hereafter too.

But *I Can't Help But Wonder Where I'm Bound* is advice
to all those tempted to hit the road to stay put, off that "long,
dusty road":

Well, if you see me passing by and you sit and
                                            wonder why
And you wish that you were a rambler too
Nail your shoes to the kitchen floor
Lace 'em up and bar the door,
Thank your stars for the roof that's over you.

Still Paxton sees no release for the man who has once got on
the rambling trail. He bids goodbye to his girl because he's "a
mighty restless man in a mighty restless land."

I have walked, I have bummed,
I have rode buses. I have rode trains,
I have ridden a time or two in a silver plane.
When I think of where I've been I have to go again
Just to see that everything is still the same.

The difference is in saying "this is how the story goes," telling
about sharecropping conditions, mine disasters and the Rural
Electrification Administration program, to urban night club audiences, folk festival, television and record audiences, instead of
directly feeding back to the hired hands and laborers themselves
their own experiences codified. Although there was among many
young Americans a post-war awakening to conditions in the
nation – dramas not only of the past but those still being struggled through around them – this generation was not involved in
a shirt-sleeves way.

Pat Foster has published poetry in the *Phoenix Magazine*,
paints, is a concert performer in East and West Coast television.

Similarly Dick Weissman's nomadism has not been so much through oil field shack towns and grain belt trailer stops, but as a banjo-picker on radio and cabaret folk shows, and his Columbia MA was in sociology. The pieces on their album *Documentary Talking Blues* are in many cases familiar – from Guthrie and Pete Seeger – and are in the talking blues idiom, that indigenous form of American bucolic poetry in which a series of dry, flatly-delivered acid comments are narrated, not sung, to a simple chord accompaniment of guitar. The talking blues is a mountain man's soapbox commentary about drought, pellagra, strikes, expressed in litotes or with poker-faced phlegmatic baldness, always with a surprise punch-line, a parenthetical wry wisecrack at the end of each verse.

The Mexican *corrido*, or newspaper ballad, the Spanish *flamenco*, the West Indian *calypso* all use a similar oral strip-cartoon technique for snap-shooting events in action, but the American talking blues has been most effectively used as a political goad, to prod the mistreated poor into militancy. Unlike the Negro blues, it is not passive but defiant, minatory. *Talking Migrant* was heard by Foster in the California citrus region and is exceptionally glum and defeatist:

> *Well, I'm down in Salinas, just pickin' cotton,*
> *Down in Georgia, just share-cropping.*
> *Wherever you see a broke-down shack,*
> *Dirty kids a-runnin' in back,*
> *That's us ex-landowners*
> *(We'll never make it ... Migratory workers,*
> *they call us)*

> *Well, we held our meeting and called our strike*
> *And the cops came by on their motorbikes*
> *Tear-gas hit us, and women were crying,*
> *Children screaming, men a-flying.*
> *(Just a big melting pot ... Never get together,*
> *too much struggle to stay where we are)*

> *Picked in Kansas, picked in Maine*
> *When the picking's done I'm on the road again*

Peach bowl, dust bowl, oranges, taters
Berries, apples, celery, tomatoes
(This song is over one minute, and I'll be on the
highway – gone again)

Talking Sharecropper is from some words found, without music, probably improvised by someone jolting along in a flivver out of dust bowl conditions, and has more of the usual belligerence:

Come on Momma, get the boys
We might as well head to Illinois,
Just as bad here, we better head South
Can't head West on account of the drouth
(That's bad for us ... Can't take it no more)

Well, come on black man and come on white
And show the rich how the poor can fight
Stand up, woman, and meet a man,
We're gonna make this country the promised land.
(We're gonna do it ... All together.
Gonna have freedom for everybody)

It is true enough of Jimmy Rodgers that "his is the music of America" in that much of America enjoyed and identified with the style of life reflected in it, but this was a Christmas card version.

The talking blues and the Negro blues contain facts about a rankness of a sub-stratum citizenship – a sort of limited-edition report on the god-forsaken – given ever rawer form by another strain of song. This dealt with suffering and hardship far beyond the woolgathering ache of a heart grown fonder through absence. These songs grew out of the fortunes – the misfortunes – of the great body of unorganized American working men on the move and whose political spearhead became the Industrial Workers of the World, the IWW.

The IWW hymnal (for although the lyrics were often savage parodies of the hymns rammed down a hobo's throat before the soup could follow, they were sacred airs in their own right) expressed with sublime din the most fervent belief that Utopia was the next stop on the American train.

PART FOUR

JOIN THE WOB, WOB, WOBBLY BAND

Look at the hands of our people. They are hard and scarred and calloused from trying to make a dream come true.

Big Bill Haywood

My experience is that the greatest aid in the efficiency of labor is a long line of men waiting at the gate.

Samuel Insull

26 : HALLELUJAH, I'M A BUM

> But singing – Christ, how we sang,
>   remember the singing
> Joe, One Big Union,
>   One Big
>   hope to be
> With thee.

> Kenneth Patchen : *Joe Hill Listens to*
> *the Praying*

"I 'VE quit rambling around this country. I just figure that a boxcar floor would be too hard on my old bones."

Fred Thompson is sixty-five now but his brush-cut, his galvanic skinniness and his gaiety give him a fifteen-year benefit. He has a steady clerical job, to which he goes and from which he returns each day to the apartment, furnished with bourgeois comfiness, on North Kedzie, Chicago.

For most of his life Fred Thompson has been a Wobbly organizer and agitator. He spent four years in jail, most of the time in San Quentin, after being arrested in April 1923 on his way to a free-speech demonstration in Stockton, California; on his person were IWW documents and leaflets, and he was charged with criminal syndicalism, as were a hundred other Wobs.

Before and after that he rode the freights around America, employed as a copper miner in Montana or digging tunnels in Oregon, wherever conditions were bad and strikes needed provoking – "I just moved around, soapboxing and organizing, living on next to nothing, a can of beans and a loaf of bread."

He began hoboing when he left his home town in New Brunswick at eighteen and crossed into America. "I always had a picture of seeing all this country," he says. "As a kid I felt that before I settled down and got saddled with wife and kids I ought to *see* this country. The people I associated with didn't think it strange that you hoboed – they just took it for granted.

"At that time it would have been thought eccentric for a construction worker to pay a fare to get anywhere. For me the

301

freights were just a practical way of getting to jobs or union assignments. I didn't hang around the jungles, chewing the fat. I always had a purpose, I was always in a hurry.

"I used to wonder why a man was going from this town with no work to that town with no work. I decided it was like lemmings. The pressure was to get out of the place where you were having a bad time. Maybe it's some notion that if you keep shuffling around you'll fall into a slot somewhere.

"Now, well, once in a while when some young hobo hits me up for the price of a coffee, I see myself in him, but I wouldn't say it's nostalgia I feel. There's not enough that's pleasant about the life to want it back.

"You remember Odysseus telling the sailors in the storm at sea that these things will be pleasanter remembered at a future time? Some things which were very unenjoyable at the time make good memories. I like to get a cup of coffee and look out of the window when there's a severe storm – we look out of a window at the past.

"That doesn't mean there weren't simple joys. I once went from Duluth to Chicago in a gondola loaded with spruce and pine boughs for decoration. It was nice, warm summer time. The odor of that balsam as the sun hit them! The boughs had a springy action. No sultan or emperor ever traveled in greater luxury than I did on that train.

"But there were some bitterly cold rides. There were times when I damaged the blood vessels in my feet from pounding them to keep the circulation going. And I've gone ravenously hungry. I traveled from Chicago to Spokane on seventy-five cents, and lived on beans and some bananas I picked up in the boxcar. There were some hens there. I watched those hens until one laid an egg.

"But I've never really understood why so much glamor is attached to hoboing, because for me it was something you didn't do unless you had to. Why did I have to? Well, I suppose it was partly for political reasons and, maybe, yes, because there was something in the life I wanted or needed."

UTOPIAN Socialism arrived in America in the 1820s with Robert Owen, the British reformer, who bought thirty thousand acres of land in Indiana and founded a sort of pilot *kibbutz* which he named New Harmony. It was based on agriculture, "the myth of the garden" in bud.

Its ideals were those which have so often planted in the breasts of men of good will the ruby of hope, which, with doleful inevitability, turns to be a clod of clay. It was to have been a community standing on its own feet, informed by selfless co-operation and a rational flow of brotherliness. New Harmony fell short of its name. It was wound up in 1828 after three increasingly discordant years, with a personal loss to Owen of £40,000.

Strangely, the nearest any movement in America came to achieving the objects of knightly beatitude was that of a rabble of nomadic roughnecks who had nowhere to call home and no meeting place other than an ever shifting horizon; who created a burning creed, their own psalmody, legend and astonishing code of heroism and chivalry; and who, within a life of monkish asceticism and hardness, fought with fists, boots, guns and sabotage – much of the time to avoid being killed or crushed first, it is true, but also out of the untrammeled belief that all capitalists should be exterminated anyway.

The IWW – the One Big Union of the Wobblies – was as quixotic and impossible as Alice's step through the looking-glass, yet for a time and for some excluded Americans it was a reality that worked.

The IWW received its contribution from Owen's "new Unionism" as it did in varying parts from many another – mostly semi-digested – political, economic and philosophical theory. It was a gallimaufry of revolutionary Marxism, English Chartism, French Syndicalism, anarchism, nihilism, and the residue of the one-for-all-and-all-for-one militancy of the defunct Knights of Labor.

What came to be the distinguishing lineament of the IWW was its make-up of, in Brissenden's words, "the unskilled and very conspicuously of the migratory and frequently jobless unskilled." The Wobbly became as token a type as the cowboy or the shantyman or the keelboatman. He was "the genuine rebel, the red-blooded working stiff."

How IWWs became known as Wobblies is as uncertain as how hobos came to be called hobos. The term seems to have materialized about four years after the official start of the party, and, as is so often the case, first as a term of disapprobation which was scornfully taken over and proudly worn as a cockade in the hat.

The nickname "Wibbly-Wobblies" was sneeringly used of them about that time by the socialist editor of the Cleveland *Citizen*, but he may not have invented it. (Other unfriendly improvisations upon the letters IWW were I Won't Work, I Want Whisky, International Wonder Workers and Irresponsible Wholesale Wreckers; an addition made after America entered the war in 1917 was Imperial Wilhelm's Warriors.) One claim is that they took their tag from the wobbling motion of the boxcars which were their transportation. Yet another explanation, given to me by an old agitator who was up in Canada in 1911 helping to unionize the Grand Trunk Railroad, is that a bunch of strikers were staying in the small town of Kamloops, and did a deal for food and board with a Chinese restaurant owner who could get no nearer the W in pronouncing IWW than wobble. Newly arrived card-holders began introducing themselves as "Wobbly-Wobbly." Perhaps the likeliest explanation is that saying IWW out in full must quickly have palled, and that Wobbly was a natural onomatopeic comic contraction.

Whichever the case, Wobblies they were almost from the start. Throughout its short tempestuous career (the IWW still exists but now as a ghostly abstraction) it was the outdoor wandering worker who personified it, romantically and realistically. The hobo, as we have seen, had already existed for several decades as a man conscious of his own identity, and he had grown a cortex of pride and obstreperousness as self-defense against the insecurity of his alienated life.

The IWW acted for these men and was made up of these men. It produced a sense of brotherhood of the dispossessed, the knowledge of solidarity against the almost invariably cheating and unscrupulous boss, a front against the antagonism of the majority toward the solo stranger, and the thrill of a possible new dawn for all those at large in the twilight regions of American life. So the IWW became a transient train-riding union and its propaganda of allegiance grew out of hobo camp fire songs and slang; and in turn the IWW completed the draughtsmanship of the hobo and convinced him that, down in the gutter or the ditch or the mine, he had not only muscles other men didn't have but also a certain berry of life. The IWW gave hundreds of thousands of "wage slaves and shovel stiffs" a face and a mental direction.

Periodically the IWW spat out the urban progressives – the long-hairs and "spittoon philosophers" – who attached themselves. From the beginning there were members who objected sniffily to those who gave the IWW its blood-and-thunder reputation – the Overall Brigade, despised as "the bummery" and "the rabble." Intellectual moderates such as Daniel DeLeon deplored these Westerners' ignorance of political science and attacked them for turning the IWW into a "purely physical force body."

Rudolph Katz primly described the Overall Brigade as consisting of "that element that traveled on freight trains from one Western town to another, holding street meetings that were opened with the song *Hallelujah, I'm a Bum*, and closing with passing the hat in regular Salvation Army fashion."

DeLeon and Katz were positively right. From the time of the founding convention in Chicago when delegates sang "We have been naught, we shall be all," the potency of the IWW was in that lucent faith – smash through to workers' rule – and not in the textual arguments of office committees about negotiation and gradualism. Not only were the rank-and-file stiffs the "dispossessed and downtrodden," they were also voteless non-citizens with no residence more permanent than a boxcar or a bunkhouse, and no property bulkier than their bedroll.

They saw no point whatsoever in parliamentary legislation and reform. They wanted industrial action – "lots of it, and right away" – for they believed they were the vanguard of the revolution. The core of the IWW was "a fighting faith."

The men who turned up at the first meeting in stagged overalls, black thousand-miler shirts, flannel blouses and red sweat rags around their throats, and who propped up their caulked boots on their blanket packs as they listened to the speeches – "a tough-looking lot," one observer reported with nervous distaste – had beat their way there on freights. Smeltermen and timberbeasts and reapers and hard-rock blasters, they had come great distances to consolidate for action, not to listen to a tutorial on civil government from men whom they must have seen in the way a seventeenth-century critic saw Hobbes – none "had ever had a finger in the mortar."

They were bitter, bellicose men, whose experience battling to survive amid an environment of giant indifference, had left them contemptuous of niceties of strategy. They wanted very direct, concrete things. They wanted their One Big Union. They wanted class war to establish a Co-operative Commonwealth, purged of class and racial distinctions, which would own and control the machinery of production and distribution. They wanted simply the overthrow of the capitalist system which sucked their blood and whose every ounce they hated.

So the Overall Brigade were solid in their loathing of the cautious, boss-conciliatory leadership of the conservative American Federation of Labor, or, as they preferred it, the American Separation of Labor.

DeLeon and his faction did not last long, and it is difficult to see how they could have, for after the 1908 convention DeLeon expressed his view of the hobo element in *The Weekly People*, fingers apparently tweezering nostrils as he wrote: ". . . . to the tune 'I'm a bum, I'm a bum,' very much like the tune of 'God wills it! God wills it!' with which Cuckoo Peter led the first mob of Crusaders against the Turks, Walsh* brought this 'Brigade' to the convention . . . Most of them, I am credibly informed, slept on the benches on the Lake Front and received from Walsh a daily stipend of thirty cents."

The first bifurcated phase of the IWW ended in 1915 when the DeLeonites changed their name to the Workers' International Industrial Union, because, reported Fellow Worker Crawford in the *Industrial Union News*, that October the "bummery" had disgraced the letters IWW, and he continued: "The name IWW

* J. H. Walsh, a national organizer of the IWW who rounded up the biggest delegation in Portland a Spokane.

has come to be associated with petty larceny and other slum tactics. It is up to us to choose a new name so as to escape the odium ..." In the same publication the general secretary-treasurer denounced "the lunatics on the rampage."

Divorce took place, but despite the IWW's move left dissension festered on below the surface like a grumbling appendix until in 1924 the lumberjack faction seceded from the main organization. A lofty contempt was still felt for the "red-blooded stiffs" by the town-based "thinkers." A 1924 pamphlet by James Rowan, one of the headquarters group, described the rogue administration as "The Grand Goblins ... the hi-jack communist machine," and continued: "The hobo is the migratory worker: the homeguard is the non-migratory worker. The former is footloose, homeless, uncouth; the latter may have a home and family, and is perhaps not so much accustomed to hardship and rude living. In the IWW the hobo and the homeguard psychology never fused."

He quoted from a General Office Bulletin complaining that the Wobs are "the industrial workers of the woods, and not of the world. That is, the migratory psychology dominates, to the disorganization of the IWW itself. Let's make this plain. In an Ohio city an IWW Headquarters is wrecked and organization almost entirely destroyed. Why? Because the migratory element emphatically insisted on making a 'flop house' of club rooms to which the homeguards wished to bring their families.

"Again, in New York City, a meeting is addressed by a migratory worker. He shouts, 'To hell with your jobs! To hell with Defense! Be independent of your jobs; throw it up and go to jail, as I do!' The result is the driving away of married homeguards, with wives and children, who cannot afford such sacrifices."

When the pro-political "yellow" doctrinaries gathered up their skirts and departed, it seemed that at last confusion had terminated an unsatisfactory situation in which two national labor organizations of incompatible aims and tactics had operated under the same title.

Left with the name, which increasingly shrilled like a burglar alarm in the ears of solid citizen America, was the Overall Brigade. The direct-action "bummery" or "red" Wobs had in any case already imposed their ferocious fundamentalist attitudes on the movement. In 1912, during a San Diego free-speech fight – the planned invasion of an industrial trouble spot to test out soapbox advocacy of strikes and militancy, which ended in pitched fights with police and mass imprisonment – the local *Tribune* put in print the way most residents spoke of these men who were agitators as well as tramps.

"Hanging is none too good for them; they would be much better dead, for they are absolutely useless in the human economy; they are the waste material of creation and should be drained off into the sewer of oblivion there to rot ... like any other excrement."

It should be remembered that the "excrement" had been holding public political meetings, as they were entitled to do under the Constitution.

The indigenous nature of the IWW, born from the insemination of peculiar American conditions by distant European revolutionary theories, became dominant: it was the party of floaters, the fraternity of hobo brothers who chalked up slogans and greetings on division point water tanks, held delegate meetings in jungles, and could count on the companionship of another red card carrier on a branch freight in the Montana mountains or in a wheat field camp in Minnesota.

This spirit had been there from the beginning, uncompromisingly, in the figure of Big Bill Haywood, one-time cowboy, miner and homesteader, blinded in one eye in a Utah mine accident, who had left Silver City to take over as organizer for the Western Federation of Miners and the Socialist Party, and who created his reputation by tramping straight through the line of militia bayonets to speak from Denver's court house steps during the Coeur d'Alene strike of 1,200 miners, when nine were indicted for murder.

At the first convention it was Haywood – "a powerful and aggressive embodiment of the frontier spirit" – who, rejecting the AF of L's craft unionism for creating "scabbery and snobbery," and setting apart the skilled from the unskilled as the "aristocracy of labor," declared: "We are going down in the gutter to get the mass of the workers and bring them up to a decent plane of living . . . the skilled worker today is exploiting the laborer beneath him, the unskilled man, just as much as the capitalist is."

The IWW's violence and ruthlessness were tempered to match the violence and ruthlessness used against the industrial laborer. It means little to refer broadly to clashes between work force and management. Some examples are necessary to give the taste of the lawlessness and cruelty that flared through industrial disputes in America until very recent times, a quality of hatred and fury not evaporated yet.

One of the first and bloodiest of the IWW organized strikes was at McKees Rocks, Pennsylvania, in July 1909, two months of bitter upheaval which set the pace of IWW militancy for the rest of its active life. Eight thousand employess of the Pressed Steel Car Company downed tools for better conditions, and the Company's instant, and predictable, reaction was to call in the "cossacks," the Pennsylvania State Constabulary, whose record was for hitting straight out into the middle of labor disturbances.

On August 12 a steel worker named Harvath was killed, "in cold blood," by the cossacks. The strikers' reply was an eye-for-an-eye ultimatum which gave McKees Rocks its niche in labor rolls. The police commander was informed that the life of a cossack would be taken in retaliation for every steel worker killed. A week later a party of steel men was attacked and a policeman was shot dead in the fray. More steel workers came gunning their way in and five guards were shot down. The battle spread. More strikers and guards fell dead and wounded before the company troops fled for cover, leaving the strikers the field and the offer of settlement around the conference table.

In June 1917 fire exploded in the Butte Speculator Mine and 200 miners clawed at the concrete bulkheads for the steel manholes that had been skimped by the company in disregard of safety regulations. There was a volitional strike and Frank Little, an IWW organizer – although already on crutches, a leg in plaster from an earlier labor brawl when he had committed the seditious act of reading the Declaration of Independence in public – arrived in Butte to take over. He made a speech that evening in the ball park. Afterward six masked armed men entered his room in the Finn Hotel and beat him up. He was dragged at the end of a rope behind a Cadillac to the Milwaukee Railroad trestle. Both kneecaps were smashed. He was found next morning, half naked, hanged on the rope from the bridge. No attempt was made to find the murderers, but next morning the town was flooded with private mine guards and State militiamen to ensure that law and order prevailed.

Atrocities of a slightly milder sort were commonplace wherever the solid citizens were determined to protect decency and American freedom – roughly translated, the employer's freedom to dictate the terms he chose. In 1917 in Arizona armed guards of the United Verde Copper Company rounded up seventy IWW strikers, herded them on cattle cars and dumped them on the far side of the California line, where they were driven back by a sheriff's posse and back again in exhausted shuttlecock.

At Bisbee vigilantes made a night raid on the homes of striking miners, held 1,162 in the ball park all night, next morning put them at rifle point on cattle cars, threw them off in the desert without food or water, and kept them out of town until the strike was broken.

At Tulsa an armed mob broke up a union meeting, rushed away the leaders in cars, roped them to trees and flogged them with blacksnake whips, afterward pouring hot tar on the lacerations and bursting pillows over them. In the Wheatland hop fields city officials rolled up in cars with sawed-off shotguns and broke up the strike meeting by killing four. Another four – lumberjacks this time – were killed at Shreveport, Louisiana, in a "daylight massacre" by timber company mercenaries, and fifty-eight strikers were jailed while other men and their families were blacklisted out of the region. In the San Diego free-speech fight Ben Reitman was stripped and his buttocks branded with the letters IWW. In Centralia, Wesley Everest, logger unionist, was beaten by a mob, castrated and hanged from a trestle of the Chehalis River bridge.

27 : DON'T WASTE TIME IN MOURNING. ORGANIZE!

Work and pray, live on hay,
You'll get pie in the sky when you die.

Joe Hill: *The Preacher and the Slave*

OF course all this brutality was not a spontaneous sport. As always, in the entire turbulent, gory history of American labor relations, such acts spouted from deeper springs: the disrespect for law in the Westering outlook, the habit of settling personal or community conflicts arbitrarily, the conditions of pioneer anarchy in which toughness ran the show. Generally employers were in a stronger position than the reckless but feckless drifters who had neither a powerful wish nor the opportunity to form permanent local bonds. And finally there was the faith in rugged individualism which was as aggressively acted out by the laborer as by the boss.

So the IWW produced a unique breed of migrant agitator, a brave utopianist who tried to put his romantic pedantry into action and invariably suffered – and quite often died – for it. One who did die, although many still believe that his execution was a frame-up, was the man who pre-eminently made the IWW a "singing organization," an immigrant Swede who took the name Joe Hill when he arrived in America in 1902 at the age of twenty.

Then he was as anonymous as a seed in the wind, among the millions transplanting themselves from the old world. Thirteen years later when he died before a firing squad in Utah State Penitentiary, he was an international hero of the left, a labor martyr whose legend has lasted.

He received the death sentence for allegedly killing a Salt Lake City grocer in a hold-up in January 1914. Hill denied it to the end, but he refused to testify, to give information about his movements on that night – or explain how he got his bullet wound, which the prosecution maintained resulted from the exchange of shots in the shop.

311

His appeal was turned down. More than 10,000 letters and telegrams arrived protesting against the decision and demonstrations were staged all round the world; the Swedish ambassador interceded and President Wilson obtained a two week stay. But Utah executed him.

In one of his last letters Hill wrote: " . . . there had to be a 'goat.' And the undersigned, being as they thought, a friendless tramp, a Swede, and worst of all, an IWW, had no right to live anyway . . . I have lived like an artist and I shall die like an artist." His farewell note to Haywood ran: "Goodbye, Bill. I die like a true rebel," and ended with the phrase that was adrenalin for the IWW's bloodstream: "Don't waste any time in mourning. Organize!"

On the afternoon before the shooting party Hill wrote out his Last Will for a newspaper reporter:

> *My will is easy to decide*
> *For there is nothing to divide.*
> *My kin don't need to fuss and moan –*
> *"Moss does not cling to rolling stone."*
>
> *My body? Ah, if I could choose,*
> *I would to ashes it reduce*
> *And let the merry breezes blow*
> *My dust to where some flowers grow.*

This was done. After his cremation pinches of his ashes were sealed in envelopes and sent to IWW members in every state in the Union, and throughout the world and they were emptied into the wind, so Joe Hill went away much as he had arrived in America.

He left behind his songs. *Casey Jones – The Union Scab* had been printed on cards and sold for strike relief in every West Coast City. More and more of his lyrics went into the "Little Red Song Book," the IWW's *Songs of the Workers*, which had on its cover the unequivocal declaration of intent: "To Fan the Flames of Discontent."

Hill invented Mr. Block, the character who stupidly placed his faith in Sam Gompers and the AF of L, and he invented

Scissor Bill, the bum too lazy and bemused by capitalist propaganda to join a union. The thousands of strikers in the Wheatland riot in 1913 were singing *Mr. Block*, and *Scissor Bill* –
sung to the tune of *Steamboat Bill* – instantly entered political
vernacular and folk lore as a booby figure.

Joe Hill's most famous song was *The Preacher and the Slave*,
set to the tune of *Sweet Bye and Bye* and better known by its
recurrent line *Pie in the Sky*:

> *You will eat, bye and bye,*
> *In that glorious land above the sky;*
> *Work and pray, live on hay,*
> *You'll get pie in the sky when you die.*

That, the lyric explained, was the preacher's message to the
"starvation army" to divert them from ideas of gaining "the
world and its wealth."

Few of Hill's songs were so bitingly good but they served their
immediate tendentious purpose: to hearten and weld together
men without protection or rights, to stimulate them to rise
against oppression, and they were scribbled quickly to fit urgent
occasions, and fitted to a current popular tune or a mission hymn
everyone knew.

The run-of-the-mill Wobbly verse was often stilted and solemn,
but these lowborn manual laborers were their own rhymesters
and poetasters, worker-buskers and tramp troubadours, and the
IWW was nothing without its song. It became the "singing organization" it was by competing on the street corners of Spokane
with the Salvation Army tambourine-and-cornet troupes. The
IWW soapbox teams lined up their own bands and roared out
their "abolition of the wage system" gospel to the idling crowds
of loggers, hobos, bums and unemployed around the tenderloin
district.

In cells in Fort Leavenworth and in country lock-ups, in the
Italian copper mine country of Michigan and in South Carolina
knitting mills, in the iron ranges of Minnesota and the cattle
ranches of Old Mexico, in the Pullman car-building shops and
in the forest camps at Little Fork River, in the seamen's local
in the Brooklyn yards and in Tenant Farmers' Association halls

in the South, in the Republic Steel Corporation tenements and on the Kansas corn plains, around water towers and in jungle camps from Cincinnati to Seattle, in freight trains and in coast-to-coast trucks – throughout all of proletarian America the IWW anthems and jingles spread like brush fire in those years between 1906 and 1917.

It seemed as if the inner door had been broken down.

The IWW philosophy and rubric were radiantly artless: direct, not political, action; sabotage "to push back, pull out or break off the fangs of Capitalism"; class war; an industrial union state and a new world order. Just that.

They were dealing with the worker of the economic level at which, in the words of Dublin Dan Liston, a Wobbly barkeep in Spokane, "he hasn't got a pot in which to spit or a window to throw it out." Their delegates and organizers were ordinary laboring blanket stiffs who preached the doctrine in the gondolas and in the orchards and in the track-laying camps where they themselves were working, and they put into the hands of the politically ignorant ingenious techniques.

The IWW started unemployed unions, chain picketing, foreign language leaflets, sticker campaigns, go-slows and sit-downs, car-caravan demonstrations, free-speech soapboxing, and it put into the members' throats bloodthirsty songs of revolution, all the new weapons of revolt.

It got to workers who felt to have fallen from grace in the American success theology, to be beyond the salvation of unionism orientated to city crafts. The IWW "job delegate system" was based on the maxim that "he who travels lightest travels fastest" and aimed at reaching agricultural and industrial workers scattered over vast territory.

This army of moving agitators worked through from the Mexican border in the New Year and closed the book on the recruiting drive in the Canadian provinces in the late fall. The opening campaign for the IWW Agricultural Workers' Organization in 1915 is described by one of the job delegates: "With pockets lined with supplies and literature we left Kansas City on every available freight train, some going into the fruit belts of Missouri and Arkansas, while others spread themselves over the states of Kansas and Oklahoma, and everywhere they went, with every slave they met on the job, in the jungles or on freight trains, they talked IWW, distributed their literature and pointed out the advantage of being organized into a real labor union."

In the face of pick-handle brigades, town marshal commandos with shotguns, and turn-outs of troops, the obscure agitator-poets and migratories (as the farmers knew them) used *The Little Red Song Book* as the empyrion, and they blew on smouldering discontent and fanned the flames.

They had inflammable material to start on, especially among the producers of raw materials, those native-born Americans "working out" away from their homes and the others – fully half of them – who were newly arrived immigrants with nothing more permanent than a mission cubicle as base. During its first decade, when the IWW rampaged through the land, America was a giant sweat-shop. When 800 dollars was officially accepted by cost-of-living studies as being the absolute bottommost of subsistence for a worker's family, one in every ten had an income of less than 300, and half the working force received less than 750 dollars a year. Then, a third of the thirty million work force were in the unskilled category that was either spasmodically or totally migratory, and unemployment in all trades passed the thirty-five per cent mark.

For those at work the kind of pay available in, for instance, the steel industry was less than eighteen cents an hour for nearly fifty per cent of employees, and twenty per cent were worked on a seven-day week and twelve-hour day basis. In a typical Chicago slaughterhouse in 1912 more than half of the men were taking home a weekly income of six dollars and thirty-seven cents.

When Woodrow Wilson said in 1913 "Don't you know that some man with eloquent tongue, without conscience, who did not care for the nation, could put this whole country in flames, don't you know that this country from one end to the other believes that something is wrong?" he meant it as a warning.

The Wobblies agreed with his general contention, and tried to tip on the fuel. When the IWW was being attacked for being unpatriotic at the outbreak of war, a Wobbly leader said: "If you were a bum without a blanket; if you had left your wife and kids when you went West for a job, and had never located them since; if your job had never kept you long enough in a place to qualify you to vote; if you slept in a lousy, sour bunkhouse, and ate food just as rotten as they could give you and get by with it; if deputy sheriffs shot your cooking cans full of holes and spilled your grub on the ground; if your wages were lowered on you when the bosses thought they had you down; if there was one law for Ford, Suhr and Mooney, and another for Harry Thaw; if every person who represented law and order and the nation beat you up, railroaded you to jail, and the good Christian people cheered and told them to go to it, how in hell do you expect a man to be patriotic?"

At that time Parker wrote: "American industrialism is guaranteeing to some half of the forty millions of our industrial population a life of such limited happiness, of such restrictions on personal development, and of such misery and desolation when sickness or accident comes ... The casual migratory laborers are the finished product of an economic environment which seems curiously efficient in turning out human beings modeled after all the standards which society abhors."

By this time the old anti-tramp psychosis had been able to find political justification. The tramp as a vague, disreputable menace had taken on the red glare of revolutionary treason. He was identifiable as a Wobbly, a striker, a pacifist, a malefactor opposed equally to the war and to the wage system, to Middletown codes and to capitalism, to the inalienable right of the employer to use scab labor and to the cash nexus that made the United States great. Now that he had a badge, he had confirmed himself in the role of an enemy to be routed and destroyed.

In the posthumous 1920 publication of Parker's *The Casual Laborer* was printed an appreciation of him by Herbert E. Cory, which had appeared in 1918 in the University of California *Chronicle*, praising Parker for being a "new frontiersman" out in the hopfields and mines and lumbercamps, studying the transient Wobblies. The value of the panegyric is what it reveals about the paucity of knowledge of and interest in migrant workmen, even though they had been teeming through the country for twenty years and had become intrinsic to the economy.

Dr. Harry Jerome undertook for the National Bureau of Economic Research an enquiry to determine the relationship of shortage and surplus of labor to immigration and emigration.

(It was an indifference, or solipsism, which continued. In 1926 *Migration and Business Cycles* did not add much more than questions. It was a piece of detection without clues. "The general seasonal character of the construction industry is a matter of common knowledge, but," confessed Dr. Jerome, "for quantitative measures of seasonal changes in the numbers employed in construction, we have been forced to rely upon estimates pieced together from fragmentary data obtained from various sources." The hobo worker was still, for all the official records cared, the invisible non-man.)

Parker's documents resemble those of an anthropologist back from studying some rum, outlandish tribe, recusant and savage, which indeed is how he did regard them – but, to his credit, as the product of a stupid, neglectful society. Parker's purpose, although he was outraged by the exploitation of the migrant worker, was to warn middle-class America that it was creating not only a new class of *canaille* but, worse, of *bonnet rouge* from whom might be expected dire acts.

But, he stressed, what else could be expected? "As the Harvard biologist words it, nurture has triumphed over nature, the environment has produced its type."

It had taken a very long time for this to be recognized in the cloisters of university departments and in the official corridors of Washington, but even now the dismay lacked some essentials. Parker's reference to the radical hobo's "euphoria" and his martyr's pride in his "stack of crowns of thorns" does not take into account the qualities of what Lerner calls the "vernacular hero" when he is discussing "the literature of a bookless world." Here he is meaning the tall tales of the bigger-than-life heroes around whom young America weaves its wish-fulfilment fantasies: the mountain men, the cow-punchers, the Paul Bunyon lumberjacks, the Pony Express drivers, the 'Forty-Niners, the river gamblers, the outlaws, the Casey Jones railroad men, the John Henry tunnel-drillers, most of whom were "organic to the growing energies of the South and West, although some were the detritus of a kind of lumpen-campfollower of the country's growth."

The hobo may often have been this lumpen-campfollower, and was beyond doubt the detritus, yet he was actually part of the atmosphere that the others blew around themselves like smoke from a dragon's nostrils – "the noise an expanding culture makes as it struts and boasts, puffing its chest a little out of cocky assurance and overbrimming energies, and a little out of the insecurity that needs reassurance. The material out of which this legendry was shaped was the everyday stuff of living; the form it took was the yarn and ballad; the setting was local, in hamlet or city, logging camp or ranch or mining town; the proportions were heroic; the mood was mock-epic; the type image was the hero who was also a bit of a charlatan and a cutter of corners, conscious of his own comic vulnerabilities."

28 : AGITATORS AND
PORK-CHOP PHILOSOPHERS

We were like the old Wesleyan preachers, only
we were preaching the gospel of discontent to a
boxcar congregation.

Old Wobbly

THE Wobbly had a political purpose which, though unsubtle
as a crowbar, set him separate from the rest of the lumpen
proletariat he mixed with. The government understood this when
it stigmatized the IWW as a rabble of 200,000 subversives (the
Federal figure, probably twice the movement's actual 1917 peak).

Reitman, an anarchist intellectual, has given his view of an
observer at the eighth IWW convention that most of the delegates "knew as much about the real labor movement as they did
about psychology, and that they cared little about the broad
principles of freedom," and, marveling at the big things the
IWW had done in its short career, he said to himself: "God!
Is it possible that this bunch of pork-chop philosophers, agitators
who have no real great organizing ability or creative brain
power, are able to frighten the capitalistic class more than any
other labor movement organized in America? . . . Are these the
men who put a song in the mouth and a sense of solidarity in
the heart of the hobo? . . . And as I looked at the delegates and
recounted their various activities, I felt that each one could say,
'Yes, I'm the guy.' And then I wondered how they did it."

They did it by means of passion and a removal, out there in
the offing of industry, from desk policies and bargaining. Their
slogans were unequivocal, cocksure: "A general strike! Tie up
all industries! Tie up all production!" and "Arise!!! Slaves of
the World!!! No God! No Master! One for all and all for one."
and "Kick your way out of wage slavery" – they were spread
by sticker (the Silent Agitator), chalked up on water towers and
factory gates, and printed in *Solidarity* and pamphlets. (But even
the IWW, it seems, drew a line. The secretary of Local No. 57

regards first with disfavor, then as a raving lunatic, Yank in Eugene O'Neill's *The Hairy Ape*, when he bursts in the office roaring: "Dynamite! Blow it offen de oith – steel – all de cages – all de factories, steamers, buildings, jails – de Steel Trust and all dat makes it go ... Dat's what I'm after – to blow up de steel, knock all de steel in de woild up to de moon. Dat'll fix things!")

The IWW did not originate their singing style any more than they invented the "flying delegate," for both were old established in radical movements that had long preceded them. What the IWW did was to emphasize their necessity in a union that had to be a fisher of men in rough tidal seas. But they were not strong enough for the weapons wheeled up against them. Mass sedition trials during the war – the "Big Pinch" – put hundreds of Wobblies in jail, and Federal suppression of the IWW led to wider purges of all radicals, which netted Wobblies who had escaped the first sweep: in California alone between 1920 and 1924 more than 500 Wobblies were indicted.

It broke the back of the IWW. In 1919 Haywood admitted openly that the organization had been shaken "as a bull dog shakes an empty sack."

But the contents of the sack had not been lost. Joyce L. Kornbluh has pointed out that the movement laid the groundwork for trade and industrial unionism in the 1930s and 1940s, and although *The Little Red Songbook* was bowdlerized, the songs had already flown the coop and were on the wing everywhere.

Many of the Wobbly songs had immediately entered the general fund of the nation's folk tradition. A song such as *Pie in the Sky*, carried by hobos through the land, and deposited with other prisoners in jail houses, with local customers in town bars, with factory workers in union halls, quickly was everyone's property. It was part of the reciprocal action of American song, for it got extended lease on small town radio shows and on commercial recordings by hillbilly stars like Carson J. Robison, Frank Luther and Vernon Dalhart in the Depression Thirties, when "pie in the sky" became a catch phrase of increased application.

This is a process that has continued, especially in the South where, as was mentioned earlier, authentic hobo songs or derivations, quasi hobo songs and imitation hobo songs, and songs in this tradition about rovers, railroaders and autobums, unwittingly transmit through juke box and receiver the old Wobbly attitudes – a peculiar virus of anarchy to find chronic in this most inoculated of commercial bloodstreams.

Perhaps it was above all its song that caused this small, shortlived movement to be loathed and feared more than any other political organization, including the Communist Party. Its voice broke through everywhere. To the tune of *Annie Laurie* people sang

When in One Union Grand, the working class shall stand
The parasites will vanish, and the workers rule the land.

To *Take it to the Lord in Prayer* they sang:

Stiffen up, you orn'ry duffer
And dump the bosses off your back.

To *Sunlight, Sunlight,* they sang:

No master class shall wine and dine while we on swill must
eat
We'll take the things we helped create and give ourselves a
treat.

And to *Barney Google* they sang:

Come on, all you workers and we'll organize so strong
That the capitalist system will soon be on the bum
So join the Wobblies, Join the Wob, Wob, Wobbly band.

The intense, exalted comradeship had the frame smashed from around it, but the spirit did not entirely expire. The Republican Senator William Borah, of Idaho, who wanted the IWW leaders summarily slaughtered, said in public, blankly, with a puzzlement he could not conceal: "It is something you cannot get at. You cannot reach it ... It is a simple understanding between men."

321

PART FIVE

GOTHS AND VANDALS

Behold, the hire of the laborers which have reaped down your fields, which is of you kept back by fraud, crieth: and the cries of them which have reaped are entered into the ears of the Lord of sabaoth.

James 5:4

29 : THE BLACK SHADOW

She say "Will you work for Jesus?"
I say "How much Jesus pay?"
She say "Jesus don't pay nothing."
I say "I won't work today."

Hobo to Salvation Army Girl in
The Swede From North Dakota

B ELOW the Dakota Bad Lands, where not a blade sprouts in
the geological freak show of clay and rock configuration,
is suddenly more of the Mid-West Wheat Belt.

This is the great granary, 300 miles wide and striding 1,000
miles from Oklahoma up to the Canadian border, in summer a
tawny Mediterranean, an inland sea always swaying with waves
and audible. The wheat plain is as big as the covering sky, leo-
nine yellow to the other's metal blue, sometimes crossed by
scampering clouds and cloud-shadows, but boundlessly, desolat-
ingly, null and empty of all but itself and the traveler.

As twilight softens the raw lines of the highway searing on
and on across mingled sky and stem, there is for the first time
a disturbance in the vacancy. Between Pine Ridge and Martin on
Nebraska's Northern rim can be seen squadrons of combine harvesters circling the plains in the gathering night, tails of dust
coiling behind them as they chew through the ripe winter-sown
wheat.

It looks like a tank battle on desert, jousting charges of scarlet
machines on a tourney ground as large as the azimuth. As the
light dies, the combines' headlamps snake about the shrinking
blocks of standing corn, and trailers loaded with the bushels
joggle through the glare of floodlights.

By eight the day-shift combine crews are clocked out of the
fields and are swarming into the Hi-Way Café, the big chrome-
sumptuous restaurant at the junction of Routes 73 and 18. All
have clown faces: a matt powdering of meally chaff dust through
which sore, red-rimmed eyes blink tiredly; the backs of their

necks are scorched lobster by the sun and their hair is cotton-wool with dust and bleaching.

They are all piratically ragged, in T-shirts and singlets black with sweat and diesel grease, in denim shirts with the sleeves ripped and collars torn off and knotted at the navel, in shirts that are no more than fluttering ribbons flying from the shoulder, in butcher-stripe dungarees and oil-stained jeans, in battered felt hats and wickerwork peaked caps. Some wear stockmans' and hunting boots, others are in sneakers, and two are barefoot. Some have slung from their belts canvas sheaths for pliers and spanners. A few sport beards, one a goatee, another a full black bush, another a spade beard with shaved upper lip, German settler mode.

A good many appear to be university students and high school boys, flamboyantly stressing the buccaneer style of the peregrinat-ing harvest hand, earning their vacation money the hard way. But there are full-time professionals here. One gigantic young man with a sun-frizzled crew-cut, who is eating his second steak dinner, is wearing green burlap slacks and blouse stencilled across the back with ROLAND MC CREERY ELEV. CO. PEKIN, IA. Outside in the car park several of the pick-up trucks and heavy duty trucks are marked JACK SCHNEIDER, LURAY, KANSAS. CUSTOM CUTTING. Across the road in an improvised open air servicing workshop are mobile sleeping vans and kit wagons which service the crews.

Rainfall has delayed the winter wheat harvest in Shannon and Bennett counties. The spring wheat is no more than sixty per cent ripe, oats seventy per cent. Rust has spoiled some fields al-together and they have been abandoned, uncut, for plowing up. But the rye is being cut and the earlier Omaha wheat and the rust-resistant Lancer and Ottawa wheat are ready for the com-bines. Some have already done their job and gone, for on the road through from Hot Springs I had met columns of caterpillar tractors mounted on bogies, following car-drawn trailers and equipment auxiliaries, thundering Northward to the next con-tract assignment, and eventually across into Alberta and Saskat-chewan: the systematic pounce from one cycle of ripeness into the next.

There is not anyway the amount of combining to do in this

region that there once was, for batches of old wheat land have been insulated under soil conservation schemes or sown with other crops under the encouragement of Federal subsidíes to check surplus production. So now the tornado of invasion that hits such barely formulated rube towns as Pine Ridge and Martin – "wide places in the road," the truckers call them – is limited to the few days of the "flash" harvest. The combine crews, whose summer hegira is through seven or eight states and into Canada – these panzer squadrons whose business is brief in the prairie towns they hardly see through the haze of their exhaust fumes and husk dust – are the mechanized remnant of the harvest hordes of only a few years ago.

FOR nearly thirty years, from the late 1890s until the sudden ubiquitous takeover of the combine in 1926, the seasonal inundation of the wheat belt by hands for hire was one of the prodigious phenomena of the American scene.

"Each season," writes McWilliams, "a great black shadow of men passed like a cloud over the plains and, with uncanny swiftness, disappeared" – a lightning sketch of both the spontaneity and the cruelty of the American catch-as-catch-can economy. The wheat belt was for those thirty years a requisite in the survival pattern of the floating worker, and for those thirty years the American farmer deftly recast the hobo from ministering angel to cloven-hooved trespasser within a few weeks, and season after season repetitively performed that same tergiversation: the warm welcome when the corn ears hung heavy, the cold shoulder when all was stubble.

Taylor recalls that in the years before World War I "one could see the freights in July moving slowly through Sioux City into the Dakotas, the roofs and doorways of boxcars literally black with men en route to the wheat fields." Grain traffic's financial importance to the railroads induced a magical tolerance at this time of the year. In an access of Christmastide benevolence, the club-swinging police patrols of the sidings and the trains, the enmity toward all with a bundle and an IWW card, the approved belligerence of train crews to the ride snagger, and the vagrancy fines and vigilante bum-rushes in the wayside halts – all, for this enchanted moratorium, was forgiven and waived.

The "blackbirds," the sought-for birds of passage, began in mid-summer to make for the depots and jumping-on points. They moved out of the flophouses in St. Paul and Kansas City and Chicago and Des Moines; construction workers in Montana and Oregon remembered that it was time for a change of locus, packed up and hurried for the freight yards; margin-land farmers in Northern Texas and the hills of Missouri kissed their families goodbye and swung aboard a local rattler; jungle camps all over the United States thinned and emptied. And all the tributaries thickened as they converged upon the midriff of America, until every freight entering the Great Plains wheat fields was heavy with human cargo.

Nobody hid or dodged then. Men rode openly on the carriage tops and crammed in the gondolas and stock cars, and no detective or station superintendent tried to sell a ticket or grab a collar – not daring to anyway when the quarry was suddenly so multitudinous.

Two hundred thousand men moved each summer in this way, then onward in a series of short hops by freight from the winter wheat areas of Oklahoma and Texas up into the spring wheat areas of Northern Nebraska, the Dakotas and Minnesota. It was like a collective fugue, a mass of men deserting their haunts and backgrounds and appearing in the identity of a harvest force.

The farmers could not do without them for cities offering pools of labor were far spaced, and most of the farming was then family-unit in size. The deliverance of help by the long-distance trains was a conjuring trick that had to work every year when the instant came for the corn to be got in.

This was no sudden caprice. Much earlier there was unease about the system of a one-crop wheat culture which produced a gun-at-head wage rate (from the farmer's viewpoint) and a hazardous existence (from the laborer's).

In 1869 John C. Burroughs, in his presidential address to the

Madison County Agricultural Society, reported in the *Transactions* of Illinois State Agricultural Society, declared: "The labor of a country is the true element of its wealth, and when we pursue that course that compels labor to be migratory, by giving it employment for but a few weeks in a year, you may expect to pay dear for your whistle."

Farmers concentrated on wheat because it was "the great money crop of the Middle Western and Pacific States." As farmers went Westward to take up new land in the Upper Mississippi Valley, wheat gave quickest cash return. Virgin soils were burstingly fertile, wheat was easy to plant.

With high value and concentrated bulk, frontier wheat could be transported to distant markets in competition with wheat from the East and from Europe. Similar conditions in the Great Central Valley of California were producing similar developments there. In the early 1860s fleets of sailing vessels began swarming into San Francisco Bay to load their hulls with wheat for the annual race to the world's markets.

Until about 1850 grain was sown by hand and harvested by hand with the cradle scythe, and the operation was contained within the family and mutual neighborly assistance. The hiring of outside labor was eschewed except for temporary help from nearby settlements. An Ohio report states that "the rush to the California gold mines in 1849 and early '50s unsettled wages a trifle, but the call for laborers to gather in the harvests was responded to by the villagers in every neighborhood, and the women in many cases came cheerfully to the fields and performed the work of men."

The Rural New Yorker in 1855 published this impressionistic but doubtless authentic description: " ... the mechanic had left his shop, the student had left his books, even those averse to labor, and those who held themselves above it, had entered the lists, for the ripened grain in wheat raising districts – *the* crop of the farmer – must be secured at the proper season ... A small army of men were in the field, paired off like dancers at a cotillion party, the reaper swinging his huge cradle in among the thick straw and laying its rich burden at the feet of the binder who followed a step behind."

The tight pattern of small interlocked units began to fracture as profit inducements swelled. The old thirty-acre, self-sustaining holding was, it was already being noted in 1845 (in *Hunt's Merchant's Magazine and Commercial Review*), giving way in Michigan and Wisconsin to "fields of 200 or 300 acres . . . and frequently 500 and 800 acres are put under a single fence." Large quantities of grain were being lost for want of hands. "Such results," it continued, "would seem to inculcate deeply the lesson, that employments should be multiplied, and a diversity of crops raised, and reliance no longer placed in a single, and that a precarious, crop. But the lesson passes off with the occasion."

Under the emerging system everyone was navigating on uncharted seas. Employers and men facing each to set the money terms for a brief, impersonal relationship lacked the steadying influence of a custom that weighed in the more leisurely arrangements for yearly hiring. Uncertain prices and the hazards of crop damage pressed upon the employing farmer; the shortness of their seasonal opportunity to earn, and the arduousness of harvest labor, impressed upon the hands. To assess a wage rate equating supply with demand was a task for trial and error; last year's rates were largely irrelevant.

Mechanization, still far off as a practicality, was being foreseen as the solution. In 1871, in *The Southern Cultivator*, a Georgia farmer welcomed mowing and reaping machines as a deliverance: "You may harvest when you please, with your machine, not subject to the whims of hand cradlers, or the disaster attending failure to get them" – a truth to be seized avidly fifty years later when cheap mass-produced machinery made it realizable.

Paradoxically in the beginning of the speed-up of mechanization, stimulated by Civil War needs, it actually increased the farmer's reliance on the bindle stiff. During the 1860s and 1870s as steam tractors, gang plows, mechanical wheat planters, drills and broadcast seeders came into their hands, farmers threw their fences wider and specialized yet more intensively in wheat, and the big scale prairie farmers required even larger armies to shock and thresh the grain. Whopping profits compensated for the annual crisis.

"There seemed to be music in the very pronunciation of that word WHEAT," said the president of the Madison County Agricultural Society of Illinois in 1869. "Year after year the contest has been as to who could sow the greatest number of acres, until Madison and adjoining counties presented, last harvest, the appearance of one vast wheat field."

And the bigger the field, the bigger the problem that the farmers were creating for themselves: the drifting flocks of hard-bargaining men without local involvement or loyalties.

A perspicacious Englishwoman writing in *The Country Gentleman* in 1869 spotted the spreading dissolution. She urged farmers' wives to "make their husbands put up cottages and employ steady married men; for this roving set of boarding hands is enough to make every woman dread the name of a farmer's wife. Most decidedly no slaves in the last or any age ever had the evils to bear, with regard to worry and drudgery, as the poor women with men to board and such help as exists here."

The migratory tide was moving; the economy was helping to create the hobo. "Reminded but undeterred," writes Taylor, "farmers first planted wheat, then afterwards sought men who could be detached from home moorings to shift from brief harvest to brief harvest, migrating hundreds of miles in following the ever-ripening grain. Almost simultaneously with sod-breaking and settlement the wheat harvest became the occasion to recruit from farther and farther a huge number of workers needed at no other time. Well to the East and South of the wheat fields of the great Northern frontier lay older, more thickly settled communities with towns growing into cities that could furnish men.

"In the venture of tapping these distant reservoirs the farmers had an ally in the railroads. Since these depended for revenue on selling land and hauling wheat they saw the farmers' interest in moving labor as their own. If the laborers rode free, the wheat paid freight and sold more land. Annual repetition molded labor through experience and expectation to a new type, matching a new need – migratory workers without ties to the farm community, traveling without women, ready to accept a succession of irregular and short employments for a season."

In Illinois and Minnesota this change was "striking men in the face." In 1868 *Harper's Magazine* published an article,

"Among The Wheat Fields of Minnesota" by G. W. Schatzel, who, "excited by the unfolding drama of an unfamiliar agriculture," described the scene in a small town as a gang of rough-looking men from Iowa and Missouri, each with a bundle or valise, disembarked from a train: "Able-bodied, hardy, of all shapes and sizes, they looked like a detachment of Goths and Vandals on a marauding expedition to our peaceful hills and vales. They were the first installment of 'fieldhands' from below, come to assist our farmers to gather in their crops."

Taylor stresses their crucial difference: "They had not come to help neighbors harvest a bumper crop. Without roots in the Minnesota community, the only connection of these migratory laborers with the farmers who had planted the wheat was the 'cash-nexus' of Carlyle – cash and board for a couple of weeks' work in the harvest. In response to an expanding market this demand by Minnesota wheat farmers for migratory seasonal laborers was creating, like cell-division, two separate men – a 'laborer' and a 'farmer,' where before there had been but one, a 'farmer-laborer' called a 'farmer' . . .''

There follows a blow-by-blow dialogue of the sparring, in Minnesota in the bumper harvest of 1867, the laborers holding out for three dollars a day and keep, the farmers refusing to cave in. The stubborn vanguard move on; others roll in; the warfare continues, until some days later, and the harvest still unstarted, the farmers drive to the depot to meet the latest train batch of laborers. This time it is different:

"Each farmer affectionately stows away his gang in the wagon. He treats them very cordially now, almost deferentially, for he fears he may lose them even yet should more than three dollars be offered by some desperate fellow who has failed to secure any. And so, whipping up his team, he drives away in hot haste . . ."

Suddenly nakedly revealed in this 1867 harvest was the new diagram of agricultural capital and labor which was to last until the 1920s. Then, the use to which this conjured legion of mobile workers could be put – despite the harshness of their demands – was suddenly understood by the frontier farmers.

They were "exploited almost immediately and on an ever

332

grander scale," Taylor says. "Greater bonanza 'farms' began to blanket the Red River Valley uniting Minnesota and North Dakota. These famous enterprises, which marked the zenith of the new development in wheat, did not grow by swallowing up small farms, like some of the plantations of the Southeast. They sprang full-blown in the early Seventies when the railroad was put through the valley and sold its virgin land to Eastern investors in great blocks at low prices."

Already by 1880 there were eighty-two farms of more than 1,000 acres in the area. In 1890 the number was 323. Averaging about 7,000 acres each, according to William Allen White in *Scribner's Magazine* in 1897, these bonanza estates rose to the towering height of 75,000 acres of the Dalrymple "farm."

"The bonanza enterprises were not farms as American settlers knew them nor were their laborers – sucked in and blown out to drift hither and thither with the seasons – hired men. Owners usually were absentees who left their properties in the hands of managers. The custom was so widespread in the wheat belt at the close of the nineteenth century that twenty-eight per cent of the wheat acreage of the entire nation was operated by managers. Few farm laborers were worked steadily."

White's report from North Dakota continues: "During the ploughing season about fifty men are employed. At the end of the ploughing season these men are discharged – all but ten of them, who find work on the farm the year round. The discharged men go back to their homes in the pineries or in the cities farther South . . .

"Except for the half-score men who are engaged upon the big farms – in ploughing season, at seeding-time, during harvest and when the season for threshing comes – the men who do the most important work are transient laborers. Frequently they are birds of passage, whose faces are familiar to the foreman, but whose homes may be a thousand miles away.

"Men of this character are not 'hoboes' – yet now and then a tramp does 'rest from his loved employ' and work with the 'harvest hands' . . . These men are regular harvesters, who begin with the early June harvest in Oklahoma, working Northward until the season closes in the Red River country.

"Men of this class never pay railroad fare. Thousands of them

– perhaps fifteen men for every thousand acres in wheat – ride into the bonanza district on the 'blind baggage' on passenger trains. When they have leisure and a taste for scenery they jolt placidly across the continent homeward-bound in what the lingo of the cult calls 'side-door sleepers.' "

There may here be confusion on the writer's part in the application of the word hobo, which he obviously takes to be a synonym for tramp or loafer, although it is possible that among the travelers themselves it had not yet taken on its later distinct meaning of a mobile casual worker. In a 1925 *Saturday Evening Post* article, Herbert Quick recalls that on his father's Iowa farm "we hired men who would now be called hoboes, but were really good industrious young fellows out to make money when wages were high."

What is also evident is that the new breed who were seasonally "sucked in and blown out to drift hither and thither" had already soaked up the zircon light of potluck adventure from the bordermen of a few decades before. Henry King in an 1879 *Scribner's Monthly* article writes that in Kansas where a few years earlier there was "all a desolate and unblest extent of buffalo-grass," the old pastoral methods had been "superseded by an epic; the plentiful reaping-machines, with their glare of paint and burnished still and their great overwhelming 'reels,' have a kind of Homeric character."

Toward the players in the Homeric ring – indeed men driven before the winds of Aeolus – there had developed the mixture of fear and envy, distrust and admiration that marks off America's necessary outcast.

Garland remembers the men who came to his father's Iowa harvests in the mid-Seventies, ex-soldiers and city bums from St. Louis and Chicago, "the errant sons of poor farmers and rough mechanics of the older States, migrating for the adventure of it." He saw them as "rough, hardy wanderers from the South, nomads who had followed the line of ripening wheat from Missouri northward . . . They reached our neighborhood in July, arriving like a flight of alien unclean birds, and vanished into the North in September as mysteriously as they had appeared."

334

Unclean they inevitably were. One of the few migrants who put his case into public print wrote an article for *The Country Gentleman* in 1900: "In the West no washing is done for farm help as a rule, and in Dakota, at least, the transient 'hobo,' who is depended on for the harvest and the threshing rush, is not provided with a bed, but catches a lousy blanket and a straw-stack or a granary, and does not see a laundry or a bath during a whole season's campaign. He pays for his meals on rainy days and between jobs, and is looked upon and treated as a necessary evil."

Twenty-one years earlier King had described, with an amused raised eyebrow, the migrants' accommodation: "Those singular huts made of rough pine boards, with canvas awnings, which you notice now and then, were set up yesterday, perhaps, and will be taken down tomorrow. They are the quarters of the men engaged in the harvesting and very odd places they are, with their rude beds of straw, their long, narrow dining-tables, their clatter of dishes, their ludicrous mimicry of towels, combs and looking-glasses."

Perhaps the economic percentage in the new labor system was totted up most baldly and honestly by an agricultural specialist from Scotland who noted in the 1870s that most of the harvest help was recruited from the Minnesota lumber regions.

"There is no difficulty in obtaining extra hands, amongst whom are many Norwegians, Scandinavians and Germans," he wrote. "During harvest and thrashing, which is done in the field, as many as five hundred men are frequently employed." He commented on the mass dismissal as the harvest finished: "Hard as such wholesale dismissal would be in Great Britain, it is no hardship here, for these men readily find lumberwork in the forests. It is obviously an enormous boon thus to get rid of men whom the farmer cannot profitably employ during the five winter months. Many an English wheat grower would gladly practice this retrenchment and send most of his staff to other vocations during the short days and bad weather of midwinter."

"Wheat farms and hoboes go together" became a byword. But the evolving system did not go altogether uncriticized. A professor at the North Dakota State Experiment Station attacked

335

wheat specialization, arguing for a return to diversification which "distributes the farm work throughout the year more uniformly ... Any plan which will dispense with careless 'hobo' labor upon the farms of this state and substitute competent, thinking men instead, will do much to advance farming interests."

Before that, Stephen Powers in his 1872 *Afoot and Alone* had deplored the upsurge of the same heartless and rootless system in the far West. In California he saw that if wheat was there also to be grown exclusively "then these immense ranches and the consequent hireling system, so baleful to California hitherto will be perpetuated."

His inventory of harvest hands was: "Runaway sailors; reformed street thieves; bankrupt German scene-painters, who carry sixty pounds of blankets; old soldiers, who drink their employer's whisky in his absence, and then fall into the ditch which they dug for a fence-row; all looking for 'jobs,' or 'little jobs,' but never steady work" but he attached the fundamental blame not to the men but to the monster wheat culture. "If the land remains in vast ranches these men will always continue hirelings and tramps.

John Hayes in *Overland Monthly* drew a picture unusually vivid and sympathetic for its period, the early 1870s, for he said there should be no surprise at the laborer's discontent:

"To see him toiling along the dusty highway, penniless, weary, and foot-sore, begging a ride from the teamsters, begging a meal of victuals from the farmers, none would suppose him a denizen of a State advertised over the world for the extent and fertility of a soil to be obtained there for nothing! Having no permanent residence, making no enduring friends, coming daily into contact with strangers whose only object is to make the most out of him and then turn him adrift, it is not a matter of much surprise that his vices attain the highest development; that his virtues become dimmed, and finally extinguished."

In 1872 the *Pacific Rural Press* also condemned this "growing evil in our State ... again the men are discharged to wander about looking for more work or idly 'killing time.'" But the same journal printed a scalding attack on laborers who after starting to harvest sought an advance of wages: "If the farmer refused to yield to the exorbitant demand and for non-compliance with contract on the part of the laborer he refuses to pay, or retains a part as a guarantee of continued work, the civilized man utterly refuses to do another day's work; leaves, and more than likely within a week, by a remarkable dispensation of divine providence (?) the farmer's stacks or grain fields are found in a blaze." The advice extended to farmers was not to engage white labor, but Chinese.

Not all the big Californian wheat growers favored cheap coolie labor but there were plenty who worked hard to block restrictions on its entry and even to step up the flow – just as was later to happen with the Mexican *braceros*.

One of the state's largest agricultural employers told the Congressional Committee on Chinese Immigration in 1876 that importations of Chinese were necessary because "the character of the labor generally in California is very bad other than that of the Chinaman. What has contributed to make the American laborer so good for nothing ... I do not know. Perhaps labor-leagues have had something to do with it. Perhaps the general disinclination to work which has grown out of the war ... At any rate, the fact is patent that the American today has made up his mind to live off his wits and not work ... I say that the rule for American laborers today is to be drunkards. They are bummers."

That is an ageless wistfulness, bedewed with nostalgic longing for days when labor was cheap and cheerful. One underdog barked back in the *Pacific Rural Press* during correspondence on laborers' conditions. Headed "A Farm Hand's Complaint," the letter ran: "If we work for a poor farmer we get a bed in the house, and sit at the same table with the family, and sit at his fire and read his papers, and enjoy the comforts of his house generally. But with the large farmers we have to furnish our own bed, if we have any; if not, maybe he will be kind enough to give us an old piece of blanket or quilt, or a few old sacks to cover ourselves with. He will tell us to go out to a barn or in the granary, or to the hay stack to sleep ... We find a place to wash ourselves out of an old barrel or a milk pan; then we wipe on the towel or piece of barley sack, that hangs there for us only ...

"If the farmer gets good steady hands, as he calls them, he will keep them just as long as he has plenty of work for them, and just the minute the work is done they must go, rain or shine. He doesn't say, 'Boys, stop until the storm is over' . . . they have to take their blankets and clothes on their back and march – to town or through the country – to look for another place to work; and thus they are treated by the rich farmers."

The growing enmity between the big employers and migratory laborers "marked the extremes among those whom one-crop wheat culture was separating." Many smaller working farmers, alarmed at the destruction of the cherished American principle of the independent, self-sufficient farming family, found themselves with the migrant on this issue.

A speaker at an Agricultural Society meeting at Ukiah, California in 1887, compared the intimacy and security of the Eastern farm worker with his counterpart from the West: "Make the employment of men brutal, and you must depend upon a brutalized class to fill the positions it offers, a class that will become more embruted by the character of its treatment."

The protests continued, here and there, now and then. "Debasing," "demoralizing," "shameful and deplorable" – these were words used by officials and investigators between the 1870s and the turn of the century against the exploitations of the "flights of alien birds," but the protest was never sufficiently fierce or unified to deflect the trend.

"If the land remains vast ranches," Powers had written, "these men will always continue hirelings and tramps." Of course it did remain so, and became more so, and the men did so continue – until it became possible to dispense with them almost entirely in the wheat belt and forget them as they smoked away into other branch lines of American life.

One of the first attempts to find out who the migrant worker was, from whence he came and whither he vanished, was made in 1923 by Don D. Lescohier. He discovered that many of the blackbirds had small farms in the South and had been "making the wheat harvest" for ten, fifteen and even twenty years, each autumn taking home with them a little cushion of dollars for the winter months on their own one-crop semi-subsistence holdings.

These were, in McWilliams' words, the Joads of yesterday. Then they traveled as single men, and indeed not all were heads of far-away households for the wheat plains army recruited too from the city hostels and the permanent hobo force.

The arrival of the harvest hands was a yearly event yet it always seemed to cause new consternation. "Drowsy little villages in the midst of the yellowing wheat fields woke to the need of providing temporary shelter for the harvest hands who landed from boxcars or came walking," reported the *Review of Reviews* in 1927. Hospitality was tempered exactly to the exigency of the moment.

A headline in the *Daily American*, in Aberdeen, South Dakota, on July 18, 1921 was MOVE ON IS ORDER OF POLICE AS TRAINS BRING HOBO THRONGS TO CITY and, no buts about it, when an area was furnished with enough hands, all later arrivals were rounded up and pushed aboard the next train out.

The labor was never, in relation to the local price structure, cheap. The migrants of those times in the breadbasket zone were Caucasian Americans; they were capably strong men and of mettlesome pride and independence, unshackled by women and children around them, or at least immediate responsibility for a family's welfare; they bargained hard and if not actual members of the IWW they leaned towards radical unionism.

The farmers were unorganized, scattered and frantically concerned to get their crops cut. The bindle stiffs strolled across the tracks out of the yards and into Main Street, squatted with their backs to the store fronts, and the farmers drove up in the buggies or T-models to conduct kerbstone deals for their labor.

McWilliams comments: "It will be noted that this migration pattern was almost the reverse in many respects of the typical present day agricultural migration. The wheat migrant was not despised: his services were eagerly sought after, and his working conditions were tolerable.

"A lord of the rods, he had no traveling expenses and never worried about a broken-down jalopy. Nor did he have a hungry family following him. He was actually received into the farm family ... Mid West farm wives prided themselves in preparing

339

good meals for harvest hands. Workers could net, for the season, around two hundred dollars, which, for many of them, was a tidy sum."

Well, they earned it. Ashleigh's description of his time as a bindle stiff in 1915 although somewhat inflamed with drama carries authenticity. Joe, his hero, is aboard the blind baggage of a passenger heading for the North Dakota harvest.

"Some frozen stars appeared. On through the sleeping land rushed the long express. Inside the passengers sat, warm and soft on the upholstered seats, or lay sleeping in their berths. And on the prow of the giant land-ship stood three muffled figures, shivering but dauntless, carried on – through bitter cold and smoke and turmoil, danger of arrest or of beating – towards the harvest jobs that would earn them sustenance for a short space, and help provide the world with bread."

Taken on, Joe follows the big machine as it scoops up the ripe wheat, lashes it in bundles and drops them behind, to be gathered and stacked. "Joe worked at shocking. Together with other slaves of the machine he worked . . . Hour after hour went by. His arms and back ached with the toil. But he must not relax: the machine went relentlessly on, and he must keep up with the machine. Under the late sun, or in the chill of the Northern wind, he must go on with his fellow-workers of the shocking crew.

"From early dawn until no light was left in the sky, by which they could work, gathering bundles and placing them in shocks – until his mind was deadened in a species of coma, and his arms performed their task with the same mechanical regularity as did the apparatus ahead of him.

"Night came and the crew ate supper, swallowing voraciously the food before going to their exhausted sleep. They slept in the barn on straw, wrapped in the threadbare unwashed blankets provided by the wheat farmer. For weeks Joe had not taken a bath nor changed his clothes. He slept in his clothes for warmth. Like the rest of the crew he had become lousy, at first to his great horror. Later he learned to joke about the lice, as did his hardened fellows."

It was in this year, 1915, that the IWW formed its Agricultural Workers' Industrial Union and began a headlong drive in the grain belt, seizing the opportunity offered by the war in Europe. Wheat prices rocketed. Great areas of new land were riven open by the plow and, as rural labor gravitated to the highly paid jobs in arms plants and factories canning export foods, harvest hands acquired a scarcity value they had never before enjoyed.

By 1918 the IWW had enrolled 50,000 in its agricultural branch, and made ever tougher deals with the farmers. Ashleigh writes: "... the IWW swept the wheat fields like a prairie fire, making thousands of new members, and raising the daily wage from three or three and a half dollars to four dollars. They also secured better food and other conditions wherever they were sufficiently powerful."

Joe finds himself in a Wobbly crew – ceiling rates. He learns the Wobs' technique: to infiltrate each crew in ones and twos, begin proselytizing, clinching an agreement to organize the job, then presenting their demands to the farmer. Concessions were not always instant and amicable. The wheat plains in those years were battle grounds of sporadic fights, strikes and raids by gun-packing citizen-territorials.

For several years before the IWW launched its campaign, the wheat belt had shaken with labor unrest. In September 1914 George Creel wrote in *Harper's Weekly*: "Since June the whole wide sweep of the Western grain belt has been the scene of ugly disorder and even actual riot.

"Thousands of men, marching in great bands, have broken down the rules of railroads, ravaged fields and gardens, robbed provision stores and acted as aggressive units in making wage demands. Towns in Oklahoma, Kansas, Nebraska and the Dakotas have been compelled to treble their police forces, the railroads have largely increased their constabulary, pitched battles are not unknown, and jails have been filled to overflowing."

Creel's rather undetailed drama is at least frank about how the farmers and chambers of commerce cast recruiting nets widely to keep down wage rates: "Wheat belt towns grew black and blacker with work hunters ... the pressure of these thousands of idle, hungry, shelterless men bore heavily on every community.

Towns people were deputized and armed with clubs, trains were met by these posses."

The wheat rush had been unleashed by stories, deliberately bruited by paid agents as distant as Chicago and St. Louis, and in newspaper advertisements throughout the Mississippi Valley, that 150,000 additional workers were needed in the wheat belt.

The anti-union plotters over-reached themselves and landed upon many a small town the graver problem of hordes of surplus men, most of whom, after hard riding across half the country, were put in a tetchy mood by learning that the announced jobs were illusory.

In some areas the scab tactics worked and wages were held or even cut. There was a song sung around the railroad network then:

> *It was on a sunny morning in the middle of July*
> *I left in a side-door Pullman that dear old town called Chi*
> *I got the harvest fever, I was going to make a stake*
> *But when I worked hard for a week I found out my*
> *mistake . . .*

> *For sixteen hours daily, oh say, oh say,*
> *John Farmer worked me very hard, so I'm going away*
> *When I left that old farmer he cussed me black and blue*
> *He says, "You goldurned hoboes, there's nothing will suit*
> *you."*
> *So back to town I'm going, and there I'm going to stay.*

Even going back to town took on additional dangers once the United States had entered the war in April 1917, for soldiers on guard at bridges and tunnels were quick to relieve their boredom by taking potshots at human targets on a boxcar roof.

Not everywhere was the bindle stiff cheated or clubbed or shot out of the county. As already mentioned, in the Northern Plains area there were many farmers whose sympathies favored the Wobblies and the laborers, the agrarian Populists who felt their enemy to be not the unionized worker but the "money baron," the "lords of industry" of the vested interests who threshed the real profits out of America's crops.

Within this variable climate of attitude, the IWW succeeded in winching up wage rates despite the Government's purge of the "One Big Union" in 1917. Lescohier reports: "From Oklahoma to Canada the hand of the IWW has been felt in the harvest. Although the Federal Government was doing everything in its power to flood the wheat belt with surplus workers as part of its efforts to crush the Wobblies, the expanding wheat acreage and other factors continued to create a relative labor shortage.

"During the war some 40,000 agricultural workers were attracted to Canada by prospect of good wages in the wheat fields ... so wages remained fairly high."

In 1920 IWW members were rejecting employment at seven and a half dollars a day. At Aberdeen, South Dakota, in that same year 400 bindle stiffs paraded through the streets protesting against the offered sixty cents an hour and chanting the implacable IWW creed: "We don't want an honest day's wage for a day's toil. We want the abolition of the wage system."

Lescohier describes a typical retaliatory ploy: "At Colby in 1921 the IWWs were in control of the situation for about a week. Approximately 1,100 harvesters were in town, the majority of whom were farmer boys from Missouri, Arkansas, Oklahoma and Eastern Kansas.

"The farmers were offering four dollars a day, with no takers ... Into this situation came three special railroad police. Guns in hand, they went into the jungles, lined up the men and brought them up to the government employment offices, where they were told to go get to work or get out – on a passenger train.

"Then began the sorting. The Southern farmer boys, factory workers, etc. stepped up and took work; the others were marched up to the Rock Island depot and over 250 dollars' worth of tickets were sold them – probably the first tickets that many of them had bought during extended travels. Within forty-eight hours not more than fifty men were left in Colby."

The tactic was applied systematically throughout the wheat belt. Wobblies, says McWilliams, were "separated from the stream of workers and rousted out of the communities, and the farm boys were treated as favorite sons. With industrial employ-

343

ment low in 1921, it became possible, moreover, to recruit city labor for the wheat harvest."

In 1923 it was estimated that of 100,000 migratory workers in the wheat belt, one-third were farm hands from the South, one-third down-and-outs roped in from the skid rows, and one-third habitual hobos.

There were other forces at work. The mechanical mower, the reaper, the gang plough, the corn sheller, the shredder, the manure spreader, the hay loader – fewer and fewer human hands were needed for the elaborate machinery rolling fast across the plains. The black shadow of men that swooped upon the corn country steadily faded from its 1915 peak until twenty-five years later the labor needed to produce a bushel of wheat had been halved.

But it was the co-operation between railroads, government agencies and anti-union farmers that exterminated the free-ranging radical bindle stiff. To help the farmers obtain a more "reliable" labor supply, in 1924 the railroads rescinded their old permissiveness when the freights were crowded like starling roosts.

Two years later sixty-five per cent of the harvesters were traveling by automobile. The old guard hobo still went by freight train but it was a more daunting ride, with closer watch at the depots, frequent raids en route, hostile train crews, and a greatly heightened likelihood of being thrown off or arrested.

This policy became possible only because of a decline already ensuing. The reduced flow could be tackled; the hobo could be subjected to ambush attack all along the line. An eloquent comparison is the railroads' defeat a decade later when the Thirties depression pushed an even bigger and more desperate horde onto the freights. In the summer of 1932 most railroads just gave up trying to fight them off, and took to coupling onto every train one or more boxcars with wide open doors to short-circuit the readiness to break into sealed cars.

When the train-riding hobo was first encountering the new auto migrant he was not especially worried. But his belief that "a chisel through the radiator, a sledgehammer on the cylinder head" would squash the competition did not prove true. The railroad bindle stiff was not only outnumbered but he was out-manoeuvred by the mobility of the car-borne who could follow the speeded-up harvest by cutting across country.

Yet as late as 1927 there was still the surprisingly huge number of 100,000 transients of all kinds involved in the wheat cutting wave starting in Texas in June and ending in Canada in October, well over half of these having followed it regularly for up to five years, and nineteen per cent for more than ten seasons.

Ironically, it was the IWW's unionization and wage rate campaign of the war years that killed off the bindle stiff's summer market. Scared and angered, farmers leaped into a mechanization that would liberate them from dependence upon the mercenaries. It was in 1926 that the combine roared into dominance through the wheat belt. In that first year it displaced 33,227 harvest hands. In the short space from 1926 to 1933, 150,000 harvest hands became redundant.

A journal of the time commented: "The carefree knights of the boxcar rods have gone to join the buffalo hunters." In 1927 the Wheat Farming Company was incorporated in Kansas and six years later was handling 64,000 acres of wheat land throughout ten counties by machine. The new age of factory farming and corporate control had arrived.

The harvest hand now had become a machinist employed by long-range companies who despatched their teams on rubber tires, vectored like air-line flights; or else he was a clock-punching shift-worker tailoring the arc-lit fields on the locally-garaged combines and tillagers. By 1940 the use of free-lance migratory harvesters, had been "almost completely eliminated" in most areas and "reduced to a trickle" in others.

A spectacular and unique phase had unfolded and closed in the American countryside; but the rural ride was not finished for Americans. Wheat was not the only "money crop."

PART SIX

RIVER'S A-RISIN'

Dat's de way we'll be soon – tore up and a-movin'
... I'd be willin' to eat dry bread de rest o' my
life if I had a place I could settle down on and
nobody could tell me I had to move no more.

Negro woman, North Carolina, 1938

30 : WRAP YOUR TROUBLES
IN DREAMS

Looks like doughnuts will be hanging too high
for the social revolution before this hard winter is
over.

Big Bill Haywood

O N the Navajo Trail south of Mexican Hat (an Indian trading post, grocery and post office skewered by the sun into
the ochre dust) is the AZ Minerals Corporation. Alone on a
rock plateau the Corporation's silver metal sheds and intestinal
pipes abut country marked on the map "Travel in this area not
recommended without guides." The plant has its own warning
screwed on the gate : CAUTION. RADIOACTIVE MATERIAL.

This part of Utah is sterile badlands on which wind-eroded
buttes and escarpments, striped with mauve and carmine, jut
like citadels in a Gothic nightmare. In the early Fifties prospectors scraped off the dead crust and revealed uranium. Hard-
rock miners migrated in to smash the deposits open with jack-
hammers, blast out open-cast sections with dynamite, and hack
at the thin sandwich of uranium by crawling flat on their
stomachs along two-foot tunnels – Finns and Swedes from Colorado, Italians and Yugoslavs who had been quarrying lead and
zinc from Montana granite.

For Dick Unger, AZ's supervisor, these past two years have
been just another spell in thirty-five years of prizing ore from
the American land mass. He is a tall rangy man with springy
gray hair, in an open-neck blue sports shirt. "My father was
raised on a farm in Minnesota, I was born in Richfield, Idaho,
and raised in Southern California – that was a good mobile start!
I finished school in the Depression but I had some mechanical
ability and I got fixed up for fifteen dollars a month running a
power unit in a mine east of Sacramento.

"From there I moved up to Colorado, screening gold, silver
and copper, just for the summer season. After that I moved up
to a gold mine at Weepah Camp, at Tonopah in Nevada, then

back to the mother lode area on the West of the Sierra Madres in California.

"That's the way it's always been. I'm in mining so I have to go where the stuff is. When I was younger I had an auto, a bedroll and a bag of tools, and if a job didn't suit me I just moved on and found another one. I've always liked traveling around through the states although it's usually zip from here to there.

"It didn't make much difference when I got married. The first place I took my wife to was a mine in central Nevada where there were twelve cabins, eleven men and us. We both like a little more freedom than you can get living in a house in town. We've never minded how remote it was. We've lived in company houses or cabins, sometimes we've rented a house wherever we've found ourselves. We've often been seventy-five miles from a doctor or a cinema, however you define civilization.

"When the uranium thing broke we were at Ouray, Colorado, with a lead and zinc company. There was this romantic thing about the gold-rush days: the uranium-rush was pretty similar. I hadn't given uranium a thought until then but when the excitement started my wife and I kicked the idea around for a few months and in 1956 we decided to come down to the hot country.

"I reckon life's been good to me. I'm a fairly adaptable person. I'm not too gregarious. I would be much more alone in a city than I am out here. There's a difference of course between a mine man and a mill man. I'm a mill man. The miner's work and life are harder physically and they get to be pretty hellroaring guys. I wouldn't say I was quite that type.

"Still I haven't owned a piece of real estate in my life. Where? It would be too much of a tie. My family now are 125 miles away. I drive up at the weekend or sometimes fly up in a charter plane. That's fine but I couldn't stand the kind of commuting they have to do in New York."

DOWN with the debris of the 1929 crash came the differentiation between the homeguard worker and the hobo worker. When, as the terrible years lengthened, and there were ten, then fourteen, million jobless men in the land, who was the better American down there in the bread line, the destitute bank teller or the stony-broke railroad ganger? The division closed: a democracy of burst boots. "Somebody had blundered," wrote Scott Fitzgerald, "and the most expensive orgy in history was over."

Also over – or punctured and deflating fast – was the fiduciary myth of the giant tycoons, the messianic cult of the Robber Baron, half good guy, half awesome monster. Those gods and their ruthless infallibility were, if not dead, wounded as mortals can be wounded, as also was the worship of success as a chalice from which all could drink.

Of 400 unemployed questioned fewer than half gave credence to the hallowed tradition of rugged individualism – "Yeah, ragged individualism," was the adjusted view. Herbert Hoover's promise of "two chickens in every pot" had turned out to be scrip for charity soup, a tar-paper tent in a Hooverville camp, and a permit to sell surplus apples, taken on credit, along the city sidewalks (and even some of New York's 6,000 apple salesmen scabbed by undercutting: *two* apples for five cents.)

Mike Gold wrote in *The New Masses*: "I enjoyed the recent music of the victim's howls and tears. Too long has one had to submit to the airs of those cockroach capitalists."

The workless man – green or seasoned at panhandling – was the new proletarian angel.

> *Once I built a railroad, made it run*
> *Made it race against time*
> *...Once I built a tower, to the sun*
> *Bricks and mortar and lime,*

sang the down-and-out in a hit song of unwonted social-realism, concluding with that familiar street cry of the Thirties, *Brother can you spare a dime?*

The girls in *Gold Diggers of 1933* shrilled with defiant mendacity *We're in the money*; outside, lovers and married couples attempted to replace fear with wry resignation with

> *No more money in the bank*
> *What's to do about it?*
> *Let's put out the lights and go to sleep*

or

> *Wrap your troubles in dreams and dream your troubles away*

or

> *Who's afraid of the big bad wolf?*

or

> *Are you makin' any money?*

Or perhaps in their bewilderment they raised their eyes with Joan Blondell as she sang from the screen, gazing beseechingly upward to some sky-based court of appeal above the heads of Hoover and J. Pierpoint Morgan, both, *Remember my forgotten man.*

There seemed too many forgotten men to be identified. "Heap o' stir an' no biscuits," was a phrase of the day that spilled out from the jungles and into everybody's parlance. At a time when Macey's department store was selling strictly for cash, when they could get it, its president, Jesse Isidor Strauss, published this article of faith (or was it a prayer?) in the New York newspapers:

> *I trust my government*
> *I trust our banks*
> *I do not expect the impossible*
> *I shall do nothing hysterical*
> *I know that if I try now to get all my cash*
>   *I shall certainly make matters worse*
> *I will not stampede. I will not lose my nerve.*
>   *I will keep my head.*

While Mr. Strauss frantically kept on conducting the band on this larger *Titanic* disaster, the question everyone was asking was: "What do you mean, there aren't any lifeboats?" Stephen Vincent Benet wrote a poem:

> *I hate to think*
> *Of the reapers, running wild in the Kansas fields,*
> *And the transport planes like hawks on a*
>   *chickenyard,*

But the horses might help, We might make a
deal with the horses.
At least, you've more chance, out there.
And they need us too.

But they didn't. And the men who knew those parts and had beaten their way around them for years, were in the cities at the soup kitchens and sleeping in ice-rimmed doorways. The billboards said, fixing the grin in place, WASN'T THE DEPRESSION TERRIBLE? A tune was commissioned for a new talking picture – *Happy Days Are Here Again.*

The public didn't believe that they were, the bankers tried to believe it, the intellectuals refused to. They had, even in the boom, on those ascending uplands of seven years' prosperity on which the hucksters and the Babbitts danced, felt a gaping alienation. " ... the virtual enemies of society," said Quincy Howe. "No common spirit possessed the people." The intellectuals, in their rush to political solutions, sought for Marxist interpretations and mimesis through their fiction and poetry and journalism, trying to find their way back to the common man. James T. Farrell found *The Buddies*, two truck drivers for the Continental Express Company, and Maxwell Bodenheim found his *Revolutionary Girl*, and Albert Maltz found *Man on a Road*, an on-the-tramp West Virginia miner with silicosis, and Clifford Odets found his strikers' committee *Waiting for Lefty*.

What they were all suddenly finding was the man who had been there all the time, and who hadn't himself noticed all that much difference, for the seven years of plenty had apparently not been long enough for Coolidge Prosperity to spread out into his area of shifting piece work and seasonal cropping; after all, it had not reached even to the stabler areas of the mill workers and the sharecropper farmers and the miners, for in 1929 when the boom was at its meridian there had been 1,800,000 unemployed in the United States. For him the boom had come and gone and he was left untouched, curiously inviolate.

The only difference now was that there were more of his kind; the freight trains were more crowded, as were the missions and the flophouses, and you had to accost many more brothers before you got that dime.

But he was at last recognized as being more than an amusing caricature of the American loser, or as menacing in his dereliction of duty to succeed, for now there were too many of him to be treated so trivially in either sense.

Hollywood discovered him, too. He was the threadbare dreamer speaking blank verse under the wet iron bridges of *Winterset*. He was the rucksacked thinker who had escaped onto the road in *The Petrified Forest*. He was, in the person of Charles Chaplin, in *City Lights* the dustbin-raking outcast shaming a ruined financier out of the thought of suicide, and in *Modern Times* the little man being crushed like a peanut between the machine age pressures, tightening bolts as he fed from the conveyor belt in a nightmare extension of the Beddoes system, until, released by a strike, stepping sideways off the industrial treadmill into the liberty of the bum's wasteland.

He was made much of in *Hallelujah, I'm a Bum*, with Al Jolson and Harry Langdon, and treated quite seriously in *White Bondage* and *Our Daily Bread* (the struggling sharecropper) and in *Millions of Us*, an underground radical production from Hollywood about the workless and the fight to unionize. Amorous escapades on the overland trek were touched upon lightly in *It Happened One Night*. In *My Man Godfrey* the hobo was drafted out of the rubbish tip shantytown to show the rich family how to live really richly.

The theater discovered him: not only the Federal Theater Project, where he had the part of ALL UNEMPLOYED, with the lines: *We need food . . . Jobs!* He was also in a musical, singing in a tender duet, *One Big Union For Two*, in the Garment Workers' Union smash, *Pins and Needles*, but Paul Kelly in *Hobo* lasted only five performances on Broadway – perhaps it lacked glitter.

Even *Vanity Fair* remembered the American forgotten man. It printed a story by Thomas Wolfe, *The Bums at Sunset*, in which a boy on the run, about to snag his first freight, is befriended by Bull, a hobo with "a curious brutal nobility; the battered and pitted face was hewn like a block of granite and on the man was legible the tremendous story of his wanderings – a legend of pounding wheel and thrumming rod, of bloody brawl and brutal shambles, of immense and lonely skies, the savage wilderness, the wild, cruel and lonely distance of America."

But already his particular kind of plight, with all its venerable associations in American folk lore, was being outdated. Where one man had stumped off to try it alone, a family was now in transit; where chance flocks of men had moved across country, now entire communities were traveling, regions on wheels. For the exodus of the Dust Bowl refugees had begun and the main flow was West to California, which, as all the advertisements said, was the Land of the Sun-Down Sea, the state of golden opportunity. Alarmed by the poverty of the new immigrants, the All-Year Club began to advertise: "Warning! Come to California for a glorious vacation. Advise anyone not to come seeking employment."

Once California's state slogan was simply: "Bring us men who match our mountains," but in the Thirties even a mountain-sized man had to have fifty dollars to get him and his family over the border; and who had fifty dollars, then?

In three years 350,000 Joads crossed the California line. Hitherto hired hands and croppers in less violent setbacks, when thrust off their plots by rising rentals or falling grain prices or the mergers of farm units, had one by one and quietly faded away "into an anomalous and shadowy obscurity." When the dust storms of the Thirties and the mechanization of agriculture and the financial ultimatums of the banks set tens of thousands adrift on the land, they unintentionally became a shadow lengthening across the broad acres of American agriculture.

It had been braked, for dispossessed rural people can hang on upon their own soil eking out a fringe existence. But when, as in the Thirties, a combination of factors accelerated, a whole population silted up in a "distressed rural area," then as the pressure mounted too high for the capacity of the frail dikes of relief and emergency aid the banks collapsed. Suddenly – apparently – there was "rural migration."

In a word California wanted, has always wanted and still wants, cheap seasonal labor – but a mobile reserve of single, passive, untroublesome ghosts, to be materialized and exorcized with a hey presto, who clear out of town and off the local budget having served their use.

The Dust Bowl refugees were different. They were not floaters. They were heads of families, with bundled up households ready for plumping down wherever permanence offered itself. More than half of those 350,000 went, between 1935 and 1939, straight in the San Joaquin Valley, the agricultural womb of the state. During those years the population of some of the Valley's twelve counties leaped by fifty per cent, in one instance by seventy per cent.

But the new wave of Neo-Californians rammed into head-on collision with a sophisticated, expertly balanced system. They were a spanner in that delicate mechanism of prices-and-wages maintenance, an ugly sore on the suburban fashion of life, and a resented burden on local fiscal structures when the harvest rush subsided.

Whereupon once again the emotional justifications for victimization flared. In the past there had been regular insurrections by natives against invaders, almost always during times of depression. The natives revolted against the Chinese, once their potential as cut-price labor had been exhausted; later against the Japanese; then against the Mexicans and Filipinos; and once before against their white American kin, against the Missouri "pikes."

There was a tankful of passion to be drawn upon. The Dust Bowlers were quickly metamorphosed into the "Migrant Menace," sub-standard alien creatures threatening Californian standards of living and morality.

There is the inevitable predisposition to see the tragedy of the Thirties slump as having been enacted by those thin hordes plodding from right to left across the vast stage of the Far West, for here was the terror of the average American's troubles distended into tribal exodus through a wilderness six times greater than Sinai.

The flight of the economic refugees from the Great Plains states was in truth but one installment of a mass disinheritance when for most Americans the leeway of privation between being in a job and being out of a job was essentially academic. Because a high proportion of those officially tabulated as employed were caught in the drop of thirty-three per cent in average weekly earnings, which meant, in terms of hard money, down to five cents an hour oscillating between idleness and a few days a month on the job.

Louis Filler, looking back on those "evil times," has written: "The dullest American who read *The Saturday Evening Post* and sat through his perishable films, who dreamed of the Big Break and voted for Landon, had no real faith in his own faith. That dull American laid down his body at night in misery and anxiety, and rose at dawn with an oppressive sense of little awaiting him."

There were more who knew that there was nothing. An anonymous Negro woman, photographed with her little clutter of possessions in the shade of a hoarding on Route 80 near El Paso in June 1938 said: "The country's in an uproar now – it's in bad shape ... Do you reckon I'd be out on the highway if I had it good at home?"

31: THEY'D TOUGHED IT OUT JUST AS LONG AS THEY COULD TAKE IT

I bought every kind of machine that's known –
Grinders, shellers, planters, mowers,
Mills and rakes and ploughs and threshers –
And all of them stood in the rain and sun,
Getting rusted, warped and battered ...

Edgar Lee Masters: *Spoon River Anthology*

THE main traveled road of that period can be followed today. They left no tracks on the hard surface and the dust that drove them out blew away like them, but this is the tack they tried. You move into the Oklahoma Panhandle through Harper County, and then it is 160 miles of flat road, dead straight but for two kinks, through the middle of the twenty-mile thick sandwich, with the weight of all Kansas above you to the North, the huge slab of Texas below. The groping, dissolved sensation so often experienced on the great curve between the two sea-boards – of being a castaway bobbing in a lifebelt in an ocean of land – assists in re-creating mentally the experience of those fugitives of thirty years ago.

Eventually Highway 64 dips across the Oklahoma state line into New Mexico, with an alternative right fork at Boise City up into Colorado. For those 160 miles you drive through the scraped brown country of Beaver, Texas and Cimarron Counties. This was the Dust Bowl, the wellhead of the great anabasis of the Thirties. At any rate, the Panhandle served a public purpose as the dramatic focal point.

The Okies, the desperate "casualties of change," crawling along the thirty-seventh parallel toward the Californian mirage in their pageant of junkyard cars, trading pans and furniture for petrol en route, became a symbol. In fact, their disaster was one that had similarly struck farming populations in a far broader realm and for a far greater span of time than just that place and period spotlit by Steinbeck's *The Grapes of Wrath*.

Oklahoma has not one natural lake. Since the Depression years reservoirs and flood-control systems have been built. Now the Panhandle is flecked with the silver of artesian wells and metal windmills. Now there is an ingrafted pattern of strip-cropping, and the roots and stems of sorghum knit together the light sandy soil.

Despite these repairs the land still has a beaten and finished-with look. It is treeless but for scraggy clumps set for weather shields around an occasional farmhouse. Sometimes there is to be seen far off the jutting gothic battlements of a grain elevator.

In daytime harriers drift across the infinite singed landscape. Small brilliant sunflowers smear the road verges; land turtles plod across the hot concrete and locusts the size of wrens on their outspread yellow vanes zoom down wind. A distant tractor plowing the skyline flies a flag of gray dust. Otherwise there is little color or movement. Sound? The unceasing scuffling rasps of stems and grasshoppers, a great pan of bacon frying.

In summer the creeks and river forks are baked fissures, quite empty and hard. There seem to be as many abandoned as occupied houses: weedpatch skeletons of timber, bleached gray and brittle as brandysnap by the sun. The farmer you now and then pass could be Pa Joad, gaunt, bristle-chinned, brown as meerschaum, in a slouch hat and bib dungarees over blue work shirt.

This is from where the Joads and the other forty-acre tenant 'croppers were blown out or tractored out by the banks and the finance companies foreclosing. You feel, as you stare ahead along the road and the unreeling changelessness of land and sky, spreading without end, killingly monotonous and without anchorage for eye or mind, that small wonder the Okies and the Arkies got the hell out of such country, and you marvel that they ever came in here voluntarily and tried to stay, to limpet onto the frail top soil which they were cutting out from under them by their hasty, clumsy deep plowing.

On the drive you begin, then, to see vestiges of the reason why they were blown off the land and in all directions by the winds that carried fogs of dust so black that lamps had to be burned all day through. There are still patches of dunes at the roadside, some scantily whiskered with grass, others bare and still creeping and realigning themselves in new perfect piles against fence posts and hillocks.

Despite the first aid – the irrigation, the Soil Conservation Agency tree-girdles, the enforced recovery of prairie and grazing pasture from the depleting crops of cotton and wheat – this is still sad, dilapidated country, threadbare as the patched overalls on a farm hand, its texture rubbed through.

H. M. Ives began working as an agricultural officer here in 1934. Now he is district agent-at-large for the U.S. Agricultural Extension Service, operating from a department of Oklahoma State University at Stillwater.

"It still blows," he says. "There was some rather serious blowing up in Cimarron County, below Boise City, this winter and in Grant and Alfalfa Counties. Some of the farmers flooded their land prior to seeding time, but there was still some blowing and fresh sanding around there.

"Of course up to 1907 this country had never been touched by a tool. The Panhandle of Oklahoma was Indian no-man's-land. They fought each other everywhere else but there was a gentlemen's agreement that they peacefully used that part as common hunting ground where they got the meat for the tribes, the antelope and buffalo.

"Even after it was settled and the cropping began, the dust conditions weren't bad everywhere: it depended on the soil type. Where the light sandy soil had been cut up by the plow there was often total blowout or at least bad duning; but in other parts the heavier adobe clay stood out not too bad during the drought.

"Yes, round here it was Cimarron County, and Dalhart in Texas, where it was really badly scoured-out. That's where the dust conditions were especially bad. Cimarron County went seven years without a crop because of the drought of 1932 to 1939, when they began to get a little bit of a crop again.

"The Federal Government program reduced the amount of grain to be grown, and ranchers used the money granted under the Range Program to impound water and drill wells, planning it out so that cattle would never have to walk more than a mile to water of some kind.

"But a lot of the people in the Dust Bowl hadn't that kind of knowledge or resource. You needed at least a three-year cushion to carry you through. It's country that in a cruel way took it out of a man, but there were some who toughed it out. We had plenty of awful hardy people out there. A lot went, and it was the hardiest of the hardy who were left.

"It wasn't felt that the people who got out were quitters. Of course some people give up easier than others. A lot of them hadn't been out there too long. They'd heard about the big crops that could be raised in the good weather patterns, but they arrived just in time for the drought. They didn't have time to get started or dug in.

"They just, in the end, told the banks 'You go out there and salvage what you can, but I've given enough of my life to it.' They were strangers to the land. Most of those who stayed *knew* the country. The trouble for those who toughed it out was that they often had to contend with the blowing from the land around, where people had pulled out, and they certainly did wish that they'd stayed and stabilized their land. Often a man *had* to spread out on to the abandoned land and put down a sorghum crop to hold it, with the result that the man sticking on had a terrible amount of work on his hands to protect himself.

"So there was some feeling about those who went. All the same, everyone was pretty philosophical. Maybe some of them thought that they'd get out too if they knew how.

"It was from the Panhandle that the big out-migration went but not all of them headed for California. A lot retracked back East into the central state, returned to places they'd come from, where they could fish and get some kind of a living, or moved in with relatives where they were familiar with the country.

"I remember seeing them going out West on Route 270 which was just a dirt road then, and coming back on Highway 64. They were in broken-down jalopies and old farm trucks that'd just about run, piled with what belongings they'd got left but no livestock, because that had all died off.

"They were worse than broke, if that's any indication. They

were desperate. They'd toughed it out just as long as they could take it.

"The Panhandle has never been repopulated up to the level it was before the exodus. It's more thinly farmed now than before the Thirties although that's because some of the men who stood out there and fought through began to pull together additional land, to take over the units too small to be farmed economically. As a matter of fact, we had a more serious drought situation in the Fifties, more concentrated than the longer period, but the man with the irrigation wells coasted through. In the Thirties most of those little people just didn't have a hope."

THE small town businessman also stuck out the drought of his spiritual faith for an amazingly long time after the crash: the Depression hadn't happened. That overwrought looking-on-the-bright-side anxiety was behind the newspaper editorial declaring that "many a family that has lost its car has found its soul," a sentiment amplified by the President of Notre Dame University who, counting the nation's blessings pointed out that a result of the Depression was that "a great portion of the American public rediscovered the home, rediscovered fireside joys, rediscovered the things of the spirit."

This was all part of the "live at home" movement of the time, but which failed to recruit the scores of thousands who were beginning to shuffle away from those fireside joys, to try to escape from the claustrophobia of poverty that was everywhere, suffocating as the dust swirling through the rainless weeks and months.

Yet they were in no sense new on the American scene. The auto migrants of the Thirties were no more bitterly off – assuredly less so – on their journey than the handcart Utah pioneers of the 1860s who *pushed* their two-wheel carriages loaded with luggage across a thousand miles of rough trail in three months, wife and children in train, to the "Valley" that was the lodestar, and many died of cold and starvation before they got there. Nor were the Okies as pressed by poverty and hardship as the families who forced through to the West in horse-drawn covered wagons.

But there were two important differences. The earlier voyageurs knew that if they stuck it out land awaited them, a place to build a home. The Okies started out from necessity, not sheer nerve, and they knew in their hearts that they had been beaten to it in the carve-up of the natural wealth ahead. Also fearsome though the earlier travail was, it was an honorable and admired enterprise, whereas the Okies were mendicants, rubbish swilling along the gutters of American life.

It was the car that gave them an identical course of action and legibility for, as the Walsh Industrial Relations Commission pointed out in 1915, there would at that time have been mass migration from Oklahoma – given the transportation. But nor were starved-out drought refugees, as a special category of émigrés, a peculiarity of 1915 and the Thirties.

The Great Plains states – the Dakotas, Nebraska, Kansas, Oklahoma, Texas, Montana, Wyoming, Colorado and New Mexico – were substantially settled in the forty years between 1870 and 1910, although this only in the sense of the slicing up of the booty, not investment of it. Since the beginning the flux and swapping of populations have continued to the present day at as impetuous a rate, a swooping in when the weather cycle is benign, a scrambling-out when the rains fail.

Before 1850, although the pioneers with the sights set on the boundless abundance of the West – the Beulah Land of the hymns that supported them on their journeys – threaded through the Great Plains, it was not until the decade between 1850 and 1860 that some began to halt short or deliberately opt for this region.

Like all the early Westerners these first home-builders on the Plains were cosmopolitan. The Eighth Census of the United States of 1860 shows that the population of Kansas in that year included persons born in every state and in twenty-eight foreign countries, ninety per cent of the 107,000; yet twelve per cent were natives of Missouri, and more than fifty per cent were born no farther east than Ohio.

This patently was short-hop settlement and until 1850 little attempt was made to hack out a living west of the ninety-sixth meridian, the vertical line that cuts through the present cities of Lincoln and Beatrice in Nebraska, Topeka and Coffeyville in Kansas and Gainesville and Houston in Texas. Those who had ventured out so far clung to the partially timbered areas and the river valleys. By 1860 the population of these ten states was 873,000, with ninety-two per cent in Texas, Kansas and New Mexico, and seventy per cent in Texas alone, and the remaining eight per cent dribbled throughout Colorado, Nebraska and the Dakota Territory. By 1890 that total had quadrupled.

But this was not a tapestry of steadily thickening design. Already the about turn and desertions had begun. For large numbers their reception in the country of big skies was drought and a malevolent sun. While the remainder of Oklahoma was being opened to the piling weight of those spilled over from the East's economic troubles, simultaneously many who had only just about hammered in their rail posts and cleared the scrub were being roasted out. Homesteads and cabins, trimly new, were abandoned; fields rippling with their first furrows were left to be combed back into blankness by the winds. Their vigor clubbed down, their hopes shriveled, the vanguard retreated from Montana and Wyoming, New Mexico and Colorado; 114 counties in Western Kansas and Western Nebraska were almost emptied; some areas were forsaken altogether. The population of Omaha and Nebraska tumbled by 37,000.

Yet – and here the saga of repeated defeat and repeated evanescence of effort begins to stamp itself upon this region – when the spell of killer summers abated and a phase of rains and coolness entered others came through to repair the crumbling houses and attack the earth again.

Between 1900 and 1910 the population of the ten states leaped thirty-eight per cent to more than three million, the armies which had withdrawn battling back again. Here is "the tragic drama frequently repeated" (in the phrase of a 1937 Works Progress Administration bulletin) beginning to shape itself into the dwelling fury.

In the forty-eight years after 1889 the Great Plains states were stricken by severe drought almost one year in six. The "excessively dry periods" occurred in 1889, 1890, 1901, 1917, 1930, 1933, 1934, and 1936. But really it may be seen with greater clarity how those early strugglers, dependent literally upon the seed they scattered from sacks by the palms of their hands, had to meet the seasons when it is put the other way: that from 1880 until the New Deal installations of irrigation equipment and the enforcement of education on crop procedure, there were no more than three naturally favorable periods for raising cultivated crops. They were 1880-1885, 1902-1906 and 1918-1923. Other than in those brief respites, drought and locusts and parching winds, while not afflicting the states uniformly, struck at them all, erratically but mutilatingly.

In all these early calamities and flights there was no urban spectator audience with economic criteria and social conscience to record, to tell, to expose the indifference to the suffering of those rolling onward. Unheard of, out of sight, they just went and found some kind of refuge and salvation, or didn't find it.

The truth is that few of them were equipped to combat the conditions they blundered into, and they further confounded their dilemma by inexperience or by experience wrong for these unfamiliar violent conditions. In 1937 the Social Research Division of the Works Progress Administration, belatedly trying to formulate a policy for correcting almost a century of mistakes and mess, came to the conclusion – not explicitly stated but intrinsic – that the Dust Bowl refugee, far from being a unique creation of the Thirties or being indigenous to Oklahoma and Arkansas, was an inevitable outcome (again, the detritus) of a free-for-all system and the obstinate, superstitious faith, immutable under recurrent evidence to the contrary, that balance could emerge from licensed anarchy.

The People of the Drought States was one of three reports on the problems of the areas of "intense drought distress" and set out to show how uncontrolled settlement had inevitably brought about dislocation between the people and the natural resources. The bulletin's frame of reference was that of the movements of the past, what became accepted as "normal export" of population.

Then in 1936, it pointed out, there were fifteen million people living in the ten Great Plains states where fifty years earlier there had been only three and a half millions, a population growth then of unprecedented speed. Once the conquest of the prairies had been made feasible by the commercial feed-lines of the railroads, by the first rudimentary interstate carriageways, by the mass production of barbed-wire whereby the small home-steader could fence off his plantings from the ranger's cattle, and by the development of the cheap bolt-together windmill which sucked up to the surface at least a sustaining trickle of water, then "a large army of restive settlers from the Eastern states and direct from Europe flocked into the Mid-West to lay their claims."

But the "demand for homesteads and the desire to bring each homestead under the plow were so insistent that no thought was given to those factors which might limit agricultural acti-vities. And when the conditions seemed unfavorable an unstable population, avoiding rather than solving its problems, simply moved on."

Where was it that this fickle, impatient army went wrong? For one thing, reported a 1926 bulletin issued by the North Dakota Agricultural Experiment Station, *Rural Changes in Wes-tern North Dakota*, "many of them were single and among the homesteaders were women, old people, excitement seekers, rovers and people from the most widely separated walks of life. Not infrequently the homesteader had never been on a farm previous to his filing.

"A study of twelve townships of Western Dakota classifies nearly one-half of the 669 farm operators who had moved out of the territory by 1925 as having come in the first place chiefly for speculative purposes. No more than one-fourth of these speculators had had any farming experience . . ."

Again in the 1870-1910 migration the vast majority of the migrants came from below the Appalachian and Allegheny Mountains, a region dominated by row-crop agriculture. At bot-tom was the fatal misconception of the Homestead Act, which was grounded in experience acquired by settling a mildly ami-able zone where humidity was uniform and relatively high, and where medium-sized farms made sense.

The Act had no relevance West of the hundredth meridian. The quarter-section originally allocated to the settler was too tiny for either grazing or for dry land farming. Later modifications – increase of land grants per person, regulation of the settlement of desert, subsidized irrigation projects – were too late, too haphazard, too piecemeal to provide material benefit. In fact the changes of policy often caused dispirited settlers to pack up and move on, and failed to put others in their place.

Equally important, as settlement reached deeper into arid country, the farming techniques themselves needed radical revision. But "the early settlers from the Eastern states or from Europe knew only the intensive moldboard culture. To them, any man who did not turn his soil completely over and pulverize it was slothful. To allow stubble to protrude, as when the soil is partially turned with disc harrow or plow, was to demonstrate his laziness. Wheat seed beds were made almost as carefully as gardens had been made in the place of original residence. Thus, adaptation to the new environment was necessarily slow and difficult ... There were no experimental stations to determine better methods, and the individual farmer could improve his efforts only through his own and his neighbors' experimentations."

One more factor was quick profits offered by government-stimulated wheat raising during and after World War I, especially between 1927 and 1930 when succulent export markets were open, which encouraged brutal over-forcing of the land.

The Grapes of Wrath were ripening for many years, the fruit of ignorance and greed, and irresponsibility toward the soil, based on the attitude that there was plenty farther on when this had been thrashed out. Prairie sod, binding safely the powdery tilth beneath, was recklessly hacked up; swamps and shallow lakes were drained to grab more wheat acreage; what woodland there was had been clear-felled for housing materials, or the bark of each tree snipped through until it died, then the whole wood burned down to extend money-making crops; pasture was improvidently over-grazed.

By the Thirties it had become obvious that drought, if not man-made in this province, had been man-worsened, and that even if some miraculous climatic endenization occurred a dependable normal rainfall could not repair the harm and ensure a firm prosperity.

The exodus of the Okies and the Arkies was an upheaval of dreadful proportions but it was really the breaking of a riptide built up from a procession of smaller waves. To stem this "aimless and expensive migration" not only interim measures were urged but "far reaching changes in attitude and policy toward land ownership and land use." Otherwise, it was warned, "a new wave of immigrants may come in to take the places of those who have recently left. Cheap land and the prospects of speculative gain are almost certain to attract new settlers. Even the most distressed portion of the area reported some migrants to farms between 1930 and 1935 . . .

"Stability of residence itself is not necessarily a desirable goal" – even here, be it noted, the American belief in the holiness of movement itself has to be dropped a curtsy – "but the high degree of mobility which has been characteristic of the Great Plains area indicates an unsatisfactory adjustment between man and his natural environment." And even this was but part of a vaster agitation, people running away, people racing to goals. A Department of Agriculture calculation is that between 1920 and 1937 thirty million persons moved from farms to towns and twenty-one million moved from towns to farms: coming and going, a minimum of fifty million migrations.

The Grapes of Wrath and the road refugees of the Thirties were prognosticated as long before as 1896 when Frederick H. Newell, chief hydrographer of the U.S. Geological Survey, wrote with a poetical power rare in official reports: "Year after year the water supply may be ample, the forage plants cover the ground with a rank growth, the herds multiply, the settlers extend their fields, when, almost imperceptibly, the climate becomes less humid, the rain clouds forming day after day disappear upon the horizon and weeks lengthen into months without a drop of moisture.

"The grasses wither, the herds wander wearily over the plains in search of water holes, the crops wilt and languish, yielding not even the seed for another year. Fall and winter come and go with occasional showers which scarcely seem to wet the earth, and the following spring opens with the soil so dry that it is blown about over the windy plains.

"Another and perhaps another season of drought occurs, the settlers depart with such of their household furniture as can be drawn away by the enfeebled draft animals, the herds disappear, and this beautiful land, once so fruitful, is now dry and brown, given over to the prairie wolf. There comes a season of ample rains. The prairie grasses, dormant through several seasons, spring into life, and with these the hopes of new pioneers. Then recurs the flood of immigration, to be continued until the next long drought."

The temper of the times was to lick this limbo into shape as you break a wild horse, with spurs, rope and muscle. The government's aim – it could not qualify as a policy – was to rid itself as swiftly as it could of the remaining public domain, and so satisfy the clamor for space that had been partly deliberately inculcated, to disembarrass itself of the surplus labor of its see-sawing Eastern industry. The pressures were irresistible.

Many of the claimants dawdled just long enough partially to chop a clearing, sell for a profit and race on toward other quick-buck speculations. After the first rush of stop-and-go settlement, although a more gradual process of adjustment unfolded, foment never faded. More than three million original homestead entries were filed between 1863 and 1963, but only fifty-eight per cent of these were finalized.

The standards by which Americans assess stability are defined by Malin's observation that by 1925 West Kansas farmers "were apparently more settled as only one half had withdrawn ten years later." The following years bore signs of roots beginning to attach, but even by 1935 only two-thirds of the farm workers present five years earlier were still ensconced or had a son there.

From the start the population of the Great Plains has been a youthful one but of course throughout the bewildering hetero-topy of Western pioneering an established custom has been for the settler to pack off his sons to fend for themselves – simply, originally, because survival on the family parcel, and with clim-atic batterings so frequent, was a hair's breadth measurement: economically, the young man ready to marry and have children of his own was forced to migrate in search of his own space and opportunities, and so with the grandchildren.

In the Great Plains states especially big families have always been the norm. Long before the First World War made corn the region's basic trading product, it was producing a human export crop: the sons who trekked deeper into the state or on to others beyond. Between 1920 and 1930 there was more emigration than immigration throughout half of the ten states, and only one showed an excess of incoming over outgoing. Despite the continued enlargement of territory for agriculture, despite the rapid national climb in birth rate – consistently highest of all in the Great Plains – there has been virtually no change in the numbers on farms here since 1910. Probably nearly three milions moved away from the points of "residence" in the years *before* the notorious exodus of the Thirties, yet these movements attracted little attention or remark.

The Thirties exodus is probably quite fairly, with clinical detachment, assessed in the official conclusion that "the interstate movement in its various aspects would indicate that drought and economic depression accentuated previously existing trends without radically altering the direction of the movement of the Twenties."

Yet there were significant differences. The "tincan tourists" were not only Okies and Arkies; and they did not all make for California.

In the *Monthly Labor Review* for February 1936 Paul S. Taylor and Tom Vasey reported on a six-month check of all motor traffic at the main highway ports-of-entry to California. Between June and December 1935 53,000 in parties and "in need of manual employment" entered California but twenty per cent of these were former California residents calling it off after trying their luck somewhere else. During nine and a half months ending September 30, 1936, another 71,000 "in need of manual employment" came across the state line in motor vehicles. Fourteen per cent of these were, again, Californians. Among the remainder were 16,500 from Oklahoma, 6,200 from Texas, 2,600 from Kansas, and about 1,500 each from Colorado, New Mexico and Nebraska.

But other surveys of the time show heavy migration also out

of the drought belt up into Minnesota and Iowa. A 1935 study, *Rural Migration and Farm Abandonment* by George W. Hill, undertaken in Tripp County, South Dakota, traced 114 families who had flitted between 1930 and 1934. A third had moved across the nearby border into Nebraska; one-twelfth had switched to Iowa, and, while many of the others had made for California, a lot had gone South.

But the Thirties exodus did and still does stand apart. In October 1935 three-tenths of all agricultural households in the Great Plains had been on relief for between fifteen and nineteen months, and one-tenth for two years or more. This was an exodus of an extremity not known before. These were not migrants but refugees, as inexorably driven as the strangely similar shuffling crocodiles moving at the same time, 10,000 miles away, down the roads of Europe from other forms of persecution, and likewise refugees who would in many cases never again find an abode. The Okies and Arkies were quondam settlers being hammered by new social forces, gipsy hordes created by, and for the use of, the evolving factory farm system.

Objectively the Dust Bowl refugees were the ones who took the rap for a maniacal exploitation of resources that, cherished and studied, would have been forever fruitful. It was soil mining. The complex skein of organic balances that had made the plains rich and green for aeons were smashed in a couple of decades, first by the land-clearers who "deadened" the land by felling and burning out forest, then rape by plow.

Conservationists measure that three of the nine inches of the vital topsoil of the American continent have been flung away, never to be replaced – gone with the wind in storms and floods into the rivers and the sea. But the refugees who themselves, or whose fathers or predecessors, skinned their country and turned the frontier into a "sump-hole of poverty" were but the victims as the land itself was a victim.

Land hawks leased great chunks of Indian lands and subleased to settlers. As this territory was untaxable there was no money to support public schools, so illiteracy was standard. By the time the tenant or sharecropper, impoverished from the start, had raked together enough dollars to buy his twenty-acre tract he had milked it dry and there was no money for equipment and improvement – for he was paying interest rates on his chattel mortgages ranging from twenty to two hundred per cent. The money vanished into the "electric light" towns, where lived the merchants and usurers who milked him as hard as he had to milk the land.

The Okie was rootless because he never had the possibility of owning a patch big enough to contain his roots; and, when finally licked by interest rates and weather, he had little to lose by packing up, quitting his slovenly land, and poking on. When in 1770 Oliver Goldsmith published his poem *The Deserted Village*, it was one of the few records of what the Enclosures had done to the English laborer, for the literature of the time had overlooked, or averted its sight from, the misery of a rural population torn from its possessions and set adrift. America's villages were deserted and her laborers thrown into vagabondage for many years before their impact upon settled communities became disturbing and alarming enough to attract notice.

In 1939 there was published *An American Exodus: A Record of Human Erosion*, text by Paul Schuster Taylor, photographs by Dorothea Lange. This was a picture of America that must have startled America, an America whose tenuous connection with the Hollywood fairy tale, then winding around the world, was the Carole Lombard and Anne Shirley poster hoardings under which nomadic families crouched from the sun.

The book's illustrations were of a terribly damaged people, like some separate, doomed aboriginal tribe: ragged, scraggy and worn, on buggies, at the wheels of gangrenous old cars packed with bedding and sticks of furniture, in mule-carts and flat trailers and hard-tire vans.

There were families in tents and roadside shelters of cardboard cartons, wooden crates and package paper. There were ghost towns, drained by drought and tumbling cotton prices. There were men, work and confidence gone, hunched on the front stoop of listing shanties, looking with haggard eyes on to bare land herringboned by erosion. There were fathers and mothers, with clusters of small children and bags under arms, trudging on foot down bleak arterials – to where? The captions were mostly from the lips of the dispossessed, those shot-gunned or bulldozed off their living.

A family on a horse-drawn cart in South-East Missouri: "I say 'A rollin' stone gathers no moss.' He says 'A settin' hen never gets fat.' I say to him 'Better stay here where people know us. We'd have to sell our team and maybe we'd be left flatfooted.' " A family from Paris, Arkansas, on the road near Webber Falls, Oklahoma: "We're bound for Kingfisher, Oklahoma, to work in the wheat, and Lubbock, Texas, to work in the cotton. We're trying not to, but we'll be in California yet."

A farmer in Oklahoma: "They're goin' in every direction and they don't know where they're goin'." A family in a car sunk on its springs under the load at Muskogee, Oklahoma: "We started from Joplin, Missouri, with five dollars. We're bound for California if we can make it in time for grape picking." On US 54 in New Mexico: "They keep the road hot a-goin' and a-comin'. They're got roamin' in their head."

Five displaced tenant farmers in North Texas: "Where we gonna go?" "How we gonna get there?" "What we gonna do?" "Who we gonna fight?" "If we fight, what we gotta whip?" A tractored-out farmer in Texas Plains: "Was waiting to see what would be the outcome of my hunt for a place, and the outlook right now is that I'll move to town and sell my team, tools and cows. I've hunted from Childress, Texas, to Haskell, Texas, a distance of 200 miles, and the answer is the same. I can stay off the relief until the first of the year. After that I don't know. I've got to make a move, but I don't know where to." A refugee, in California, from Cimarron County: "No, I didn't *sell* out back there. I *give* out."

373

32 : WHO WE GONNA FIGHT?

> *In what way were we trapped? where, our mis-*
> *take? what, how, when, what way, might all*
> *these things have been different, if only we had*
> *done otherwise? If only we might have known ...*
> *How did we get caught?*
>
> James Agee: *Let Us Now Praise Famous Men*

"INTENSIVE, large-scale and highly seasonal agriculture have created in California the largest wage-earning class, proportionately, of any important agricultural state," writes Taylor. "They have produced a large, landless and mobile proletariat ... Like fresh sores which open by over-irritation of the skin and close under the growth of protective cover, dust bowls form and heal.

"The winds churned the soil, leaving vast stretches of farms blown and hummocked like deserts or the margins of beaches. They loosened the hold of settlers on the land, and like particles of dust drove them rolling down ribbons of highway."

The particles of dust said in various places: "We just make enough for beans, and when we have to buy gas it comes out of the beans." "What bothers us travelin' people most is we can't get no place to stay still." "People got to stop somewhere. Even a bird has got a nest."

The following year a book entitled *Land of the Free* was published. It was again a frieze of photographs of the unknown, unbelievable American povertyscape of the Thirties, photographs taken mostly for the Resettlement Administration, the Tennessee Valley Authority and the Soil Conservation Administration. The commentary was in free verse by Archibald Macleish:

> *... All you needed for freedom was being American*
> *All you needed for freedom was grit in your craw*
> *And the gall to get out on a limb and crow before sunup*
> *... There was always some place else a man could head for*
> *... We looked West from a rise and we saw forever*

374

Now that the land's behind us we get wondering
You need your heelhold on a country steady
You need a continent against your feet
. . . Blown out on the wheat
Tractored off the cotton in the Brazos
Sawed out in the timber on the Lakes
Washed out on the grassland in Kentucky
Shot-gunned off in Arkansas
. . . We've got the road to go by where it takes us
. . . We've got the cotton choppers' road from Corpus
                                                    Christie
North over Texas; West over Arizona
Over the mesas; over the mile-high mountains
Over the waterless country; on West
We've got the pea-pickers' road out of California
North into Oregon; back into Arizona
East to Colorado for the melons
North to Billings for the beet crop . . . back again . . .
We've got the fruit tramps' road from Florida northward
Tangipahoa Parish Louisiana
North to Judsonia, Arkansas: east to Paducah
North to Vermilion Illinois . . . into Michigan
. . . We've got the road to go by where it takes us
We've got the narrow acre of the road
To go by when the land's gone
. . . Men don't talk much standing by the roadside
We wonder whether the dream of American liberty
Was two hundred years of pine and hardwood
And three generations of the grass
And the generations are up: the years over . . . We wonder
We don't know
We're asking.

33 : DUST CAN'T KILL ME

Los Angeles wants no duds, loafers and paupers;
people who have no means and trust to luck, cheap
politicians, failures, bummers, scrubs, impecunious
clerks, bookkeepers, lawyers, doctors. We need
workers! Hustlers! Men of brains, brawn and
guts! Men who have a little capital and a good
deal of energy – first-class men.

Colonel Harrison Gray Otis,
editor of the Los Angeles *Times*, 1886.

SOME of the answers were given by a tramp guitarist and
radical whose anger at what he had seen on the road and
in the Federal Work Camps went into documentary songs about
human fortitude and hard times of the American kind. They
were not politically partisan but more in the tradition of the
Western come-all-ye autobiographical ballads and the Southern
dam'-fool ditties, which recounted real happenings to real people
– gun-fights, hangings, train wrecks, strikes and elections, and
prodigious feats of labor, which were oral newspapers about
events and luminaries in the turbulent, mysteriously wayward
working-class world of America.

Woody Guthrie was himself an Oklahoman, from Okemeh,
an early oil boom town. He sold newspapers, jig-danced on the
sidewalk for pennies, then at thirteen hit the road South to Houston, Galveston and the Gulf, and back, hoeing figs, weeding
orchards, gathering grapes, hauling timber, helping cement men
and well-drillers.

He carried a harmonica and gigged in barber shops and pool
halls, around truckstops and shoe shine stands. During a store
job in Pampa he learned the guitar and began entertaining at
ranch and town dances, at rodeos, fairs, carnivals and "bust-
down parties." He hustled his way to California as a sign painter,
playing and painting his way along the highway, and in Los
Angeles got onto a radio country programme, which he used as
the outlet for propaganda union songs he had begun writing,

about cotton strikers, canning house workers and dispossessed dirt farmers.

Although he sang around the wayside jungles and fruit pickers' camps, it was oddly enough after seeing the film of *The Grapes of Wrath* in New York that he wrote his *Dust Bowl Ballads*, for Guthrie had been ahead of the mainstream of tincan tourists. All the same he had mingled with plenty who had taken that route.

He told Lomax: "For the last few years I've been a rambling man. From Oklahoma to California and back, by freight train and thumb – I've been stranded and disbanded, busted and disgusted with people of all sorts, shapes, sizes and calibers – folks that wandered all over the country looking for work, down and outers, and hungry half the time.

"I slept with their feet in my face and my feet in theirs, with Okies and Arkies that were rambling like a herd of lost buffalo with the hot hoof and empty mouth disease. Pretty soon I found out I had relatives under every railroad bridge between Oklahoma and California.

"Walking down the big road, no money, no job, no home, no nothing, nights I slept in jails, and the cells were piled high with young boys, strong men and old men. They talked and they sung and they told the story of their lives – how it used to be, how it got to be, how the home went to pieces, how the young wife died or left, how Dad tried to kill himself, how the banks sent out tractors and tractored down the houses. So somehow I picked up an old rusty guitar and started to picking and playing the songs I heard and making up new ones about what folks said."

In the West, he wrote in his book *Bound for Glory*, he met "the hard-rock miners, old prospectors, desert rats and whole swarms of hitch-hikers, migratory workers – squatted with their little piles of belongings in the shade of the big signboards, out across the flat, hard-crust, graveling desert. Kids chasing around in the blistering sun. Ladies cooking scrappy meals in sooty buckets, scouring the plates clean with sand. All waiting for some kind of a chance to get across the California line.

"Yes, guess I'm what you'd call a migrant worker ... I ain't nothing much but a guy walking along ... Thumbing it. Hitching it. Walking it and talking it ... From Barstow to San Bernadino to Los Angeles to everywhere, I set my hat on the back of my head and strolled from town to town with my guitar slung over my shoulder.

"I sung along a lot of boweries, back streets and skid rows. I sung on Reno Avenue in Oklahoma City, and Community Camp and Hooversville, on the flea-bit rim of the garbage dump; in the city jail in Denver, in Raton and Dodge City. I sung long tales and ballads for the railroad gangs on the Texas plains, the road workers along the border.

"In Portland I sung for a lot of ship scalers, inland boatmen, and timber workers; I hit Chicago on a wild cattle train from Minneapolis and sung in a dozen saloons across the street from the big packing-houses, with the Swedes, the Slavs, Russians, Norwegians, Irish, Negroes.

"It looked like everybody leaned on everybody's shoulder, and the songs and tunes didn't have any race or colour much, because what's right for a man anywhere is right for you wherever you are ... I am out to sing songs that will prove to you that this is your world and that if it has hit you pretty hard and knocked you for a dozen loops, no matter how hard it's run you down and rolled you over, no matter what color, what size you are, how you are built, I am out to sing the songs that make you take pride in yourself and your work."

In the late Thirties Guthrie was in New York meeting with formulating politically-conscious "progressive" song writers and folk groups. He was by then deeply involved in union campaigns. He sang at IWO lodges, at Hoovervilles and camptowns of the unemployed through the South into Oklahoma, in union halls and in factory workers' clubs, and on New York radio shows and for Moe Asch's record company. He composed and sang – or "talked", for he perfected the mountain idiom of the "talking blues", which isn't really the blues at all – about the building of the huge New Deal public utility project, the Grand Coulee Dam of the Bonnerville Power Administration, about anti-fascism, about union-busting vigilantes with tear gas and blackjacks, about strikes and lockouts, about the homeless and unorganized and destitute, and about their loss of faith in what has been called "story-book democracy".

Guthrie's voice, or rather his simplism, worked better in song than in prose. In print his folk-say steams a bit discomfortingly with a theatrical ordinariness, although that has in itself an honourable lineage from the ring-tailed roarer, the half slapstick, half romantic teller of tall tales and the epic brag, who both made and was made by the frontier myth.

Guthrie's proselytizing pilgrimage through the Northern American continent is, when set down on the page, self-regardingly Homeric. Yet he has conveyed uniquely well the bravura and the wonderment and the vehemence and the profligacy, both of waste and muscle, that have all collided together in every crossing of this immense land. He has grasped the "whole big flood of all these kinds of new wide open, free airish, sky clear feelings" in Oregon and the Pacific North-West mountain towns, and where "the neon signs splutter and crackle" on to the "hock-shop windows, the coffee joints, slippery stool dives, hash counters" of the city skid rows.

It is in his songs that Guthrie is most bony and poetical, the voice of a hard-travellin' minstrel who had relevant statements to make on behalf of the common man off the rails. "Sharecropper before I hit th' road", he comments in his adaptation of the hymn *Heaven Will Be My Home, I Ain't Got No Home In This World Anymore*. "I got th' share. Boss got th' crop. You think they's lots of us out loose on th' roads. River's a-risin' an' it's gonna be more," and then he sings:

I ain't got no home
I'm just a ramblin' round
I'm just a wanderin' workin' man
I go from town to town
Police make it hard where I may go
And I ain't got no home in this world any more.

Tenaciously Guthrie kept with strict literalness to the "untrained" acumen of the broadsheet commentator whose like is still to be found in both church and sugar shack in the South and West, the narrow-eyed, alert tension behind the lazy expression, that is a ubiquitous American manner, from the cow-puncher to the truck driver, from the jazz musician to the soda jerk. In all of Guthrie's songs, conversational, throw-away, poker-faced, he kept to the hillbilly delayed action, the succinct slyness, but his tongue was that of a political evangelist. He was a poet of the sort who used to earn the pioneer audience plaudit: "True as steel – that's exactly like it happened."

Long before folk song became the best-selling commodity it did in the 1960s, before it had a paying audience and before it became essential armament for the Civil Rights movement and the peace marchers, Guthrie was delivering social messages in his topical, "radio ballads" to the people they were about, which included himself.

We come with the dust and we go with the wind, was a line in his *Pastures of Plenty*, about the migrant workers who crop the Californian peach trees, pick the hops in Oregon and dig up the beets and gather the wine grapes:

> *It's a mighty hard road that my poor hands has hoed*
> *And my poor feet has traveled a hot dusty road.*

He had this to say about the unemployed's improvised igloos that grew like tumors on every Depression city:

> *Ramblin', gamblin', rickety shacks*
> *That's Hooversville*
> *Rusty tin an' raggedy sacks*
> *Makes Hooversville.*
> *On the skeeter bit end of the garbage dump*
> *Thirty million people slump*
> *Down where the big rats run 'n' jump*
> *In Hooversville.*

This was Guthrie's requiem for generations of laboring men who built tracks, roads and industry across the United States:

> *I hammered in the water, hammered in the rock*
> *Hammered on the railroad, hammered on the dock*
> *Hammered in the mill, hammered in the mine*
> *I been in jail about a thousand times.*

There was again the language and hand-lines of the card-carrying oilfield hand in *Boomtown Bill*:

> *I held down jobs of roustabout, roughneck, and driller*
> > *too,*
> *Coke knocker, gauger, fireman and bucked the casing*
> > *crew,*
> *Fought fires with Happy Owell, a man you all know well,*
> *I worked the cross and cracking still, my name is*
> > *Boomtown Bill.*
> *I polished bits in Texas dust from the ocean to the*
> > *plains,*
> *Worked every field in forty-eight states and half way*
> > *back again,*
> *Six million CIO workers just naturally can't be wrong,*
> *We'll work to win the union way and I hope it don't*
> > *take long.*

Yet nowhere is the passion more corrosive than in his *Dust Bowl Ballads*, perhaps because these were his own people and their journey had been his. His *Tom Joad*, written on a typewriter in a New York apartment the night after seeing *The Grapes of Wrath*, is the novel's plot, narrative, background and densely worked overtones condensed into seventeen verses with meticulous clarity. "The people back in Oklahoma haven't got two bucks to buy the book, or even thirty-five cents to see the movie," he said, "but the song will get back to them."

His *Dust Can't Kill Me* again has the heroic plainness: a tenant farmer's catalogue of the disasters that have belabored him. The pawnshop has got his furniture, "but it can't get me"; the tractor has run his home down, "but it can't run me down"; the dust storm has blown his barn down, "but it can't blow me down"; the landlord has got his homestead, "but he can't get me" and, the final defiant affirmation, the dry spell has killed his crop, his baby, his family – "but it can't kill me."

What happened to the Great Plains refugees who lived through it? Some – 456,000 between 1930 and 1940 – transferred to Washington and Oregon. This was not drifting but determined resettlement, a re-grouping with their own neighbors, the transplanting of communities. McWilliams found that in Kitsap County, Washington, there were ninety people who had previously lived in or around a South Dakota town of 300. Whenever they could they stuck together.

At first they settled in camps – just the unladenings of their cars, where they could park – which were resented and fought off by the older established. They had little choice of land: "shoestring" valleys in clearings amid brush scrub, in once-forested stump lands of sour soil, in deserted marginal farms. Real estate sharks saw the opportunity for profit and quickly ran up cheap subdivisions of "farmettes," plots for rabbit farms and goat farms, and sold at extortionate hire-purchase rates.

To earn money the Okies and Arkies invaded the seasonal market of the North-West with its fever peaks of activity when 35,000 hands were needed in the hop fields and apple and cherry orchards, after which State Highway patrolmen saw to it that the migrants vacated the Yakima Valley.

In California the half-million drought refugees who slid in under the bar, and who pussyfooted in after the bums' blockade was abandoned, found land all appropriated and steady jobs as rare as a spare acre. They, even more imperatively than their neighbors who went North, were sucked into the straggling hordes servicing the brimming productive bowls of the San Joaquin and Imperial Valleys. From their squatter shacktowns around Salinas (there had grown a resident camp population in California of 150,000) they went off at the bidding of fruit and vegetable growers when the times of heavy labor need came round.

They did find a niche. Cotton had but recently been introduced, and the Okies knew about cotton. During that decade an almost total change occurred in the labor pattern in rural California. The Anglo-American took over from the Mexican who, displaced, retreated across the border. The final external factor which crucially affected the man from the Dust Bowl was the outbreak of World War II, when booming defence factories – aircraft plants and shipyards – lifted him off the soil of the Valleys, and the Mexican came back.

The Grapes of Wrath sold 420,565 copies in its first year. So

382

in 1939 the Okies were suddenly renowned and their plight sent a quiver through the nation. The novel, the release of the film in February 1940 and the publication of Carey McWilliams's *Factories in the Fields*, had an earthquake effect on state politics, and the commotion aroused throughout the country brought the La Follette Committee investigations into being.

Yet a year later retaliatory propaganda by the Associated Farmers (who denounced *The Grapes of Wrath* as obscene, vulgar and immoral, and got it banned from libraries) and public boredom had largely killed the issue, and the Okies were, if not forgotten, relegated to history and not regarded as a continuing, unsolved problem – for the drift of migrants had not stopped.

In California as the "Migrant Menace" cooled off there was some grudging acceptance of them. They integrated, after a fashion. They were not proud of their famous sobriquet, and a large number submerged their Okie name and their Dust Bowl background as soon as they could. Small islets of them are still to be found, in Colorado, in New Mexico, in the Pacific North-West, as well as in California. A post-mortem study at the end of the decade found that in a sample group in Monterey County a majority were "somewhat better off financially" than when they arrived (not difficult) but a third were worse off. Ninety per cent declared their intention of staying in California but their outlook on their future was "generally colored by pessimism."

Subsequently some dug themselves in with relative security. Some even prospered.

Their methods of attaining security and prosperity would not in every case have been the right material for a Woody Guthrie song. When in 1941 Mexican citrus workers struck in Southern California, Okies from the San Joaquin Valley – who themselves had fought in many a strike and pay dispute – enrolled as strike breakers, and, says McWilliams, "promptly attempted to drive the remaining Mexicans from the fields."

The family of man is frail in its kinship loyalties; the oppressed often learn not only dignity and courage but also the technique of how to oppress others.

"It's a funny thing," a Baptist migrant missionary said as we drove through the fat vineyards of Kern County, "but some of the very nicely off fruit farmers around here who are most guilty of exploiting the Mexican field hands are old Okies and Arkies, who were taken to the cleaners in exactly the same way when they got here. Maybe they feel they're entitled to their turn, because they showed like real Americans that they could pull themselves up by their bootstraps."

In the ballad *Tom Joad*, on the run again from police and the vengeance of authority, he bids his mother farewell:

> *Wherever little children are hungry and cry*
> *Wherever people ain't free*
> *Wherever men are fightin' for their rights*
> *That's where I'm gonna be, Ma,*
> *That's where I'm gonna be.*

34 : RENTASLAVE

*Between Augusta and Charlotte I met a man, his
wife, and seven children ... The family was
stranded on the highway. It was late evening, and
neither the mother or the father seemed to know
what to do. They just stood there on the outskirts
of a little town, hoping.*

The American Worker in the Twentieth Century

FIDEL MENCHACA is 2,400 miles from his home in McAllen
in the extreme foot of Texas. He is as usual spending the
summer months in the state of Washington, which he reached
after a seventy-two hour trip by Greyhound bus with an overnight stop in Salt Lake City.

He is not a *bracero*, one of the 180,000 Mexicans who until
1965 were given permits to enter the United States for the seasonal stoop labor in the fields (or, permitless, came across the
river border as "wetbacks"). Fidel Menchaca, makes it understood that both his grandfathers were born in Texas: he is officially described as a Spanish-American. It was in fact the *braceros* who pushed him and his father and his brothers on the exploration north. The cheap labor flooding across the Rio Grande
and the eager undercutting by local farmers so depressed wages
that the Menchacas and their kind had to range ever farther
afield to maintain their rates.

This is Walla Walla, one of the first settled stages on the
Oregon Trail beyond the Rockies, battleground in bloody skir-
mishes with the Cayuse Indians and a roughneck frontier town
during the 1860s gold mining. Now the Blue Mountain valleys
are rich with grain and vegetables. At this time the pea, aspara-
gus and beet harvests are finished and the prunes and tomatoes
not yet ready, and the migrant labor camp four miles out of
town is only half full. Most of the occupants are Spanish-
Americans from Texas, and about ten per cent whites who have
converged in from Missouri, California and Illinois. The single
men have signed on for the wheat cutting, bunkhouse-living out
on the ranches all week. Others are temporarily in the processing

plants, where each year seven million cases of vegetables are canned and 165 million pounds frozen.

"This is a long haul to find work," Menchaca says, "but it is worth the trip. Around home until May there are the citrus seedlings to be transplanted and grafted, but after that work is rather sad down there. Mechanization is coming in and reducing the old jobs. Here there is clipping the apple trees to start with, then the peas and spinach and lima beans and prunes and onions to pick. Some, the beet blockers, move on North to other beet fields when they've finished, but you can earn the whole summer through just staying here, maybe working in the canneries too.

"I began coming to Walla Walla with my father in 1958. It was necessary because the *braceros* were entering Texas and taking jobs at thirty-five cents an hour and we could not afford to accept that. The end of the *bracero* programme has not made much difference. They still pay more up here.

"We could stop earlier, in California, but none of us like the attitude of the people there. They try to cheat you in the stores, at least that is the feeling I get, and the rents they charge are extortionate. My father has always been very distrustful of the *gringo*. He is growing out of that, with my help.

"But, let's face it, he learned from experience that the *gringo* are always out to get you. It is why we live in the labor camp and not out on the farms if we can help it. No, my gosh, we are not slaves. They squeeze all they can out of you. It is a better bargaining position, living away from the farm.

"Most of my group get here in cars, in family groups, or in pickup wagons. Some come up in crew buses run by contractors. It was pitiful the way they used to bring our people up here, like cattle. It used to be wide open.

"But now in Texas they are stricter about conditions. Even so it is a very long way from home, it is a long way to come for work, and my father is getting old; yet the way we feel, we would rather do this – starve, even – than go on public assistance.

Daybreak in Cottonwood Row (Dingetown, you're likelier to hear it called), the Negro ghetto of Bakersfield, California, and the clumpy shadows of hundreds of waiting men – Negroes, Mexican, a few white – dissolve as they hasten to the farmers' buses pulling up: pay rates stated, no argument, and they bear off their day-haul gangs for picking the plums, nectarines and peaches, for cutting cotton field weeds, thinning grapes and topping sugar beets. But many are left behind, no work that day, so most probably no food.

On Highway 441 approaching Athens, Georgia, and the Oconee River peanut plantations, an old truck with smooth tires, canvas sides and a Florida number plate, and brimming over the tail-gate with Negro men, women and children: their grand tour, of which each stop for them is the middle of another field, the tin shack corner of another town.

In New York State, around Rochester and Utica where the snap beans and tomatoes are being gathered, across in South-Western Idaho where this is the time for onions and sweet corn, in Maryland where the peppers and squashes are ripe, in Minnesota for the cucumbers and potatoes – in almost every state in the Union except perhaps Nevada and Montana in these late summer weeks the migrant pickers are out, working usually from "can't to can't" – from when you can't see the sun in the morning until you can't see it any more at night, getting money that forbids an adequate existence, living in shelters that stink and crawl.

At any given daylight moment in the fruitful seasons there are perhaps two million bent backs in the fields of the Great Society, an African servitude in the meadows of plenty.

Statistics differ uncertainly in these shifting sands for the population of this America is never permanently still enough for a head count – between crops, shaking along the roads in those rattletrap trucks – but there appears to be no official dis-agreement about that two million. They are a petrol-driven peasantry living in a sort of revolving slum which never more than brushes the suburbs and towns of affluent America. They are destitute and sunk in a way that the old harvest force of ornery individuals never was, in a way that the surviving hobo with his prickly, even pathological, pride in his own volition is not. The hobo has always hung on to the conviction that the next train ride may have a special significance; even the Okies had an objective, that dream California. These migrants cannot raise their eyes above the next row of beans.

During all the emerging mobility patterns of the unmarried hobo worker of the West, who made his presence known by his invasion of main street and by raising his voice loud in song and self-aggrandizement, in protest and boasts of prowess, other movements of Negro labor were starting up their present paths, but these were passive herds. When the U.S. Industrial Commission reported in 1901 on changing employment conditions, it found that thousands of Southern Negroes were already in worn grooves. The movement from Virginia up to Rhode Island and other New England states, "from crop to crop and area to area" was established, a custom that apparently began in the 1880s when Negro battalions were imported by steamboat from Norfolk to gather vegetable crops around Providence. At about the same time the Mexican shepherds and cowboys who had begun crossing the border to the new Texan ranches beat the path for the foot laborers who entered the East Texas cotton fields in increasing numbers.

These trickles became the sluggish flood. Each spring now 50,000 Negroes move up from their winter jobbing in the Florida glades, 50,000 from just one part. Until the ending in December 1964 of the *bracero* programme (the licensed admittance of Mexicans approved as an emergency scheme in 1951 and indefinitely extended, to the detriment of American wage standards and opportunities) the annual influx reached 178,000 – and they still come in, as "wetbacks," illegal job-hunters who, figuratively anyway, swim the Rio Grande. Now, since 1950, the Puerto Ricans are found drifting in the Middle Atlantic States, originally transported by farmers' agents direct from their homeland and left trapped in the tide.

––––––––––

THERE are in present-day America six major streams of seasonal migrants in constant monkey-on-a-stick movement. All have Southern sources and they flow Northward and ebb back when the crops are in.

There is the one originating in Florida, mostly Negroes, which climbs the Atlantic Seaboard, through the Old South into Delaware, New Jersey, New York and Pennsylvania, engaging in a great variety of harvests. There is one of Mexican-Americans which goes from Texas up into the North Central and Mountain States, most of the way on sugar beet but also picking vegetables and fruits. There is another wholly Mexican-American stream which leaves Texas and passes through Montana and North Dakota on wheat and small-grain harvests. There is a third from Texas, Spanish-American and Negroes, which splits – one working the cotton crops Westward to New Mexico, Arizona and Southern California, the other making for the Mississippi Delta. There is one, mainly whites of early American stock, which goes from Oklahoma, Arkansas, and Western Tennessee, and fans North and West on fruit and tomatoes. There is the sixth, composed of migrants of mixed races, which shuttles up and down the Pacific Coast, harvesting and processing fruits and vegetables.

They go in families, even in communities, in single cars, in motorcades, in buses and trucks led by middlemen crew organizers who contract with farmers to deliver the manpower, and the woman and child power, and collect the better part of the financial reward. The migrants move because they have no other way of earning any money.

Since 1940 two and a half million farms have gone, simply wiped off the agricultural map of America by being either wrung dry and returning to scrub or being cannibalized by agribusiness units. The expropriated tenants, sharecroppers and small owners have been sucked into the migrant streams.

There are about three million Americans doing some work for wages in agriculture but only a fifth of those are in employment of nominal regularity. There are also 1,400,000 unemployed farm workers, some of them partly and patchily migratory in an increasingly mechanized and automated food-producing industry that needs occasional snatches of manual labor.

Among these migrants there are about 75,000 working, schoolless children over ten years of age. The number under ten who work is not known, but one indication of the volume of child labor in the "blue-sky sweatshop" ("There are no sweatshops on the farms of America," said North Carolina's Congressman Cooley. "On the farms of our nation, children labor with their parents out under the blue skies," a viewpoint not unanimously concurred with) is that in 1964 five- to nine-year-olds accounted for one-fifth of all the agricultural child labor violations found under the very limited protection of the Fair Labor Standards Act.

In point of fact farm workers continue to be excluded from virtually all workmen's compensation laws. They have no minimum wage, no unemployment insurance, no right to collective bargaining. As disenfranchised non-residents of anywhere, they have no vote and cannot make their wishes felt. President Roosevelt placed importance upon this when Congress was debating the Fair Labor Standards Act, and he called for minimum wage coverage for both "those who toil in factory and on farm." That was in 1937. The farm workers were left out.

In this century there have been in the neighborhood of 150 separate attempts to improve the conditions of farm workers through legislative and administrative action, with scant success. For nearly thirty years one of the most adamant and bellicose Washington employers' lobbies, composed of the American Farm Bureau, the National Association of Manufacturers and similar groups has succeeded in keeping the land worker just about where he has ever been. Against this (the "toughest lobby I have ever met," James P. Mitchell, former Secretary of Labor, described it) the land worker has had neither the economic nor the political power to mobilize in his own defence. He has always been somewhere in the middle of a field, stooped.

His insecurity is extreme. At the end of a 1,000 mile trip he can discover that the crop is late or failed or already hired for. If he hands himself over to a crew leader he is often in all senses taken for a ride. If there is work it is for piece rates that pin him firmly to a degraded standard of living. He can find himself staying in this type of accommodation, a Baedeker compiled by National Association for the Advancement of Colored People investigators : dilapidated barns, chicken coops, old school buses, tents, shanties, tar-paper shacks, barracks, machine storage sheds and pigpens. Ordinarily there are no windows, no heat, no cooking facilities, no sanitation. Rent is charged by the farmer or land steward on the luxury level of the prices charged at the company store for groceries.

Conditions are not always so foul. The camps vary. Some are moderately maintained and reasonably clean. Also the migrant hand can, in short bursts, earn enough to get by if he picks his steps carefully. The U.S. Department of Labor issues guides to peak areas and the better camps, a necessarily skeleton map, which is an acceptable but apologetic substitute for real action.

Some young whites, reared to it and relaxed about a feckless, unambitious life they can enjoy, ride the bad breaks philosophically; it is among the Negroes that there is encountered what appears to be a mass psychological depression and loss of contact with hope. But adjustment, even when it can be and is made, cannot justify the toleration of poverty of this ingrained quality in a society of such abundance. In any event, however fly the migrant's planning and however happy-go-lucky he manages to stay, it is a beastly, disproportionate way of staying alive, for there are seldom the means, once in the migrant stream, of avoiding fourteen-hour days when employed and desperate scourings of the country when not employed, of seeing your children inexorably drawn into the same bondage of poverty, of having no comforts or background or local attachment, of having no future expectations, of being shackled to an inhuman level of labor whose wage status is actually declining. In the 1910-14 period the farm laborer's average hourly wage was sixty-seven per cent of the average factory hand's; by 1945 it had dropped to forty-seven per cent; by 1963 it was down to thirty-six per cent.

"A hundred years ago we owned slaves," a Congressman from a South-Western state said of the contract labor system. "Today we just rent them."

There seems no defensible cause for conditions to be such. The small grower a lot of the time shaves the economic danger line uncomfortably close, but agriculture *is* America's largest single industry, whose productivity is rising faster than almost any other, whose overall labor costs against production costs steadily fall (barely eleven per cent a year), and it is the industry which rakes in more than forty billion dollars a year from marketing and government subsidies.

It should be possible for so rich and powerful an industry to spare a better share for its necessary task-force, these two million people, "comparable," the Negro leader Herbert Hill has said, "in their destitution to feudal serfs, save that they are bound to no land."

A religious committee reviewing the problem declared: "The conditions of these American migratory farm workers and their families are an affront to the conscience of the nation." But they do not seem to be.

There is nothing new or revolutionary in the above facts. They have been publicized many times, angrily, passionately. Quite regularly they cause an uneasy flutter, which then subsides. In 1960 Ed Murrow's CBS television film *Harvest of Shame* showed the dismal convoys of black labour on their way up the East coast from Belle Glade, Florida, and eventually returned to Belle Glade. Summed up one: "We broke even. We were broke when we left. We were broke when we came back."

In 1965 there appeared Truman Moore's *The Slaves We Rent* and Dale Wright's *They Harvest Despair*, two honest, muckraking books which again aroused much controversy and public oath-taking that something should be done. But during the long history of this sewer-bed migration – against which the roughest going of the career freight-rider and the sweaty trudges of the old-timer bindle stiff have the airy dash of a peregrine falcon – there have been many printed denunciations, many senate investigations and hearings, many, many individual campaigns.

Meanwhile for millions life carries on much the same in the stoop crop fields, and there seems little sign of change in the vagabond farm hand's lot. In his testimony to the National Advisory Committee on Farm Labor in 1959 Dr. Hector Garcia said: "As a migrant, his world will be from the Atlantic to the Pacific, from the Great Lakes to the Rio Grande. It will be his world, however, only in that the only piece of property he will own will be his grave."

That is descriptively true but perhaps what is more factually affecting is the statement of another physician to yet another enquiring body, the President's Commission on Migratory Labour, when he pointed to: ". . . evidence of ordinary starvation among many of these people." His survey in Texas labor camps showed that "ninety-six per cent of the children in that camp had not consumed any milk whatsoever in the last six months. It also showed that eight out of ten adults had not eaten any meat in the last six months . . . they could not afford it with the money they were making."

It is strange that, while "this national scandal" should have been so nailed for all to see across such expanses of print and film, that a migratory worker could still be right when he said "It seems like of all the forgotten men, we're the most forgottenest." The forgetting comes of long practice.

The color bar has, overtly at least, been erased in America. The migrant bar has not. In towns with migrant camps shoved away on the fringes, behind the tar-paper curtain, there can be seen on cinemas, on restaurants, on shops these notices; MIGRANTS NOT ADMITTED and NO MIGRANTS.

A Department of Labor booklet, *The Community Meets the Migrant Worker*, designed to foster educational and welfare programmes that will take the curse off the migrant in the eyes of residents, says: "Local people avoided the migrants when possible; they feared they were dirty, might spread disease, or steal . . . Gradually, however, people in a good many communities have come to realize that this is not a true picture of the migrants; that they have an obligation to these workers who are necessary to their economy . . ."

It would be nice to believe so. In Arkansas the Reverend Sam Allen, area head of the National Council of Churches and active in the migrant ministry which for forty-six years had toured the camps with literacy classes, entertainment, distribution of clothes, food and, of course, religion, says: "There is an enormous gulf between residents of anywhere and the migrants from somewhere else, which we try to bridge a little, but there are seventeen thousand migrants a year come into this state, all strangers.

"Or look at Memphis, from where they ship out three to five thousand laborers a day, gone at dawn, back at sunset. How can they identify with the town? My fear is that in five years' time, when mechanization has done away with the migrant in Arkansas, he won't be integrated anywhere. He'll just go to swell another pocket of poverty, all of his own kind."

Up at Grove Park, Mrs. Marion Lunden looks after 36,000

chickens in her husband's batteries, and when through with the hens goes down to the migrants' camp to teach the women crafts. "I don't know whether it's hopeless or whether they don't want to better themselves," she says. "But then the cabins down at the Labor Camp are terrible. I don't know how they stand it. Then, almost every woman is pregnant every year. There are children of thirteen and fifteen with three babies. They're very polite and pleasant but they are totally inbred and don't want anything outside the camp.

"They're proud, not a bit grabby, and they don't beg even when they're hungry. But, you see, the town attitude to them isn't very good. We've just had some middle class teenagers who said they weren't going in the swimming pool with those dirty things. Yet we have less trouble with the migrant teenagers than with our own.

"I think most of the American people have a wrong attitude about the migrants. They think they're scum. They're not scum. They are under-privileged."

Harry Wilson is a high school teacher who helps in the evenings with classes for the migrant children at the Springdale Labor Camp, a voluntary chore which seems to leave him palely despondent: "If you ask the children what they want to be when they grow up they say they want to be bean pickers. Why? They just don't know. That's all they know, picking beans and chopping cotton.

"They're not dumb. They're just behind, because their parents aren't interested in them having an education. They need to take them travelling, to earn money in the fields. If you take the kids to see the rodeo they crawl around on the floor looking for money people have dropped.

"They're loud and noisy, but they don't know how to play organized games. Most of them never did finish high school and never knew anything about sport. The teenagers go out in the fields and just hang around. There's a baseball field just a block away where the local kids play every night, but these kids won't go out and mix with the town children. Probably it's because they feel odd men out."

PART SEVEN

PICTURE-BOOK HEROES

I am divided from mankind, a solitaire, one banished from humane society.

Daniel Defoe

35 : YOU'VE BEEN TO THAT TOWN A THOUSAND TIMES

The perpetually shifting frontier that lies between ordinary life and the terror that would seem to be more real ...How long the road is from my inner anguish.

Franz Kafka : *Diaries*

JACK MALONE'S story has the cadence of the closing 1890s when America was still a wild bronco of a country and those who were breaking it in were necessarily themselves wild and lived with gusto, with a contemptuous disregard for humdrum law and order. Since then America, with bewildering speed and magnitude, has been subdued and civilized. The ideal of the Garden of the World was never consummated but the roughness was smoothed over with subtopia. The pioneer hardship, danger and nihilism have been eradicated, but Jack Malone and his kind have managed to preserve themselves in a reliquary of the pristine American life, for Malone keeps on hoboing.

He is now forty-five. His father was Polish-American, his mother Irish, and he was born in the East End of London where his sailor father hung around for a time. When he was fourteen they left for the United States, for Seattle which his father remembered as "a friendly port." Malone, who took his mother's maiden name, did not go to school a great deal once there; he began doing odd turns at laboring, loading trucks, working on the coastal shipping, and in 1939 returned to Britain to join the Army. In the Welsh Regiment he fought in France and Belgium, and his foot and hand were injured in a booby trap. In 1946 he bought a passage to New York with his discharge pay and moved in with an aunt.

"Then after two months," Malone says, "she told me, 'Jack, maybe you'd better move on.' It was a small apartment and I understood her difficulties. So I grabbed a Greyhound and landed in Cleveland, one of the few times I ever paid a fare after that. Since then, for twenty years, I've been on the road.

'I knew nothing about hoboing when I hit Cleveland but I found myself down in the slave market off Euclid Avenue and saw this gang of men waiting around. They were shipping out on the railroad and told me you didn't have to have cash or gear or nothing. So I went in to see the clerk in this employment office and he said he was sending me up to Western Ohio for the New York Central line.

'I was given a work-slip with my name and social security number on it and we all travelled out on a mail train with one passenger coach. At the other end the bull-cook met us and took us out to the rolling camp, old 1870 coaches on a side track fitted out as dining-car, sleeping-car and shower-car, and we were issued with blankets and sheets from the store-car. Next morning we were pulled up to Toledo where they were re-laying track and resurfacing the road bed with fresh ballast.

"I was a shovel and pick man. This is the kind of work you take up as a last, I mean last, resort. At first it hits you so hard that you're too bushed to eat. It takes you ten days to break in. I was there two weeks. I started at seventy-eight cents an hour, working from six in the morning until five at night, and quite often overtime after that.

"I did seven years broken service with the railroad. My next job was with the Chicago, Burlington and Quincy up at Wisconsin, then on the western railroads at Minneapolis and in North Dakota with the Big G, the Great Northern. The camps were totally different out in the West: very good. Laundered sheets, good bunk houses, not lousy like in the East, and all the food you could swallow – I seen one man eat eighteen fried eggs for breakfast.

"Pretty soon I became a gandy dancer. You use a spike-maul, that's a ten-pound hammer with a foot-long narrow head, and you really have to roll that spike-maul – you hit the spike, which is inch-and-half diameter, with a twirling action. Two of you work on each spike, hitting it in turn, whirling that hammer to keep it whipping. In just one second – zzzzssss! – that spike's right in. You're not allowed too many misses. They don't like you hitting the rail. If you show yourself not to be too much of a marksman you don't last. Finally I became a gauge spiker, leading a section.

"You have to line up the new rail with the old rail, put an iron gauge on the old and the new, and keep them in position while you drive in the gauge spike as a guide for the gandy dancers behind you. This has to be done with speed and precision. You're setting the pace. With a gang of sixty men you'd lay or re-lay three miles of track, one length of single line, in a day. With overtime you can pull down eighty dollars a week, less deductions for board, but that's cheap at a dollar fifty a day.

"When you finish a job you're a one-day millionaire. You grab a freight and run down into town and live it up for a while. One reason I rode freights was that there wasn't too much motor traffic on the roads out in those Western parts even just a few years ago. Quite early I found a lot of guys use these shipments out to get to a jumping-off point for wherever they're heading. I met a couple of new arrivals up on a job at Dickinson, North Dakota, who said they were picking up supper and breakfast before pushing off for Seattle so I went with them.

"I had a few days' money coming and arranged to pick it up at the Butte, Montana, division point. We hitch-hiked it, really struggled away in that hot sunshine, but we were given a ride in a station wagon and got to Butte easy and we celebrated there a little bit. After that I fixed up to join another gang at Missoula and when that was finished I collected sixty dollars. I grabbed a freight for Spokane with a couple of old timers, and when I got to skid row I fitted myself up with new shirt and pants, and booked in at a hotel. The clerk said 'With or without?' I thought he meant with or without a bath, but he meant with or without a girl, so I said with.

"After two days the money had gone and as it was getting 'round time of year for the pea harvest I joined some of the crews engaged by farmers who came into Spokane with trucks to ride you out to the fields. Then I went logging in Colorado, at Kremmling. That was at an elevation of seven thousand feet, piece-work, and using a cross-cut at that height was impossible for more than fifteen minutes at a time. I'd been in Denver before that and down on Market Street skid row a contractor came in with a lorry finding men to fall spruce on government land. First he took us to a hardware store to buy axes and saws. He told us he had a camp up there, but we found we had to live in a hotel and eat in a restaurant. That was a poor job. There wasn't much big timber and at the end of two weeks he deducted the cost of the tools and accommodation and we had just ten dollars apiece coming.

"So I hopped over to Salt Lake City on the Denver, Rio Grande and Western Railroad, gandy dancing again. After that I decided to make Klamath Falls for the potato harvest – that's a really rugged way of earning your dough. Then I took a trip up to Portland and shipped out for the Southern Pacific to a place called Eugene where I worked for about a month re-laying track. Checked out of there and up to Seattle, and I decided to lay off gandy dancing for a while and proceeded to hustle the city, just doing odd jobs and using the missions. There's one there, Jack and Jenny's, run by two hot gospellers where to earn yourself a supper and a bed you have to take an ear-beating for three hours, and if you happen to fall asleep you're tossed out of the door. There's another, Sister Dorothy, who really enjoys throwing the winos out. There must be at least thirty missions in Seattle, because of all the loggers and sea-going men, so you can get by there for quite a while.

"I've averaged forty thousand miles a year, and must have done near a million miles, mostly on freights. I've worked through nearly all the states, except some of those quiet New England states, forty or fifty times apiece. That includes the South, although it's bad for a hobo down there. If they see you've got heavy gear on they know you're from the North – a snow-bird, they call you – and the cops are on to you damned quick.

"I hold two records for hoboing. Once I rode the fastest freight there is, the Berry Special, which carries fruit on a complete run from Seattle to Chicago, but you can't hold it down all that distance because of the speed it does. It's a diesel service now but they were still using steam then. I grabbed it at Fargo, North Dakota, in the Dilworth Yards and I rode it through to Minneapolis. I covered 265 miles in three hours forty minutes, that's an average of eighty miles an hour. There are only four or five guys who've done this and lived to tell the tale. It was carrying cherries and strawberries and all the cars were closed up with a government seal, so I had to ride the roof. You have to contend with the swaying of the coaches because it really whips round those curves.

"When I got off the train in Minneapolis yards it took me an hour to wash all the coal dust off. I told this story at the Britt hobo convention and they all said 'Here's a guy who rode the Berry Special, give him a hand,' and they applauded me. Most hobos seeing the Berry Special coming say 'I ain't gonna ride that baby,' because they know the kind of speed it does.

"My other record was hitching from Portland, Oregon, to New York, 3,300 miles in ninety-six hours, in mid-December which is the roughest time for hitch-hiking. I was in Portland with five cents in my pocket and I had this urge to get to New York. I was on Highway 30 and after two hours got a lift 100 miles in a Cadillac. By five that afternoon I'd done 300 miles and by six next morning I'd been taken by a guy in a Buick to Salt Lake City. So I thought 'Things are going good, why stop now?' So I hitched up to Ogden, Utah, stayed overnight and got a lift to Evanston, Wyoming, and the next guy drove me right through to Omaha. On the third day I was half way across the States. I panhandled a breakfast and the next car was a Mercury to Philadelphia, where I had some sandwiches. On the fourth day I made New York.

"I've taken the occasional job inside, like working for the post office as a sorter, but I always feel hemmed in, claustrophobia, or sump'n. On one inside job the boss liked me and he began calling me by my first name, and when a boss starts calling you by your first name a hobo resents it. He thinks 'I got to move on.' You think you've been there too long. A hobo doesn't like to establish too much of a routine. It's like the philosophy of the American Indian. He doesn't like to make too much of a close friend because if he loses that friend he'll never get over it. Just the same if you save an Indian's life. He'll never forgive you – because he can't repay you.

"People see a hobo as a no-good hopeless sort of guy. But in fact he can never let up if he's going to remain self-sufficient. He always has to know where to find water, how to trap a rabbit like the old time trappers, how to forage to keep himself alive. He likes to feel he's capable of making out for himself. After he's been a hobo for a while he doesn't feel he comes within the scope of ordinary settled people any more.

"Even if occasionally he decides to clean himself up and try for a steady job it doesn't work out. The outlook of the people you come into contact with makes it impossible. In the States they don't ask for references and that sort of stuff – they'll always try you out on a job, which is not the case in England. But, even so, in a small town you just aren't accepted. They say 'Who is this guy?' If you're just drifting through, okay, but if you try to settle there's a lot of suspicion and distrust.

"In a big city there's the pace of the competition and inevitably you're living in some cheap flophouse and you can't break through from there. Often you feel you're excluded from society. In your twenties and thirties you don't mind this, and anyway there's always this dream that the young hobo has of being taken into some family. I've known this happen. A family says 'Hey, this guy looks like our boy who left home years ago,' and they take him in and treat him like a son.*

"But there's always the enjoyment of beating society, of winning over local law enforcement, of getting by when officially you're not supposed to get by. The important thing is not to get entangled with people because if you meet somebody you could really get to like, male or female, and it ends, then you have a hard time getting over it.

"It's a lonely life but you have this picture in your mind that you're battling against adversity all the time, and although that can make you feel bitter it's also satisfying that you can win. I suppose every kid of seventeen or eighteen gets the idea of leaving home and hitch-hiking around the country for a bit – but he goes back. Usually a hobo has left for a different reason, because there was no home there to begin with, so he's nowhere to return to. What's the point of him trying to settle down somewhere? Suppose he gets a steady job and takes a room, what does he go back to at night? Just four empty walls around

* This may have become part of a hobo's supporting fantasy. On the other hand it may have happened oftener than might seem probable. W. H. Davies, in *The Autobiography of a Super Tramp*, describes how in the summer of 1894, after fruit-picking on a farm at St. Joseph, Michigan, the old German couple with no son of their own offer to adopt him and bequeath him the farm upon their death. He turns the offer down.

him. No, when you're on the road, hitting the freights and jungles, there's a feeling of brotherhood. You see a guy and say 'Hey, Joe, we met up in Washington state,' and you remember he stood you a meal and this time you have a hundred dollars in your pocket after a rail job and you buy him a meal, and you talk over old times and you really have experiences in common that ordinary people just don't know about.

"Let me put it this way. In the hobo's mind he's the last of the pioneers and the last of the wandering minstrels. It gets tougher all the time. Everything's getting automated, all those jobs he's worked at, and he has to be careful he doesn't become just a mission stiff. A hobo has to be something a little above average if he's going to be successful. When he gets off a train in a small town he may look like he's just crawled out of a coal yard, but he has to present a happy-go-lucky character to show he's not ashamed of his appearance and that he really has something there.

"He's got to be open and forceful. A fly-by-night beginner gives up. You have to have nerve to approach people and show them that you're not crawling, that you're a man worth helping along. The toughest years for a hobo are between forty and sixty, because he's too old to be given sympathy as a kid on the road and too young to be helped as an old man. Between those years people look at you and say 'You should have made your money, don't expect nothing from me, bud.' Aw, well, you can get by if you travel light and keep your wits about you. I travel light. West of the Mississippi you need a sleeping bag or a bed roll – couple of blankets or a quilt; a couple of shirts; spare pair of pants and socks; toothbrush, razor, soap, maybe some cooking utensils; but just the essentials.

"A hobo gets wore out if he tries to carry too much. And he should never expect too much from others. I remember in one jungle in Montana beside the Northern Pacific Railroad, it was a very cold night and there was three of us around a fire, and one old timer beside his own fire, and a young hobo just off a train walks up to the old guy and says 'Hey, pop, can I warm up around your fire?' The old timer pulls out a match and says 'Go build yourself a fire.' The young hobo goes off and I says to the old timer 'Why didn't you let him warm up?' and he said 'I could have done that, but what'll he do when he's on his own? He'll freeze to death.' You see that philosophy?

"I have my regrets about my way of life. I feel maybe I could have done something better. But you get to feel what has to be has to be. The hobo lives for today and tomorrow can take care of itself. When you lay down for sleep you think tonight will take care of all your troubles and tribulations, even if you are sleeping on a rough, hard floor. And next morning you again have the feeling to go on. Part of it's the old traveler's dream of things being better over the other side of the hill. You always have the feeling that that day you'll meet someone who'll give you a hand, even though most people in America say 'Sure, I'd like to be traveling and seeing the country, too, but I have to work to support my wife and family, so why should you be gallivanting around? No, I don't believe in helping people like you.'

"On the other hand you often do meet people who feel in tune with you, even though they're stuck somewhere: maybe they've done it themselves in their young days but anyway they know what it's like because, being a young nation, they're not so far removed from the difficulties of the pioneer days.

"Like any profession you got to learn the technique. You get to know which is a hot town for law enforcement and to avoid it; you get to know that often the cops are friendly and the people aren't, and vice-versa. You get to know the good railroads. Now the Southern Pacific is known as 'the friendly SP.' They're easy going and they help you all they can. If an engineer sees you wandering around the freight yards he'll call 'Hey, where are you going?' And if you say Phoenix or somewhere he'll say 'Cross over to track twelve and there's an empty boxcar on that train.' I remember in 1956 from Pasco, Washington, to Walla Walla, that's just a branch line of the SP, there were 300 hobos riding on a freight train of fifteen cars but that engineer didn't mind although he was pulling more tonnage of hobos than freight.

"I been at a conservative estimate in jail 500 times, usually just overnight but also for two weeks at a time for what they call investigation. They're bad conditions in city jails but the county jails are usually comfortable and well stocked up with food. One night in a town in Southern Illinois I couldn't find anywhere to sleep, so I rang the bell of the deputy sheriff's house and explained and he handed over his bunch of keys and said 'Let yourself in the jail. There's some kindling there, so build yourself a fire in the stove, and bring the keys back in the morning.'

"You can survive when you're treated decent occasionally. The authentic hobo, the man who does it because he just has to, has a rebounding mind. He may get the blues but an hour later he feels he's going to fight back. However bad things are you don't really believe it's the end of the world. You feel 'Well, I been hungry before, I know what the score is.' Even if you haven't eaten for twelve hours and get off a freight feeling punch drunk – because you can take an awful pounding on them trains – and a guy in the main street says 'Hey, help me unload this truck and I'll give you a few dollars' you don't tell him you haven't had no breakfast. You do the work and eat after.

"But, you know, during these twenty years it's got tougher and tougher to make out. The cops all have instructions now to keep the hobo moving. They don't want you around their town. They say 'Get yourself back on that highway and keep moving.' At least with the new inter-state turnpikes you're always sure of a long ride, but now you really have to know your railroads to ride the freights. You can't snag rides the way you once could. On the steam trains you always jumped on an up gradient but the diesels make almost the same speed uphill, so you have to know those points where they take on fuel every 1,000 miles and get services every 500, or the crossings where the trains have to stop with a red block showing against them.

"Still it hasn't closed down. Not all the freights are metal. They still have to use the old wooden sliding-door cars on the grain trains because the grain would get too hot inside metal, so you can get inside those. Or you can still ride the blinds, although you run the danger of being seen at stops. But you can't ride the rods no more. There haven't been rods on trains for years. But, sure, you can still, out in the West anyway, ride the trains.

"The important thing is to have an aim in life. You have to decide when to quit a town because you know you've wore it out. You have to settle on a destination in your mind so that you don't just wander aimlessly and feel that you're in a daze. When you get to that point you're finished, you're just an old wino or mission stiff. So you always say 'I'm heading for 'Frisco or Baltimore' to give yourself a goal.

"But you know something? Eventually it comes into your mind that you must be crazy because you've been to that town a thousand times already and it's difficult to convince yourself that it's worthwhile going anywhere, and you begin to wonder if you should have grabbed some of the chances you had of settling down. It happened to me early in my career around Missoula in July one year, on my first trip out to the West Coast, and a couple in a Chrysler stopped right up in the Rocky Mountains. I told them I was heading for Seattle and they said they'd take me within 100 miles and we got on well.

"Then a month later, coming back on that same road, I met them again and they were going back to Minneapolis. They tried to talk me into staying with them. They said they had a spare room and that they'd get me a job in the local hospital and help me settle down. Well, I did stay with them for coupla nights. It was genuine hospitality. Then they said to me 'What do you think?' and I said 'Look, it's okay, but I got to move on.' I didn't feel ready to compose my mind. I was starting out on this hobo career and I felt I had to keep moving. If it had happened a few years later I'd have taken them up on it.

"It's a life that makes you able to get through anything. If you fall sick you just have to fight your way through it. In Pittsburgh I was working for the Salvation Army collecting articles door to door. I had holes in my shoes and there was snow on the ground. I woke up one morning with a fever, and in fact had a severe attack of bronchial pneumonia, but they got me up out of bed and gave me a couple of pills and I had to go out on that truck. Another time I was hitching out of New York and got a lift on a pickup truck, and the driver went into a spin and flipped the truck. I busted three ribs and was taken to hospital but they strapped me up and said 'You can't stay here. This is for local people and anyway you got no cash.' So they told me to hit the road. Those ribs never have set properly. But three months later I was working on the railroad again.

"I've never felt I wanted to get myself organized politically or anything of that nature. You meet a lot of old Wobblies around the jungle fires and there's a fair amount of political talk but it's usually in a humorous vein, like 'There ought to be a two-hour working day with an hour off for lunch.'

"It may sound sort of funny but even as a hobo you do feel to have a share in the American system. You come off a railroad job with a couple of hundred dollars and even if you don't exactly join the system you can enjoy the luxury for a couple of days. Cleaned up and with a new shirt, you can walk through the supermarket and say 'I'll have some of that and some of this,' just like everybody else.

"Now, well I don't know. I done just about every kind of job, from picking cotton to baling wheat, and you can always look forward to a happy time in the spring and summer, shipping out on a harvest or railroad gang with your old buddies, and a binge at the end of it, but automation's caught up on the railroads and you have to be a regular payroll man to do much work for them. It's not so easy these days to fix yourself up with a coupla hundred dollars, and there are these rubber tire tramps who consider themselves a cut above the real hobo and who wouldn't use a freight and who drive around for the harvest work.

"Yeh, it's tougher now. It's easier to get ragged and dirty so you can't recognize yourself, with everyone trying to drag you down to their level. Maybe now you either got to change your ways or resign to being just floating flotsam."

Nathaniel Morgan is willowy and slight with a translucent tubercular look, but he has been living the hard roving life, "following the farm work around," for twenty-four years since he was six. That goes back to the time when his father finished the hay crop down in Oklahoma and set off on the annual excursion, driving the family North in a rattletrap and picking up a few dollars where any flapped.

Nathaniel did like his daddy. In recent months he came up from Russellville, Arkansas, and was enlisted for the bean crop near Fayetteville. Beans in, he turned to grading birds in a turkey processing plant; 9,000 got oven-ready in an eight-hour day in that shop, he says with an admiring eye for such advanced technology from his precarious position on the agribusiness fringe.

The plant has now begun laying off, and Nathaniel is lounging on the boardwalk, very natty in country rover style, in a shirt of green-and-white candy stripes and chinos, and high, tight suede boots; his butter-hued hair is bunched and pasted in art nouveau whorls. "Just turning it over in my mind," he says, "whether to make it up to Michigan, or maybe even over to California again. Last year I stayed on in Michigan after the crops was through and fished, and that was real nice, so I may do that again. Sure, it's an uncertain life – but isn't any job? I just like traveling free, don't know why, just like it. I'm just a drifter, I guess."

Glyn Grant checked in at the employment office in Springdale, Arkansas, at five a.m. to see if any day hands were wanted. Although the heavy rain has abated it is now nine-thirty and no farmers have turned up or telephoned, for the bean crop is almost picked. Until the grape harvest begins in a month's time there is unlikely to be much steady work, perhaps an occasional replacement needed in the peach orchards or in the turkey processing plant.

So Glyn Grant is just loafing, like a dozen other men outside the grocery store, while barefoot children play around the hutments where up to ten people sleep on pallets in each small room. Most of them are Okies and Arkies, poor whites from the old Dust Bowl area of the Oklahoma Panhandle and the Ozark Mountains of Arkansas, but there are also some here from farther afield, from New Mexico, Texas, Kansas and Iowa.

Glyn Grant comes from Fort Smith, only seventy-five miles south. He is a vivacious young man with sculpted sideboards and dark hair coiffured in a dated high bouquet, early Elvis, and wearing a white T-shirt and black hunting boots with side buckles.

"I been traveling since I was three years old, my parents used to go off most of the year through to Texas and California or Missouri and Michigan. When we went traveling there'd be seven or ten cars, all the family and kinfolk and neighbors.

"Some folk call us road tramps but I don't mind that too much. They also say that it's rough on the kids but I don't see that. The kids learn a whole lot from traveling, they learn history and geography and about farming. I reckon they learn a whole lot better that way than just settin' in a school.

"Myself, I been following the harvests for about fifteen years. I winter down home in Fort Smith for about two months around Christmas time. You can work around there then. There's the arragation and there's the peanut harvest and some boll-pulling, but I like the traveling. There's the excitement and everything like that, the scenery and stuff like that. Best place I ever been to is Oregon, that's the prettiest state I ever seen. I also been as far as the Michigan coast, cherry picking up there, and sometimes I drive a tractor for the wheat harvest.

"Mostly I live in camps but if I hit a place where there ain't no camp I just buy me a tarpaulin. Us harvest people are used to the weather, not that we like the bad weather but we can put up with it. I reckon that most of them who have a studying job would do this work if they could take the weather.

"Yep, on the whole I enjoy the life. Sometimes you can make more money a week than you can in a steady job; sometimes you can double it. It just depends the way the crop is. I'm a drifter, I guess, but I've always liked it. Even if I get married I guess I'll keep on with this life, traveling on. Just keep rolling."

J. H. Kavanaugh, assistant manager in the Farm Labor Office at Bakersfield in the San Joaquin Valley of California, is happy that the cantaloup crop is in ahead of schedule, and that there are plenty of Portuguese, Swiss-Italians and Filipinos down from Los Banos and Dos Palos offering themselves for the grape-picking which is due to start.

"It's a tricky operation," he says, "keeping all the balls in the air. There are 2,021 farms in Kern County and farmers'll cut their staff down to one man, then come round and say 'I'm going to start the sprinklers Monday, get me men on the job.' That can be a headache sometimes.

"Right now there are about 22,000 workers, permanent and casual, around here: that's potato pickers and diesel mechanics, combine operators and unskilled field hands, a conglomeration, we get 'em all in this office. Every morning they'll be waiting here from four a.m., Mexicans from Texas and Arizona, and bottom-of-the-barrel whites, too, teeth decayed, raggedy clothes, but if he can get up and down a sixteen-foot ladder with a fifty-pound sack round his neck for all the daylight hours, he can work. They say 'Ah hoed weeds' or 'Ah picked cotton,' and a lot of them can't do much else.

"I used to counsel these people and ask them why they floated but they just say 'Ah was born this way and Ah like it.' Still, we don't lower the boom on them unless they repeatedly show us that they can't do a job or have whisky on their breath. Everyone gets a chance.

"There are twenty buses owned by contractors which come in to collect workers around seven a.m. and you can see the crumbums trying to get aboard. Some get up here in old wrecks with wired-up cylinders; some have got flatbed trucks with tents built on top for the whole family. They go out on Highway 58 into the sand dunes and start a little bonfire and cook their supper. Or they go up to Weed Patch – that's an old time Western town – or Cottonwood Row, where the houses are built out of five-gallon oil cans, and you can get drunk cheap in those nickel bars.

"But they're not as dumb as they look. They can make twenty-five to thirty dollars a day on speciality crops so it's worth them coming up from Tennessee or New Mexico."

Professor Paul S. Taylor, of the Department of Economics, University of California, at Berkeley, has been enfilading the "streamlined plantation system of the West" for many years: a land-ownership pattern which, he says, has denuded the country of people.

"The biggest land-owners in America are in the Kern County Land Corporation, here in California. Back in the Eighties they cut off the water of the little men and cleared them out. They wanted slaves who vanish at the right moment and return when the next crop's due. This is the California story.

"How can a man put down roots in the San Joaquin Valley when there's not an inch left for him, when he can't own land? The migration across America has been glamorized but the Dust Bowl refugees weren't glamorous. They were victims of, a product of, an increasing rootlessness in American life.

410

"They were not deeply rooted people themselves. They were easily shaken loose from that Oklahoma country and although the dream of the West, of California, drew them here the big men had already carved it up. These refugees became like the leaves of autumn that are blown by the wind, like the dust that drowned them out. Once sand is blown by the wind it makes little ripples and then the dust cloud gathers in volume and velocity. The sense of community disappears.

"Once you start moving you roll; once the tap-root is severed, you roll."

The radio program of Spanish-language pop requests – "for Margate Trujillo," "for Angel Otobe," "for Victor Astro" – clattering out across the cafe tables is sponsored by the First National Bank of Walsenburg, which is offering, the disc jockey excitedly bays, "A deposit service for people who do not wish to keep large sums of money in the house overnight."

This seems a diploma test of salesmanship for it is hard to believe that it is a decision many of the occupants are wrestling with. All around, styptically beautiful, are the snow-coned peaks of the Sangre de Cristo and Culebra ranges of the Southern Rockies, a set of stupendously incongruous grandeur for the fly-blown litter that is this Colorado town which once dug more than two million tons of coal a year out of the foothills.

This is now a Mextown, a "pocket of poverty." On the outskirts along rutted dirt roads – Maple Street, Pine Street – higgledy-piggledy among the weed patches and scrub, are shacks of adobe and packing-case planks, dribbling away toward the rusted gates of closed mines and slag-tips whiskered with grass. In Main Street paint flakes off empty shops and office buildings, and at every corner squat groups of men on the broken sidewalks, squinting under straw brims through the brilliant mountain air at nothing.

The Spanish came early, the first time fifty years after Columbus under Captain-General Francisco Coronado, a Conquistadore band in search of the fabled Seven Cities of Cibola; later Mexican homesteaders settled and the town was named Plaza de los Leones. Coal mining began to boom after the railroad arrived, and then came the reinforcements, whites from Georgia, German settlers led by Fred Walsenburg for whom the town was renamed. At the clamorous, grimy climax Walsenburg and Huerfano County were the prosperous home of 18,000. From then, in 1930, it sank to 7,867 and, says a redevelopment report, "the largest part of the labor force continues to be unemployed." Cause: "decline in coal mining, production and agriculture, business depression, weather conditions and labor disputes, and new substitute industries have not come in ... a running down of facilities and buildings, deterioration, obsolete public utilities, apathy and despair, and outright suspicion of any group advocating change."

Out-migration completed the death and the emptiness. Between interviewing dark young girls with swarms of children and old scrawny men, Mrs. Haynes in the Welfare Office seems unable to conjure even any official hope: "King Coal has long abdicated but most of the unemployed miners who've hung on here *will* still regard the area as a coal mining center. They're not ready to accept the fact that their living has gone for ever and won't come back.

"The county has lost two-thirds of its population. All the Italians and the Slavs cut their losses and moved on. The only job left for the Spanish-Americans is ditch digging. We're left with the elderly, the incapacitated, the illiterate."

Where did the others go?

William H. Metzler, an agricultural economist at the University of California at Davis, says: "In California we had a lot of miners come in who didn't make the grade here, who couldn't find the land to get dug into. They became bindle stiffs and wanderers, a special class of people who have never become part of the community.

"In America there is a myth about movement. Well, it's ninety per cent myth and not enough reality. Mechanization, efficiency, profits – they are put first, before people. Crops are sacred. Workers are cheap. If they go hungry nobody gives a durn about them.

"There is a gradual depositing that goes through all the states, people who are being pushed out of the plantation system and drifting into the migration stream, a distributing agency which

412

is in perpetual motion. I don't see it stopping for a long time, not while there are unskilled cut-price laborers and the farmers want a kind of hobo peasantry.

"The drifters and floaters and derelicts are part of the system. It destroys people. The fellow here in this country who isn't able to move up gets pounded down into the pavement. You can destroy people by developing so much competition, by developing a society in which there is bitterness and animosity, instead of one that is democratic and sound.

"Yet at the same time, I honestly believe that the migrant farm workers are happier than the growers in this part of the country. They are a friendlier and happier group than the agribusiness operators who've made a million and have to go on to make the next million, and are worried about it because they grab harder and sweat more, and their tenseness and unhappiness increases. They have got in a rat race and don't know how to get out of it.

"The migratory workers are the last free folk we have. They are the last free Americans. They're staying outside organized society; they're against regimented society. Even when a farmer finds a good man, wants to keep him and offers him a monthly salary and a house, that worker often packs his bag in a few weeks. He feels he has got into something he hasn't figured on.

"His future may be guaranteed for the rest of his life but he doesn't want to get up every morning in that same confounded little house and go through that confounded routine every day. Even if this farmer is a good guy, the migrant doesn't want to be obliged to him because he wouldn't be a free man any more.

Leaning over the desk of the Cedar Lake Motel on U.S. Highway 97 at Chemult, Oregon, on the edge of the Winema National Forest, Ray Haynes says: "We see a lot of people who just flunk about. You'd be surprised. You know – people who just go from job to job, going from place to place, get a few dollars and then walk out.

"This sorta people, they're never satisfied, always looking for greener pastures. There's one guy I see going through town every year, with whiskers and long sideburns, carrying a bedpack and a few tools, he told me he'd been in every state in the Union six times. We get even young girls through, they'll work for us for a month and then move on, to a café or something: they like working in these truckstop cafés where the truckdrivers shoot the bull with the waitresses and maybe take them along.

"Now last spring we had a family stop one night, in a panel-door truck with one of those U-haul trailers, a guy with a wife and two kids. He said he was a cement-finisher from Spokane and they were heading for California. He said 'My gosh, cement finishers get twice the money down there and there's a heap of work, so I figured we might just as well go there.' Well, two weeks ago on a Sunday afternoon I said to my wife, 'Here's a repeat customer, I bet you four bits.' It was that same guy, the cement finisher. He said he'd been down there in Los Angeles seven months and all he'd got was ulcers, and they were heading North.

"See what I mean? They look over the fence and figure the pastures are greener, if they keep going, but those people will always be broke. They'll get that bumming habit and end up like the bums who drop off from the Southern Pacific freights just across the road and hit the town.

"Now even whole families get up and quit their jobs with nothing else in view. Government welfare has a lot to do with it. They figure they can always be fed."

Up and down the aisles in the South State Street chapel the preacher is prowling predatorily to and fro under the black letters on the wall: *ALL WE LIKE SHEEP HAVE GONE ASTRAY; WE HAVE TURNED EVERY ONE TO HIS OWN WAY: AND THE LORD HATH LAID ON HIM THE INIQUITY OF US ALL. Isaiah 53:6.* He is exhorting the 200 worshippers at the noon-tide service to come forward and be saved.

"Dear friends, you're stubborn," he shouts furiously. "The impenitent, rebellious sinner winds up in the lake of fire! God's been real good to you, REAL GOOD. You *should* be in that lake of fire RIGHT NOW!"

An old man – or perhaps he is not all that old – with shorn white head hinged down on the white fuzz of his chest, bursting like ivy through the tear in his Hawaiian shirt, snores a bubbly beery snore.

"Make a break for it! Make Jesus your friend and you'll no longer be lonely! Make a break for it! Yessir, you'll never know real joy until you do." Several heads turn, without concealment, to look at the clock and check how long to go before the soup can be got at. "Wouldn't it be something if someone offered to die for you? Man, wouldn't that be something?

"But wait until that grim reaper comes your way. You can't pass the buck. A lot of you guys think you can. You can't pass the bucket either, friends. You may kick that bucket tonight. Get up out of your seat and come down the aisle and be saved." No one moves. "The Lord knows all about you. Oh, yes, boy, he's known every little thing about you since the second you were born. You can't spring anything new on my heavenly Father. He loves you and he wants you to know him.

"The devil's a burner and a crook and a thief, and he's the one who's broken up everything in your lives. He's out to kill you and he would today if he could and if the Lord's hand didn't stay him." The Lord's hand moves the clock to midday. The preacher ends abruptly, appearing neither uplifted nor cast down by the non-committal blankness of the congregation which, as suddenly electrified into motion, including the snorer, is flooding through the door to the soup kitchen, to which access has been gained through the turnstile of nominal atonement.

In the lobby, as the army of black and white, young and old, but all in the uniform of overworn work clothes, shuffles urgently by, Dick McCalum, the assistant superintendent of the Chicago mission, watches them as a production manager might watch the assembly line, falcon-eyed for the alcoholic flaw. He has a face reminiscent of Norman Vincent Peale's: shaven smooth as a mushroom, spectacles alert with a mica-like glitter which suggests that mercy is not promiscuously squandered upon this alterant flock.

"It's estimated that there are five million homeless men in the United States," he says. "Sometimes you'd think we had 'em all here. Most of them here wouldn't be accepted in the established church, but all the same we aren't a welfare agency. Our purpose is to get out the Gospel. Just as God sends missions to foreign lands, he sends out the Gospel here to men who have drifted out of society.

"A good many of these are non-conformists. They've deliberately opted out. Their line of least resistance is to say 'I don't need you or anything.' A lot of them are weak-willed individuals all the same. They don't hold a job because they have no purpose in working except to exist. They're content to rest, to go into taverns, buy a few drinks and feel like a big shot for a moment.

"They idealize themselves. They think there's romance in being on the road. They're picture-book heroes in their own mind, that's the only way they can make something of themselves, by seeing themselves as gallant, bold individuals and by thinking they're showing their families that they're really roughing it out.

"The trouble is that life's too easy here in America. In Europe and countries where food is hard to come by every crumb of bread is of value. Here they scoff at it. Everywhere else in the world you have to struggle for existence. Here you can go anywhere and make it.

"There's a spirit of unrest in America. These men figure the world owes them a living and without making any effort to get out of the rut they're in they just drift around, by bus or hitchhiking, or freight train, expecting to have it handed out to them.

"We treat them here like gentlemen. If they have any gumption at all they want to get over the hump and we try to help them, to make them feel they are somebody. But a lot see themselves as tied down to the drudgery of factory machines and can't take it. They don't think about tomorrow. They just stop fighting. They're not ashamed about that. They don't see themselves as humble. They see themselves as big shots. Big shots on skid row."

THE WOODS ARE FULL OF WARDENS

*Travel on, there is help for you. You will come
to a good place; there is plenty*

The man in the vision of Patience Loader,
on the Mormon Trail, 1856

*The little hobo standing under a sad street lamp
with his thumb stuck out – poor forlorn man,
poor lost sometime boy, now broken ghost of the
penniless wilds.*

Jack Kerouac: *On The Road*

PART EIGHT

THE WOODS ARE FULL OF WARDENS

36 : THE AMERICAN SPECTER

I have no plans
No dates
No appointments with anybody

Jack Kerouac : *Mexico City Blues*

FROM the Top o' the Strip cocktail lounge of the twenty
million dollar Dunes Hotel, the frail and rickety anatomy
of Las Vegas is laid naked. At night at street level the Strip's
four miles of gyrating, throbbing neon are an electrical fire-
storm in gold, kingfisher green and vermilion. Downtown the
massed bulbs of the gambling joints, the Golden Nugget and
The Mint and Diamond Jim's, throw a cold livid glare bright
as summer noon. All shudder together into an hallucinatory
metropolis. But from this daylight eyrie Las Vegas can be seen
to be a half-pint shantytown, a village of flimsy pre-fab shells
behind the gargantuan sign superstructure.

Below, the gimcrack little fruit-machine parlors and bars fry
in a sun like a laser beam. In the Dunes – which offers "ankle-
thick wall-to-wall carpeting" and for the Dome of the Sea diners
a "diaphanous blond mermaid harpist providing seascapes in
music while floating" – piped show tunes seep through the artificially dimmed and chilled air. This is the latitude traveled by
Sam Landy, the Professor of Chance and peripatetic gambling
man.

He is dapperly dressed in yellow silk shirt with monogram
on the pocket, blue slacks, black suede shoes and a minuscule
gold watch with snaky gold strap; he has shiny gray hair and
moustache, and a beautiful tan soaked up from many a costly
resort-in-the-sun. Ignoring the coffee poured out for him, Sam
Landy stares musingly and unseeingly toward the biscuit colored
horizon where, at Frenchman's Flat, they test atomic devices.

"I'm known as the Professor of Chance," he explains, "because
I give humorous lectures about gambling to Rotarians and the
Lions and Women's Clubs, see? My father intended me to be-
come a rabbi, and I went to theological college for four years in

419

Chicago, where I was born. I quit. I didn't like the importance attached to money in the clergy. I didn't want any part of that atmosphere.

"I went to the University of Illinois and became a physical education instructor, but – this was in the Thirties – jobs were hard to find. Finally I went to work in a horse parlor, a bookie shop. It was just a job as far as I was concerned. I wasn't interested in the gambling, never, never.

"But one day they needed extra help on the Kentucky Derby and they found I had a natural talent. Natural. It was just there. They trained me as a dice croupier. I worked myself up to be the top craps and blackjack dealer in the country. It wouldn't be right to say I like the life: I love it. *Love* it, I had the natural instinct. If you move your eyelid I can tell what your next bet's going to be; I can tell from the way you handle your chips whether you're winning or losing.

"There's an epitome to every situation. I wanted to work all over America in the top places. I'm nomadic by inclination. When gambling was illegal I worked the casinos everywhere, Ben Martin's Riviera Club just across Washington Bridge, in New Jersey, which was the top gambling place in the land, and in a gambling boat outside the three-mile limit off the California coast. I dealt in a place in Washington DC where I played with the top ambassadors and statesmen, and I've worked in Hollywood and Miami Beach.

"A lot of people think that because this is your profession, and you work Miami and Las Vegas, that you must be gangster, a hoodlum or racketeer or some sort. Let me tell you something, I've lived a very clean life. I don't smoke or drink or gamble – not with my own money. What I like to do is to get up and go, not because I have some place in particular to go, but just to see if I can make it to the top in the next place."

Sandy Lehmann-Haupt is a young record engineer who at this moment in this Greenwich Village pad is in the middle of tailoring a television series which will re-create the capricious career of jazz through all its periods and fads. Sitting among mounds of LPs and old 78s of Count Basie and Mildred Bailey and Willie the Lion Smith and Bix Beiderbecke, he recalls his arrival in

New York by bus, but not a Greyhound.

"There was this whole bunch of us out in San Francisco who'd just sort of floated in from all directions," he says. "We thought we'd have a kind of mobile party right across to the East. Somebody found a bus, it was a 1938 International Harvester school bus which had been used as living quarters by a family, and we all chipped in and bought it.

"We spent a long time getting it the way we wanted. There were seven of us, two writers, an ex-Army lieutenant, a philosophy student, a couple of painters and myself, and it was a team job. We painted that bus from back to front in phosphorescent colors and we painted everything in it – even the fridge was covered in collages.

"We decided to film the trip, so we built a platform on the back, and put a bench, a motorcycle mount and an old barbershop chair for panning shots. We sawed out a hole in the roof and fenced round an area for a mattress. I spent two months fitting the bus throughout with an intercom system, stereo and reels of taped jazz.

"We had a lot of briefings but we never really succeeded in defining why we were doing this except that we all wanted to get out on the road and this seemed a new way of doing it. We had a shakedown trip from San Francisco to Los Angeles and that went okay so then we pushed off on the real trip.

"By then there were fourteen men and one girl and we all had our movie names: there was Intrepid Traveler, Swashbuckler, Highly Charged, and so on. One of the men was the original Dean Moriarty in Kerouac's *On The Road*. It was really great – flying across the Nevada desert at sixty miles an hour, sunbathing on the roof, all the way with Ornette Coleman coming across the intercom. That's the way to travel."

PROFESSOR J. K. GALBRAITH has drawn attention to the similarity between the American system and the bumblebee, whose aerodynamics and wing-loading are such that in principle it cannot fly. The fact that it does fly in defiance of the authority of Isaac Newton and Orville Wright must, Professor Galbraith thinks, keep the bee in constant fear of crack-up. It is a successful but insecure insect and he believes that there is among Americans a corresponding "depression psychosis," a deep undercurrent of insecurity about an economy which obviously flies high but flouts the rules with a dangerous combination of audacity and apprehension.

As we have seen, however, there are in the American beehive many who never even get airborne, who from the outset reside in the Other America, that half-life lapping at the buttresses of the Great Society. Here beyond the edge is the homeless and workless man, the Odets eidolon of the Thirties still on the street corner: " ... a beggar with the face of a dead man. Hungry, miserable, unkempt, an American specter." The American specter, thirty years later, is still not an anachronism, a wingless survival of an earlier evolutionary stage of the insect colony. He continues to be in a lively state of mass production.

Until the draft call for Vietnam, the American economy maintained an unemployment pool among under twenties of sixteen per cent, and a million jobless young people between sixteen and twenty-five, a gristly lump of undigestible workless amid unprecedented boom conditions. This is mass despair and defeat, which in most magazine surveys of the state of the nation is parcelled briskly in such a phrase as "unemployment sank to an eight-year low of 4.5 per cent." It fluctuates, but it has stuck around the five to six per cent mark for about eight years. That official estimate is based on statistics of insured wage-earners and those statistics omit multifold groups of workers, many of whom in despondency have lapsed from labor exchange registers and have gone into social limbo. Six million may be the more realistic level of fairly steady unemployment.

Despite President Johnson's "War on Poverty," thirty-five million (or perhaps forty, or fifty, no one is sure) of the nation's 198 million continue to live below the line of sufficiency and security, badly housed, badly fed, badly paid, in want: the central paradox in a nation whose destiny, a plausible pipedream, has been repeatedly celebrated as upward into ever more sumptuous plateaux of affluence.

It is a lopsided ascendancy, with the prosperous escalating away and leaving the poor behind across a widening gap of disparity. When President Johnson appointed R. Sargent Shriver as generalissimo of the new Office of Economic Opportunity, charged with running such vital-sounding departments as Vista, Community Action Programs, Neighborhood Youth Corps and a Job Corps (conservation camps and urban training centers, strongly echoing the New Deal CCC, for 25,000 illiterate or impoverished adolescents) the bugle call was "to weed out poverty at the grass roots." At that time a cynical Republican remarked: "Lyndon Johnson is the only man who could run on a platform of poverty and plenty at the same time." The subsequent waning of enthusiasm to get at those grass roots of poverty may connect with the result of a Gallup poll, in which forty-six per cent of the electorate expressed the opinion that poverty is a result of lack of effort rather than force of circumstances.

Old myths never die and don't often fade away. Move. Go West, young man. Look slippy. Git up and go. Go places and do things, as they used to say in the Twenties. Faith is unshaken even when disproved, and that same discredited faith is preserved, in companionship with guilt, in the breasts of the illiterate, the impoverished, the unskilled, the untaught, the untrained, the displaced, the disrupted, the defeated. Many in modern America sit hopelessly in defunct areas, made superfluous by automation or vanished styles of manufacture; but most respond to the social praxis and move. They move along the interstices of the American Good Life and just keep rolling along, for perhaps the coal pits are closing in Allegheny County, Pennsylvania, but there may be an opening in Colorado, and if Colorado is dying too, let's try California where the sun shines on everyone, and if that's crowded out then Chicago's worth a throw. The journey continues along the freight tracks and in city-bound fruit trucks, in Greyhound buses and salesmen's cars; stays in skid row cage-hotels or the Muni or a rundown tourist court; meals in beaneries and hash houses with the menu written in soap on the window; drinks on a panhandled quarter in sawdust saloons where the muscatel can be spiked with raw alcohol.

As the social pyramid towers higher, the rubble of poor at its foundations thickens. Yet the man without job or home rarely impinges, even as a shadow, upon the citizen with fresh laundry each morning, however concerned he may be about the default from the grammar of sound economy when he reads the figures in his newspaper. Inevitably, the fact that millions of his countrymen are in permanent destitution is an abstraction most of the time, an academic debate of conscience. For the commuter trains arrow from country club land to the city's business heart; the expressways girdle towns without touching them; the cars glide between the billboard screens along the cement crosshatchings. Beyond those traffic conduits, the rejected man is geographically ever more distant, either a small bent-over figure in the sun of a factory farm or a face, glimpsed at night, etiolated by the sodium lamps of the city. And in his traditional hobo version he remains secure in the curio corner of stock American folk fiction. There is a break in circuit between the caricature and its physical truth. To the prosperous citizen the hobo of his fancy has about the same relation to the man turned away from the employment office grille, or to the derelict sleeping off dope or bay-rum on a park bench, as has Li'l Abner to the redundant Appalachian miner in a ghost shack town of the East Kentucky field, or as Baby Doll has to a sharecropper's child of the hookworm belt.

The fiction continues to be perpetuated in terms of whimsy derision. There are always the useful light relief newspaper filler paragraphs to be got out of hobolore. It is reported from Santa Barbara that "county supervisors ordered the District Attorney to look into complaints that hoboes have been using up electricity by plugging in their electric blankets at deserted homes." From Buffalo comes the despatch that a hobo in from Chicago by de luxe coach complains: "It was terrible. The coach was either too hot or too cold. You couldn't get a seat and when you weren't standing you were sitting or lying down in the aisle. Give me the good old days when a 'bo could ride the rods in comfort." When Harry Baronion, editor of *The Bowery News* and late of *The Hobo News*, died in 1965 the New York *Times* reported a friend as saying: "Harry was planning to bat the hell out of the war on poverty. He said there were hardly any old-time bums left, anyhow, and President Johnson looked like he was trying to wipe them out altogether."

So can be provided not only a wry grin, but comfort for the conscience.

Down in the boondocks, across the tracks, out in the jungles, in niggertown and Mextown, over the hill, on skid row – however it is labeled, this is the ghetto of "internal aliens," those immersed in a depth of failure which they can move through horizontally but not vertically. They are all the easier to over-look because their ghetto's boundaries are the borders of the United States and individually they are hard to focus upon. Their very mobility is no identity marker, for also mobile are the technicians and managers and high-grade artisans and special-ists, and through the unpopulated mechanized tracts which were the countryside, along the inter-town highways, proceed the giant shuntings of a restless population. Why, among this ebullition, should the hobo be noticed? Yet he does enter into the anxieties and preoccupations of the others. Machine culture brought unparalleled ease of convenience and efficiency to the better-off American. Deliverance from frontier drudgery came, nature was whipped and overcome, but to be replaced by another wilderness, that of the apparatus of mass production, mass liv-ing, mass organization, at the heart of which lingers the fear that something irreplaceable and unique has been extinguished, and something less tangible than that "depression psychosis," Gal-braith's worm in the apple of abundance.

It would seem ingenuous to accept *in toto* Metzler's conver-sational statement that the migrant worker, the drifter, the landless stranger on his home soil, is "the last free American." It can on the contrary be argued that the hobo has, since he was created in the kinetic American pattern, been a prisoner in a chain-gang of limited possibilities, oppressed and harassed, with access neither to his own hearth and family nor to sustaining relationships in which other men find a truer freedom of security and love. Therefore, the hobo had to invent his consolations. He had to wring a little poetry and pride out of his rag of a life, to make a simulacrum of himself.

Yet it is a curiously insidious and seductive myth and, as has been shown on these pages, for nearly a hundred years it has been a tantalizing melody in the air, a wild, wood-wind note heard by most Americans. However imaginary that freedom of the man on the road, it makes no less real the repining, in the middle of mass plenty, that something of value has drained away. Ironically it is the dispossessed – the joke hobo figure – who is believed to have retained that possession still coveted by the others. He is the infidel excommunicated from the consumer theology, yet he seems to have in his moneyless state an American prize not to be got by planned payments or credit card. That he does have the prize is doubtful, but the salaried suburban American endlessly strives to reach through his suffusion of goods to grope for it.

"As pants the hart for cooling streams, so does his spirit pant for money, the only wealth," wrote Karl Marx: but the conflict in the American has always been to want both money, meaning machine civilization and culture, and the cooling streams, meaning the repose of nymphs in the Garden of the World. The bucolic balm – or at least its synthetics – can be seen in America in a thousand forms and fantasies. The roadscape is pustuled with services for a population of rubber tire romantics, so the tubular alloy cabins that have obliterated the countryside are tacked over with crusty clapboard and called Aunt Jemima's Pancake Cottage. White picket fences cosily surround the drive-in banks. Motels and weekend fun compounds are disguised with lacy white Colonial wrought iron or knotty timber. Everywhere is "the piety towards the out-of-doors." The flight from the ticky-tacky boxes on hunting and camping trips is a vacation ceremonial, and the wilderness cult is an advertising mode for anything from a sedan to a cigarette: wool shirts and whipcord for the models, mountains and elk trails for the setting. Kits for frying hamburgers by starlight, so recreating a whiff of the overlander heritage, are a ten million dollar chain store sales item, maintained by the American who seeks his historical roots by chewing a charred Frankfurter with his Martini. The small town, its sleepy, warm, hi-neighbor serenity of life around the court house and the catfish ponds is obsolescent, and perhaps just about obsolete, by-passed by the highways, pruned off by rationalized railroads, strangled by absentee agriculture, and its hitching posts and spinning wheels and general stores are embalmed in Disneyland. So, quite recently, twelve writers collaborated to produce *A Vanishing America*, a faded, sepia daguerreotype proffered as "a hymn to lost simplicity" – a simplicity that has drowned in the cream-whip of the 400 billion dollar consumer economy. Its epitaph is the words of Jack Isidor Strauss of Macy's: "Our economy keeps growing because our ability to consume is endless ... The luxuries of today are the necessities of tomorrow." And the necessities of yesterday – options, resource, independence – now seem to be the luxuries of today, priceless, unobtainable, not to be bought.

It would be misleading to draw too much inference from that half-hearted rebellion against mass organization, the beatnik movement, yet it was in fact traditional in its impulse to dodge beyond the lasso of regimentation, and Jack Kerouac had some statements to make that are worth recalling. Kerouac ("Joys of the open road," one journal summed him up, "myth of the glamorous wastrel") in *On The Road* attempted for his generation a twentieth-century restatement of *The Pilgrim's Progress*. It was an incoherent shout of disaffiliation, a cry to be free: "I felt like an arrow that could shoot out all the way ... I heard the Denver and Rio Grande locomotive howling off to the mountains. I wanted to pursue my star further ... I suddenly saw the whole country like an oyster for us to open; and the pearl was there, the pearl was there."

The pearl appears not to be there, but who can scoff at the search for it? Much of Kerouac – and the tense, obsessional cross-country lunges in stolen cars – seems to be a frenetic extension of Huxley's *furor Americanus*, the American cult of action. Perhaps more exactly it can be seen as the last spurt of the "democracy of haste," not now the expansionist stampede of whole townships and populations and industry, but here the agonized rush back into an idea of sapling energy and liberty. This wrenching free from hindrance and habit was, in the Kerouac idiom, mindless and immaturely excitable, yet poignantly right at heart and oddly heroic. It was a try at hacking a path back across an American range of life that has been built over, expunged. The spaces have shrunk, the wheat prairies are mechanized, the timber stands clear-felled, the trains are too fast for a man of an ambling disposition, the highways swoop from coast to coast, and the Wobbly union battles are won or forever lost.

What is there left to travel for once you have reached the end of the Kerouac trail? To be sure America is still the same prodigious and awesome bulk, but somehow Utah where Joe Hill went before the firing squad, the miners' union halls in Butte, Montana, the apple orchards of Washington, the water tank towers of remote Western freight yards, the North Dakota steppes of corn – none has the same blood-singing stature of distance and adventure. The archetypal hobos who still stubbornly push around the circuit are ghosts on a path whose St. Elmo's fire fades. The very group to which the hobo belonged in a class or toil sense – that of the industrial machine operator – has performed its Marxian trajectory, and, after growing for seventy-five years to be the biggest single group, has now attenuated and been replaced by a new majority, the managerial technocrat.

Both the trade and the dream have, functionally, gone. It is therefore extraordinary that the spell stays. It is entered by every new generation. In a smallish book, *I See By My Outfit*, published in 1965 by a young New Yorker named Peter S. Beagle, there was renewed the same glow of an enchanted journey – the two Bronx beatniks, motor-scooting across to San Francisco, "slide in and out among the cars like moonlight on railroad tracks," into "the kind of country you dream of running away to when you are very young and innocently hungry, before you learn that all the land is owned by somebody."

It is an ache that is constantly there. It was present in the strange, scaly quality of Truman Capote's *In Cold Blood*: the nihilism and random violence of the two killers, Perry Smith and Dick Hickock, who come out of space into the windy breadth of Kansas, that "gospel-haunted strip of United States territory," and destroy the Clutter family. Capote said to me after the book was published: "There is in America a whole sub-culture, a universe, of wandering, desperate, rootless people, who move always in an aimless, drifting, dangerous way, and there was the collision between these peculiar wanderers and a race of pious, quiet, rooted people: the two great extremities, the greatest polarities."

There seems to me to be nothing astonishing about this collision of opposites. Perry Smith and Dick Hickock belonged in that terrain just as much as did the Clutters – part of the fauna.

The previous summer when I was about to leave New York on a 9,000 mile round-trip, I had been repeatedly advised – warned – not to take chances, not to pick up hitch-hikers, not to sleep at the roadside, not to lodge in dubious motels. "The whole goddam United States is full of screwballs roaming around," a friend told me, very seriously. "Don't come back dead." I had no wish to but I was, after all, looking for Perry Smith and Dick Hickock, not necessarily psychopathic murderers but men following their noses to nowhere in particular around the continental mass. I wanted to intercept some wild goose chases. I was driving out into a Kerouac landscape: " . . . we came to sundry sullen towns where we stopped for gas and nothing but bluejeaned Elvis Presleys in the road, waiting to beat somebody up." And I remembered Humbert Humbert's sharpening eye, during his dark, doting year of motel-hopping with his nymphet, for "the curious roadside species Hitchhiking Man, *Homo pollex*, of science, with all its many sub-species and forms: the modest soldier, spic and span . . .; the schoolboy wishing to go two blocks; the killer wishing to go 2,000 miles." I tried to cultivate a similar ornithological eye, especially for the killers, and obviously succeeded; yet I did meet those in whom one recognized the genetic embodiment of that phrase of D. H. Lawrence: "The essential American soul is hard, isolate, stoic, and a killer." Elsewhere Lawrence wrote of the black side of the pioneer experience: " . . . the grimness of it, the savage fight and the savage failure which broke the back of the country but also broke something in the human soul. The spirit and the will survived: but something in the soul perished: the softness, the floweriness, the natural tenderness."

Lawrence stopped short of the complete explanation, which is that the essential American soul hardened itself to stoicism and violence not only to endure isolation but to keep the dream alive. It had to have a carapace, the yolk of that egg. But in modern America the yolk has addled in the shell. The confident, solitary man who once could find exactly the sort of impersonal *éclat* his temperament needed among the awkward squad on the outgoing rail tracks and in the wild country of the North-West, has now been shouldered off into a different role: he is the baffled, alienated Camus stranger, without obligations or moral restrictions, and in a changed context. He is a disrupted personality, still performing an American drama that has been completed, the Pyrrhic contest between man and his environment. The collision between the Clutters and their two killers was of especial terror and 'motivelessness,' yet it was the logical extension of the commoner conflict between "the world of safety" and "the world of non-safety" – the first increasingly encroaching upon the other, squeezing it into more concentrated and desperate paths of action, until it seems that such rolling stones as Smith and Hickock are hemmed inevitably into their role ("fate burns gasoline along the endless highways") for this is the only alley of free movement left to them.

A British reviewer of *In Cold Blood* described the sensation of watching "two strange, inhuman, sharklike monsters swim to the surface out of the lower depths of American life" – actually, not out of the depths, merely across into the mainstream. He touched the nerve more precisely later when likening their wanderings, after the murder, to "some modern and corrupt version of *Huckleberry Finn;* the beautiful epic has turned sour, Huck and Tom Sawyer, though they still retain a pale shadow of their former charm, have acquired hearts that are cold, callous and depraved, boyish dreams of adventure have given way to futile hopes of living without work by impossible lagoons, and all human relationships have become those of *homo homini lupus."*

As a temporary fellow traveler through that soured epic, the foreigner in the United States, and particularly the Englishman from his damp, meek climate, is constantly, edgily, aware of an electricity of violence; it is like the tremble of summer lightning on any skyline. It can explode in such casual slaughter as in that Kansas farm house or in the outburst of racial frustration or in the most routine little ugly city crimes and gratuitous gang carnage, but these are perverse distortions of its true nature which is that of energy, and the conflict between the imperative of fusion into one national, manageable entity and the resistance of American individuality against being so managed and fused. It is the persistence of that quest for "the boundless licence of a new region" which Timothy Flint wrote of in 1826 and which, even then, he said with melancholy, was "something we crave and have not."

The neon of the American sign carnival, showering the night with cold, empty color – the marsh gas of urbanism – signals sameness and safety to the traveler. Risk of the unfamiliar has been screened out: WMCA THE GOOD GUY SERVICE, trailers for sale or rent, Gulf Gas, Litebite Bakerette, Country Ham Steak, Ancient Age Bourbon, Optimo Cigars, Beltway Toll, Howard Johnson, Trailway Post House, Lazy Susan Ranch-Style Meals, See You In Church On Sunday, Budweiser, S Public Shelter, Chok Full o' Nuts, Save Supermart, Flamingo Tourtel, Stoppe Shoppe, English Muffins, Leisure World Community for Senior Citizens, The Methodist Men Welcome You, Big Chief Motor Court, Snax, Eat, Kumrite Inn: Anywhere USA, go where you like, it won't feel different. Yet over the dazzling promises of indistinguishability that earlier craving for "boundless licence" still hangs like moonwrack. Which do people want? The man who made his choice, the hobo, now does not have the strength of numbers, the variety of job, the private gazetteer of way-stages, the ease of companionable stowaway rides, all of which gave him a conviction of free decision, of elbow room and of fraternity. His kind has now dwindled away into different strands the ageing blear-eyed fauns in any skid row; the man from a "poverty pocket" striking out for any place offering hope of no longer being on the outside looking in; the fruit migrants scouting around on their own wheels with the family packed behind; the loner – hitch-hiker or rubber tire tramp – who is often that deeply dislocated man with Perry Smith's "aura of an exiled animal"; the boys finding their way on the old freight train routes that have become tribal lore; and the protean bindle stiff who still contrives to scrape a perilous living on the motorized wheat belt ranches and in the Pacific shore lumber "shows."

The longing for reprise, the need to will back into existence all that was marvellously inchoate in the American story, is everywhere. It remains as part of the credentials of most successful, settled, middle-aged men. On my excursion, meeting with an assortment of hospitable sober citizens, I never had to wait two shakes, when they discovered my reason for being in America, for each one's personal Odyssey of his apprenticeship on the highway or railroad. "I was raised in a staid middle-class family in Philadelphia," said a New York magazine editor, "and when I was sixteen my idea of tasting life with a capital L was to get out on the highway, put up my thumb and see where I ended up." "I was on the bum for years," said a foreign editor, "and that's the way I educated myself for journalism, by riding the rods and getting to know for myself how ordinary people felt and thought." "I went hoboing at eighteen," said an Illinois school teacher. "I'd been reading Jack London. It seemed to me that in this country everyone had to go somewhere else; there was a pioneering spirit still about. I was convinced that it was a good life and that every man should have that experience."

Now there is atavism among the present generation, the old *Drang nach Westen*. In the Solidarity Bookshop, at 713 Armitage Road, Chicago, Bernard Marszalek, pinkly youthful behind his beard, was running off mimeographs of a declamatory pamphlet. "I'm going up to Washington in September to lend a helping hand organizing the apple pickers," he said. "I shall go largely for romantic reasons. My old man was up there, organizing in the Twenties. The people now taking this kind of action are the permanently unemployed, the completely dissatisfied people who used to be called beats. There's a difference in them now. They're developing an ideology. They're urban kids trying to break out into new fields of activity. The freedom riders were beatniks. We're trying to go even further out into this country, not just politically but individually." Pat Ellington, young wife of the administrator of the Oakland, California, Orchestra, said: "The IWW is more active than's generally realized. A new generation has joined. When my husband took out his card in 1957 some of the older members didn't like us 'dirty, upstart anarchists,' as they called us, but then one day an old guy got up and said, 'The kids may run this organization into the ground but they won't let it die on the vine.' We'd much rather the IWW went out in a blaze of something, rather than sit around in a dusty hall playing pea-knuckle. A lot of us have this urge to move out, a sort of wanderlust, and organize. You can't in this day and age walk up to a farmhouse back door and ask for a hand-out. You're right away picked up for vagrancy. But that's the

432

longing we have, to get out into this country the way the old Wobs used to."

Aside from those with a political purpose there are the others who may be said to draw sustenance from post-war maladjustment, who believe that it is more neurotic to adjust to a society of the style that is offered as normal. The rebel who rejects life's goals was first defined by John Clellon Holmes in 1952 in *Go*: "all of them, like children of the night; everywhere wild, everywhere lost, everywhere loveless, faithless, homeless. All with some terrible flaw." Clellon Holmes's world, there, is of "dingy backstairs 'pads,' Times Square cafeterias, bebop joints, nightlong wanderings, meetings on street corners, hitchhiking, a myriad of 'hip' bars all over the city, and the streets themselves ... connected by the invisible threads of need, petty crimes of long ago, or a strange recognition of affinity. They kept going all the time, living by night, rushing around to 'make contact,' suddenly disappearing into jail or on the road ... They had a view of life that was underground, mysterious."

When Kerouac's *On The Road* appeared in 1958, attracting the first wide acknowledgement of the beats and their mysterious, underground life, there was the accompanying reaction of outrage against such ingrates who rejected, so insolently, the fecundity of mid-century America. Since then beats have, of course, become an international phenomenon in societies and economies of all hue and stripe, but, it must be conceded, only where the living has some upholstery. As has been pointed out, if you tried to be a beat in India or Cairo you would die without being noticed. Nevertheless, there are beats in Israel and beats in Paris, beats in Western Germany and beats of a sort behind the Iron Curtain, beats in the Greek Islands and beats in Tangier, and there are beats in the English seaside towns and rundown London tideland areas, mostly teenage, mostly working class, not asking for much except the few shillings they can scrounge and a dossing space on the beach or in an abandoned house. They do not regard themselves as the surplus men of economists' tables. They are on the lam from the factory daily grind; they have chosen not to enter the industrial system. They are incurious about each other's identity and background, but generous with a cosmopolitan code of chipping in without question, generous with the offer of succor. They have an insect instinct for homing in on the beat hang-outs in whichever city or country they arrive in with their sleeping bag and toothbrush. If they have a political attitude it is vaguely pacifist and brotherly. They have elected their own representatives and minstrels, in such persons as Bob Dylan and Donovan, free-form poets in the old Woody Guthrie form, with neck-frame harmonica and guitar. They are self-elected outsiders with a mild, sardonic woodenness and dismissal of the clock-controlled world.

One hostile American critic, Paul Goodman, discerned behind the hosannas of *On The Road* "the woeful emptiness of running away from even loneliness and vague discontent ... The narrator finally finds himself betrayed, abandoned, penniless and hungry in a strange city. The theme of the rhapsody is metempsychosis." Transmigration of souls is exactly what Kerouac was trying to convey in his frenzied but evocative writing, a return to "the beautiful epic" of Huck Finn, but at the point of Huck's valediction on his last page. "Aunt Polly she's going to ... civilize me, and I can't stand it. I been there before." And he decides to "light out for the territories."

Where are the territories now but in metempsychosis? Where can the American wanderer go to compensate for the elegiac weight of forfeiture, to find the *déjà vu* that haunts the more tormentingly because it is recognition of an idyll that may never really have existed? The "emphasis on the will, on conquest, and on a kind of materialistic asceticism" served its pioneer purpose and had to end, but the old hobo and the nomadic ranch hand and the recidivist beat are alike in finding it insupportable that America has shriveled to a suburb and the independent man to a commuter.

I return to Kerouac because, although his importance as a writer is not large, he did express the yearning anew and because he is a praiser of life, and it is that which makes all the keener the heartsoreness with which he invokes in his *Lonesome Traveller* what may be the last, doomed "vision of America that had no end." In Brueghel's time, he says, children danced around the hobo. Today "mothers hold tight their children when the hobo passes through town because of what newspapers made the hobo to be – the rapist, the strangler, child-eater. Stay away from strangers, they'll give you poison candy. The Brueghel hobo and the hobo today are the same, the children are different ... What about Shirley Temple, to whom the hobo gave the Bluebird? Are the young Temples bluebirdless?"

And Kerouac describes how he concludes his own rather dilettante sallies by freight and thumbed lift after being surrounded by three of those "5,000-dollar police cars with the two-way Dick Tracy radios" while on his way, haversack on back, at two a.m. "for a night's sweet sleep in the red moon desert." He relates the dialogue:

"Where are you going?"

"Sleep."

'Sleep where?"

"On the sand."

"Why?"

"Got my sleeping bag."

"Why?"

"Studyin' the great outdoors."

"Who are you? Let's see your identification."

(I just spent the summer with the Forest Service.)

"Did you get paid?"

"Yeah."

"Then why don't you go to a hotel?"

"I like it better outdoors and it's free."

"Why?"

"Because I'm studying hobo."

"What's so good about that?"

He ends: "There's something strange going on ... There ain't a sheriff or fire warden in any of the new fifty states who will let you cook a little meal over some burning sticks in the tule brake or the hidden valley or anyplace any more because he has nothing to do but pick on what he sees out there on the landscape moving independently of the gasoline power army police station. I have no ax to grind: 'I'm simply going to another world ... The woods are full of wardens."

The warden's attitude to the mobile man is, today as ever, governed by the manner of that mobility. Mobility is unarguably

435

an indispensable component in an economy of the American character and in a nation of America's size, and so is justifiably prized and commended. But the idea itself has come to be qualified by a cluster of subordinate clauses. Mobility with money is, of course, laudable and desirable – you are then a tourist or an envoy of business. Mobility between firms and cities is proof of a professional man's initiative and ambition. Mobility is also proof of a workless working man's grit, of his determination to hunt down the breach in the wall and find readmission to the commonweal. Finally, mobility without those objectives or rationalizations – therefore mobility for its own feckless sake – must be held to be bad, for it is the act of a renegade and puts in jeopardy the American declaration of intent.

So the wardens patrol the woods to keep the runaways on the move or in custody, and the vagabond misfits and the inept, hopelessly poor – those who by their existence are an offence against the immutable ideals of success – are punished for their failure by being ignored or counted out. Yet although there is officially now no room any more in America for the wayward man, there are those who do manage still to steer their own wilful course through the closing barriers, and from afar the hobo, the traveling man, is eyed with disquiet, with a mixture of envy and nostalgia, by the majority who must, to uphold their own choice of life, condemn his. The "American specter" seems, unwarrantably, to have a charisma not vouchsafed them: all the gains that have made America so dazzling and so powerful cannot wholly fill the sense of loss that, of all people, the hobo seems not to have suffered.

AARON, DANIEL *Writers on the Left*, Harcourt, Brace and World, 1961.

ALLEN, F. L. *Only Yesterday*, Pelican, 1938.

ANDERSON, NELS *The Hobo: The Sociology of the Homeless Man*, University of Chicago Press, 1923.

—— *Men on the Move*, University of Chicago Press, 1940.

—— (as "Dean Stiff") *The Milk and Honey Route*, Vanguard Press, 1931.

ARMITAGE, MERLE *The Railroads of America*, Duell, Sloan and Pearce-Little, Brown, 1952.

ASHLEIGH, CHARLES *Rambling Kid*, Faber, 1930.

BAGDIKIAN, BEN H. *In The Midst of Plenty*, Beacon Press, 1964.

BENDINER, ELMER *The Bowery Man*, Nelson (New York), 1961.

BOORSTIN, DANIEL J. *The Colonial Experience*, Penguin, 1958.

BOTKIN, B. A. (edited by) *The American People*, Pilot Press, 1946.

BOTKIN, B. A., and HARLOW, ALVIN F. *A Treasury of Railroad Folklore*, Crown, 1953.

BRISSENDEN, PAUL FREDERICK *The I.W.W.: A Study of American Syndicalism*, Columbia University Press, 1920.

CALDWELL, ERSKINE, and BOURKE-WHITE, MARGARET *You Have Seen Their Faces*, Modern Age Books, 1937.

—— *Say, Is This the USA?* Duell, Sloan and Pearce, 1941

CHAPLIN, RALPH *Wobbly*, University of Chicago Press, 1948.

CHARTERS, SAMUEL B. *The Country Blues*, Michael Joseph, 1960.

COLEMAN, TERRY *The Railway Navvies*, Hutchinson, 1965.

DAHLBERG, EDWARD *Bottom Dogs*, Mandarin Books, 1930.

DAVIES, W. H. *The Autobiography of a Super-Tramp*, Cape, 1907.

DE GRAZIA, SEBASTIAN *Of Time, Work, and Leisure*, The Twentieth Century Fund Inc., 1962.

DERBER, MILTON, and YOUNG, EDWIN *Labor and the New Deal*, University of Wisconsin Press, 1957.

EDGE, WILLIAM *The Main Stem*, Vanguard Press, 1927.

FEIED, FREDERICK *No Pie in the Sky*, Citadel Press, 1964.

FILLER, LOUIS (edited by) *The Anxious Years*, Putnam (New York), 1963.

GALARZA, ERNESTO *Merchants of Labor*, Rosicrucian Press, 1964.

GALBRAITH, J. K. *American Capitalism*, Pelican, 1963.

GALLAHER, JR. ART *Plainville Fifteen Years Later*, Columbia University Press, 1961

GAMBS, JOHN S. *The Decline of the I.W.W.*, Columbia University Press, 1932.

GARLAND, HAMLYN *Son of the Middle Border*, John Lane, 1917.

GELLERT, LAWRENCE *Me and My Captain*, Hours Press, 1939.

437

GINZBERG, ELI, and BERMAN, HYMAN *The American Worker in the Twentieth Century*, Free Press of Glencoe, 1963.

GOURFINKEL, NINA *Gorky*, Evergreen Books, 1960.

GUTHRIE, WOODY *Bound for Glory*, Doubleday, 1943.

GREENWAY, JOHN *American Folksongs of Protest*, University of Pennsylvania Press, 1953.

HANDLIN, OSCAR *The American People*, Hutchinson, 1963.

HARE, RICHARD *Maxim Gorky*, Oxford University Press, 1962.

HARRINGTON, MICHAEL *The Other America*, Penguin, 1962.

HOBSBAWM, E. J. *Labouring Men*, Weidenfeld and Nicolson, 1964.

HOFFER, ERIC *The Ordeal of Change*, Sidgwick and Jackson, 1964.

HOLBROOK, STEWART H. *Story of the American Railroads*, Crown, 1947.

JAFFE, A. J., and CARLETON, R. O. *Occupational Mobility in the U.S.*, King's Crown Press, 1954.

JOSEPHSON, MATTHEW *The Robber Barons*, Eyre and Spottiswoode, 1934.

KARSON, MARC *American Labor Unions and Politics, 1900-1918*, Southern Illinois University Press, 1958.

KNIBBS, HENRY HERBERT *Songs of the Outlands*, Houghton, Mifflin, 1914.

KORNBLUH, JOYCE L. (edited by) *Rebel Voices*, University of Michigan Press, 1964.

KROMER, TOM *Waiting For Nothing*, Knopf, 1935.

LAUBACH, FRANK C. *Why There Are Vagrants*, Columbia University Press, 1916.

LERNER, MAX *America as a Civilization*, Simon and Schuster, 1957.

LESTER, RICHARD A. *As Unions Mature*, Princeton University Press, 1958.

LEWIS, EDWARD E. *The Mobility of the Negro*, Columbia University Press, 1931.

LITWACK, LEON *The American Labor Movement*, Prentice-Hall, 1962.

LOMAX, ALAN *Folk Songs of North America*, Cassell, 1960.

McWILLIAMS, CAREY *Ill Fares the Land*, Faber, 1945.

—— *Factories in the Fields*, Little, Brown, 1940.

MARX, LEO *The Machine in the Garden*, Oxford University Press, 1965.

MILBURN, GEORGE *The Hobo's Hornbook*, Ives Washburn, 1930.

MINEHAN, THOMAS *Boy and Girl Tramps of America*, Farrar and Rinehart, 1934.

—— *Lonesome Road*, Row, Peterson, 1941.

MOORE, TURMAN E. *The Slaves We Rent*, Random House, 1965.

MULLIN, GLEN H. *Adventures of a Scholar Tramp*, Century, 1925.

MYRDAL, GUNNAR *Challenge to Affluence*, Gollancz, 1963.

ODUM, HOWARD W. *Rainbow Round My Shoulder*, Bobs, Merill, 1928.

OLIVER, PAUL *Blues Fell This Morning*, Cassell, 1960.

—— *Conversation with the Blues*, Cassell, 1965.

OUTLAND, GEORGE E. *Boy Transiency in America*, Santa Barbara State College Press, 1939.

PARKER, CARLETON H. *The Casual Laborer*, Harcourt, Brace and Howe, 1920.

PARKES, HENRY BAMFORD *The American People*, Eyre and Spottiswoode, 1949.

PARRINGTON, VERNON L. *Main Currents in American Thought*, Hart-Davis, 1927.

PAYNE, ROGER *The Hobo Philosopher*, Puente, California, 1920.

PEELE, JOHN *From North Carolina to South California*, Edwards, Broughton, 1907.

PELLING, HENRY *American Labor*, University of Chicago Press, 1960.

PINKERTON, ALAN *Strikers, Communists, Tramps and Detectives*, Carleton, 1878.

POLLACK, NORMAN *The Populist Response to Industrial America*, Harvard University Press, 1962.

RAMSEY, JR., FREDERIC *Been Here and Gone*, Cassell, 1960.

REITMAN, BEN L. *Sister of the Road*, Werner Laurie, 1937.

RAYBACK, JOSEPH G. *A History of American Labor*, Macmillan (New York), 1959.

RICH, BENNETT MILTON *The Presidents and Civil Disorder*, The Brookings Institution, 1941.

REIGEL, ROBERT E. *America Moves West*, Henry Holt, 1947.

SHANNON, DAVID A. *The Socialist Party of America*, Macmillan (New York), 1955.

SHOCKMAN, CARL S. *We Turned Hobo*, F. J. Heer, 1937,

SINCLAIR, UPTON *Singing Jailbirds*, published by the author, California, 1924.

SILVERMAN, JERRY *Folk Blues*, Macmillan (New York), 1958.

SMITH, HENRY NASH *Virgin Land*, Harvard University Press, 1950.

STEINBECK, JOHN *The Grapes of Wrath*, Heinemann, 1939.

—— *Travels With Charlie*, Heinemann, 1962.

TAFT, PHILIP *The A.F. of L. in the Time of Gompers*, Harper, 1957.

—— *The A.F. of L. From the Death of Gomphers to the Merger*, Harper, 1959.

TAYLOR, PAUL S., and DOROTHEA LANGE *An American Exodus*, Reynal and Hitchcock, 1939.

THERNSTROM, STEPHAN *Poverty and Progress*, Harvard University Press, 1964.

THISTLETHAITE, FRANK *The Great Experiment*, Cambridge University Press, 1961.

TULLY, JIM *Beggars of Life*, Chatto and Windus, 1925.

UDALL, STEWART L. *The Quiet Crisis*, Holt, Rinehart and Winston, 1963.

VON BORCH, HERBERT *The Unfinished Society*, Sidgwick and Jackson, 1963.

WECTER DIXON *The Age of the Great Depression*, Macmillan (New York), 1948.
WILCOCK, RICHARD C., and FRANKE, WALTER H. *Unwanted Workers* Free Press of Glencoe, 1963.
WILLIAMS, JOHN A. *This is My Country Too*, NAL-World, 1964.
WITHERS, CARL *Plainville U.S.A.*, Columbia University Press, 1945.
WRIGHT, DALE *They Harvest Despair*, Beacon Press, 1965.
WYLLIE, STEPHEN *The Self-Made Man in America*, Free Press, 1966.
ZORBAUGH, HARVEY W. *The Gold Coast and the Sun*, University of Chicago Press, 1929.

REPORTS AND STUDIES

ADAMS, LEONARD P., and ARONSON, ROBERT L. *Workers and Industrial Changes*, Cornell Studies in Industrial and Labor Relations, 1957.
BAKKE, E. WIGHT, and others *Labor Mobility and Economic Opportunity*, Technology Press of Massachusetts, 1954.
BLUMEN, ISADORE, and others *The Industrial Mobility of Labor as a Probability Process*, Cornell Studies in Industrial and Labor Relations, 1955.
GORDON, MARGARET S. *Employment Expansion and Population Growth, the California Experience 1900-1950*, University of California Press, 1954.
La Follette Committee hearings *Democracy on the Land*, Congressional Record, October 19, 1942.
MYERS, C. A. and MACLAURIN, W. R. *Movement of Factory Workers*, Wiley, 1943.
PALMER, GLADYS L., and BRAINERD, C. P. *Labor Mobility in Six Cities, 1940-1950*, New York Social Science Research Council, 1954.
PALMER, GLADYS L., and others *The Reluctant Job Changer: Studies in Work Attachments and Aspirations*, University of Pennsylvania Press, 1962.
PARNES, HERBERT S. *Research on Labor Mobility*, New York Social Science Research Council, 1954.
PETERSON, FLORENCE *Strikes in the U.S. 1880-1936*, Bulletin 651 U.S. Department of Labor, 1937.
RASMUSSEN, WAYNE D. *History of the Emergency Farm Labor Supply*, U.S. Department of Agriculture, 1951.
Reports to the President on Domestic Migratory Farm Labor, U.S. Department of Labor, 1951-1963.
ROGOFF, NATALIE *Recent Trends in Occupational Mobility*, Free Press of Glencoe, 1953.

Taylor, Paul S. *Adrift on the Land*, Public Affairs Pamphlets, 1940.
Tolan Committee hearings *Interstate Migration of Destitute Citizens, 1940-43.*
Vagrancies and Public Charities Reports, U.S. Bureau of Foreign Commerce, 1893.
Wolman, Leo *The Growth of American Trade Unions, 1880-1923,* National Bureau of Economic Research, 1924.

446

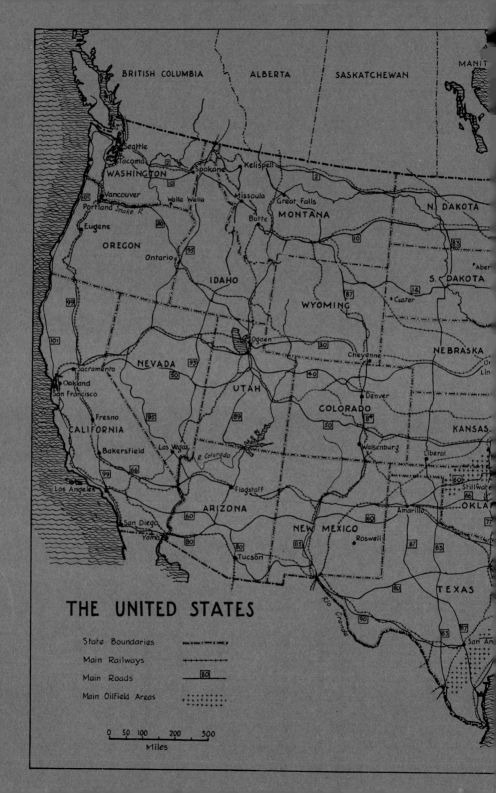

THE UNITED STATES

State Boundaries

Main Railways

Main Roads

Main Oilfield Areas

0 50 100   200   300

Miles